The Young Victims of the Nazi Regime

The Young Victims of the Nazi Regime

Migration, the Holocaust and Postwar Displacement

EDITED BY
SIMONE GIGLIOTTI
AND MONICA TEMPIAN

Bloomsbury Academic
An imprint of Bloomsbury Publishing Plc

BLOOMSBURY
LONDON · OXFORD · NEW YORK · NEW DELHI · SYDNEY

Bloomsbury Academic

An imprint of Bloomsbury Publishing Plc

50 Bedford Square
London
WC1B 3DP
UK

1385 Broadway
New York
NY 10018
USA

www.bloomsbury.com

BLOOMSBURY and the Diana logo are trademarks of Bloomsbury Publishing Plc

First published 2016

© Simone Gigliotti, Monica Tempian and Contributors, 2016

All rights reserved. No part of this publication may be reproduced or transmitted in any form or by any means, electronic or mechanical, including photocopying, recording, or any information storage or retrieval system, without prior permission in writing from the publishers.

No responsibility for loss caused to any individual or organization acting on or refraining from action as a result of the material in this publication can be accepted by Bloomsbury or the authors.

British Library Cataloguing-in-Publication Data
A catalogue record for this book is available from the British Library.

ISBN: HB: 978-1-4725-3075-2
      PB: 978-1-4725-2711-0
      ePDF: 978-1-4725-2822-3
      ePub: 978-1-4725-2390-7

Library of Congress Cataloging-in-Publication Data
The young victims of the Nazi regime : migration, the Holocaust, and postwar displacement / edited by Simone Gigliotti, Monica Tempian.
       pages cm
ISBN 978-1-4725-2711-0 (paperback) — ISBN 978-1-4725-3075-2 (hardback)
1. Jewish children in the Holocaust. 2. World War, 1939–1945—Children.
   3. Holocaust, Jewish (1939–1945) I. Gigliotti, Simone, editor.
             D804.48.Y66 2016
             940.53'18083—dc23
               2015034261

Typeset by RefineCatch Limited, Bungay, Suffolk

CONTENTS

List of Illustrations vii
Notes on Contributors viii
Acknowledgements xiii
Acronyms and Abbreviations xiv

Introduction *Simone Gigliotti and Monica Tempian* 1

PART ONE Migration: Departures to new homelands: Adaptation and belonging in refugee countries 9

1 Jewish refugee children in the USA (1934–45): Flight, resettlement, absorption
 Judith Tydor Baumel-Schwartz 11

2 'Detour to Canada': The fate of juvenile Austrian-Jewish refugees after the 'Anschluss' of 1938 *Andrea Strutz* 31

3 'This tear remains forever . . .' German-Jewish refugee children and youth in Brazil (1933–45): Resettlement, acculturation, integration *Marlen Eckl* 51

4 A distant sanctuary: Australia and child Holocaust survivors *Suzanne D. Rutland* 71

5 'The children are a triumph': New Zealand's response to Europe's children and youth, 1933–49
 Ann Beaglehole 91

6 'No common mother tongue or fatherland': Jewish refugee children in British Kenya
 Jennifer Reeve 113

PART TWO The Holocaust: Ghetto and camp battlegrounds: Imprisonment, activism and forced labour 133

7 Polish and Soviet child forced labourers in National Socialist Germany and German-occupied Eastern Europe, 1939–45 *Johannes-Dieter Steinert* 135

8 The forced relocation to the Krakow Ghetto as remembered by child survivors *Joanna Sliwa* 153

9 The fate of children at the Majdanek Concentration Camp *Marta Grudzińska* 171

10 Children and youth in Auschwitz: Experiences of life and labour *Gideon Greif* 201

11 The legend of the ghetto fighters: Zionist youth movements and resistance during and after the Holocaust *Avinoam J. Patt* 215

PART THREE Postwar displacement: War childhoods in an unforgiving world: Memory, rehabilitation and silence 237

12 The Kinder's children: Second generation and the *Kindertransport* *Andrea Hammel* 239

13 Remembering the 'pain of belonging': Jewish children hidden as Catholics in Second World War France *Mary Fraser Kirsh* 257

14 Unaccompanied children and the Allied Child Search: 'The right . . . a child has to his own heritage' *Susanne Urban* 277

15 Children of Lidice: Searches, shadows and histories *J. E. Smyth* 299

16 Europe's children across the borders of memory *Roger Hillman* 321

Index 337

ILLUSTRATIONS

Tables

2.1 Outflow of Jews from Austria 1938–41. 34

Figures

11.1 Cover page of the collective diary kept by Kibbutz Lochamei HaGetaot al shem Tosia Altman. 231
15.1 Montgomery Clift, Fred Zinnemann and Ivan Jandl on location in Munich, 1947. 314
15.2 A page from Zinnemann's research dossier on the Holocaust. 315

NOTES ON CONTRIBUTORS

Judith Tydor Baumel-Schwartz is the Chair of the Graduate Program in Contemporary Jewry and Professor at the Israel and Golda Koschitsky Jewish History Department at Bar-Ilan University in Ramat-Gan, Israel. She is the author of numerous books and articles, and she specializes in topics pertaining to the Holocaust, gender, memory, the State of Israel and commemoration. Among her books are *Unfulfilled Promise* (1990), *Kibbutz Buchenwald: Survivors and Pioneers* (1997), *Double Jeopardy: Gender and the Holocaust* (1998) and *Perfect Heroes: The World War II Parachutists and the Making of Collective Israeli Memory* (2010). She is also co-editor of *The Holocaust Encyclopedia* (2001).

Ann Beaglehole is a New Zealand historian and fiction writer. She held senior roles in the New Zealand public service in Maori Development and in Ethnic Affairs and is currently engaged in research for the Waitangi Tribunal, a commission which addresses the grievances of New Zealand's indigenous Maori people. Her publications include *A Small Price to Pay: Refugees from Hitler in New Zealand, 1936–1946* (1988), *Facing the Past: Looking Back at Refugee Childhood in New Zealand* (1990) and *Refuge New Zealand: A Nation's Response to Refugees and Asylum Seekers* (2013).

Marlen Eckl is Senior Researcher at the Laboratório de Estudos sobre Etnicidade, Racismo e Discriminação (LEER) at the University of São Paulo, Brazil. Her research interests include German-speaking exile in Brazil, Brazilian history (1930–45) and Brazilian-Jewish literature. She is the author of numerous publications, including *'Das Paradies ist überall verloren.' Das Brasilienbild von Flüchtlingen des Nationalsozialismus* (2010) and co-editor of *'. . . mehr vorwärts als rückwärts schauen . . .' Das deutschsprachige Exil in Brasilien 1933–1945 / '. . . olhando mais para frente do que para trás . . .' O Exílio de língua alemã no Brasil 1933–1945* (2013).

Simone Gigliotti is Senior Lecturer in the History Programme at Victoria University of Wellington, New Zealand. She publishes in the fields of Holocaust studies, Central European refugee history and comparative genocide. Her publications include *The Holocaust: a Reader* (2005, co-editor), *The Train Journey: Transit, Captivity, and Witnessing in the Holocaust* (2009) and *The Memorialization of Genocide* (editor, 2016).

NOTES ON CONTRIBUTORS

Gideon Greif is Chief Historian at the 'Shem Olam' – Faith and the Holocaust Institute for Education, Documentation and Research in Israel, and Chief Historian and Researcher at the Foundation for Holocaust Education Projects, Miami, USA. He specializes in the history of the Holocaust, the history of the extermination camp of Auschwitz and the Jewish 'Sonderkommando' in Auschwitz. His publications include *My Brother's Keeper. Jews who Saved Oher Jews During the Holocaust* (2004) and *We Wept without Tears ... the Testimonies of the Jewish Sonderkommando in Auschwitz* (in German, first edition 1995; second edition 1999; in Hebrew, 1999; in Polish, 2002; in English, 2005).

Marta Grudzińska is an academic researcher at the State Museum at Majdanek in Lublin, Poland. She specializes in, among other areas, the methodology, development and implementation of interviews with (amongst others) former prisoners of Majdanek, their families and those who remember the years of the Second World War as part of oral histories. She is the author of educational projects about the prisoner community in KL Lublin, has been a co-curator of several exhibitions on that topic, and has published extensively about the history of Majdanek and its Jewish and non-Jewish prisoners. She is the editor of the publications *Przewodnik po zbiorze relacji i pamiętników znajdujących się w zasobie Państwowego Muzeum na Majdanku* (2011) and *Majdanek. Obóz koncentracyjny w relacjach więźniów i świadków* (2011).

Andrea Hammel is Senior Lecturer in German at Aberystwyth University, UK, and Co-director of the Arts and Humanities Research Council (AHRC) Network *Holocaust Writing and Translation*. Her research interests focus on the literature and history of German-speaking refugees, autobiographies and memoirs, and the *Kindertransport*. She is the author of numerous publications, including *Everyday Life as Alternative Space in Exile Writing: The Novels of Anna Gmeyner, Selma Kahn, Hilde Spiel, Martina Wied and Hermynia Zur Mühlen* (2008), and co-editor of *The Kindertransport to Britain 1938/39: New Perspectives*. Yearbook of the Research Centre for German and Austrian Exile (2012) and *Not an Essence, but a Positioning: German-Jewish Women Writers, 1900–1938* (2009).

Roger Hillman is an emeritus fellow in the School of Languages, Literature and Linguistics of the Australian National University, Canberra, ACT. His research interests focus on film and history, European cinema and modern European literature. His publications include *Unsettling Scores: German Film, Music, and Ideology* (2005), 'Film adaptations of Guenther Grass's prose work', in Stuart Taberner (ed.), *The Cambridge Companion to Gunther Grass* (2009), and 'Transnationalism in the films of Fatih Akin', in Paul Gifford and Tessa Hauswedell (eds), *Europe and its Others: Essays on Interperception and Identity* (2010).

Mary Fraser Kirsh is an adjunct professor at the College of William and Mary in Williamsburg, Virginia, USA. She earned her Masters Degree in Jewish Studies from Oxford University and her PhD in history from the University of Wisconsin-Madison. Her doctoral dissertation is entitled 'The Lost Children of Europe: Narrating the Rehabilitation of Child Holocaust Survivors in Great Britain and Israel'. Dr Kirsh has held fellowships at the United States Holocaust Memorial Museum and the American Jewish Joint Distribution Committee Archives. Her publications include 'La politique de placement des enfants en Grande-Bretagne et en Palestine', in Ivan Jablonka (ed.), *L'enfant-Shoah* (2014).

Avinoam J. Patt is the Philip D. Feltman Professor of Modern Jewish History at the Maurice Greenberg Center for Judaic Studies at the University of Hartford, Connecticut, USA, where he is also Director of the Museum of Jewish Civilization. Previously, he worked as the Miles Lerman Applied Research Scholar for Jewish Life and Culture at the Center for Advanced Holocaust Studies of the United States Holocaust Memorial Museum. He is the author of *Finding Home and Homeland: Jewish Youth and Zionism in the Aftermath of the Holocaust* (2009), co-editor of *We are Here: New Approaches to the Study of Jewish Displaced Persons in Postwar Germany* (2010) and co-author of *Jewish Responses to Persecution, 1938–1940* (2011).

Jennifer Reeve is a doctoral candidate in the School of History at the University of East Anglia, UK. She researches British colonial policy towards Jewish refugees during the 1930s and 1940s. She is the author of a chapter in *The Routledge History of Genocide* (forthcoming) and is looking forward to broadening her research interests in areas of race and immigration in future projects.

Suzanne D. Rutland is Professor in the Department of Hebrew, Biblical and Jewish Studies in the Faculty of Arts and Social Sciences at the University of Sydney, Australia. Her major history of Australian Jewry, *Edge of the Diaspora: Two Centuries of Jewish Settlement in Australia*, was first published in 1988 and has had two subsequent editions (1997 and 2001). Her recent publications include *The Jews in Australia* (2005) and, with Sam Lipski, *Let My People Go: The Untold Story of Australia and the Soviet Jews 1959–1989* (2015). In 2008, she received a Medal of the Order of Australia (OAM), for services to Higher Jewish Education and interfaith dialogue.

Joanna Sliwa is a PhD candidate at the Strassler Center for Holocaust and Genocide Studies at Clark University in Worcester, MA, USA, and David and Fela Shapell Fellow conducting research for her project 'Jewish Children in German-Occupied Kraków'. Her publications include 'Jewish Humor as Source of Research on Polish-Jewish Relations', in Leonard Greenspoon (ed.), *Jews and Humor: Studies in Jewish Civilization* (2009) and 'Coping with Distorted Reality: Children in the Kraków Ghetto', in Thomas Kühne and Tom Lawson (eds), *The Holocaust and Local History* (2011).

J. E. Smyth is Associate Professor of History at the University of Warwick (UK). She is the author of *Reconstructing American Historical Cinema* (2006), *Edna Ferber's Hollywood* (2009), *Hollywood and the American Historical Film* (ed., 2012), and *Fred Zinnemann and the Cinema of Resistance* (2014).

Johannes-Dieter Steinert is Professor of Modern European History and Migration Studies at the University of Wolverhampton (UK). His research interests focus on German, British and European social and political history, with special emphasis on international migration and minorities, forced migration, forced labour, survivors of Nazi persecution and international humanitarian assistance. He is the author of numerous publications, including *Germans in Post-War Britain: An Enemy Embrace* (2005), *Nach Holocaust und Zwangsarbeit. Britische humanitäre Hilfe in Deutschland. Die Helfer, die Befreiten und die Deutschen* (2007) and *Deportation und Zwangsarbeit. Polnische und sowjetische Kinder im nationalsozialistischen Deutschland und im besetzten Osteuropa 1939–1945* (2013).

Andrea Strutz is Senior Researcher at the Ludwig Boltzmann Institute for History of Society and Culture and Lecturer at the Institute of History at the University of Graz, Austria. Her research interests include transatlantic migration movements, with special emphasis on North America and Canada, questions of Jewish displacement, memory and migration, National Socialism and restitution matters, biographical studies, and methodological questions of oral and video history. She is the author of *Wieder gut gemacht? Opferfürsorge in Österreich am Beispiel der Steiermark 1945 bis 1964* (2006), and co-editor of *Mapping Contemporary History. Zeitgeschichten im Diskurs* (2008), and *'Nach Amerika nämlich!' Jüdische Migrationen in die Amerikas im 19. und 20. Jahrhundert* (2012).

Monica Tempian is Senior Lecturer in the German Programme at Victoria University of Wellington, New Zealand. She specializes in topics pertaining to Holocaust literature, memory studies, diaspora and exile studies, and is currently working on the first *Critical Edition of Manfred Winkler's Poetry*. Her publications include *Minnie Maria Korten. Ein Schauspielerleben rund um die Welt* (2015), and '"They had a foot in every century and every world . . .". Deutsch-sprachige EmigrantInnen zwischen europäischer Herkunft und neuseeländischer Zukunft', in Daniel Azuelos (ed.), *Alltag im Exil* (2011).

Susanne Urban was from 2009 to November 2015 Head of Historical Research and Education at the International Tracing Service (ITS) in Bad

Arolsen, Germany. Since then she is Executive Manager for the Jewish Heritage in the three cities of Mainz, Worms and Speyer (Schum-cities). Her recent publications focus on survivor testimonies, the death marches, and Displaced Persons/DP children. She has published on topics such as the *Bricha*, *Youth Aliyah* and anti-Semitism. Her book *Surviving in Fear: Jewish Slave Labor and Jews with False Papers at Volkswagen Werk during 1943 to 1945* (2005) is in print for the fourth edition in German and the third in English. She is now writing a book on early testimonies of surviving children and Displaced Persons.

ACKNOWLEDGEMENTS

The editors very gratefully acknowledge the staff at Bloomsbury Academic in London for guiding the project from commission to completion, particularly Rhodri Mogford and Emma Goode. We also very much appreciated the response from peer reviewers to our first proposal. Their feedback gave the project additional cohesion and affirmation of the content and historiographical intervention of the book.

Funding from the School of History, Philosophy, Political Science and International Relations at Victoria University of Wellington, New Zealand, covered the translation of Marta Grudzińska's chapter on Majdanek (Chapter 9). To that end, we thank Małgorzata Paprota who translated the chapter so very meticulously, Karolina Piwowarczyk from the agency, Biuro Tłumaczeń Alpha, who managed the translation process extremely efficiently, and Krystyna Duszniak in Melbourne who recommended the translation agency. Our research assistant Stephen Clarke worked assiduously on formatting the chapters and liaising with contributors to produce the final manuscript. We are deeply grateful to him and to the Faculty of Humanities and Social Sciences at Victoria University of Wellington for a small grant that funded his work.

Finally, we acknowledge the excellent contributions of our authors – younger scholars, museum educators, mid-career and senior professors – from Australia, Brazil, Germany, Israel, New Zealand, Poland, the United Kingdom and the United States. This book is possible because of their commitment and scholarly professionalism.

ACRONYMS AND ABBREVIATIONS

AAJ: Archive of Australian Judaica
AFSC: American Friends Service Committee
AJC: American Jewish Committee
AJR: Association of Jewish Refugees in the United Kingdom
AJW&RS: Australian Jewish Welfare & Relief Society
AJWS: Australian Jewish Welfare Society
ANZ: Archives New Zealand
APMAB: *Archiwum Państwowego Muzeum Auschwitz-Birkenau* (Archives of the Auschwitz-Birkenau State Museum)
APMM: *Archiwum Państwowego Muzeum na Majdanku* (Archives of the State Museum at Majdanek)
ARI: *Associação Religiosa Israelita* (Israelite Religious Association)
BdM: *Bund deutscher Mädchen* (Federation of German Girls)
CIP: *Congregação Israelita Paulista* (São Paulo Israelite Congregation)
CNCR: Canadian National Committee on Refugees
CSB: Child Search Branch
CTB: Central Tracing Bureau
CTS: Child Tracing Section
DP: Displaced Person
EJCA: European Jewish Children's Aid
FAJWS: Federation of Australian Jewish Welfare Societies
FDRL: Franklin Delano Roosevelt Library
FKL: *Frauenkonzentrationslager* (women's concentration camp)
GJCA: German-Jewish Children's Aid

HEU:	*Heimatlos – Elternlos – Unterkunftslos* (uprooted, orphaned, homeless)
HIAS:	Hebrew Immigrant Aid Society
HICOG:	Allied High Commission for Germany
ICRC:	International Committee of the Red Cross
IGCR:	Intergovernmental Committee on Refugees
IRO:	International Refugee Organization
ITS:	International Tracing Service
JDC:	Joint Distribution Committee
JUVA:	*Judenvermögensabgabe* (Jewish Property Levy)
KL:	*Konzentrationslager* (concentration camp)
KTA:	North American *Kindertransport* Association
LRP:	Limited Registration Plan
NCJW:	National Council of Jewish Women
NKWD:	*Narodnij Komissariat Wnutrennych Del* (People's Office for Interior; Soviet Secret Service 1937–46)
NRS:	National Refugee Service
OHD:	Oral History Division, Institute for Contemporary Jewry, Hebrew University of Jerusalem
OSE:	*Oeuvre de Secours aux Enfants*, initially *Obczestyo Sdravokhraneniye Evreyev* (Children's Aid Society)
OTC:	One Thousand Children
PJA:	Philadelphia Jewish Archives Center
POW:	Prisoner of war
RCM:	Refugee Children's Movement
RMS:	Refugee and Migrant Service
ROK:	Reunion of *Kindertransports*
RSHA:	*Reichssicherheitshauptamt* (Reich Security Main Office)
SIBRA:	*Sociedade Israelita Brasileira de Cultura e Beneficência* (Brazilian-Jewish Cultural and Beneficent Society)
SOE:	British Special Operations Executive
SS:	*Schutzstaffel* (Protection Squadron)

UN:	United Nations
UNRRA:	United Nations Relief and Rehabilitation Administration
UNSCOP:	United Nations Special Committee on Palestine
USC:	United States Committee for the Care of European Children
USHMM:	United States Holocaust Memorial Museum
WVHA:	*Wirtschafts- und Verwaltungshauptamt* (SS Main Economic and Administrative Department)
YIVO:	*Yidisher Visnshaftlekher Institut* (Yiddish Scientific Institute)
ZOB:	*Żydowska Organizacja Bojowa* (Jewish Fighting Organization)
ZZW:	*Zydowski Zwiazek Wojskowski* (Jewish Military Union)

Introduction

Simone Gigliotti and Monica Tempian

The Young Victims of the Nazi Regime: Migration, the Holocaust and Postwar Displacement is an edited collection of research chapters about the experiences of children and youth whose lives were indelibly affected by National Socialist ideology and policy. The time period of 1933 to 1949 covers the inception of the Nazi regime through to the division of Germany into a Western and an Eastern sector, the British Dominions and Commonwealth policy regarding refugee relief, British colonial governance in Africa and the Middle East, the emerging Cold War in Europe, and the creation of Israel. The book is unique in that it places the experiences of children and youth in a transnational context, shifting the conversation of displacement and refuge to countries that have remained under-examined in a comparative context. Moreover, it provides new perspectives on how the experiences and fates of Jewish children and youth intersected with and diverged from those of non-Jews (forced labour camps, concentration camps with victims from Poland, the Soviet Union and Baltic States), and offers an opportunity to contribute to recent debates about Germans as victims of war.

Children's experiences during war and genocide are a burgeoning research area and there is certainly room for books on the topic from the nineteenth century to contemporary times. Scholars such as Lynn Nicholas (*Cruel World: The Children of Europe in the Nazi Web*, 2006) and Nicholas Stargardt (*Witnesses of War: Children's Lives under the Nazis*, 2007) have gestured in that direction. This volume, however, is focused on children's experiences of war and displacement during the Nazi regime, and issues of rehabilitation in the postwar period. Seventy years after the Holocaust, those who survived as children and youth now form the majority of survivors still alive and physically able and willing to speak about their experiences. In the last decade, their accounts have gained recognition as essential voices to inform historical representation. Collaborative research programmes such as *Kindertransport 1938/39. Rescue and Integration* (2004), *The Kindertransport to Britain: New Developments in Research* (2009/11) and *Alltag im Exil* (*Everyday Life in Exile*, 2009/11) have made the children's refugee experience a focal point of Diaspora and Exile Studies. Nevertheless, the study of childhood exile has so far mainly concerned itself with the biographical narratives of children and youth who remained in Europe (particularly in Britain) during and after the war. Consequently, the life stories of child refugees who were relocated to transatlantic and transpacific countries have been only marginally considered and certainly not systematically examined from a comparative and multidisciplinary perspective. This book takes a significant step in that direction, guiding readers to make a spatial and geographical argument about routes of escape for Jewish refugee children as well as places of confinement in Nazi-occupied Europe as segregated spaces but at the same time fused with non-Jewish populations. This volume's ultimate scope is that of representing the range, diversity and experiential drama of children and youth living in Europe and of those whose lives were uprooted by Nazi policies which resulted in relocation to all corners of the globe. This global geography of resettlement and refuge is also reflected in the disciplinary backgrounds of the book's contributors in Modern European history, German Studies, Jewish Studies, film, literature and cultural studies, the locations of archival repositories consulted, and the languages on which their chapters are based: Czech, English, French, German, Hebrew, Polish, Portuguese and Yiddish. The book's principal goal is to contextualize attention to the 1.5 million Jewish and non-Jewish children killed during the Holocaust with the experiences of those who survived in Europe and other places of refuge through the actions of individuals, Jewish and non-Jewish aid organizations, community groups and public responses to refugee crises in Nazi-occupied Europe.

The Young Victims of the Nazi Regime examines the fate of children and youth in their pan-European and global locations of experience. Prevailing notions of the Holocaust's extreme geography locate its main traumatic and experiential core in the ghettos, concentration and extermination camps of East-Central Europe. This book aims to expand that geography in three sections: Part One: Migration: Departures to New Homelands – Adaptation and Belonging in Refugee Countries; Part Two: The Holocaust: Ghetto and Camp Battlegrounds – Imprisonment, Activism and Forced Labour; and Part Three: Postwar Displacement: War Childhoods in an Unforgiving World – Memory, Rehabilitation and Silence.

Part One, 'Migration: Departures to New Homelands – Adaptation and Belonging in Refugee Countries' includes a geographical range that highlights settler and colonial societies' inconsistent policies which guided the acceptance or rejection of young victims of Nazi persecution. Jewish populations existed in varying sizes in all countries examined by the authors in this section: the United States, Canada, Brazil, Australia, New Zealand and Kenya. British Commonwealth policies influenced the fate of young potential refugees (including Kindertransportees) to these countries, as did the tireless activism of Jewish aid organizations which battled against substantial doses of fear, xenophobia, anti-Semitism and hostility.

Judith Tydor Baumel-Schwartz examines the case of the United States where more than one thousand unaccompanied, mostly Jewish refugee children found haven between 1934 and 1945. Unlike in Britain, the children were not exceptionalized as 'refugees' but were treated as immigrants which tested the public's humanitarian limits. Andrea Strutz's chapter brings the colonial dimension into view, when Austrian-Jewish children who escaped to Britain after the 'Anschluss' in March 1938, were declared 'enemy aliens' at the outbreak of the Second World War and deported to Canada. Using oral histories and other archival materials, Strutz follows the journeys of five young Viennese boys who were deported to Canada and rebuilt their lives after the war in distinguished occupations in North America. Marlen Eckl's chapter on the experiences of German-Jewish refugee children and youth in Brazil highlights the tensions and challenges of adapting to new cultural homelands in South America. Brazil was, after Argentina, the most popular location for refugees from Nazi Europe in Latin America, receiving between 16,000 and 19,000 German-speaking refugees between 1933 and 1945. Her chapter highlights the work of Jewish aid organizations in São Paulo, Porto Alegre and Rio de Janeiro in responding to local pressures on refugees, which included measures to 'brazilianize' their European identities through language use and restrictions on professional practices, among other examples.

Attitudes towards the care and relocation of orphaned and refugee children in Australia and New Zealand are examined by Suzanne Rutland and Ann Beaglehole, respectively. Rutland examines the measures introduced in Melbourne and Sydney, the largest urban destinations for Jewish refugees and Holocaust survivors. Focusing mainly on the years between 1946 and 1950, Rutland addresses the fundraising efforts of children and guardian schemes and the transnational activities of Jewish relief agencies such as the *American Jewish Joint Distribution Committee*, the *Hebrew Immigrant Aid Society* and the *Organization to Save the Children* (*Oeuvre de Secours aux Enfants*, OSE).

Beaglehole traces the background to and impact of New Zealand's restrictive immigration policies from 1933 to 1949 which in the main privileged young children, irrespective of their ethnicity, as they were deemed particularly adaptable to placement in foster or other care facilities compared to working-age prospective refugees from different ethnic and minority groups. During this time, New Zealand admitted around 1,000 young Jewish and non-Jewish refugees. This figure included children who arrived under personal sponsorship (such as the 'Deckston children' from Poland) in the mid-1930s, Kindertransportees, Polish (mainly Catholic) children who arrived in 1944 through direct sponsorship from the New Zealand government, Holocaust survivors in the postwar period, and those who arrived under the

Displaced Persons (DP) intake in 1949. Beaglehole provides a comparative perspective on the migration and settlement experiences of children from these different groups.

Concerns of empire arise in Jennifer Reeve's chapter on Kenya. She uses British Colonial Office files, refugee testimony and autobiographical literature to assess how the refugees' once-persecuted Jewishness in Nazi Germany was promoted to an elite social position in a racially hierarchical colonial society with competing socio-economic and territorial interests: the British white colonials, the Indian settler community and the indigenous African communities. Once in Kenya, Jewish refugees were perceived to threaten the socio-economic infrastructure in some regions, and restrictions were put in place, not unusually so in refugee diasporas in non-European locations, to move them into agricultural occupations to introduce skills and modernize farm and agricultural land management.

Whereas Part One focuses on the impact of migration, refugee diasporas and disrupted childhoods, its parallel time focus in Europe is the concern of Part Two, 'The Holocaust: Ghetto and Camp Battlegrounds – Imprisonment, Activism and Forced Labour'. Historians' neglect of children as forced labourers under the Nazi regime is the focus of Johannes-Dieter Steinert's contribution. They worked, as he notes, in all branches of industry, in agriculture and in German households, and the *Wehrmacht* and SS used children for construction work on fortifications, bridges, roads and airfields. Using testimony and archival sources in multiple languages, Steinert examines the lives of Polish and Soviet child forced labourers, who, in addition to Jewish children, endured the most dehumanizing working and living conditions under Nazi occupation policies.

Joanna Sliwa continues the focus on memories of forced movement by examining how children recalled their abrupt and harrowing movement to the Krakow ghetto from March to October 1941, elucidating aspects of the territorial and spatial emphases of experience that are sometimes overlooked in critical analyses of survivor testimony. The attention to Krakow expands the ghettoization geographies beyond the two largest that dominate historians' interpretations of a ghetto childhood in the Holocaust – Lodz and Warsaw. It also prioritizes children as vocal agents of memory, an agency that was acknowledged and affirmed in the immediate postwar years by the historical commission, the *Central Committee of Jews in Poland*, which facilitated these interviews, and by the *Shoah Foundation Institute for Visual History* in Los Angeles, which began its global interviewing project in the mid-1990s.

The terrible fate of Jewish, Polish and Belarusian children is reported in Marta Grudzińska's chapter on KL Lublin (more commonly known as Majdanek) and through its evolving uses as a prisoner of war (POW), concentration, penal, transit, labour and extermination camp. The children featured at each stage of the camp's evolution and arrived there via deportations from numerous locations, including nearby ghettos and prisons in Belarus. Grudzińska examines the camp experiences of different child victim groups, many of whom did not remain in the camp for longer than six months. Their age, ethnicity and perceived utility contributed to their fate, which was in some cases, closely associated with the experiences of their mothers in the camp who tried to vigilantly protect them from removal or death.

The concentrationary universe that was Auschwitz is examined through the lives of children in Gideon Greif's chapter. What was an Auschwitz 'childhood' like? To be subjected to camp registration as adults and receive degrading treatment, to be deemed fit for work if they were or could pass for twelve years of age, or to live a relatively short life in the camp once they passed its first and subsequent selections, if they survived the deportation to the camp? These are just a few of the topics Greif examines. Auschwitz's singular legacy is its international claim on the fate of Jewish and non-Jewish children and by implication, Europe's lost cultural potential. No other camp was as responsible for destroying the future of Jewish children from Poland, France, the Netherlands, Belgium, Slovakia, Yugoslavia, Germany and Austria, Greece, Hungary and Italy.

In contrast to these analyses of omnipotent power and paths to destruction was the activism of youth during and after the Holocaust in DP camps. Avinoam Patt charts the evolution of the concept of and meaning given to 'resistance' among Zionist youth movements such as the *Hashomer Hatzair* and the means by which their chosen activism empowered a surviving generation and communicated it to a mainstream Jewish public in the early postwar years. Patt examines the locations, leaders, spirit and geographies of activism that connected the two homelands of the Jewish past and future: Poland and Palestine.

Part Three, 'Postwar Displacement: War Childhoods in an Unforgiving World – Memory, Rehabilitation and Silence' moves into the difficult postwar years. Andrea Hammel's chapter returns attention to the impact of *Kindertransport* migration to Britain. Specifically, she examines the social history of a transgenerational complexity – the 'second generation' identity of children of Kindertransportees. Questions of inherited and constructed identity are analysed in Second Generation activities, reunions, organizations and reluctant discussion of an 'absent' past.

Bifurcated identities are the focus of Mary Fraser Kirsh's fascinating foray into Jewish children who were hidden in France. While children's reactions to persecution, she argues, were shaped by parental decisions, their personal, inner worlds were lively spaces for personal autonomy and negotiation of Jewish cultural identity in Catholic environments. Drawing on the testimonies of around fifty Jewish children who survived on hidden identities, she suggests that an attraction to Catholicism enabled attachments to Judaism though not without ambiguous legacies about their religious identity in adulthood. This 'lonely marranism', as she terms it, was a social strategy of survival that evokes prior Jewish historical experiences of private truth and public conformism in times of religious and state persecution.

'Liberated but not free' was the familiar refrain from survivors who had become stateless dependents and asylum seekers in the early postwar period under military administration and humanitarian management. More generally, they and their war histories were flattened by the administrative term under which they would be managed in the Western Occupation Zones in Germany and Austria: 'Displaced Persons' (DPs). Children were also DPs. Other associated terms of their non-belonging included 'unaccompanied' and 'orphan'. Susanne Urban explores how the *United Nations Relief and Rehabilitation Administration* (UNRRA) addressed this non-belonging through attempts to restore children to their biological and cultural heritage through reunification and *Child Tracing* Programmes, the latter of which in 1950 became affiliated to the *International Tracing Service* (ITS). She examines the different locations of children's liberation – concentration camps, forced labour camps, and *Lebensborn* homes, and the challenges that these liberated children presented to administrators, welfare workers and psychologists. Many of them could not remember their names, had survived through repeated exposure to violent behaviour, were classed as so-called infiltrees from the Soviet Union or were 'germanized' through placement in *Lebensborn* homes. The UNRRA and the ITS had to balance welfare, geo-politics and different ideological agendas in assessing the 'best needs' of the child in the postwar world.

Cultural memory of the war and its aftermath was also expressed in visual and literary terms. Displaced children were the principal object of pity and neglect in postwar journalism, film and humanitarian reportage. While readers might object to the ideological bent of some representations, the focus was grounded in historical truth, not all of which could be represented or was known at the time. Fred Zinnemann's *The Search* (1948) was among a crop of postwar films to focus on Europe's displaced and 'wolf'-like war children. J. E. Smyth investigates *The Search* in the context of the local history of Lidice, Czechoslovakia, the site of a major Nazi massacre in June 1942 during which children were abducted, deported and killed. Drawing on archival and film sources, she explores how the remembering of that massacre by the Allies, anti-fascist resistance groups, and the American public shaped representations of the Czech war orphan in Hollywood and European cinema.

Finally, intertextual intersections of cultural memory in post-Wall Germany are explored in Roger Hillman's chapter on German war-affected childhoods in the novel *The Dark Room* (2001), its cinematic adaptation, *Lore* (2012), and in the acclaimed novel *Austerlitz* (2001) by W. G. Sebald. Hillman provides an innovative reading of traumatic memory pollinating across generations, landscapes and visual fields, connecting European origins of the Holocaust with its German centre, and its diasporic legacy in Australia. The chapter is a fitting conclusion to the book's preoccupation with cultural representations as dialogic mediations of contemporary displacement.

Though this volume's focus is largely historical, the issues addressed within it are not. Postwar humanitarian organizations struggled to recognize the fundamental catastrophic impact of the Nazi regime and the Second World War on children. They still struggle. Initiatives to recognize the rights of children as members of family units and also as young individuals with rights have enshrined minimum protections in terms of education and labour. But governments and other non-government organizations face immense obstacles to prevent the co-option of children into terrorist organizations, militia groups and child soldier corps among other dangerous and psychologically destructive activities. Conferences on 'Children and War', such as that organized by one of our contributors, Johannes-Dieter Steinert in conjunction with the *UN Office of the Special Representative of the Secretary-General for Children and Armed Conflict*, demonstrate children's continuing vulnerability as primary victims of insurgent activity and political, ethnic and religious conflict. The contribution of *The Young Victims of the Nazi Regime: Migration, the Holocaust and Postwar Displacement* to these ongoing global and humanitarian debates illustrates the convergence of scholarship and activism devoted to preventing the continuing victimization of children during wartime.

The book aims to spur continued research and interventions into the destructive impacts of political extremism, nation-building agendas, and war and genocide on society's most vulnerable victims. The children and youth whose life histories are treated respectfully and sensitively by all contributors affirm that they were no minor witnesses to the indelible legacies of the Nazi regime.

PART ONE

Migration:

Departures to New Homelands: Adaptation and Belonging in Refugee Countries

CHAPTER ONE

Jewish Refugee Children in the USA (1934–45): Flight, Resettlement, Absorption

Judith Tydor Baumel-Schwartz

Between 1934 and 1945 over a thousand unaccompanied refugee children from Central Europe, most of them of Jewish origin, found refuge in the United States of America. More than two-thirds arrived before the outbreak of war; the rest came directly from occupied Europe during the 1940s with a small number arriving from England from 1939 onwards, usually to join family members already in the United States. The story of their migration, all as legal immigrants and not under any special 'refugee' category as occurred in other countries such as Britain, is part of the saga of Jewish refugee children during the Hitler era and sheds light on a number of issues. Among them are the American attitude towards refugees, child resettlement law in the United States during the years in question, the activities of American and American-Jewish refugee organizations during the 1930s and the 1940s and the American public's attitude towards immigration in general and refugee children in particular at that time. This chapter will describe and analyse these aspects in brief, in order to present an overview of the issues relating to the flight, resettlement and absorption of Jewish refugee children in the United States during the Holocaust.

Our story begins in early 1933, only weeks after Hitler came to power, when the plight of Jewish children in Nazi Germany moved several American-Jewish organizations to suggest various means of assistance. In the middle of that year, the executive committee of the *American Jewish Congress*, a Zionist-oriented organization connected with the *World Jewish Congress*, adopted a resolution expressing the hope that some 40,000 German-Jewish children would be cared for by private families throughout the world. A considerable number of these children were expected to reach the United States. Not all Jewish groups, however, reacted with enthusiasm to this resolution and a number of influential *American Jewish Committee* (AJC) members, those belonging to the political organization of the non-Zionist elite of American Jewry, privately expressed their chagrin that figures had been mentioned. Side by side with this criticism they began charting the first steps towards putting together a practical plan to bring Jewish refugee children from Germany to the United States.[1]

Why not adult refugees? AJC members preferred children over adult refugees for a number of reasons. First, they would not compete with labour during the economic depression that had gone on since the beginning of the decade. Second, American immigration regulations already stipulated that the Secretary of Labour would accept bonds for unaccompanied children, something that would allow them to enter with relatively little bureaucratic difficulty. Third, as opposed to adult refugees which might arouse antipathy from various populations, children would arouse more sympathy than any other group.[2]

Throughout the end of 1933 and early 1934 a subcommittee composed of representatives from the AJC, the *American Jewish Congress* and *B'nai Brith* worked on a programme that would bring 250 German-Jewish children to the United States.[3] Only children born in Germany would be considered in order to enable them to enter under the German quota and 18 per cent of the children would be of Eastern European parentage.[4] The organizers hoped that one thousand children could eventually be brought out of Germany and resettled in the United States. Originally, they set the age limit at fourteen as the fourteen- to sixteen-year-olds were the most difficult to place, but the committee soon determined that sixteen would be the upper age limit.

Ideas generate bureaucracy and bureaucracy requires organization, or in this case, a central organization to deal with the undertaking at hand. This case was no exception. In April 1934 an organization known as *German-Jewish Children's Aid* (GJCA) was created in order to post bonds for the refugee children, prevent their becoming public charges, arrange their transfer to the United States and care for them after their arrival.[5]

One of the prominent figures involved in GJCA was Cecilia Razovsky. Razovsky had been born in St Louis to an immigrant family and had been active for many years in refugee transfer and resettlement organizations where she used both her knowledge of immigration rules and procedures and her personal acquaintance with those responsible for administrating the laws. Now she began using these abilities in order to further the work of GJCA, convincing American government officials of the need to assist the scheme and not hinder it with administrational stumbling blocks. Luckily for the former refugee children and their families, in most cases she was successful.[6]

After more than a year of planning, the first group of nine German-Jewish refugee boys, aged eleven to fourteen, arrived in New York on Friday, 9 November 1934, accompanied from Cherbourg by Dr Gabrielle Kaufmann, a Jewish professor of philosophy. Immediately upon arrival, the boys were sent to Jewish foster families in and around New York City, a resettlement policy that would be changed as time went on and the organizations responsible for the children feared creating a refugee enclave in New York and its surroundings.[7]

Due to Razovsky's efforts, and those of other GJCA activists, these boys were supposed to have been the first of 250 unaccompanied refugee children that the American government would permit into the country. But, as time went on, the organization was faced with various difficulties that threatened to stop the rescue operation. The first was lack of funds. Within a year of its inception GJCA found itself functioning on a reduced scale and unable to pay foster families the sums promised for the children's upkeep. A second problem was the ironic situation of having permission to bring children to the United States but lacking sufficient foster homes in which to resettle them.

By American law, children could only be placed in foster homes of their own religion and these homes had to be able to offer a certain minimum economic standard that included a separate bed for each child and no more than two children in a room. As these were the years of the Great Depression few lower middle-class or lower-class Jewish families – the groups to which a large number of American Jews belonged – could provide such a standard. Fostering requests from traditional and Orthodox Jewish families, often more attuned to the need for benevolent activities, were often rejected as such families usually had an even smaller income, larger family and even more crowded homes than others.

A Jewish family in Philadelphia which desired to help refugee children turned to the local Jewish board assisting the GJCA with an offer to foster a Jewish refugee child from Germany. When inspected by the *Child Welfare Bureau* the offer was rejected as they already had two daughters who slept in the family's one bedroom while the parents slept in a separate living room. Despite their desire to assist a Jewish refugee girl, this family's offer was rejected by the child welfare services which claimed that they couldn't offer a refugee child the minimum conditions demanded by the *Children's Bureau*, two children to a room.[8]

Thus GJCA found itself facing opposition on several fronts: Jewish social workers in Germany were still not attuned to a project that would separate children from their families and were protesting the scheme; each refugee child cost GJCA $500 a year that was paid to his or her foster family; and to top everything off, even with the meagre number of children signed up for the project, there were not enough families to go around. Those few wonderful families that had taken refugee children had heard of the programme through word of mouth, organizational affiliation and the rare pulpit appeals in synagogues. No large-scale public appeals were being made in the fear of giving the project too much publicity which could cause a greater rise in anti-Semitism than already existed in the United States.[9] Consequently, by March 1938 GJCA had only 351 children under its auspices, including a number of 'non-Aryan' children from Germany, and its directors were contemplating terminating the scheme.[10]

The events of the spring, summer and autumn of 1938 – the 'Anschluss' (the Nazi invasion of Austria), the Évian Refugee Conference, the Munich Agreement and the Nazi takeover of the Sudetenland in Czechoslovakia, the deportation of thousands of Polish Jews from Germany and finally, 'Reichskristallnacht', the pogrom of 9–10 November 1938 – were turning points for Central European Jewry and with it, for the refugee organizations dealing with its plight. Not only was it obvious to the refugee organizations that their work was not coming to an end but just beginning, but at the end of 1938 there began a series of legislative battles in the American Congress regarding German refugees in general and refugee children in particular.

The most notable of these proposals was a joint resolution submitted by US Senator Robert Wagner of New York and Representative Edith Nourse Rogers of Massachusetts in early 1939 calling for extra-quota legislation to permit the entry of 10,000 German children each year during 1939–40 in excess of the existing quota. Children would be under fourteen years of age and had to have resided in Germany or German-occupied territory during the period following 1 January 1933.[11] The idea was to create a framework that would circumvent the American quota system of the time, which permitted only about 150,000 immigrants a year to enter the country, some 26,000 of whom could come from Germany. Shortly after the bills' introduction, the *Non-Sectarian Committee for German Refugee Children* was formed under the directorship of Quaker activist Clarence E. Pickett to lobby for the bill's passage.[12] Supporters of the bill were found among almost all religious denominations and organized labour.

Nevertheless, the bill had little hope of passing. As the hearings were held, advocates and opponents debated the American birth rate, the economic threat to employment, the children's value as future consumers, separation of families and a reiteration of the theme that 'charity begins at home'.[13] US President Franklin Delano Roosevelt remained silent over the extra-quota bill from the day of its introduction, in spite of the fact that his wife Eleanor Roosevelt, Secretary of the Interior Harold Ickes and Secretary of Labour Frances Perkins were among those inside the administration who were sympathetic to the bill. His only response was in June 1939 when he received a memo from his Secretary 'Pa' Watson stating that Caroline O'Day, the Democratic Congressional Representative from New York, had asked if the president would express his views on the Wagner–Rogers Bill. Roosevelt's response, recorded for posterity, lay across the top of the page – 'File, no action, FDR'.[14]

How does one explain the contradiction between his initial sympathetic attitude towards such legislation before its introduction and his later reticence? One explanation is that Roosevelt sought Congressional approval for military expansion and was therefore hesitant in pressuring Congress on the child refugee bill. Another explanation is that sixty 'anti-alien' bills had already been proposed before the 76th Congress and Roosevelt preferred to remain silent rather than be a catalyst for additional outbursts of restrictionist sentiments. However, a third argument was that Roosevelt's early steps in the child refugee issue were solely pro forma and did not represent his true feelings on the matter.[15]

As a result of pressures from isolationist groups which tried to stranglehold the bill, after committee hearings during the first half of the year, the final bill gave preference to child immigrants from Germany over adult immigrants, but all within the existing quota. In order to not discriminate against refugee adults who might be in more danger than children, Wagner and Rogers ultimately withdrew the Congressional Bill, in the hope that the isolationists would also withdraw their bills to limit immigration even more. Its timing had been off – in June 1939 the Congress wanted no problematic debates delaying the anticipated speedy adjournment. The outbreak of war in September 1939 demolished any false hopes about a miraculous resurrection of the amendment-choked corpse. In view of the prohibitive transport costs since the war's outbreak and the restrictionist promise to maintain a status quo if no extra-quota legislation would be introduced, Wagner and Rogers decided not to re-introduce the bill during the second session of Congress. Thus, the Wagner–Rogers Bill did not really die, but rather faded away between the two sessions of Congress in 1939.

Between 1934 and 1945 there were several dozen national organizations active in the transfer and resettlement of European refugees in the United States. Five of these worked only with the transfer and resettlement of refugee children. None of these organizations functioned in a bureaucratic vacuum and throughout their existence they maintained contact with close to a dozen advisory, finance, special services and government organizations. Among the groups dealing with refugee children in the United States were large-scale refugee organizations offering special services to refugee children such as the *National Coordinating Committee* and the *National Refugee Service* (NRS);[16] child refugee organizations such as GJCA (which was renamed *European Jewish Children's Aid* in December 1942)[17] and the Russian–French *Organization to Save the Children* (*Oeuvre de Secours aux Enfants*, OSE), with its small branch in the United States.[18] Founded as a health protection organization in St Petersburg in 1912, the organization was active in health and child care both during and after the First World War. In the nineteen years following its creation, the organization's main office moved twice – to Berlin after the Russian Revolution and to Paris following Hitler's rise to power. Retaining its former initials the group adapted its Russian name to a French one. Eventually the OSE also established a small branch in the United States.

There were also small-scale refugee organizations offering special services to refugee children in the United States, such as the *United Fund* and *Selfhelp*, funding organizations such as the *National Council of Jewish Women* (NCJW), *Hebrew Immigrant Aid Society* (HIAS) or the *Joint Distribution Committee* (JDC), special care bodies such as the Quaker movement, the *American Friends Service Committee* (AFSC), and government organizations such as the *United States Children's Bureau* and the *President's Advisory Committee on Political Refugees*.[19] Another important group was the *United States Committee for the Care of European Children* (USC), originally established to bring British children to North America during the Blitz, but later dealing with several groups of primarily Jewish refugee children from France who were brought to the USA between 1941 and 1943 with the assistance of the OSE and the AFSC.[20] There were also small Jewish organizations, such as the *Brith Sholom Lodge* in Philadelphia, whose activists, Gilbert and Eleanor Kraus, travelled to Europe at great personal risk in 1939 and rescued children threatened by Nazi persecution.[21]

Not only did the number of American organizations dealing with refugee children grow. Their European counterparts also grew in number, particularly Jewish social welfare and refugee organizations that dealt with choosing the children, preparing their documentation, and making their travel arrangements. The *Reich's Deputation of the German Jews* (*Reichsvertretung der Juden in Deutschland*) headquartered in Berlin, coordinated with Jewish organizations worldwide to find emigration opportunities for children at risk. Preference was given to two categories of children whose removal from Germany was considered urgent: young boys in concentration camps and children where one or both of their parents were in such a camp or had been deported.[22]

Despite its position as nerve centre for the emigration of Jewish children from Germany from the mid-1930s onward, the *Children's Emigration Department* (*Kinderauswanderungsabteilung*) of this organization, headed by Käte Rosenheim, was seriously understaffed. The cultured, elderly, highly educated and hard of hearing Rosenheim, affectionately known by some as 'Rosie' was less respectfully nicknamed *Täubchen* ('little dove', also 'little deaf one') by her youthful co-workers. Rosenheim was the guiding force behind the department until her eleventh hour departure to the United States in 1940. The daughter of a famous Berlin surgeon and a trained social worker, Rosenheim had been dismissed from her position in the civil service after Hitler's rise to power at which time she joined the *Reich's Deputation of the German Jews*. Extremely social, even after she and her exhausted staff had worked continuously for several days running to successfully send off a children's transport, she was known to turn to them late in the evening and delightedly exclaim, 'Let's have a party!'[23]

Although this department had been in existence for several years prior to the *Kindertransport* scheme, the large influx of applications in late 1938 necessitated hiring additional workers. Apart from Rosenheim, the staff consisted of Norbert Wollheim, Herta Souhami and a Miss Springer who assisted with various tasks. Wollheim, who had recently lost his job at a Jewish import–export business, joined the *Kinderauswanderungsabteilung* after 'Reichskristallnacht', having been asked to do so by Otto Hirsch, one of the heads of the *Reich's Deputation of the German Jews*. Years later, Wollheim described the scene he encountered when he first entered the department:

> When I went there, I almost fainted when I saw the disorder. There was a big conference room in the office and a big table covered with heaps of cards and a desk which was covered with papers, and the telephone was constantly ringing. The staff were mostly social workers and although they were doing their very best, they had no experience in technical matters like the transports . . . the first thing I did was to try and organize the cards into alphabetical and geographical order . . . Then you had to organize the people from places outside Berlin to come to Berlin and assemble on a certain day, at a certain time. There was also a lot of technical work at the last moment. Children got sick, or parents said, 'No, we can't afford to let our children go', and the lists had to be changed; we had to be in constant contact with London . . . this wasn't a nine-to-five job. We worked deep into the night . . . but it was work that had to be done.[24]

Herta Souhami, a former Westphalian Jewish social worker who worked in the *Children's Emigration Department* even prior to 'Reichskristallnacht' described the procedure used to select unguaranteed children in Germany: the children's parents would submit applications and pictures to the provincial social worker who would evaluate the case's urgency. The paperwork, including health certificates, school certificates, pictures, statements regarding the parents' health, geographical and financial situation and other related documentation would then be forwarded to the Central Office in Berlin which received thousands of applications each month. As the combination of huge volumes of applications received daily and the lack of help in the social work offices precluded the possibility of reading them all, irate and desperate parents often came directly to the Central Office complaining that they had not received replies. Perseverance often paid off. In such cases, the social worker would frequently sift through the pile of applications from that parent's district, and having found the application would deal with it as soon as possible. This system was not the most efficient, but under the circumstances there appeared to be little alternative.[25]

These people, young and old, who spent day and night trying to ease the transfer of refugee children fleeing Nazism, had their American counterparts.

Among the American activists who deserve special mention with regard to the fate of the *One Thousand Children* (OTC) are Cecilia Razovsky, who was also the assistant to the executive director of the NRS, and Lotte Marcuse of GJCA. Until 1937 Marcuse had also been a worker in the NRS; however, in March 1937 she became placement director of GJCA. Marcuse had received a diploma in social work from the Prussian Ministry of the Interior in recognition of her services in aiding military families. After coming to the United States in 1921, she gained experience in the field of children's social services and, following her move to GJCA, she became active in all activities concerning the transfer and resettlement of Jewish refugee children. Marcuse had her difficult side, and had a strong bias against traditional and observant children, but without her assistance, dozens if not hundreds of children would have had a harder bureaucratic struggle in their transatlantic odyssey.[26] Another important activist was Dr Ernst Papanek, a political refugee from Vienna who became an OSE educator in France, later moving to the United States where he tried to assist in the resettlement of several hundred children brought to the USA from OSE homes in France. Papanek, the more easygoing educator and Marcuse, the more rigid bureaucrat, clashed over the question of the children's upbringing, with refugee children becoming objects of organizational struggle in issues such as keeping them together to make them feel more at home or distancing them from each other during resettlement in order to force them to mix rapidly with American children. Luckily, few, if any of the children were aware of these struggles at the time.[27]

Let us turn now to the various waves of refugee children who began reaching the United States during the Holocaust. Several groups of unaccompanied Jewish refugee children reached the United States between 1934 and 1945: 590 from Central Europe, Belgium and the Netherlands; over 350 from France, Spain and Portugal; and several dozen from Great Britain. Most of the children coming from the continent had lived in Central Europe. This was true for some of the children coming from Britain as well. From 1934 to 1940 children arrived directly from Germany and Austria. Most of the children from Britain, Belgium and Holland came to the United States during the summer of 1940. The children from France arrived primarily between June 1941 and October 1942 and from that time on, only those refugee children already in Spain and Portugal could reach the United States.

The first children came from Germany from 1934 onwards – the bureaucratic process for their immigration will be detailed later on in this essay. From early 1939 onward, the efforts of GJCA to bring refugee children to the United States entered into high gear. When war broke out in Europe, the major transportation routes through Western Europe were closed to children trying to leave Greater Germany. Most children had come by boat via Southampton, England. However, there were still children from Germany who managed to leave even after that date, travelling via Italy and later through occupied France, and on to Portugal, or via Holland and Sweden. A few children even came to the United States via Siberia and Japan, landing in San Francisco. There is documentation of isolated attempts to bring children from Norway and Sweden to the United States under the auspices of GJCA. Although the refugee girl who originated in Germany[28] and spent two years in transit in Sweden eventually reached the USA, there is no documentation regarding the success of the Norwegian endeavour.[29]

In 1939, another small group of children came to the United States from Belgium and the Netherlands. Most were unaccompanied children from Germany and Austria, who had been sent there until they could be joined by their parents and were cared for privately by Jewish refugee committees. Soon after reaching Western Europe, these organizations tried to send children to the United States.[30] Additional children from these countries escaped to England and were brought to America with the next group of refugee children, those coming from Great Britain.

In 1940, a new group of children reached the USA, children who were fleeing the Blitz, including some refugee children who had reached Britain from Central Europe in 1939. Most of the British children were not Jewish, not considered 'non-Aryan', and not included in the 'refugee child issue', as it was known. These British children who, unlike the refugee children from Germany, were welcomed publicly by various groups with open arms, were transferred through and cared for by USC, which would later play a part in the rescue of Jewish and 'non-Aryan' Christian refugee children. Some 861 children were brought to the United States under this scheme.[31]

Throughout 1941, larger groups of refugee children began reaching the United States, this time from another location: France. Almost all of these children were actually refugee children from Central Europe, who had found refuge in children's homes in France. Most of these orphanages were connected with the OSE and had been established in the late 1930s. In late 1940, rescue organizations agreed that the children should be chosen by members of the AFSC in Southern France. As placement of teenage children was often difficult, the AFSC suggested an upper limit of twelve years of age. Nevertheless, in order not to separate siblings, a number of young teenagers were allowed to join the transport.[32]

Meanwhile, OSE activists began directing efforts to making the children's transition to American culture easier. Early in 1941, Papanek, who prior to his emigration to the United States, had directed an OSE home in France, sent the words and music of several songs to his former institution with the request that they be taught to the children coming to the United States. The songs included 'The Star Spangled Banner', 'America' and 'God Bless America'. Forty years later, former refugee children vividly recalled practising these songs in war-torn France as they prepared for their arrival in a new homeland.[33]

The last group of children reached the United States between 1943 and 1945 from Spain and Portugal. These were mostly refugee children from

Germany, Austria, Czechoslovakia and France, who had found refuge there during the war years, at times with their families, infrequently on their own. Dozens of these children were brought to the United States by the end of the war.

And what of the refugee children and their foster families? Children coming from Germany went through one bureaucratic process, those coming from France went through another, and the children arriving from Spain and Portugal went through a third bureaucratic sequence. Children from Germany were usually selected through the office in Berlin, went through preliminary physical examinations, and GJCA was informed in order to make travel arrangements. A great number of the bureaucratic details involved in the children's immigration pertained to regulations set down by the American Department of Labour and Department of State, requiring photographs, birth certificates, affidavits and other documents, usually in triplicate. As a student, studying about American immigration laws, one of our lecturers decided to illustrate how much documentation was necessary for a person to enter the United States from Europe in the 1930s. He held out to the class what looked like one very long sheet of paper, with many lines of small print that were to be filled in. Then he stood up on the desk at the front of the room (and he was not short), held the document in his hand, held his hand high above his head, and still holding the first pages in his hand, he let what turned out to be an accordion sheet of paper open up, until the last page reached the floor. Showing us this incredibly long document, he stated laconically: 'This is what people requesting a visa to the United States had to fill out . . . in triplicate'.

Following the German takeover of Austria and Czechoslovakia, similar emigration procedures were followed in Vienna and Prague.[34] After receiving permission to immigrate, families of refugee children were informed of the travel arrangements, the amount of luggage they were permitted to take, and permissible items. Although instructed to keep luggage to a minimum, it was a rare parent that did not take the opportunity to try and save a few valuable items, family photo albums, and the like. Not knowing what the children would be given in the United States, there were those families in Germany which sold all their possessions and sent children with steamer trunks full of clothing in sizes that would keep them until age twenty-one! As a result, there are the stories of the uncle who meets his ten-year-old niece at the pier, saying 'I thought you were a poor refugee and here you come with three suitcases!'

The other groups of refugee children followed a different procedure. Children in France were chosen from OSE homes by activists of the AFSC, and brought out through Spain and Portugal. After France was cut off following the German invasion of late 1942, Spanish Loyalist children, French and German-Jewish refugee children in Spain and Portugal, and 'non-Aryan' Christian children of the same background reached the United States by boat via Lisbon. The story of the first group going through Portugal taught refugee activists a lesson for further groups. Before putting the children on the boat for America, the dedicated activists wanted to compensate them for their years of deprivation and fed them unlimited amounts of chocolate and candies, something that the children had not seen in years. Like most normal children would do, they gorged themselves and spent the first two days of the journey sick to their stomachs. Learning from the mistake, refugee activists decided to dole out the sweets very sparingly while the children got on board, in order to avoid this problem.[35]

Care upon arrival differed for the various groups. The first children to arrive received minimal reception care and within hours of their arrival were often placed in a foster home. While the rapid transfer from boat to foster home suited many of the young refugees arriving from Germany in the mid-1930s, this was no longer true for the traumatized children arriving after 1938. Social workers had already noted this trauma in the late 1930s, yet general awareness of the importance of a transition stage between arrival and placement in a foster home began to develop only during the 1940s.[36]

After the first years during which children went directly to foster parents, most groups of refugee children reaching the United States went through a few days of reception care. During this time, children who had gone through 'refugee shock' – the trauma of flight through several countries – could recover from their ordeal before having to meet their foster family and begin acclimatizing to life in America.

Throughout this period of reception, the children underwent medical examinations, had time to relax and orient themselves, and the agencies could allocate children to child agencies throughout the United States. Among the institutions where the children were temporarily placed in and around New York City were the *Clara De Hirsch Home*, the *Gould Foundation*, the *Seaman's Church Institute*, the *Academy*, the *Hebrew Orphans Asylum* and the *Pleasantville College School*.[37] While the earlier groups were first taken on excursions around New York, the experience of later groups made it preferable to bring them directly to the reception centre. This was particularly true with regard to the groups arriving after the outbreak of war whose members were much more traumatized than those in the earlier groups. For example, a group from Austria arriving in April 1940 was taken to see *Pinocchio* and a gangster film but only two of the children could appreciate them. Some of the children arrived undernourished, needing immediate medical care. This was particularly true of the children arriving from France, and later from Spain and Portugal, who had gone through difficult wartime experiences.[38]

Children coming from OSE homes in France showed the greatest signs of wartime trauma. There were children who hoarded food for the first few days until it was explained to them that there was enough food for them in the reception shelter. Some of the older boys, who had spent time in camps, were rowdy and there were even cases of stealing, a survival technique they had learned in occupied Europe. Then there was the problem of language. Most of the children spoke German, a few knew French, and the workers dealing with them spoke to them in German and Yiddish until the children began to pick up American expressions, which some already did at the reception centre. These were the languages which some of the foster families initially used with the refugee children that came to live with them. There were also cases of mix up until they learned the language. One girl thought the word 'juice' was really 'Jews' and that it was a special drink for refugees only.[39]

This brings us to the area of foster families and resettlement. Foster families in the United States who agreed to take refugee children stated that they would care for them until they reached the age of twenty-one, see that they were educated, and guarantee they would not become charges of the state. Most of the children were assigned a social worker from a local social service agency to oversee the child's resettlement process. Difficulties sometimes arose in cases where relatives offered to care for refugee children. Although they were often given preferential consideration, these homes were subject to investigation and supervision by the accredited child care agencies. Relatives' homes did not always meet the necessary standing and in addition, the responsibilities and expenses of caring for refugee children were not always clear to the relatives.[40] As a result, there were families who, once faced with the reality, requested that their young relative be removed from their home and given to another foster family. In some cases, this caused resentment among the children who felt abandoned by their flesh and blood. In other cases, where there had been a lack of chemistry from the onset between the young refugees and their relatives, both breathed a sigh of relief at parting. Regina Dembo's experiences were typical in this matter:

> On arrival we stayed a week with a European friend of mother's who had arrived in the US shortly before we did. After about a week our uncle, my mother's brother, rented an apartment in Brooklyn, where we lived for three months. Since he was about to be married and he did not realize how expensive and difficult it would be to keep us, he requested aid from the Jewish Federation of Philanthropies in New York.[41]

Regina Dembo and her two sisters were sent to the *Pleasantville* reception centre and over two and a half years were placed with three different Jewish foster families.

However, most of the foster families had no family connection to the refugee children that they offered to house. The majority were decent, genuinely wishing to offer a home to a refugee child. However, there were those whose motives were not always pure. Some wanted children to act as companions to their own children, and one agency received a request for a thirteen-year-old girl who, it turned out, was to be a companion for the seventeen-year-old disabled daughter of the family. In another community people had the mistaken impression that GJCA was bringing over children to be servants.[42]

Families requesting to foster refugee children were examined by the child welfare organizations which obviously rejected those which were unsuitable. This situation was very different than that of the refugee children who had found homes in Great Britain where larger numbers in fact ended up serving as companions and maids. This was due to the discombobulation of thousands of refugee children in Britain due to their evacuation at the war's outbreak and the larger scope of the British rescue operation which involved over 10,000 refugee children from Central Europe as opposed to the 1,000 or so refugee children who made their new home in the United States.

The lack of suitable homes, which during the mid-1930s nearly caused the termination of the GJCA operation, continued to plague the agency throughout most of its existence. Rabbis were occasionally asked to appeal for homes. From the late 1930s, the policy of GJCA avoided resettling children in and around New York City, thereby hastening the assimilation into American society and avoiding the formation of conspicuous groups of refugee children. This policy was an outgrowth of the general resettlement policy of the NRS ('New York is big, America is bigger') which actively encouraged immigrants to settle in areas outside the east coast in general and New York City in particular in order to avoid creating refugee enclaves and encouraging anti-Semitism.[43]

Most of the refugee children in the United States were ultimately placed in large cities with approximately 27 per cent in the greater New York area. Other cities where refugee children were resettled included Chicago, Philadelphia, St Louis, Los Angeles, Cleveland, Detroit, Baltimore, Boston, Newark, Atlanta, Pittsburgh, Cincinnati and Kansas City. Cities having between two and ten children included Albany, Bridgeport, Buffalo, Columbus, Dallas, New Orleans, Omaha, Portland, Rochester, Seattle, Dayton, Denver, Hartford, Indianapolis, Louisville, Milwaukee, Minneapolis, New Haven, Washington DC and Wilmington. El Paso, Houston, Manchester, Nashville, Oklahoma City, Providence, San Antonio, Shreveport, Spokane and Stockton had one refugee child each.

Once the children were settled, the local child care agencies were responsible for them along with their foster parents. Children maintained contact with a social worker until their discharge at age twenty-one. Contact was usually on a monthly basis and these meetings were often used for purchasing clothes with money from the local child care agency. 'Shopping was a dreaded task',[44] said a fifteen-year-old girl from Munich. 'I was always torn between what any teenager wanted and having to take very forceful "suggestions" on what was proper from my social worker'.[45] During these shopping jaunts the child was given a chance to make his or her own selection under the social worker's guidance and within a budget. In practice, it usually meant purchasing only utilitarian clothing since public money could not be wasted on fashionable items. 'I always wanted saddle shoes', recalled Camilla Maas. 'All the girls in my class had them and probably every Jewish girl from a middle-class family in the city had them. Yet, my social worker was adamant in insisting that they were a luxury I did not need, as saddle shoes, being black and white, would dirty much quicker than the standard utilitarian all black or brown'.[46]

How did refugee children react to the adventure that they were undergoing? Among the important issues that they dealt with were their attitude towards their parents and foster parents, learning a new language, their education and future. Many, if not most of the children, had left their parents in Europe, with communication after the outbreak of war becoming difficult, if not non-existent. There were children who were angry with their parents for having sent them away. 'My most vivid memories were a constant desire to be reunited with my family and occasionally I would be angry for having been sent here', stated Freda Grab who reached the United States in 1939.[47] With the outbreak of war, those children who had reached the United States before September 1939 were naturally frantic about their parents' fate. Those arriving during wartime had often already been cut off from parents for weeks, months and even years. This, however, did not lessen their fears regarding what was unfolding in Europe in general and regarding their parents' fate in particular.

Foster parents were another issue. Some of the children took very well to their new families, others less so. There were children who needed re-placement several times until the social services found an environment which was suitable for them. While the large majority of foster parents were people who out of the goodness of their hearts wanted to host a refugee child, there were still many cases of expectations versus reality. Young blond, blue-eyed girls were much in demand. Older children of both sexes were considered harder to place than younger ones and foster parents usually preferred girls to boys. These difficulties were illustrated by the number of boys who needed re-placing in foster homes throughout the prewar and war years. Potential foster parents were at times only ready to accept refugee children under their own terms. Upon discovering that the children were predominantly older boys, just ordinary children, not 'geniuses' and not for adoption, more than one family reneged on the offer of a home.[48]

Language was an important issue in the children's Americanization. Very few of the children knew any English upon arrival. However, most of them picked up English quickly, depending, of course, upon their age at arrival. According to most scholars of language, the cut-off date for accents is around age fifteen. If a child moves to a new country before the age of ten he or she will usually speak without an accent. Between ten and fifteen years of age, the child's accent will depend upon how good an ear they have for languages. After the age of fifteen most children will retain some foreign inflection and at times, even a completely foreign accent in their new language. This seems to have held true for most of the refugee children who came to the United States. School-age children rapidly acquired a reading and writing knowledge of the language. Fluency in spoken English was usually achieved in six months or a year. Ursula Pels Block attributed her fluency in English to the fact that she did not live in New York. 'If one stayed in New York and lived in Washington Heights', she wrote, 'one could communicate in German forever'.[49]

Education was a concern of all those involved in the refugee child issue: the refugee organizations, the children, their parents, foster parents, social workers and of course, educators. The release form which parents or guardians had signed in Europe entrusted GJCA with the education and training of their children. Due to their interrupted education and language difficulties, some refugee children were initially put back several grades or placed in a combined class for foreigners of all ages. Within a short period, however, most children were permitted to enter their regular grades. 'I received some extra tutoring in language', recalled Eric Greene about his early school days in America, 'but was ahead of my age in math and geography and sciences'.[50]

Two studies on the education of young refugees concluded that the children enjoyed learning and viewed school as a challenge and not a chore.[51] This was supported by the children themselves. 'It was hard getting back into a regular school routine', said a girl from Munich, 'but it became a challenge to see how long it would take me to catch up to my American schoolmates'.[52] Accustomed to the rigid European system of education, most refugee children adapted rapidly to the more flexible American system. Viewing education as a challenge there were refugee children who received educational prizes or grants for exceptional scholarship. For example, a fifteen-year-old refugee girl in New York City won a citywide high school contest for her essay 'What it means to me to be an American' and another refugee girl received first prize in a national contest for her essay entitled 'Why national unity is important to my country'.[53]

Academic excellence, however, could not always be translated into professional training. Although many of the children had come from families with white-collar professional backgrounds, budgetary limitations of child welfare services often made it difficult to obtain higher education and training. After completing high school children were expected to earn a living. 'No one even brought up the possibility of my going on for higher education', wrote Helga.[54] 'Although both my real and foster families were intellectual it was understood that as early as possible I was to go out and earn my keep'.[55] Information sheets distributed to parents while the children were still in Europe warned of this contingency and requested parents to prepare their children accordingly.[56]

Nevertheless, family tradition, the desire for education, and the Servicemen's Readjustment Act of 1944, commonly known as the GI Bill, were among the factors that enabled refugee children who managed to complete professional training later in life, often after their military service. Among former refugee children one finds college professors, nurses, physicians, lawyers, business people, insurance agents, writers, manufacturers and restaurant owners. All of those I interviewed for my study appeared to be loyal Americans, aware of the wonderful qualities of the country which gave them a home and the unique society which absorbed them. It is probably for that reason that the Jewish refugee children who came to the United States did not exhibit two characteristics I found in my study of those children who went to Great Britain.[57] While a not inconsiderable number of the children who came to Britain ended up in Israel and an equally striking number ended up converting to Christianity, I found almost no parallels among the children who came to America. By placing children with families of their own religion, the American child care agencies made sure that they would not be pressured through proselytizing by their foster families. Similarly, the unique nature of American society – originally a melting pot of immigrants – made almost all refugee children feel at home enough to not want to leave the country that became their home. These two qualities of the child refugee experience in the United States are unparalleled in any other country which I examined that gave refuge to children persecuted by the Nazis during the prewar and wartime period.

'What is past is prologue' reads the inscription on the base of one of the statues flanking the entrance to the *National Archives* in Washington DC The refugee issue of the 1930s was a harbinger of the postwar Displaced Persons (DP), the exodus of Eastern Europe and more recently the displacement of millions from the Third World. Throughout the decade following the end of the Second World War and as a result of lessons learned during the Hitler era, United States immigration policy and even popular attitudes towards refugees, both young and old, began to undergo drastic changes. American contrition over restrictionist policies served as a successful lubricant for subsequent liberalized immigration policies. While neither overthrowing the quota system, nor ignoring previously existing restrictions, American legislation would begin righting the wrong done by the United States government to the hapless refugees of the Third Reich. Postwar displaced children would, at least in this respect, reap the fruits sown by the bitter tears of their refugee counterparts during the 1930s.

What would be the reaction of the American legislature today if asked to pass emergency rescue bills to bring tens of thousands of children for an unspecified amount of time to the United States, just like the Wagner–Rogers Bill of 1939? And more specifically, what would happen if these children were Jewish? Would the American administration risk going against a worldwide growing tide of anti-Semitism in order to back such a step? Would American-Jewish organizations be willing to pressure the government on this matter, take out full page advertisements appealing for the large-scale rescue of Jewish children, and turn to Jews throughout the United States to open their homes to young unaccompanied refugees? And if given cold 'logical' reasons why such a plan would be unfeasible, for how long would these organizations continue to 'buck the system' in order to generate enough publicity that would pressure the government into bringing these children to America?

Government regulations aside, what would be the attitude of the American people? Would Americans open their arms to these hordes of children who would not know a word of English, have different customs, and – on top of everything else – not for a month, or a year, but for an unspecified amount of time? Would their charitable nature extend to doing much more than writing a cheque, or making a one-time gesture, to taking on a full-time responsibility which would probably upset their household ways, and change every facet of their daily life? Would they be willing to short-change their own children in order to divide up their emotional and even financial resources among a group that included one more child, a refugee, a stranger? Would they be willing and able to cope with the traumas that such children would bring into a household, and be subject to pressure from some of those children to vouch for their parents who were still overseas and save them as well?

When put that way the refugee child issue suddenly sounds very different than the bland title 'Jewish Refugee Children in the USA'. One can only hope that in the future the topic will remain a historical one and that no government or people would ever be asked again to rise to the hour and be put to the test of what they would do under such circumstances.

Notes

1   Minutes of the executive committee of the American Jewish Committee, 1 September 1933, v. 4 pt. 1, American Jewish Committee Archives, New York (henceforth: AJC archives).

2   Barbara M. Steward, *United States Government Policy on Refugees from Nazism 1933–1940*, PhD dissertation (New York: Columbia University 1969), pp. 76–7.

3   Kohler to Perkins, 6 April 1934, Morris D. Waldman files, RG 1, EX0-29, file 3 AJC Archives.

4   Children arriving with their parents were listed under the parents' quota and thus, children born in Germany of Polish parents were ineligible for the German quota if travelling with their parents. Dubinsky to Galter, 24 January 1940, Local German-Jewish Children's Aid (henceforth: GJCA) committee papers, box 4, folder 10, Philadelphia Jewish Archives Center, Philadelphia, PA (henceforth: PJA); meeting on aid to German children of GJCA, 3 January 1934, AJC chronological files, RG 17 GEN – 3, fox 3, folder 1, January–February 1934, AJC Archives.

5   AJC Archives, GJCA papers, file group 249; 'Statement of incorporation of GJCA', GJCA papers, file 1, Yidisher Visnshaftlekher Institut Archives, New York (henceforth: YIVO). The underlying premise was 'to establish in the United States a kind of Youth Aliyah', Arieh Tartakower and Kurt R. Grossman, *The Jewish Refugee* (New York: Institute of Jewish Affairs 1944), p. 476.

6   Bat Ami Zucker, *Cecilia Razovsky and the American Jewish Women's Rescue Operation in the Second World War* (London: Vallentine Mitchell 2008).

7   *The New York Times*, 10 November 1934, p. 5.
8   Author's interview with Marilyn Stavisky, Philadelphia, 26 August 1982.
9   Report, 31 December 1940, GJCA file 127, YIVO. See also Haim Genizi, 'New York is Big – America is Bigger: The Resettlement of Refugees from Nazism, 1936–1945', *Jewish Social Studies* 66 (Winter 1984), pp. 61–72.
10 Minutes GJCA, 13 May 1937; 20 January 1938, Chamberlain papers, file 14, YIVO archives.
11 *Congressional Record* v. 84, pt. 2, 1278, text of SJR 64.
12 *The New York Times*, 2 March 1939, p. 10.
13 *Refugee Facts* (Philadelphia: American Friends Service Committee 1939), pp. 13–15; Henry Smith Leiper, 'Those German Refugees', *Current History* (May 1939), pp.19–22; 'An Appeal for Refugee Children', *School and Society* (15 April 1939), p. 474.
14 EMW to FDR, 2 June 1939, OF 3186, Franklin Delano Roosevelt Library (FDRL), Hyde Park, New York.
15 McIntyre to Cantor, 27 January 1939, PPF 1018, FDRL.
16 Activity on children's programmes, 12 January 1942; publicity division discussion with Hannah Ziegler, 9 June 1942; Levy to Ziegler, 14 May 1942, memo NRS, 7 May 1942 from Ziegler, Levy to Ziegler, 27 April 1942 all in National Refugee Service (NRS) papers file 197, YIVO.
17 GJCA incorporation notice, GJCA file 5, YIVO.
18 The original Russian name, *Obczestyo Sdravokhraneniye Evreyev* meant the Society for the Health of the Jewish Population. An alternative definition of the initials was *Organization pour la Santé et l'Education* (Organization for Health and Education). Regarding the organization's history see Ernst Papanek and Edward Linn, *Out of the Fire* (New York: William Morrow 1975).
19 Selfhelp of Emigres from Central Europe, *Selfhelp in Action: Report on the Activities of the Selfhelp for German Emigres, Inc. 1938–1939* (New York: Selfhelp 1939); *National Information Bureau Bulletin* (4 March 1941), Morris D. Waldman Files RGI=EXO-29 file 3, AJC Archives; American Friends Service Committee (AFSC) programme in France, 1940–1, Foreign service. France. Relief general, 11940, American Friends Service Committee Archives, Philadelphia, PA.
20 Excerpts from board meeting of the USC, 12 March 1943, published on 28 April 1943, file: refugee children, 1943–1945, JDC Archives.
21 Judith Tydor Baumel, *Unfulfilled Promise: Rescue and Resettlement of Jewish Refugee Children in the United States 1934–1945* (Juneau: Denali 1990), pp. 29–30; Minutes of meeting held at Dr Kenworthy's home, 29 June 1939, 7. AFSC Archives; Messersmith to Geist, 6 February 1939 and Kraus to Messersmith, 9 February 1939, both in State Department files 150:626J. RG 59 b. 150 National Archives, Washington D.C.
22 Interview with Käte Rosenheim, head of the Children's Emigration Department, Oral History Division (OHD), Institute for Contemporary Jewry, the Hebrew University, Jerusalem 63 (27).

23 Author's interview with Norbert Wollheim, New York, 11 April 1981; author's interview with Hilda Matzdorf, Jerusalem, 3 December 1981.
24 Mark Jonathan Harris and Deborah Oppenheimer, *Into the Arms of Strangers: Stories of the Kindertransport* (London: Bloomsbury 2000), pp. 77–8.
25 Herta Souhami, OHD 50 (27).
26 Marcuse's curriculum vitae appears in *Review of EJCA*, GJCA file 161 YIVO.
27 *New York Post* (28 December 1940), OSE file 86, YIVO. Castendyck to Lovejoy, 26 April 1940, Children's Bureau files, box 592. National Archives, Washington D.C.
28 The girl requested to remain anonymous.
29 Morris to Non-Sectarian Foundation, 30 April 1940, GJCA file 112; Marcuse to Kepecs, 3 October 1941, GJCA file 127; Lang to GJCA, 13 November 1941, GJCA file 290, YIVO.
30 Van-Tijn Cohn of the Dutch refugee's committee to Marcuse, undated, GJCA file 7, YIVO.
31 Katherine F. Lenroot, 'The Untied States Program for the Care of Refugee Children', *Proceedings of the National Conference of Social Work 1941*, (1941), p. 203.
32 Frawley to Noble, 28 July 1941, AFSC foreign service, France-relief. Marseilles – letters, May–August 1941, AFSC Archives.
33 Papanek to OSE Montintin, 14 January 1941, OSE file 104, YIVO. Author's interview with Camilla Maas, New York, April 1981.
34 Shaughnessey to Secretary of State, 5 January 1938 and State Department to consul Berlin, 9 August 1938, State Department files, RG 59, B 148, National Archives, Examples in GJCA file 25, YIVO.
35 Report on children arriving on Serpa Pinto, March 1943, GJCA file 165, YIVO.
36 Marcuse to Wise, 13 October 1941, GJCA file 82, YIVO.
37 Report on children arriving in September 1941, GJCA file 485, YIVO.
38 Report on children coming from Vienna, 1 April 1940, GJCA file 477, YIVO.
39 Author's correspondence with Lillian Kramer, November 1981.
40 Marcuse to Vienna Kultusgemeinde, 12 February 1941, Central Archive for the history of the Jewish People, A/W 2001, Jerusalem, Israel.
41 Questionnaire, Regina M. Dembo, Meeting Juvenile Aid Society, 28 November 1939, GJCA committee, box 5 folder 2, Philadelphia Jewish Archives.
42 *Review of EJCA*. GJCA file 161, YIVO.
43 Report, 31 December 1940, GJCA file 127, YIVO.
44 Author's interview with Camilla Maas, New York, 1 April 1981.
45 Ibid.
46 Ibid.
47 Questionnaire, Freda Grab.
48 *Review of EJCA*. GJCA file 161, YIVO.

49 Questionnaire, Ursula Pels Block.
50 Questionnaire, Eric G. Greene.
51 Elisabeth Tilly Gutman, *Refugee Children Adjustment in the United States* (New York: Columbia University School of Social Work 1947), p. 23, found in Papanek papers, box 9, New York Public Library. Gunther Gerald Gates, *A Study of the Achievement and Adjustment of German Refugee Students in American Public High Schools in the San Francisco Bay Area*, PhD dissertation (Berkeley: University of California 1955), p. 94.
52 Questionnaire, W.Y. The girl requested to remain anonymous.
53 *Intermountain Jewish News*, 22 August 1941, p. 2; *The Jewish Way*, 13 February 1944, p. 10; *Newscast* 4, November–December 1943, p. 3.
54 Family names of the interviewees are not disclosed to respect the wishes of some of the participants for confidentiality.
55 Questionnaire, H. B.
56 Report on children arriving May–October 1943, GJCA file 485, Central Archive for the history of the Jewish People A/W 2000. *Merkblatt für die nach Amerika ausgewanderten Kinder und ihre Eltern* (Berlin, n.d).
57 Judith Tydor Baumel-Schwartz, *Never Look Back: The Jewish Refugee Children in Great Britain 1938–1945* (West Lafayette: Purdue University Press 2012).

CHAPTER TWO

'Detour to Canada':

The Fate of Juvenile Austrian-Jewish Refugees after the 'Anschluss' of 1938

Andrea Strutz

Viennese-born Peter Heller, Josef Kates, Bryan Sterling, Eric Kruh and Josef Eisinger were teenage boys when German troops marched into Austria on 12 March 1938. As youths they experienced humiliation and persecution by the Nazi regime due to their Jewish descent and, ultimately, they had to flee. The five boys in the centre of this study share a common destiny: As youths they managed to flee to Great Britain, where, after the outbreak of the Second World War, they were all interned as 'enemy aliens'. Moreover in 1940, they were deported to Canada, together with 2,290 other, mostly Jewish refugees. Although a few historical and sociological studies researched the reasons for German and Austrian-Jewish refugees being deported from Great Britain to Canada and some of these studies also focused on individual experiences and memories of internees,[1] the life stories of nearly all the Austrians in that group have not yet been examined in detail.[2]

The aim of this chapter is to overcome that neglect by examining the life stories of these five Viennese Jews who were teenagers at the time of their deportation as 'enemy aliens' to Canada.[3] The chapter draws on oral histories, a diary and archival material, to trace their memories and experiences as youths particularly with regard to their escape from Austria to Great Britain in 1938 and the internment experience in Canada from 1940–2.[4] The 'detour' to Canada in 1940 affected the biographies of these juvenile Austrian refugees from Nazism significantly; they ended up rebuilding their lives in North America and never returned to their birth country.

The systematic persecution on racist grounds against the Jewish population started in Austria with great force right after the 'Anschluss', the Nazi invasion of Austria in March 1938. Due to a series of discriminating laws, Jews were deprived of their civil rights, removed from economic and public life, and their property was looted and expropriated.[5] Jewish businesses, real estates, apartments and all other assets had to be registered ('property notice' from April 1938), and most of it was 'aryanized' by the so-called *Nazi Property Transaction Office* (*Vermögensverkehrsstelle*). Jews increasingly lost their means of existence, e.g. only a few weeks after the 'Anschluss' Jewish school teachers, university scholars and Jewish civil servants in all working fields were dismissed. Jews were forbidden to practise certain professions, which particularly affected laywers, tax accountants, artists, pharmacists, veterinarians and dentists. Medical doctors lost their licence to practise and were permitted to treat Jewish patients only. Jewish schoolchildren were separated from non-Jewish pupils and were required to attend Jewish collection schools.[6]

Terror and violence in the course of the November pogrom of 1938 increased the pressure upon the Jewish population to flee Austria.[7] In the 'Reichskristallnacht', Jewish-owned businesses and homes were plundered and destroyed, synagogues were burnt down and thousands of Jewish men were arrested and deported to concentrations camps such as Dachau and Buchenwald.[8] In the following months, Jews were even further excluded from public life and virtually lost their means of existence by decrees and regulations; by now it also became nearly impossible for them to find employment in the private sector. They were banned from public parks, swimming pools and all other athletic facilities, and they were forbidden to attend any form of entertainment such as theatres or cinemas. Strict restrictions were furthermore introduced for the use of public transport, the purchase of groceries or medical treatment.[9] In 1939, Jews had to add 'Sara' or 'Israel' to their names, and their passports were marked with a red 'J' on the cover. Moreover, Jews were driven out of their apartments and were required to move into collection flats located in Vienna, from where in spring 1941 the first deportations were carried out.

In Austria, called 'Ostmark' after the 'Anschluss', roughly 200,000 persons – 3 per cent of the residential population – were considered Jews by the racial Nuremberg Laws.[10] At the beginning, the anti-Jewish Nazi policy aimed at the expulsion of the Jewish population. The *Office for Jewish Emigration* (*Zentralstelle für jüdische Auswanderung*), established in August 1938 in Vienna and headed until 1939 by Adolf Eichmann, played a crucial role. It was the only authority that issued exit permits, which were an absolute prerequisite for anyone to leave the country. To obtain such an exit permit, discriminatory taxes had to be paid, such as the *Reichsfluchtsteuer*, a tax imposed on people leaving the Reich, or the *Judenvermögensabgabe* (JUVA), the Jewish Property Levy, which was calculated on the basis of the registered assets' purchase price.[11]

By the end of 1938, already 68,000 Jews had fled Austria, and until September 1939 the number of Jewish refugees almost doubled to 120,000. Afterwards the waves of refugees abated due to the outbreak of the Second World War; the peak was reached by October 1941 when 130,742 – two-thirds of the Austrian-Jewish population – had left their home country.[12] At that moment, the anti-Jewish Nazi policy had already turned from expulsion to systematic extinction and genocide. In October 1941, a full stop to Jewish emigration was ordered, which caused a life-threatening situation for the remaining Jewish population in the country.[13] Already in the spring of 1941 deportations from Vienna to ghettos and extermination camps such as Auschwitz, Sobibor, Theresienstadt and Lodz had begun. Those who were considered unfit for work ('arbeitsunfähig'), which especially concerned children and elderly and often frail people, were at a high risk to be murdered right after their arrival in the camps. In about forty-five transports more than 48,000 persons were deported from Austria, less than 2,000 of them survived the Nazi camps. Furthermore, roughly 16,600 refugees were caught by Nazi persecutors on the run in countries that later became occupied by the regime. Altogether about 65,400 Austrian Jews were murdered, which means that almost a third of the Austrian Jews fell victim to the Shoah.[14]

Jewish refugees had to overcome considerable obstacles by Nazi authorities in order to receive exit permits and passports. As a result, when the papers were finally issued, the necessary expenses usually left them penniless due to expropriation and the payment of all the anti-Jewish taxes. They were also in urgent need to obtain affidavits from sponsors, entry visas, and tickets for timely transportation. However, strict quota systems, such as the immigration rules of the United States of America,[15] and the introduction of a visa requirement for Great Britain[16] for Austrians and Germans, as well as the reluctance of numerous countries to accept mainly impoverished Jewish refugees, severly hampered or even prevented emigration. The following table shows that more than 50 per cent of the Austrian-Jewish refugees first fled to other European countries (70,000), of whom Great Britain absorbed a great share (31,000). Another 30,000 Austrians (23 per cent) went directly to the United States of America. Roughly 17 per cent emigrated to Asia and the Near East, where the major flow of refugees was directed to Palestine (15,200) and China/Shanghai (6,220). A further 6,845 Austrians (around 5 per cent) were granted asylum in Latin America, and about 2 per cent survived in Australia and Africa.

At the beginning of the twentieth century, Vienna was the centre of Jewish life, where over 90 per cent of the Austrian Jewry lived. As a matter of fact, Vienna was home to the third-largest Jewish community in Europe. Prior to 1938, Jews played a significant role in various fields such as literature, music and psychoanalysis. They were amongst the most important figures who

Table 2.1 Outflow of Jews from Austria 1938–41.

Continent	Number of refugees	percentage	Destinations (selected)	Refugees admitted
Europe	69,390	53.2	Great Britain	31,050
			Switzerland	5,800
			France	4,850
			Belgium	4,670
			Hungary	4,400
			Czechoslovakia	4,100
			Italy	3,870
			other	10,650
North America	29,942	22.9	USA	29,860
			Canada	82
Asia incl. Near East	22,390	17.1	Palestine	15,200
			China/Shanghai	6,220
			India	250
			other	720
Latin America	6,845	5.2	Argentina	1,690
			Bolivia	940
			Uruguay	560
			Cuba	532
			Columbia	530
			Brazil	360
			other	2,233
Africa	1,125	0.9	South Africa	332
			Uganda	120

			Tunisia	150
			Morocco	100
			other	423
Australia	1,050	0.8	Australia	970
			New Zealand	80
Total	130,742	100.0		

Source: Jonny Moser, *Demographie der jüdischen Bevölkerung Österreichs 1938–1945* (Vienna: DÖW 1999), pp. 65–71.

created the cultural milieu known as 'Viennese Modernism'. Although anti-Semitism was manifest in Austria before the 'Anschluss', many testimonies of Holocaust survivors indicate that Jews felt very much at home in Austria before 1938 and were also deeply rooted in the Austrian culture. At the same time, many also treasured their Jewish heritage, including the practice of various forms of religious traditions from liberal to Orthodox. The testimonies of the young Viennese boys in this study include clear references to multiple identities and identifications.

Peter Heller, born January 1920 in Vienna, was the only son of Hans Heller,[17] a Viennese industrialist, owner of the well-known confectionary factory Gustav & Wilhelm Heller, and his wife Margarete. Peter grew up in a wealthy upper-class family with left-liberal political views and an interest in psychoanalysis; his father had close connections to the artistic and literary avant-garde of the time, often supporting their activities financially and even writing himself. Since Peter's parents identified as atheists and humanists, Jewish religion did not play any role in the boy's upbringing.[18] After his parents' divorce, the four-year-old lived mainly with his father. As he was deeply affected by the situation created, Peter attended between 1929 and 1932 child psychoanalysis sessions with Anna Freud. His school education started at an evangelical primary school but then at age eight he moved to a small private school[19] in the Viennese district of *Hietzing*, and later on attended a public grammar school, *Realschule Diefenbachgasse*, in the fifteenth district. Peter remembers that he was sometimes insulted by schoolmates and teachers who called him 'Saujud', but he never experienced physical violence. Within a few weeks after the 'Anschluss', Jewish schoolchildren were separated from their Gentile peers, and Peter was transferred to the largest Jewish collection school, the *Realschule* in *Kleine Sperlgasse* in the second district *Leopoldstadt*.[20] There, he completed his high school education in May 1938 along with sixty other Jewish students.[21] Soon after the 'Anschluss', it became very clear to the Hellers that they had to leave. Peter was the first one to leave for Paris together with his two-years' younger cousin from where they continued their journey to London. They arrived in England on 23 July 1938, where they were supposed to work as volunteers in a candy factory owned by one of Hans Heller's business partners. Following the liquidation of his candy factory, Hans also escaped to London together with his second, non-Jewish wife. Peter remembers his time in London as a stressful and unsatisfactory one.[22] In his diary, he states that he often lived just for the day; he soon stopped working at the candy factory and tried to follow his dream of becoming a pianist. In the end, Peter was indeed accepted at the University of Cambridge as a student of music, and moved to Cambridge in February 1940.

Josef Kates was born in May 1921 to a Jewish middle-class family and was the second youngest of six children.[23] His parents, Anna and Bernhard Katz, were both from Galicia (today part of Western Ukraine), a former crownland of Austria-Hungary. They owned a poultry shop in Vienna's fifth district, *Margarethen*. Josef remembers that his parents spoke Yiddish with each other, but only German with their children. Judaism was not particularly important, but the family attended the synagogue to celebrate the Jewish holidays. As a boy, Josef enjoyed playing soccer, biking in the Viennese Woods and skiing in the mountains. However, his childhood recollections also reflect that he was affected by anti-Semitism. He remembers a hostile climate in a city plastered with anti-Semitic stickers and posters as well as being physically attacked by schoolmates. Until the 'Anschluss', Josef attended the *Goethe Realschule*. When after the annexation of Austria, he found himself placed in the last row together with two other Jewish boys of his class, Josef left school and started preparations to leave Austria.[24] In June 1938, he left Vienna on his own – heading to Italy first and then to Switzerland. Late in 1938, he was joined in Zurich by some of his siblings and his father. As they all had temporary permits for Switzerland, Josef's elder sisters did their best to obtain British visas for the whole family. In February 1939, Josef arrived in London and by the summer of 1939, he was reunited with his mother there.

In London, Josef became an apprentice in an optical company. His income was very small and he could barely make a living, so he decided to move to the industrial city of Leeds, where his parents and three siblings had a small apartment. He joined his family in Leeds on 1 September 1939, the day the Second World War broke out.

Bryan Sterling, originally Bruno Zwerling, was born in January 1922 in Vienna; he was the only child of Hermann Zwerling, the owner of a textile shop, and his wife Klara.[25] His father was from Galicia and his mother came from the southern region of today's Czech Republic. Bryan grew up in a middle-class household in the ninth district *Alsergrund*, surrounded by domestic servants including a nanny and a cook. His mother kept a kosher kitchen at home, and all the religious holidays were observed in the family.

As a boy, Bryan enjoyed playing soccer; he was a big fan of the soccer club *Admira Wien*, and also a supporter of the famous *Hakoah*-team of Vienna. Education was greatly valued by the Viennese Jewish middle class;[26] also by Bryan's family, who wanted him to become a physician. As with Josef Katz, Bryan's recollections of Vienna after the 'Anschluss' focused on the hostile atmosphere he perceived in the streets. With his blond hair and *Lederhosen*,[27] he was spared insults and attacks, but was also relegated from the sixth grade of his grammar school *Realgymnasium Stubenbastei* to the Jewish collection school in *Sperlgasse*. A few weeks later, his Austrian schooling came to an end. His father, on a business trip in Olomouc on the day of Austria's 'Anschluss', organized from Czechoslovakia the escape of his family, and had his wife and son cross the border illegally on a night train on 23 June 1938. Bryan spent about two months in Olomouc, and then escaped to Great Britain on a student visa organized by an uncle in Manchester. In May 1939, his parents too obtained a life-changing British visa and came out to England to work as a cook and a chauffeur. After one year of schooling in Britain, in August 1939 Bryan was granted permission to become a toolmaking apprentice (making measuring instruments for ships) in Pendleton, north of Manchester.[28]

Eric(h) Kruh was born to Anna and Isaak Kruh in February 1922.[29] The family lived in Vienna's first district and Eric's father ran a sports clothing shop that secured their existence. As many other acculturated Jews in Vienna, Eric's family practised the Jewish faith in a liberal way and generally attended services in the synagogue only on high holidays such as Yom Kippur, Rosh Hashanah and Passover. In his interview, Eric mentioned that he and his family did not experience anti-Semitism before 1938. The family embraced social democratic values, which Eric held on to for his entire life.[30] Eric's main interest as a boy was soccer. He often went to games with his father and he was a soccer player himself at the grammar school *Realgymnasium Stubenbastei*. His favourite soccer team was *Austria Wien*. Although the Kruh family was very aware of political developments in Germany – an uncle left for Italy before 1938 – they did not take any precautions. Like the other Viennese boys in this chapter, Eric, too, was transferred to the collection school in *Sperlgasse* shortly after the 'Anschluss'. He was able to finish sixth grade, but then was banned from school. His parents' sports clothing shop was looted and the Kruh family lost their means of existence. They desperately tried to acquire visas and affidavits but without any success. Finally, Eric was accepted on a *Kindertransport* to Great Britain in February 1939. After his arrival in Britain, he was sent to Leeds, and placed in the care of the local Jewish community. Roughly 2,300 Austrian-Jewish children like Eric were saved by the *Kindertransports*;[31] these life-saving transports from Vienna to Great Britain took place between December 1938 and August 1939.[32] Eric's parents, however, had to stay behind until August 1939 when they escaped, travelling illegally to Italy and from there to Switzerland. In Leeds, sixteen-year-old Eric became a labourer in a textile factory. For a boy who in Vienna was preparing for his university studies, the new realities of life meant a culture shock. In his interview, Eric recalled life in Leeds as dreadful and emotionally draining, particularly because he was unaware of the fate of his parents and other relatives who had stayed back in Vienna.[33]

The youngest of the Austrian child refugees in this study is Josef Eisinger; he was born in Vienna in March 1924. Together with his older sister he grew up in the third Viennese district, *Landstrasse*.[34] The family, of Galician origin, was liberal in its outlook, although his parents were observant and kept a kosher home. Like Eric and Bryan, Josef also attended *Realgymnasium Stubenbastei* (until fourth grade) and he, too, was very much interested in soccer. In his interview, Josef vividly described all the soccer tournaments that the schoolboys organized. Furthermore, Josef mentioned that he rarely experienced anti-Semitism personally, but he did sense anti-Semitic attitudes during his childhood: 'Anti-Semitism was always a part of Vienna, but one didn't take it so seriously, one made jokes about it'.[35] However, after the 'Anschluss' the climate in Vienna became hostile. Like the other Jewish boys, Josef was relegated to the Jewish collection school in *Sperlgasse*. When their drug store was looted, the Eisinger family lost their means of existence and realized they could no longer live in Austria. As they could not obtain affidavits and visas for the whole family, they had to flee one by one. At first, Josef's sister Ilse was granted a visa for Great Britain and immigrated as an au-pair girl aided by a British business partner of the family. Luckily, Josef could join a *Kindertransport* and left for London in March 1939. Since in Vienna juvenile boys were in high danger of being arrested in the streets, many of the transports carried out between December 1938 and March 1939 consisted mainly of teenage boys (at least half and sometimes even up to two-thirds).[36] After his escape, fourteen-year-old Josef ended up in the region of Yorkshire on a remote and primitive farm (without running water, and hardly any electricity) and became a hard-working stable lad. In his interview, he pointed out that he felt very lonely and uprooted there, because he had no one to share his worries and fears with.[37] However, luckily, he could keep in contact with his family via letters to his sister in London and his parents, who fled Austria as late as December 1939 on an illegal ship taking them down the Danube to Palestine.[38] In spring 1940, Josef, who had just turned sixteen, moved down to Brighton on the south coast, where his sister had found him a job as dish washer at a hotel.

At this moment in time, the paths of the five juvenile Austrian escapees in Great Britain intersected. The developments in Europe and the great fear of a German invasion in Great Britain, in particular, affected their future destiny crucially. After the outbreak of the war, British authorities classified all nationals of a power they were at war with as 'enemy aliens'. In mid-September 1939 112 'alien tribunals' – twenty-three of them in London alone – were established across Britain to review the foreigners' status, which also included refugees.[39] Approximately 84,000 foreign nationals were under observation by those tribunals and judged according to their loyalty or resentment to Nazi Germany. The vast majority of them (64,200) was alloted to category 'C' ('friendly alien', no restrictions of freedom of movement), 86 per cent of which (55,400 persons) were classified as 'refugees from Nazi oppression'. Persons categorized under category 'B' ('friendly enemy alien') came under police observation and experienced certain restrictions on freedom of movement. However, only a small share of the investigated foreigners were regarded as disloyal and therefore allocated to category 'A', leading to immediate internment as 'dangerous enemy aliens'.[40]

Although initial policies against Austrian and German refugees from Nazism were less restrictive, this changed in the course of the German war of expansion in May 1940 and the pressures from the British right-wing press. Now the hostility against German-speaking residents, irrespective of their status, radically increased. Finally 'the government gave way to those who argued that the refugees posed a threat to national security, as potential fifth columnists who might sabotage British defences'.[41] As a result, German-speaking foreigners assigned to category 'B' and 'C' were also interned.[42] From 12 May 1940 onwards, arrests without prior notice took place and also affected minors aged sixteen and above, notwithstanding that many had just escaped from Nazi Germany on *Kindertransports*. That very day, Peter Heller was arrested in his boarding house in Cambridge and a detective brought him to a town hall crowded with Austrian and German refugees.[43] Josef Eisinger remembers that two friendly policemen picked him up at his work place in a Brighton hotel and that he was detained for several days in the racecourse building of the city. Eric Kruh and Josef Kates were also arrested around mid-May in Leeds, as well as Bryan Sterling, who then lived near Manchester. At first they all thought that the arrest would only be a temporary measure, but this turned out to be just the beginning of a hastily organized mass internment of 'enemy aliens'. Soon they were transported to Huyton near Liverpool, where an improvised camp for approximately 5,000 'enemy aliens' was erected on a newly constructed but unfinished council estate.[44] Whereas Josef Eisinger and Peter Heller were later transferred to the Isle of Man – the island was quickly turned into the biggest British internment site with approximately 14,000 internees –[45] the other Viennese youths stayed in Huyton. Despite all these precautions, the British public and the cabinet still worried about potential fascist spies among the internees. Therefore, it was decided to send prisoners of war (POWs) and dangerous 'enemy aliens' (category 'A') abroad to the British Dominions. Canada assisted the British motherland and gave permission for the intake of 3,000 POWs and 4,000 category 'A' internees.[46] As the number of potentially dangerous Germans, Austrians and Italians in the camps was lower than the Canadian quota, the British added young and preferably unmarried male internees of category 'B' and 'C'. Most of them were refugees from Nazism and the five juvenile Viennese Jews were among them.[47]

By 15 July 1940, some 6,750 prisoners of war and internees had arrived in Canada on three prison ships (*Duchess of York, Ettrick, Sobieski*); the group of deportees consisted of about 1,900 POWs, 2,100 dangerous internees, 400 civilian Italians and 2,290 refugees from Nazism, almost all of them Jews.[48] The Canadian government was informed by the British about the switch in categories of the deportees on 8 July,[49] but at the beginning there were no concessions.[50] Refugees were interned alongside dangerous Nazi leaders, Nazi sympathizers and POWs in several camps in the provinces of Ontario, Quebec and New Brunswick, and had to wear prisoner of war uniforms. But soon, in order to put a stop to the physical violence that aroused due to antagonisms between inmates, the Canadian Army had to divide the camps into sectors segregated by barbed wire fences. Only in October 1940, camps were reorganized according to different groups of internees. Most of the Jewish refugees were transferred to camp 'N' (near Sherbrooke, Quebec) and to camp 'B' (Little River near Fredericton, New Brunswick).[51] To run the camps, internees had to engage in everyday routines such as kitchen work, but there were also (small) paid work programmes. For instance, Bryan Sterling produced camouflage nets for the military and both Josef Eisinger and Josef Kates worked hard as lumberjacks.[52] Although it was obvious to them that they were exploited as cheap labour,[53] their interviews revealed quite positive memories of that time. One possible explanation is that work helped to kill time as Bryan Sterling emphasized in an interview:

> You had to do something to prevent going crazy. Your own country kicks you out; you end up in another country in a prison camp in a uniform with red stripes and a big red dot at the back, so that the guards know where to shoot. Apparently you are in a camp for the whole war.[54]

Furthermore, they could afford to buy delicacies or cigarettes at the camp canteen from time to time. The fact that Canada provided plenty of food for the internees, while nutrition in the British detainment was very scarce, also coloured their memories positively. In his diary, Peter Heller repeatedly took note of his constant hunger on the Isle of Man. On 31 August 1940, he described his contradictory experiences overseas as well as his emotions:

> Enormous amounts of food. We will never forget that. Brown trout! And how much salmon I ate in Canada. You are ashamed, but you eat (anyway). You are ashamed that you do not feel so much shame at all and you are eating voraciously.[55]

Furthermore, there was also spiritual food: despite many limitations, internees created a colourful cultural life over time.[56] For instance, they performed classical concerts[57] and stage plays or organized soccer and ice hockey games for entertainment. However, negative memories about the internment were also mentioned such as the constant noise in the camps or the lack of places of retreat over the whole period of detention.

In order to improve the chances for a release, internees established camp schools. This was a very important step, since many of the interned refugees were quite young and had not finished any schooling due to Nazi persecution.[58] Therefore, great pains were taken to prepare especially the young internees for university education or for certain occupations that Canada needed. Elder internees, of whom many had been highly qualified scholars and university professors before their expulsion, gave lessons in subjects such as mathematics, physics, engineering, English language, history and art history, but also agricultural training was established.[59] The *Canadian National Committee on Refugees* (CNCR) that had been established for the support of the interned refugees in January 1941, strongly supported the school programme by providing books and other needed material. Later they also helped to find sponsors for the students' release. Three of the interned Viennese teenagers – Eric Kruh, Josef Eisinger and Josef Kates – took the chance and successfully completed their interrupted high school education during the internment in the fall of 1941.[60]

About a year after their deportation, the Canadian government accepted the insistent demand of the CNCR and changed the refugee's status from 'enemy aliens' to 'friendly aliens'. Thus, refugees were granted rights in everyday camp life (e.g. to wear civilian clothes instead of the POW-uniform or to be granted access to camps for refugees and church organizations). However, it did not mean that they were released.[61] In late 1940, a return possibility was offered by the British government to the refugees deported to Canada on condition that they would enlist in the British Army and join the non-combat Pioneer Corps.[62] In the end some 900 refugees from Nazism returned to Great Britain between December 1940 and July 1941; it can be estimated that about a quarter of them were Austrians.

For the remaining interned refugees a release became possible only late in 1941 after lengthy negotiations of the refugee lobby with the director of the immigration branch, Frederick Charles Blair. The immigration director, who was known for his anti-Jewish attitude, favoured the return of the interned refugees to Europe if possible. Hence, he created numerous bureaucratic hurdles and rigorously reviewed almost every single case in person. Therefore, releases from the camps proceeded slowly and took until 1943.[63] Refugees could gain freedom for employment preferably in war-related businesses or in agriculture, and as students if they were younger than twenty-one, had been accepted at an educational institution and had found an individual Canadian sponsor. But Blair limited the number of student releases to only 100 cases, although at least some 300 interned refugees could have been prospective students. Only a small number of the juvenile refugees was given the chance for a student release.[64]

Fortunately, three of the Austrian juveniles in this chapter were granted the opportunity to study: Peter Heller, Josef Eisinger and Eric Kruh. Peter was released on 17 November 1941[65] and went to Montreal, where he was accepted at McGill University to study music and German literature. Josef Eisinger was accepted at Toronto University to study mathematics and physics; he was released from camp 'N' on 15 December 1941. Eric Kruh's release was delayed until 26 June 1942, due to difficulties in finding a sponsor, but he was finally allowed to study German literature and European history and culture at Toronto University. Although Josef Kates was an excellent student at the camp school, he was not granted a student's release. He failed to find a sponsor as there were not enough for all the juvenile refugees eager to study. Instead, Josef was released on 19 March 1942, due to the offer of roughly thirty jobs in the optical business in Toronto for which he qualified because of his one year working experience in Great Britain. Nevertheless, Josef strongly wished to study physics and mathematics and a year after his release enrolled for extra occupational night courses at Toronto University. Bryan Sterling was interned for the longest period of time. He was released only after two and a half years of internment on 17 November 1942 and went to Toronto, where he had to accept a poorly paid factory job. To support himself, he further worked as an usher in a burlesque house at night and lent his voice to radio plays on weekends.

Only a small number of the 130,000 Austrian-Jewish refugees returned to Austria after 1945; it is estimated that some 8,000 went back.[66] Since nobody in Austria gave serious thought to the reintegration of former Jewish refugees, the low quota is not surprising. For the young men featured in this chapter a return was completely unthinkable. Also countries such as the United States and Canada provided at that point great opportunities for a new beginning overseas, which in particular applied to youth and child survivors. Indeed, the five Viennese youths in this study all look back at an extraordinary career in Canada and the United States of America.

Josef Kates is the only one who permanently settled in Canada. After his release, he settled in Toronto, where he still lives today. Many of his family members were reunited in postwar Canada; three of his sisters and also his mother came to Toronto, following Josef's father's death in Great Britain in 1969. Although he was working full time after his release from the camp, he finished his studies at Toronto University within a short period of time with a BA in Mathematics and Physics in 1948, an MA in Applied Mathematics in 1949 and a PhD in Physics in 1951. Thereupon, Josef became a successful business executive, a distinguished scientist and Canadian computer pioneer.[67]

Peter Heller immigrated to New York after his graduation from McGill University in 1944 with a BA in German Literature.[68] He completed his university education in German literature at Columbia University with an MA in 1945 and a PhD in 1951, and became an instructor in German at Harvard University (1951–4). Between 1954 and 1968, he was Associate Professor, Professor and Commonwealth Professor at the University of Massachusetts, Amherst. From 1968 until his retirement in 1990, Peter

Heller was Professor of German and Comparative Literature at the State University of New York in Buffalo. He died in Buffalo in November 1998.

At the end of the Second World War, Eric Kruh learned that his parents had survived in Switzerland and helped them move to Toronto.[69] After finishing his BA in German Literature at Toronto University, he received a fellowship from the University of Chicago and left Canada in 1946. He completed his postgraduate studies in German literature at the University of Chicago and started teaching German at the newly established Roosevelt University. Eric kept in close contact with his parents and often travelled to Toronto, where his parents spent their remaining years. After teaching in Philadephia for a short period of time, Eric was appointed Professor for European Literature at Long Island University (Brooklyn Campus), New York in 1964. He settled in Easthampton, where he lived until his death in March 2011.

Bryan Sterling was reunited with his mother early in 1946 in Toronto, but never saw his father again; he had died of pneumonia during his internment on the Isle of Man. Five years later, Bryan moved to New York City with his Canadian wife Frances. He was planning on a career as a writer and actor and assumed that the United States would be a better work place for his career plans. He succeeded and became a writer who gained nationwide recognition as an expert on the work of American entertainer Will Rogers, whose biography he published. After a rich and fulfilling life as a writer of books and newspaper articles, Bryan Sterling passed away in New York in March 2008.

Josef Eisinger first interrupted his undergraduate studies at Toronto University, choosing to serve in the Canadian Army for about two years in order to express his gratitude toward his host country. After that, he graduated from Toronto University with a BA in Mathematics and Physics in 1945, and an MA in Physics in 1948. He continued his university education at the Massachusetts Institute of Technology in Cambridge, USA, and completed a doctorate in atomic physics in 1951. Josef subsequently returned to Toronto and worked for the *National Research Council* in Ottawa. After many years of separation, the family finally joined him in Toronto: sister Ilse immigrated in 1947 and his parents came from Israel in 1952. When Josef was offered a research position at Rice University, Texas in 1953, he left Canada, but always kept in touch with his family. In 1954, he moved to New York City and for about thirty years worked at the Bell Laboratories in New Jersey. Later he became a professor at Mount Sinai School of Medicine in New York and retired from the Department of Structural and Chemical Biology in 1998. He still lives in New York with his family and has recently published a biographical study based on Albert Einstein's travel diaries from 1922 to 1933.[70]

Clearly, the five Viennese young men have all succeeded in reaching outstanding heights in their professional life. Nevertheless, the traumatic experience of expulsion, uprooting and internment during their youth had a lifelong effect on all of them. The great emotional burden is manifest in their statements and narratives, in particular when they talk about 'home'

(*Heimat*) and 'belonging'. Although some of them integrated certain cultural or culinary facets of their childhood in Vienna into their new lives overseas – Austrian dishes such as *Wiener Schnitzel* and *Palatschinken*, Viennese songs (*Wienerlieder*), classical music and opera, German literature – they had all lost a genuine feeling of belonging. Instead, they expressed alienation and also ambivalence. Eric Kruh described his feelings for Austria as a love–hate relationship and especially blamed Austrians for their lack of honesty in dealing with the Nazi past.[71] Bryan Sterling also expressed his disappointment in the Austrian government's hesitation to admit its complicity in National Socialism and its failure to apologize to the victims of Nazism for a very long period of time after the war.[72] While Bryan Sterling calls the city of New York his home and Josef Kates regards Canada as his homeland,[73] Josef Eisinger explained that he feels like falling between two stools. On the one hand, America is his home, but it is still a foreign country to him, since he did not grow up there. On the other hand, Austria has remained his home with respect to certain things, such as food and humour, although, according to his own statement, he certainly cannot call himself Austrian anymore.[74] Peter Heller, too, dealt with a fragmented identity throughout his life; he tried to come to terms with the traumatic experience of his youth by writing. He neither felt American, nor Austrian; instead, he described himself as an 'inbetweener',[75] not being at home anywhere.

In the generation of youth survivors, feelings of fragmentation and rootlessness such as those expressed in the narratives above seem to be a common reaction as they all suffered throughout life from a great emotional strain triggered by the traumatic experience of the racial persecution and expulsion by the Nazi regime. After 1945, only a few thousand Jewish refugees decided to return to Austria; for most of the survivors a return was unthinkable because of the humiliations suffered, and the younger exiles in particular saw no reason for returning to their birth country. That was also true for Peter Heller, Josef Kates, Bryan Sterling, Eric Kruh and Josef Eisinger. Their future after the war's end was in North America that offered them an opportunity for a new beginning and a new home. The life stories and particularly the distinguished careers of the former Viennese boys demonstrate that they belong to that exceptional group of youth survivors from Central Europe, who, despite their past trauma, reached prominence in various professional, academic and cultural fields and made an extraordinary contribution to American and Canadian life.

Notes

1   The most relevant publications are: Paula Jean Draper, 'The Accidental Immigrants. Canada and the Interned Refugees: Part 1', *Canadian Jewish Historical Society Journal* 2/1 (Spring 1978), pp. 1–38 and 'The Accidental Immigrants. Canada and the Interned Refugees: Part 2', *Canadian Jewish*

Historical Society Journal 2/1 (Fall 1978), pp. 80–112; Eric Koch, *Deemed Suspect. A Wartime Blunder* (Toronto: Methuen 1980); Genevieve Susemihl, '. . . *and it became my home'. Die Assimilation und Integration der deutschjüdischen Hitlerflüchtlinge in New York und Toronto* (Münster: LIT Verlag 2004); Annette Puckhaber, *Ein Privileg für wenige. Die deutschsprachige Migration nach Kanada im Schatten des Nationalsozialismus* (Münster, Hamburg, London: LIT Verlag 2002).

2   An exception is the work of Eugen Banauch. He analysed the literary work and cultural production of Jewish writers in Canada who came as internees in 1940 and stayed on after 1945. See Eugen Banauch, *Fluid Exile. Jewish Exile Writers in Canada 1940–2006* (Heidelberg: Universitätsverlag Winter 2009).

3   According to recently investigated archival material from the Canadian Jewish Congress Charities Committee National Archives approximately 600 Austrian refugees had been deported as 'enemy aliens' from Great Britain to Canada. The current research of the author aims at creating a sociological profile of the Austrian deportees as well as to trace their subsequent lives after release from Canadian internment.

4   The collection of interviews is a very time-sensitive matter due to the age of survivors. Today we can only speak with those who were youths at the time of internment. These testimonies are most valuable since many of the older refugees died before researchers in Exile Studies even became aware of this subject matter. The life stories of Josef Kates, Eric Kruh, Bryan Sterling and Josef Eisinger were recorded by the author in 1996 and 2010. Peter Heller's memories were published in several articles and the author is in the possession of a copy of his unpublished manuscript written in the mid-1980s which contains his memories about the escape from Austria to Great Britain and the Canadian internment 1940 to 1941.

5   Compared to Germany, the terror against the Austrian Jewry after the 'Anschluss', and their mass expulsion, was more brutal. At the beginning 'wild aryanizations' took place, e.g. neighbours stole from Jewish tenants or even forced them out of their apartments. For more details see Albert Lichtblau, 'Integration, Vernichtungsversuch und Neubeginn', in *Geschichte der Juden in Österreich*, ed. by Eveline Brugger et al. (Vienna: Ueberreuter 2006), pp. 447–566, here pp. 519–36; Helga Embacher, ' "Plötzlich war man vogelfrei". Flucht und Vertreibung europäischer Juden', in *Ausweisung – Abschiebung – Vertreibung in Europa 16.–20. Jahrhundert*, ed. by Sylvia Hahn, Andrea Komlosy and Ilse Reiter (Innsbruck: Studienverlag 2006), pp. 219–40, here pp. 222–4.

6   See Renate Göllner, *Schule und Verbrechen. Die Vertreibung jüdischer Schülerinnen und Schüler von Wiens Mittelschulen* (Frankfurt/Main, New York: Peter Lang Verlag 2009), pp. 77–85.

7   Albert Lichtblau, 'Integration, Vernichtungsversuch und Neubeginn', pp. 519–36.

8   Ironically, the Nazi regime blamed the Jews for the damage caused by the pogrom and imposed a punitive fine ('Sühneabgabe') of one billion Reichsmark on them.

9   Albert Lichtblau, 'Integration, Vernichtungsversuch und Neubeginn', pp. 520–1; Helga Embacher, 'Plötzlich war man vogelfrei', p. 224.

10 Jonny Moser, *Demographie der jüdischen Bevölkerung Österreichs 1938–1945* (Vienna: DÖW 1999), pp. 16–17. Approximately 180,000 were officially of Jewish faith but not all of them practised their religion.

11 Gabriele Anderl, Dirk Rupnow and Alexandra-Eileen Wenck, *Die Zentralstelle für jüdische Auswanderung als Beraubungsinstitution, Veröffentlichungen der Österreichischen Historikerkommission* (Vienna, Munich: Oldenbourg Verlag 2004), pp. 109–54.

12 Jonny Moser, *Demographie der jüdischen Bevölkerung Österreichs 1938–1945*, pp. 27–9. Specific data relating to the number of Austrian refugee children and youth are not available.

13 Gabriele Anderl, 'Emigration und Vertreibung', in *Vertreibung und Neubeginn. Israelische Bürger österreichischer Herkunft*, ed. by Erika Weinzierl and Otto D. Kulka (Vienna: Böhlau Verlag 1992), pp. 167–337, here p. 171.

14 Florian Freund and Hans Safrian, 'Die Verfolgung der österreichischen Juden 1938–1945', in *NS-Herrschaft in Österreich. Ein Handbuch*, ed. by Emmerich Tálos et al., 2nd rev. ed. (Vienna: öbv und hpt 2000), pp. 767–94, here pp. 772–82 and p. 789.

15 US immigration quotas were based on the country of birth, and 50 per cent were allocated to immigrants from the United Kingdom. This regulation had significant adverse consequences for Austrian Jews born in the territories of the former Austro-Hungarian monarchy. Immigration quotas for Eastern European countries were low, which caused very long waiting times. Many of them fell victim to the Shoah, because they could not leave in time.

16 With the significant increase in the number of refugees after the 'Anschluss' in 1938, Great Britain introduced visa requirements for Austrians and Germans, respectively. Initially, visas were granted according to the 'value' that the immigrant represented for the UK. Thus, renowned persons had a certain advantage, but there was also a special quota for domestics. After the November pogrom, entry requirements were loosened due to public pressure but with the restriction that these refugees should migrate further within two years. *Österreicher im Exil. Großbritannien 1938–1945. Eine Dokumentation*, ed. by Dokumentationsarchiv des österreichischen Widerstands (Vienna: Österreichischer Bundesverlag 1992), pp. 50–3; Gabriele Anderl, 'Flucht und Vertreibung 1938–1945', in *Auswanderungen aus Österreich. Von der Mitte des 19. Jahrhunderts bis zur Gegenwart*, ed. by Traude Horvath and Gerda Neyer (Vienna: Böhlau Verlag 1996), pp. 235–75, here pp. 245–7.

17 The biographical details of Peter Heller in this paragraph originate from the work of Beatrix Müller-Kampel. See *Lebenswege und Lektüren*, ed. by Beatrix Müller-Kampel, pp. 71–116; ibid., Peter Heller, pp. 1–5, https://www.sbg.ac.at/exil/multimedia/pdf/hellermuellerkampel.pdf (accessed 24 November 2013).

18 His parents did not deny being Jewish but had an agnostic-humanist view of the world and did not practise any religion. However, Peter was registered with the Jewish temple community in Vienna on the request of his grandfather Gustav Heller but never entered a synagogue as long as he lived in Austria.

19 The private school was founded by Dorothy Burlingham, who in the 1920s moved to Vienna with her four children for an analysis by Sigmund Freud. She

opened the school for her children and others who were involved in child psychoanalysis by Anna Freud.
20 *Leopoldstadt* was a traditional district, particularly for Orthodox Jewry, who moved to the Austrian capital before or during the First World War.
21 Renate Göllner, *Schule und Verbrechen: Die Vertreibung jüdischer Schülerinnen und Schüler von Wiens Mittelschulen* (Frankfurt/Main, New York: Peter Lang 2009), pp. 77–85.
22 Peter Heller, *Über die Internierung der Emigranten (1940),* unpublished typescript (1985), pp. 17–20.
23 Biographical details in this paragraph were collected by the author in an interview with Josef Kates on 12 September 2010, Toronto, Canada. His original name was Josef Katz and was changed into Kates in the early 1950s.
24 '*spuren*:suche', Broschüre Goethe Gymnasium (Edition Virtuelle Bibliothek 2005), 'Josef Kates' pp. 14–20, http://www.astgasse.net/cms/images/stories/schule_allg/spurensuche.pdf (accessed 20 August 2015).
25 Personal details were collected by the author in an interview with Bryan Sterling on 13 March 1996, New York, USA.
26 Erika Weinzierl, 'The Jewish Middle Class in Vienna in the Late Nineteenth and Early Twentieth Century', Working paper 01–1, University of Minnesota, Center for Austrian Studies, October 2003, pp. 1–18, here p. 3, http://cas.umn.edu/assets/pdf/WP011.PDF (accessed 27 November 2013).
27 In the 1930s, *Lederhosen* were an everyday attire for many Austrian schoolboys.
28 Canadian Jewish Congress Charity Committee National Archives (CJCCC NA), UJRA Collection, Series B, Interned Refugees, Case files (WIL-ZYT), box 24; file: questionnaire Bloomsbury House, Bruno Zwerling, 1 August 1941, Z2212.
29 Biographical details were collected by the author in an interview with Eric Kruh on 29 February 1996, East Hampton, Suffolk, USA. During emigration he adjusted his first name 'Erich' to fit the English spelling.
30 The Social Democratic Party was the leading political power in Vienna at that time, and significantly shaped the city during the interwar period through certain reforms geared at improving public housing, social welfare, education and the health system. The phenomenon is known as 'Red Vienna' (*Rotes Wien*) and until today these reforms are visible in the urban image signalled by the residential houses built at the time.
31 Following internationally established research standards, the editors use the term, Kindertransports, throughout the book to denote the plural (instead of the German *Kindertransporte*).
32 Gerda Hofreiter, *Allein in der Fremde. Kindertransporte von Österreich nach Frankreich, Großbritannien und in die USA 1938–1941* (Innsbruck: Studienverlag 2010), p. 46.
33 Whereas Eric's parents were able to flee to Switzerland, three siblings of Eric's mother, as well as his Viennese grandmother, did not survive the Holocaust.

34   The biographical details were collected by the author in interviews with Josef Eisinger on 16 February 1996, and 6 August 2010; both took place in New York, USA.
35   Interview with Josef Eisinger, 16 February 1996.
36   Claudia Curio, 'Flucht, Fürsorge und Anpassungsdruck. Die Rettung von Kindern nach Großbritannien 1938/39', *Exilforschung. Ein Internationales Jahrbuch*, 26 (2006), pp. 62–72, here pp. 64–5.
37   Interview with Josef Eisinger, 16 February 1996.
38   The illegal transport started in Bratislava and reached Palestine in November 1940 after a very dangerous odyssey full of privation. Rudolf and Grete Eisinger survived and lived in Palestine/Israel until 1953. For more information concerning the so-called *Perl-Transporte* see Anderl, 'Emigration und Vertreibung', pp. 256–308.
39   Dokumentationsarchiv des österreichischen Widerstands, *Österreicher im Exil*, p. 53.
40   Anthony Grenville, *Jewish Refugees from Germany and Austria in Britain 1933–1970. Their Image in AJR Information* (London/Portland, OR: Vallentine Mitchell 2010), p. 28.
41   Ibid., p. 29.
42   Some 27,000 Austrian and German refugees as well as 4,500 Italians were interned after Italy declared war on Great Britain in June 1940; for more details, see Peter Gillman and Leni Gillman, *'Collar the Lot!' How Britain Interned and Expelled its Wartime Refugees* (London, Melbourne, New York: Quartett Books 1980), pp. 105–59 and p. 173; Lucio Sponza, 'The Internment of Italians 1940–1945', in *'Totally Un-English' Britain's Internment of 'Enemy Aliens' in Two World Wars,* ed. by Richard Dove (Amsterdam, New York: Rodopi 2005), pp. 153–63.
43   Peter Heller, *Internment Diary*, translated by the author, p. 40.
44   Former internees describe Huyton as a disorganized and chaotic place. Twelve internees shared a house; rooms were unfurnished, they slept on straw sacks, and those who arrived later had to sleep in quickly erected tents; see Peter Gillman and Leni Gillman, *'Collar the Lot'*, pp. 135–45; Jennifer Taylor, 'Internment', in *Changing Countries: The Experience and Achievement of German-speaking Exiles from Hitler in Britain, 1933 to Today*, ed. by Marian Malet and Anthony Grenville (London: Libris 2002), pp. 127–51, here 135–7.
45   Dokumentationsarchiv des österreichischen Widerstands, *Österreicher im Exil*, p. 59.
46   Peter Gillman and Leni Gillman, *'Collar the Lot'*, p. 164.
47   Australia also accepted POWs and dangerous internees and aboard the ship *Dunera* quite a number of Austrian and German Jewish juveniles were deported to the former colony; Alexandra Ludewig, 'The Last of the *Kindertransports*. Britain to Australia, 1940', in *The Kindertransport to Britain 1938/39. New Perspectives*, ed. by Andrea Hammel and Bea Lewkowicz (Amsterdam: Rodopi 2012), pp. 81–102.

48 Eric Koch, *Deemed Suspect*, pp. 262–3. A fourth ship intended for Canada, the *Arandora Star*, loaded with about 1,600 men, was torpedoed and sank. Approximately 800 passengers drowned, about 450 Italian civilians and 150 'B' and 'C' internees. Despite that traumatic experience, the British authorities sent surviving internees on the *Dunera* to Australia shortly thereafter; Dokumentationsarchiv des österreichischen Widerstands, *Österreicher im Exil*, p. 56.
49 Peter Gillman and Leni Gillman, *'Collar the Lot'*, pp. 205–6.
50 Canadian policy and treatment of interned refugees from Nazism, as well as camp life, can only be outlined here. For details, see Paula Jean Draper, 'The Accidental Immigrants'; ibid., 'The Accidental Immigrants. Canada and the Interned Refugees, Part 1', *Canadian Jewish Historical Society Journal*, 2/1 (Spring 1978), pp. 1–37; ibid., 'The Accidental Immigrants. Canada and the Interned Refugees, Part 2', *Canadian Jewish Historical Society Journal*, 2/2 (Fall 1978), pp. 80–112.
51 Some camps were in very poor condition such as camp 'N', which was filled with about 700 interned refugees. It consisted of two abandoned railway repair stations, full of soot with leaking roofs and broken windows. Refugees strongly protested against their treatment but were strictly ordered by the camp's commander to collaborate in the improvement work, which granted them a compensation of 20 cents a day for repair work done.
52 Internees were seen as a cheap labour force that benefitted governmental and private industries. The work programmes varied from camp to camp; interned refugees, for example, produced various defence items, as Bryan Sterling did. Furthermore, internees produced socks, kitbags and pillow cases, grew and harvested tons of vegetables, and some, working as draughtsmen, produced technical drawings for 25-pounder guns for the Canadian military; Paula Jean Draper, 'The Accidental Immigrants', pp. 279–84.
53 At first, internees were paid twenty cents a day and in autumn 1941 the payment increased to up to fifty cents per day.
54 Interview with Bryan Sterling 1996, translated by the author.
55 Peter Heller, *Internment Diary*, p. 157, translated by the author.
56 See Eric Koch, *Deemed Suspect*, pp. 153–7; Paula Jean Draper, 'The Accidental Immigrants', p. 90.
57 Peter Heller gave several piano concerts; musical instruments were frequently donated to the camps.
58 About a third of the interned refugees were teenagers under twenty; Eric Koch, *Deemed Suspect*, p. 146.
59 Paula Jean Draper, 'The Accidental Immigrants', pp. 284–304.
60 Many of the interviewees who attended these camp schools as teenagers emphasized in retrospect that the outstanding schooling in the camps and their European education had a strong impact on their subsequent professional careers in North America.
61 Paula Jean Draper, 'The Accidental Immigrants', pp. 84–5.
62 Peter Gillman and Leni Gillman, *'Collar the Lot'*, pp. 267–70.

63 Paula Jean Draper, 'The Accidental Immigrants', pp. 346–58. Released internees had to report regularly to the Royal Canadian Mountain Police and often were threatened with re-internment, if they dared to complain about poor working conditions or low payment.

64 Ibid., p. 347.

65 All release dates presented here were taken from the list 'Interned refugees (friendly aliens) from the United Kingdom', Library and Archives Canada, Department of External Affairs, RG 25, file: 1939–842-AF.

66 Albert Lichtblau, 'Integration, Vernichtungsversuch und Neubeginn', p. 538.

67 Josef Kates, for example, created the world's first automated traffic signal system (Toronto, 1954) and solved the congestion problem of the St Lawrence Seaway by optimizing the locks in the mid-1960s. Kates is the founder of KCS Limited, the first Canadian computer consulting business. He was chair of the Canadian Science Council 1975–8 and Chancellor of the University of Waterloo 1979–85. In 2011, Canada rewarded his outstanding lifetime achievement with the Order of Canada. For more details on the career of Josef Kates and the career of Josef Eisinger, who befriended each other in the camp school, see Andrea Strutz, 'Effects of the Cultural Capital in Careers of Young Austrian Jewish Refugees in Canada. A Biographical Approach to their Life Stories', in *Cultural Challenges of Migration in Canada / Les défis culturels de la migration au Canada*, ed. by Patrick Imbert and Klaus-Dieter Ertler (Frankfurt/Main: Peter Lang Verlag 2013), pp. 175–93, here pp. 188–91.

68 His first wife was an American citizen from New York and his father, John (Hans) Heller, had also resided there since 1940; Beatrix Müller-Kampel, *Lebenswege und Lektüren*, pp. 94–6.

69 Between 1945 and 1956 approximately 30,000 Holocaust survivors immigrated to and remained in Canada. Franklin Bialystock, *Delayed Impact. The Holocaust and the Canadian Jewish Community* (Montreal, Kingston, London, Ithaca: McGill-Queens University Press 2000), p. 73.

70 Josef Eisinger, *Einstein on the Road* (Amherst, NY: Prometheus Books 2011).

71 Interview with Eric Kruh in 1996.

72 Interview with Bryan Sterling, 1996. Austria's complicity in Nazi crimes was admitted for the first time by an Austrian official, Chancellor Franz Vranitzky, in 1994. Until then, Austria defined itself as the 'first victim of National Socialism'.

73 Interview with Josef Kates, 2010.

74 Interview with Josef Eisinger, 1996.

75 Peter Heller, *In Transit: Prose and Verse in German and English* (New York: Peter Lang Verlag 1995), pp. 72–8.

CHAPTER THREE

'This tear remains forever...'[1] German-Jewish Refugee Children and Youth in Brazil (1933–45):

Resettlement, Acculturation, Integration

Marlen Eckl

> In my old age, many years later, I tend to describe that as the last chapter of Herr Hitler's hideous persecutions.... these separated family members, these lonely elderly people without the proximity of their nearest relatives. Instead of being able to be together, we survivors and widows are scattered around the world in our old age and are alone, which weighs heavily on us to this day. This tear remains forever, and the incomprehensible fate Herr Hitler inflicted upon us is without end.[2]

Eva Sopher thus describes the fracture the expulsion from the homeland wrought in the lives of those affected. Born in 1923 in Frankfurt on the Main, the banker's daughter had witnessed the National Socialist rise to power as a ten-year-old. With the forced emigration 'what was until now a peaceful and sheltered childhood ... transitioned into an uncertain and hectic youth, beset with constant hardship'[3] – an experience shared by many in Eva Sopher's generation who underwent the same fate. Consequent to the

Nazi persecutions, thousands of children and young people lost everything treasured and familiar to them overnight and were compelled to make their way within strange languages and countries, often growing up and becoming independent at an early age. The abrupt end to youth and childhood would potentially have a long-lasting impact on the lives and careers of this generation.

> We crossed the ocean without knowing what awaited us, without speaking the language of the destined country. We knew absolutely nothing about our new homeland. It's hardly surprising that I expected to see monkeys on the streets. [4]

Eva Sopher's comment illustrates the uncertainty accompanying her and her family as they travelled, like many other refugees from Hitler, to Brazil in 1937.

This chapter examines the experiences of German-Jewish refugee children and youth in Brazil, the tensions and contradictions between successful integration on the one hand, and loss of homeland on the other hand, with specific reference to the work of the *São Paulo Israelite Congregation* (*Congregação Israelita Paulista*, CIP), the background and history of German-speaking cultural agents in Brazil, and the adaptation of refugee children to life in agricultural settlements.

As with all South American countries, Brazil was very much a 'second choice', if one can speak of 'choice' in respect to the urgency for those fleeing Nazi persecution. Although the country remained well below its potential intake capacity in proportion to area and population count, 16,000 to 19,000 German-speaking exiles found refuge there between 1933 and 1945.[5] As there were no humanitarian operations and organizations to save children and youth from Nazi-occupied Europe, and refugee children entered the country with their families as 'immigrants', there are also no reliable statistics available, that would support an estimate of Brazil's refugee youth intake from 1933 onwards. Generally speaking, Brazil was, after Argentina, the second largest destination for refugees from Hitler in Latin America. Unlike in other Latin American countries where the German-speaking refugee population was concentrated in the capital cities, the majority of the refugees in Brazil settled in Rio de Janeiro, São Paulo and Porto Alegre, the capital of Rio Grande do Sul, Brazil's southernmost state, as well as in the agricultural settlements in the southern states.

On the one hand, Brazil, like most other countries in the world, pursued a progressively restrictive immigration policy, in particular towards Jews. On the other hand, it was deeply engaged in a debate on *brasilidade* (brazilianization). Brazilian national identity was promoted by the so-called *campanha de nacionalização* (nationalization campaign) in order to ensure a better 'integration' of immigrant minorities, such as the Italian, Japanese, German or Jewish communities into Brazilian mainstream culture. As part of this campaign the use of foreign languages in education and religious services as well as in the publication of newspapers was prohibited and immigrant organizations had to 'nationalize' their names and elect native-born Brazilians to their boards of directors. Finding a job was complicated by the regulations of the nationalization campaign which also promoted the 'nationalization' of the Brazilian economy. Some professions were reserved for native-born Brazilians. After Brazil entered the war on the side of the Allies in August 1942 – Brazil was the only Latin American country to send an expeditionary force to Europe – the regime of President Getúlio Vargas promulgated numerous laws aimed against the so-called *súditos do Eixo* (subjects of the Axis). Legal resident aliens from the Axis Powers and Brazilians of German, Italian or Japanese descent were now considered enemy aliens. The authorities, thereby, did not distinguish between Jewish refugees fleeing from Nazism and Brazilians of German or Austrian descent or immigrants potentially sympathizing with fascism. These special circumstances considerably affected the refugees' daily life. Their freedom of movement was restricted. The government required a permit for all travels, a so-called '*salvo conduto*'. Moreover, the prohibition of the public use of the languages of the Axis Powers faced the refugees, particularly the older ones, with a real challenge. Quite often, refugees were denounced and arrested by the police for speaking German in public. In most cases, they were released after a short time.

Consequently, the refugees – adults and children – were forced to learn Portuguese in a short time in order to achieve their social and economic integration into Brazilian society. Unlike most other Latin American countries, where the German-speaking refugees maintained the use of their native language for a long time, the refugees in Brazil changed their language soon, without, however, forgetting their German origins. In contrast to Argentina where the refugees could choose between three German anti-Nazi schools, among them the famous *Pestalozzi* School founded in 1934, the exiled children in Brazil had no alternative but to attend Brazilian schools. Compared to other Latin American countries, the integration process of refugees in Brazil proceeded in a different way as result of the nationalization campaign. Therefore, the communities and aid organizations which, as a result of the growing number of refugees from 1933 onwards, were soon formed in Rio de Janeiro, São Paulo and Porto Alegre played an important role in this context.

By 1936, German-Jewish exiles had already formed their own communities in the latter two cities – the CIP in São Paulo and the communal organization *Brazilian-Jewish Cultural and Beneficent Society* (*Sociedade Israelita Brasileira de Cultura e Beneficência*, SIBRA) in Porto Alegre. The establishment of the *Associação Religiosa Israelita* (ARI) in Rio de Janeiro did not follow until 1942. With their comprehensive social infrastructure, career, legal, business and women's advisory services and cultural activities, the communities represented more than mere religious affiliation, and disseminated feelings of home and belonging amongst those seeking refuge in the midst of the unknown.

Right from the outset, the community placed much value on the care and upbringing of Jewish refugee children, particularly with regards to furthering their integration into Brazilian society, as is evidenced by the CIP institutions devoted to serving the younger generation. As early as 1937, a children's home, the *Lar das Crianças*, had been established with the help of the *American Jewish Joint Distribution Committee*. The home was primarily for children whose parents were temporarily unable to provide adequate care for them on account of health, occupation or owing to circumstances of forced emigration, but also for orphans. The home's founders and for many years, its directors, Ida Hofmann and Charlotte Hamburger, the latter a trained kindergarten teacher, were themselves refugees who had emigrated to Brazil with their young families in 1936.

The early years saw *Lar das Crianças* confronted with a difficult balancing act between imparting principles for life in the new home and retaining the values its directors had brought with them from Europe.

> What stories should we tell our children? The wonderful fairy tales of the Grimm Brothers or the folkloristic fantasies of Saci? Which songs should we sing? *Hänschen klein*, a Portuguese translation, or modinhas [a type of sentimental, lyrical song which arose in the eighteenth century as Brazilian street songs] and Brazilian melodies?[6]

These were the questions people asked themselves. It was just as important that the children celebrated the Jewish holidays and the beginning of Shabbat on Friday evening together as it was that they participated in school celebrations on national holidays. Charlotte Hamburger was thus able to demonstrate a successful balance in the integration work of *Lar das Crianças* in her retrospective account written for the twenty-fifth birthday of CIP, titled *A Critical Study of the Outcomes Achieved through the Humanitarian and Educational Activities of the Congregação Paulista Israelita's Children's Home*:

> When comparing the desperate situations in which the children and their families found themselves at the time of the children's acceptance into the home with their present situations, the results must be regarded as extremely gratifying, even when taking into account the failures.[7]

That 'many children who visited the home in the early years – or their parents' would go on to become 'members or even co-workers of the community' was 'a very welcome yet unintended by-product of our work'.[8]

Many of the former refugee children and youth did indeed remain connected with the community as adults. For some of the children, this is explained in that their parents had actively contributed to the CIP as founding members and co-workers, so participating in the children's and youth activities was a matter of course for them. They had grown up in the community, just like the family of Charlotte Hamburger whose husband Hans was active in the CIP in various capacities, the community's administration being one of them. Among others also the Gotthilf and Koch families were heavily involved in community activities. Siegfried Gotthilf performed a variety of roles in community leadership, and his son Francisco led the scout group *Avanhandava* for several years. Ernst Koch, Leopold Ullstein's grandson, led the CIP for over ten years, and during this time, his wife Adelheid, who was initially the only training analyst in Brazil, carried out pioneering work in psychoanalysis and was involved in the community's youth work. It is hardly surprising that the Kochs' daughter attended the activities and later served as a scout group leader every now and then. But young refugees whose parents cultivated only loose or even no ties with the CIP, also appreciated what the community had to offer in terms of education and recreation. The CIP made an effort to be a contact point for juvenile refugees who felt lost, to enable them to come together and interact with their own kind.[9]

Hence, in 1940, Anita and Wilhelm Speyer were put in charge of establishing a youth department and were assigned its management. Before the couple's emigration in 1937, these two educators had taught at Jewish schools in Berlin and had then been employed as private tutors in Rolândia, an agricultural settlement in interior Brazil in the state of Paraná. In 1939, Wilhelm Speyer outlined the following fundamental aspects of youth work in his 'Report on the role and potential of a proposed youth department of the Congregação Israelita Paulista':

1. In order to unite the Jewish youth of São Paulo, the formation of a youth department and the simultaneous creation of a 'Youth House' is recommended.
2. A fundamental goal of all work that must be carried out for Jewish immigrant youth is the facilitation of their integration into the new environment.
3. Another fundamental goal lies in introducing the youth to the world of Judaism through engagement with Jewish history. This is not intended to lead to a biased position within Judaism but rather to an attitude of collective Jewish solidarity.
4. The achievement of these goals lies as much in the interests of collective Jewry as it does in the interests of the individual young people; recovering a clear position on these vital issues has a much stronger influence on the practical life skills of young immigrants than is commonly assumed.[10]

The youth house, the *Casa da Juventude*, was created in 1941. According to Wilhelm Speyer it was to serve a threefold purpose: 'as a place for study groups, as a recreation space for young people in inadequate housing and as the home of the youth guidance service'.[11] The young people found not only a new circle of friends there but in addition to leisure activities, they were also able to attend seminars on topics like German literature, Jewish history, or Portuguese language courses according to their needs and interests, which of course differed because:

> [f]or the young Jewish refugees the question of 'cultural background' could not be answered consistently ... The older ones, who had not gone through Brazilian schooling, still clung to the cultural background of Germany while the younger group seemed to have already adapted to their Brazilian surroundings effortlessly.[12]

Egon Schwarz, who managed to flee to Bolivia in 1939 at the age of sixteen, singles out age as a deciding factor for successful acculturation and integration into the receiving society. After the war, he went to the USA and there became one of the most important promoters of German literature. For him, emigration at this age came:

> [i]n a particularly unsuitable phase of development ... when I was no longer a child and not yet an adult, bringing with me only the expectations Europe had poured into me but none of its accomplishments, and was thus unable to adapt to the new setting as someone who was not yet moulded or prejudiced could. Had I been a little younger – a single year might have tipped the balance – if I could not have become a Bolivian, since that is something one is and cannot become, I might yet have been able to become a Latin American in a broader sense. And if I had been a little older with a fully-formed identity and individuality, with a fixed Europeanness, I would have perhaps viewed this period of my life as an interlude, ... and taken from it that which suited me or at least, that which was obtainable. Instead I was neither one nor the other and have remained till this day someone who is essentially at home nowhere but in another sense, at home everywhere.[13]

It is common knowledge that youth groups formed in exile contributed significantly to the creation of identity and supported the young refugees' integration in their host country. They certainly played a significant role in the social lives of young refugees in São Paulo. There were the groups *Kanaken* and *Shalshelet* for example, and also the scout group *Avanhandava*. This name, taken from the Amerindian Tupi language and meaning 'place of the rapids', was intended to accommodate President Vargas' nationalization campaign which aimed to ensure that the Portuguese language would have a fixed position in the communities of immigrants and refugees. Founded in 1938, *Avanhandava* became affiliated with the youth house following its establishment in 1941. In the view of the historians Roney Cytrynowicz and Judith Zuquim:

[S]couting became the central core of youth activities within CIP. Wilhelm Speyer considered scouting the best method to raise children and youth, and he was willing to create a system of pedagogic values brought from his education in Germany. For him, scouting would be the ideal instrument to integrate the descendants of immigrants to their Brazilian reality. Boy scouting and girl scouting were therefore disseminated to every centre of the Jewish community in São Paulo.[14]

Speyer's perspective, which saw no contradiction between Jewish values and the virtues of the scout movement, and in fact embraced all these emphatically as being for the collective good of the young generation, differed markedly from the position of the *Asociación de Boy Scouts El Cóndor*. This group came about in 1943 in Bolivia as an amalgamation of the two scouting associations *Jewish Youth Association (Jüdischer Jugendbund)* and *Brigade Baden-Powell*, both founded in 1940. The *Asociación*, whose members were comprised primarily of German-Jewish and Austrian-Jewish refugee children, but with a few Czechs and Hungarians and a small number of children from non-Jewish political refugees, rejected all identification with Judaism. Care was given to 'being completely inter-faith'.[15] By the end of the 1940s, the *Asociación* had already dissolved, yet *Avanhandava*, whose Jewish programme is recognized by the *Union of Brazilian Scouts (União dos Escoteiros Brasileiros)*, continues today.

By observing all regulations within the parameters of the nationalization campaign and all stipulations for the subjects of the Axis powers known as *súditos do Eixo*, that came into place once Brazil entered the war on the side of the Allies, *Avanhandava* and the *Casa da Juventude* were able to provide a place for the exiled children and adolescents that fully catered to their concerns and desires. Not only did they impart the values and traditions of the children's familiar German-Jewish culture enabling these to live on, but they also imparted practical help with life as well as guidance for building their own futures in Brazil and support regarding training.

The shared experiences in *Avanhandava* and the *Casa da Juventude*, the collaboration of *Avanhandava* with Brazilian scout groups and the sense of belonging this generated, all had a role in allowing the majority of the exiled children and adolescents to integrate successfully into Brazilian society and find a new home. Several of those belonging to the early *Avanhandava* generation and of those who attended the *Casa da Juventude* made a name for themselves as mediators between worlds and cultures. Among these are Alice Brill Czapski, Hans Günter Flieg, Francisco Gotthilf and Eleonore Koch. Friendships and contacts that were created and are still created in *Avanhandava* and the *Casa da Juventude* remain long-lasting, which was understandably particularly the case for the exiled children and teenagers, knitted together by their shared experiences of forced emigration.

Anita and Wilhelm Speyers' contact with Rolândia enabled them also to meet the children and young people living in this agrarian colony. Eleven of the Jewish refugee families who settled in Rolândia joined the CIP.[16] But it was not only the community's youth work which created a connection between the cities and rural areas. The exiles themselves sought out interaction and exchange on a personal level. Children and young people from Rio de Janeiro, São Paulo and Porto Alegre spent holidays or other extended visits with friends and relatives in Rolândia. Conversely, children and young people from Rolândia came to the city to do things such as attending schools, and stayed either with the Speyers or with families who were friends of the Speyers. All of this worked towards strengthening solidarity.

While in the cities the refugee-founded communities attempted to promote the integration of children and youth into the receiving society and provided every support needed during their accommodation, the young refugees in the agricultural settlements in Inland Brazil were experiencing a very different kind of adjustment. Unlike the children and youth in the cities, they not only had the deprivation of their familiar way of life and accustomed routines to overcome, but found themselves confronted with the inhospitable nature of an as yet undeveloped backcountry. 'Nature showed herself to be tropically magnificent, yet chaotic and dangerous. Merely expecting children to stay healthy in such an environment, let alone raising and educating them there, seemed downright scandalous to me',[17] wrote Karin Schauff of her first impression.

Together with Oswald Nixdorf and Erich Koch-Weser, the former Germany's Minister of the Interior and Minister of Justice, Schauff's husband Johannes, a settlement politician and centre party MP, was responsible for developing an exchange transaction warranting refugees from Hitler entry into Brazil, despite the Third Reich's strict exchange control regulations and Getúlio Vargas's restrictive, clearly anti-Semitic immigration policies. In his biography of Johannes Schauff the historian Dieter Marc Schneider describes this exchange transaction as follows:

> Anyone who paid for railway materials for the 'Paraná Plantation' in Germany, received a certificate for land shares in return; this permitted entry to and residency in Brazil. The Paraná-Gesellschaft had their own visa quota which was made available for this purpose.[18]

As a result of a contract negotiated between the *Society for Economic Research (Gesellschaft für wirtschaftliche Studien)* and the *Companhia de Terras Norte do Paraná* in 1932, over the course of the 1930s, the settlement of Rolândia developed into a refuge in the Brazilian jungle.[19] Reports regarding the number of refugees who came to Rolândia in these years are contradictory. According to an estimate by Geert Koch-Weser, who, like his father Erich Koch-Weser, immigrated to Brazil in 1934, there were eighty families, twenty-five of which were Jewish.[20] Many of the refugees were part of the political opposition or were Catholics. The Schauff family, who came to Brazil through Italy with seven children, belonged to this category. Two further children were born in Rolândia. Despite seemingly insurmountable obstacles, the battle with the unaccustomed climate and the challenges of untamed nature, Karin Schauff vowed during her first pregnancy in Brazil:

> [t]o embrace with my whole heart the country in which it [i.e. the child] will see the light of day and to love it as it is. Might the brains of adults be dulled and the children remain illiterate! Life itself, the life of the land on which we now subsist, is what counts.[21]

Although Rolândia, in contrast to agricultural projects in other Latin American countries, ultimately proved to be a success, where many refugees were able to build new lives and find a home, one should not be deceived by such words over the depth of the rupture the flight into the jungle wrought. Coming for the most part from bourgeois backgrounds and the urban upper or middle classes, the refugees found themselves forced to exchange their earlier cultured lives for what was initially a primitive existence. Lawyers, doctors and scientists often acquired a piece of farmland without any prior agricultural experience. For the young children, who had only a vague idea of the seriousness of the situation at best, the whole thing was still something of an adventure.

> Of course we had read books, usually about the Amazon, but in any case there was enough jungle here that one did not feel disappointed. No Indians. There were no Indians. But it was still a matter of excitement anyhow. Now and then a snake was seen, and at times, one might encounter monkeys.[22]

Unlike the parents, the children accepted their new circumstances as par for the course, which Hilde Wiedemann was able to observe with her three-year-old daughter Dorothea. The young family had acquired land in the settlement of Terra Nova, also in Paraná, and had immigrated to Brazil in 1933. Hilde Wiedemann wrote in her memoirs:

> The primitive lifestyle agreed with our child splendidly.... Two months after our arrival my husband wrote to his mother, 'Dorothe [sic] already knows all the tools by name and wants all sorts of things like a handsaw and an axe for her birthday. On weekdays she runs around in her little blue panties like a dirty little farm boy. Only on Sundays is she a clean little girl in a pretty wee frock.' 'Is it not dangerous to let a child run *around* so freely in the wild nature?' the worried grandmother wrote back from home.[23]

The younger children explored their new surroundings playfully – warnings and orders not to mess about with snakes, spiders, worms, opossums and toads were of little avail.[24] For the older ones, on the other hand, the carefree childhood tended to be over. The situation required them either to help with looking after their younger siblings or to make themselves useful on the farms. To relieve the family and earn their keep, some worked as home help or hired hands for other refugee families. Since work also needed to be carried out on the weekends, they had very little free time.

Despite adverse conditions, great importance was placed on learning and education. Right at the start, the refugees were anxious for their offspring to receive the best possible schooling. Several families brought private tutors with them.[25] In doing so, the exiles had recourse to the extensive libraries they had brought into exile with them from Germany. Hertha Levy, who came to Rolândia in 1936 as a young bride, declared retrospectively that 'We prized the German culture which was collapsing in Germany at that time. Which was then burnt down there, in fact. Here people gave lectures and loaned books and that is still the case today'.[26] And Michael Traumann emphasized that 'Literature [was] so important for us that we may have felt closer to the people in books than to our own people'.[27] The Traumann family's *fazenda* Gilgala was one of the *fazendas* around which the emigrant community's cultural life revolved. As a trained singer, Else Traumann not only put on small concerts but also gave music and piano lessons to countless children who rode to Gilgala from their own *fazendas* specifically for lessons.

On the *fazenda* Jaú belonging to the Kaphan and Maier families, Mathilde Maier taught Hebrew and Jewish religion.[28] The building known as the *Pupil's House* was also built here. Maier and the Kaphans were committed champions of the emigration to Brazil of Jewish adolescents who had received as preparation for their new life an agricultural education on a training farm in the Silesian village of Gross Breesen. However, the resettlement of this group of young Jews foundered in the end against the German bureaucracy and the anti-Semitism of the Vargas regime which denied them their entry visa.[29] A few succeeded in escaping to other countries after being released from the concentration camp of Buchenwald on condition of immediate emigration, but many of the 'Gross Breeseners' did not survive the Nazi persecution. 'Thus a dark shadow that we could not shake off, nor desired to shake off, was cast over our new beginnings'.[30]

Only one 'Gross Breesener', Hans Rosenthal, made his way to Rolândia, where he continued his education with Heinrich Kaphan, one of the few exiles who was a trained agriculturalist. In 1941, 'Juwa', as Hans Rosenthal had been called by his fellow 'Gross Breeseners' who escaped concentration camp and kept in touch with each other for decades through a newsletter, reported what great fortune he had had to be able to work for the Kaphans:

> In the one year that I spent there as a year of apprentice, I have been able to learn a fabulous lot ... After Mr Kaphan had recently obtained the management of the *fazenda* of Dr Stinnes, he took me there as his assistant manager. ... The *fazenda* is among the largest estates in the local area

and is not only equipped agriculturally on a large scale but also constructed industrially with a sawmill and brickworks.... my work here consists now in the supervision of the stock, the supervision of the agriculture and the workers.[31]

After the war, Hans Rosenthal became acquainted with Inge Sachs in the USA. They married and moved to Rolândia. As Inge Sachs had arrived in England through the *Kindertransports* in 1939 and had gone on to the USA in 1947, Hans and her were united by a common fate of having survived the Nazi persecution thanks to targeted emigration initiatives for children and youth, thanks to the *Hachschara* and the non-Zionist agricultural training and preparation courses, and of the course the *Kindertransports*. In memory of Gross Breesen, they named their *fazenda* Nova Breesen, New Breesen.[32]

In contrast to the Rosenthals, who had to conquer the obstacles of forging a new existence largely on their own, the refugee families with children saw the ever-at-hand generational conflicts re-emerging with particular significance. The children acknowledged what their parents had gone through and respected them for their acceptance of events and for effecting a role change from members of higher society to agriculturalists, for the large part without complaint. The extent to which the older ones suffered under a longing for home and their previous lives was often hidden from the children, who, in their ignorance, criticized them on account of their purported 'romantic aesthetic and fastidiousness'. It became apparent to the younger ones only in retrospect that the planting of flowers, trees and herbs one had known as a child served to mitigate 'something of the piercing fierceness of the pain in our longing'.[33] Michael Traumann did not understand until much later how much his father had suffered by being displaced. 'He acted as if he was a British lord from the eighteenth century. I said to him quite sharply once, "You're not a British lord, you're an emigrant". That was rather harsh and cruel'.[34]

Understanding each other could only come with time. Right in that phase of life in which young people are still searching for and believing in the fulfilment of their own dreams and plans, they were forced to accept that these dreams and plans would, invariably, change. They demonstrated a sense of responsibility earlier than usual, doing things like taking over the management of the family *fazenda* or making their own living.

The same was also true for the young people who, supported through the activities of the Jewish communities in São Paulo, Rio de Janeiro and Porto Alegre, sought to find their place in Brazilian society. To improve the situation of their families, they attempted to become independent and earn their own wages very early on. Sometimes they even dropped out of school against the will of their parents to look for employment, or even without their parents' knowledge. For financial reasons (and reasons of time), tertiary education was frequently out of the question. A few, however, did complete a course of study later on. Lacking an education they tried to find an occupation that would accommodate their interests and aptitudes. As the majority originated from the German-Jewish *Bildungsbürgertum* class, they had already been introduced to art, music, literature and theatre by their parents in Germany. It is hardly surprising therefore that people like Eva Sopher, Alice Brill Czapski and Eleonore Koch began working in art dealerships and bookshops as sixteen- and seventeen-year-olds. Hans Günter Flieg and Kurt Klagsbrunn had already delved into photography in Europe and had brought cameras and even manuals into exile with them. Both young men turned this into their profession in Brazil. Others started companies.

With the help of their work, into which they were able to incorporate their European cultural heritage, the young refugees became important cultural mediators. The outlined career paths of Hans Stern, Eva Sopher, Bruno Kiefer, Francisco Gotthilf, Eleonore Koch, Gisela Eichbaum, Alice Brill Czapski, Kurt Klagsbrunn and Hans Günter Flieg which follow are but a small representation of many more.

Hans Stern (1922–2007) came to Rio de Janeiro from Essen as a sixteen-year-old with his parents shortly before the outbreak of the Second World War. As an electrical engineer, his father found work in north-eastern Brazil. Since Hans Stern preferred to remain in what was then the capital, he was left to his own devices early on. In an export company, he came to know the world of minerals and precious stones and its secrets. In 1945, he opened his own business, from which H. Stern, the first jewellery company in Latin America, emerged. With over 160 stores in twelve countries, it is one of the most eminent in the world today. Hans Stern was poised to set new standards within the gemstone industry nationally and internationally right from the start. H. Stern made Brazilian gemstones famous worldwide and, furthermore, laid the groundwork for the relationship between technological progress and creative design, cementing the quality and perfection of the jewellery. What Stern appreciated about his profession was 'the challenge to create something, to develop a company, and the opportunity to witness the transformation of an ordinary stone into a beautiful piece of jewellery'.[35]

Hans Stern's pioneering spirit and power of determination – he continued visiting mines in Inland Brazil well into old age – is perhaps also characteristic of the generation who went into exile as adolescents. They all had seen the money and titles that had been won with pride in Europe prove themselves to be fleeting and of little value in exile. In this sense, Eva Sopher (born 1923) also took her life into her own hands at a young age. As previously mentioned, she found work in a shop for art objects with an attached gallery called *Casa e Jardim*. The owner Theodor Heuberger was also the founder of *Pró Arte*, a society for art, science and literature which had made its goal the promotion of cultural exchange between Germany and Brazil. The relationship with *Pró Arte* and Theodor Heuberger was to give strong direction to Eva Sopher's cultural development. After moving to Porto Alegre in 1960, her offer to be of service to *Pró Arte* there, received in response the terse 'assignment' to reactivate the Porto Alegre branch. The programme of *Pró Arte*, developed under Eva Sopher's direction and initiative, changed the cultural life of Porto Alegre from the bottom up. It was important to her from the outset not only to bring nationally and internationally recognized artists to Rio Grande do Sul and to create dialogue between them, but also to be constantly propelling new talent onto the stage. Unsurprisingly then, in 1975, she received an offer to manage the *Theatro São Paulo* and supervize its renovation. In 1984, it was reopened and has held a key position in the cultural landscape of Brazil since then. Eva Sopher has received countless accolades in Brazil and internationally for her work in cultural mediation. Today she works tirelessly for the *Projeto Multipalco Theatro São Paulo*, one of the biggest theatre complexes in Latin America, as its long-time director.

Rio de Grande do Sul also became the new home of Bruno Kiefer (1923–87), who came to Brazil with his family at age eleven. He completed his music study under Hans-Joachim Koellreutter, likewise a refugee from Hitler. Koellreutter introduced twelve-tone composition to Brazil and set up a music school with the support of *Pró Arte*, where he taught alongside other exiled musicians. He also started the *Música Viva* movement, which united diverse musical genres and promoted new ideas. *Música Viva*'s influence can been seen in Kiefer's compositional work and musicology. 'What is unique in the works of Kiefer is that he often interweaves melodic material typical of medieval music, Brazilian popular and folk music, or jazz within a harmonic context steeped in Second Viennese School'.[36] His study about the *History of Brazilian Music* remains authoritative.[37]

Wrocław-born Francisco Gotthilf (1923–2012), who immigrated to Brazil with his parents as a fifteen-year-old in 1938, also acted as a cultural mediator, although in a very different capacity. He called into being what is today the longest-running Brazilian television show called 'Mosaico na TV', broadcasting without interruption since its inception. It began with the daily radio show 'Hora Israelita', which Francisco's father Siegfried produced and directed from 1940 onwards, assisted by Francisco. Listening to the show quickly became a firmly entrenched household ritual for many Jewish families in São Paulo. After his father's death in 1952, Francisco continued the radio show and in July 1961, took it to air on television under the name 'Mosaico na TV'. The Jewish community's 'mouthpiece' now became a 'window' through which one could also reach into non-Jewish society. Not only does 'Mosaico na TV' continue today to provide Brazil's Jewish communities with news from Brazil and the rest of the world, but it also brings Jewish faith, culture and tradition closer to the non-Jewish population. Over the course of time, the programme has documented a unique record of Jewish life in Brazil.[38]

Countless well-known artists and photographers came out of the German-Jewish refugee community. 'Art: a refuge and hope, the dream of freedom lost too soon to fortune's slings and arrows',[39] wrote Alice Brill Czapski in her 1988 book *Da arte e da linguagem*, answering the question of why art became a lifeline for young refugees. As with Brill Czapski, Gisela Eichbaum and Eleonore Koch also found a chance for expression in painting, design or sculpture, that not only allowed their artistic talent to unfold but also allowed them to unite the cultures of both worlds, that of their European homeland and that of their receiving country Brazil. Influenced by the directions in art that emerged in Europe in the interwar years, their works contributed to the development of a strong sensibility for modern art in Brazil.

Although the work of these artists differed in their choices of preferred motifs and style, their German-Jewish origins and the circumstances that had brought them to Brazil bound them together, as did the fact that they had in common notable Brazilian artists as teachers. In addition to studying with Samson Flexor, Bruno Giorgi, Yolanda Mohalyi, Elisabeth Nobiling and Poty, contact with the group Santa Helena, to which Aldo Bonadei, Paulo Rossi Osir, Francisco Rebolo, Alfredo Volpi and Mario Zanini belonged,[40] was of great importance for the artistic development and careers of the young refugees.

While Alice Brill Czapski and Gisela Eichbaum came from artist families, the career choice of Eleonore Koch was not particularly close to home. The works of Eleonore Koch, too, are noticeably influenced by her European cultural heritage. Born in 1926 in Berlin to the psychoanalyst Adelheid Koch, and the lawyer Ernst Koch, Eleonore emigrated to São Paulo in 1936 with her family. Although she began a course of study at the *Museu de Belas Artes* at the age of seventeen, she soon found it did not suit her and left. At her parents' suggestion, she began learning book-binding instead and worked in bookshops such as *Livraria Nobel* and *Editora e Livraria Kosmos*, both established and run by emigrants. Following private study with different artists, she became the sole student of Alfredo Volpi. Koch's pictures signal first and foremost the sanctification of items from the profane. A period of several years in Europe was of crucial importance in furthering her artistic progression and recognition, yet on returning to Brazil, she confessed her return to be the most valuable experience of the past years.

> In Europe I felt a little like an intruder. . . . I did not belong to the setting in which I lived, which perhaps is why it made perception sharper and the experience enriching. My return . . . brought back my vision of landscapes, which in my affective plane had never disappeared.[41]

Brazil was more than a country of safety. It had become a new home.

This was also the case for Gisela Eichbaum (1920–96). The daughter of Mannheim pianists Hans Bruch and Lene Weiller-Bruch, Eichbaum came to São Paulo in 1935 at the age of fifteen.[42] She abandoned the piano studies she had begun in 1940 and turned her attention to drawing and painting. Her images exemplify inner release and the influence of the country of exile on artistic development. While her earlier works depict fear and morbid fantasies in dark colours, neutral or luminous colours and Brazilian motifs distinguish her later works. Musicality is another characteristic feature of Eichbaum's work, which clearly shows the significance of the European cultural heritage alongside Brazilian influences.

> There is a very intimate relationship between music and painting ... Since Kandinsky, this approach has been clearly noted. ... Gisela Eichbaum is a musical painter. She understood from an early age just what harmony, melody, rhythm and counterpoint were.[43]

Like Eichbaum, Cologne-born Alice Brill Czapski (1920–2013) was one of the artists who brought a commitment to Expressionism to Brazil with them.[44] For Brill Czapski, it was her father, painter Erich Brill, whose work had already been denounced as 'Judenkunst' by 1932, who was her first teacher. Shortly after their arrival in Brazil in 1934,[45] the two of them spent a few months on the island of Paquetá and used the time to paint. Brill Czapski later took lessons from Brazilian art colleagues whom her father had met in Brazil, some of whom had become their friends. She was also aware that it was not only the talent inherited from her parents, 'but also the fact that their life's work had been interrupted in its early stages that moved me to carry out that which they had begun'.[46] She sought inspiration in her indirect surroundings and took urban life and its effects on humankind as the preferred subject of her imagery – the loneliness of the individual, a sense of being lost when surrounded by buildings, the lack of nature and the rat race. While this subject matter in Brill Czapski's paintings reveals cultural imprints of Europe, her photography portrays a kind of 'exploration' or 'discovery' of the land of exile and adds an important contribution to the history of Brazilian photography.

Brill Czapski belonged to the group of exiles destined to modernize Brazilian photography and cement it as a genre. Their images reflect an influence of Bauhaus and cinema in their camera positioning, lighting and meaning, some of which can also be ascribed to architectural influences.[47] This new pragmatic approach reveals itself in unconventional perspectives and compositions. The works of these photographers hauntingly document the architectural, technical, industrial and cultural progress of their country of resettlement, such as the so-called *verticalização* of São Paulo[48] and the building of Brasília. They play a significant role in the history of Brazilian photography. Moreover, these photographers made a strong impact on photojournalism, which, at that time, was just beginning to emerge in Brazil, and they discovered rich scope for activity further afield in advertising.

Among the photographers exiled in Brazil there were four – Alice Brill Czapski, Fredi Kleemann, Kurt Klagsbrunn and Hans Günter Flieg – who were forced to leave Germany as children or adolescents. Born Alfred Kleemann in Berlin, Fredi Kleemann (1927–74) came to Brazil as a six-year-old, where he became an actor at *Teatro Brasileiro da Comédia* in São Paulo in 1949 and where he would go on to become one of the most famous theatre photographers with his pictures of the *Teatro*'s productions.

When Hans Günter Flieg, born in 1923 in Chemnitz, arrived in Brazil in 1939, he had already completed a three-month apprenticeship under Grete Karplus, the photographer of the former Berlin Jewish Museum. The technical details he had learned in this course provided the basis for his later capabilities. Along with a Leica set-up, he also brought two books into exile with him: *Die neue Foto-Schule* by Hans Windisch and *Meine Erfahrungen mit der Leica* by Paul Wolff. The Viennese medical student Kurt Klagsbrunn (1918–2005), who likewise reached Brazil with his family in 1939, also had Windisch's book, a Leica and a Super-Baldina in his luggage.[49] With the assistance of other emigrated photographers, Klagsbrunn and Flieg were both able to receive their first assignments and in time, made a name for themselves.

Kurt Klagsbrunn chronicled life in Rio de Janeiro. As a freelance photographer, he worked for *Time* and *Life* magazines from 1941, but primarily for the magazine *O Cruzeiro*, whose photo articles played a central role in the photojournalism that was starting to emerge in Brazil. His camera documented everything from student culture to large social events. He took portraits of artists and intellectuals as well as Brazilian and foreign statesmen and political VIPs. Interpreting the emergence of Brasília as a sign of progress and modernization, Klagsbrunn followed this happening with particular attention. He explored Brazil further in numerous trips and constructed a picture of the country in both senses.

Klagsbrunn's career path resembles that of Flieg in many respects. Flieg's works also captured São Paulo's development from a major city into the commercial metropolis of Latin America. He, too, photographed cultural and political celebrities. Advertising photography and photo articles were as much a part of his work as they were of Klagsbrunn's. Yet, unlike Klagsbrunn, who is considered a 'specialist and pioneer of society photography',[50] Flieg grew his reputation primarily in industrial photography. Mercedes, Volkswagen, Pirelli, Olivetti, Ipiranga and Brown & Boveri were just some of his clients. His pictures of monumental industrial buildings and production halls testify to the fascination for progress and modernization that was characteristic of Brazil in these years. The theme of construction pervading Flieg's works is multifaceted. With his camera, he captures the quite literal ascent of the city of São Paulo in the buildings of several of the most important Brazilian architects of the twentieth century – Oscar Niemeyer, Lúcio Costa, Lina Bo Bardi, Gregori Warchavski and Rino Levi.

As previously mentioned, he participated in the activities of *Avanhandava* and the CIP-directed *Casa da Juventude*, and traced the day-to-day life of this German-Jewish community and its members with his camera. These moments caught on film witness the construction of a new existence and the integration process of refugees in their country of resettlement, and in doing so, also tell the story of the photographer himself.

Taking in the pulsating life of the cities and the lively culture and shared life of diverse groups in Brazil was also an attempt on the part of the young photographers to free themselves from the intangible, fear-filling memories of their old, now destroyed world and an attempt to be part of the aspirations their host country had in those years. The work represented the link between the old and new homes.

The experience of an abrupt end to childhood and youth and expulsion from the homeland of Germany left its mark not only on the generation directly affected. The consequences also left effects on those who followed. As far as Brazil goes, most of the exiled children and adolescents 'conquered' the initially foreign country of safety using very different means and paths. It became a new home for the majority of them, who have become an integral part of Brazilian society and belong, like the small selection of mediators between cultures and worlds that have been introduced in this essay, not only to the history of Brazilian industry but above all, to the history of Brazilian culture.

Notes

1   See Eva Sopher, 'Dieser Riss bleibt für immer . . .', in '. . . *auf brasilianischem Boden fand ich eine neue Heimat.' Autobiographische Texte deutscher Flüchtlinge des Nationalsozialismus 1933–1945*, ed. by Marlen Eckl (Remscheid: Gardez! Verlag 2005), pp. 168–77.
2   Ibid., p. 170.
3   Ibid.
4   Ibid., p. 171, p. 172.
5   Patrik von zur Mühlen, *Fluchtziel Lateinamerika. Die deutsche Emigration 1933–1945: politische Aktivitäten und soziokulturelle Integration* (Bonn: Verlag Neue Gesellschaft 1988), pp. 48–9.
6   Charlotte Hamburger cited in Roney Cytrynowicz, *A 'Congregação Israelita dos Pequenos'. História do Lar das Crianças da Congregação Israelita Paulista 65 anos* (São Paulo: Editora Narrativa-um 2003), p. 43. Regarding the history of the *Congregação Israelita Paulista*, see Alice Irene Hirschberg, *Desafio e resposta. A história da Congregação Israelita Paulista desde a sua fundação* (São Paulo: Edição especial por ocasião do quadrigenário da Congregação Israelita Paulista 1976).
7   Charlotte Hamburger, *Kritische Studie ueber die Resultate der Hilfs- und Erziehungsarbeit des Kinderheims der Congregação Paulista Israelita seit der Eröffnung im September 1937 bis Dezember 1960* (São Paulo: Congregação Israelita Paulista 1961), p. 12. Margit Herzberg, who worked in the home from 1972 and was the educational director of the institute until 2012, participated in CIP activities as a child and teenager.
8   Ibid., p. 17.
9   See also Eva Froehlich cited in Elisa Caner, 'Judeus-alemães no Brasil – Um estudo dos depoimentos das vítimas do nazismo', unpublished Master's thesis, Universidade de São Paulo, 1996, p. 224.

10 Wilhelm Speyer, *Gutachten ueber Aufgaben und Moeglichkeiten eines etwaigen Jugend-Dezernats der Congregação Israelita Paulista*, São Paulo, 3 November 1939, p. 6, Wilhelm Jonas Speyer Collection, CP 0016 Jonas Speyer, Arquivo Histórico Judaico Brasileiro, São Paulo.

11 Ibid.

12 Ibid., p. 2.

13 Egon Schwarz, *Keine Zeit für Eichendorff. Chronik unfreiwilliger Wanderjahre* (Frankfurt am Main: Büchergilde Gutenberg 1992), p. 151, p. 152.

14 Roney Cytrynowicz and Judith Zuquim, *60 anos de escotismo e judaísmo 1938–1998. A construção de um projeto para a juventude. Uma história do Grupo Escoteiro e Distrito Bandeirante Avanhandava* (São Paulo: Editora Congregação Israelita Paulista 1999), p. 214.

15 Heinz Wilhelm Kalmar cited in León Bieber, *Jüdisches Leben in Bolivien. Die Einwanderungswelle 1938–1940* (Berlin: Metropol Verlag 2012), p. 131.

16 For more details, see Ethel Volfzon Kominsky, *Rolândia, a terra prometida. Judeus refugiados do nazismo no norte do Paraná* (São Paulo: FFLCH/Centro de Estudos Judaicos/USP 1985), p. 80.

17 Karin Schauff cited in Dieter Marc Schneider, *Johannes Schauff (1902–1990). Migration und 'Stabilitas' im Zeitalter der Totalitarismen* (Munich: R. Oldenbourg Verlag 2001), p. 75, p. 76.

18 Ibid., p. 74. The above mentioned 'Parana Gesellschaft' is commonly known as the Paraná Plantation Ltd. with its headquarters in London and its Brazilian branch at *Companhia de Terras Norte do Paraná*.

19 Regarding the history of Rolândia, see Peter Johann Mainka, *Roland und Rolândia im Nordosten von Paraná. Gründungs- und Frühgeschichte einer deutschen Kolonie in Brasilien (1932–1944/45)* (São Paulo: Cultura Acadêmica/Instituto Martius-Staden 2008).

20 Ibid., p. 173.

21 Karin Schauff, *Brasilianischer Garten. Bericht aus dem Urwald* (Pfullingen: Verlag Günther Neske 1971), p. 52, p. 53.

22 Michael Traumann, in *Flucht in den Dschungel. Eine deutsch-brasilianische Geschichte*, film by Michael Juncker (Munich: Bayerischer Rundfunk 1999).

23 Hilde Wiedemann, *Der Weg ist das Ziel* (Rio de Janeiro: Selbstverlag 1979), p. 59.

24 Karin Schauff, *Brasilianischer Garten*, p. 114.

25 See among others Eleanor Alexander, 'A Year in the Brazilian Interior', in *Between Sorrow and Strength. Women Refugees of the Nazi Period*, ed. by Sibylle Quack (Cambridge: Cambridge University Press 2002), pp. 159–66.

26 Hertha Levy cited in Gudrun Fischer, *'Unser Land spie uns aus'. Jüdische Frauen auf der Flucht vor dem Naziterror nach Brasilien* (Offenbach: Verlag Olga Benario und Herbert Baum 1998), p. 36.

27 Michael Traumann in *Flucht in den Dschungel*, film by Michael Juncker.

28 Max Hermann Maier, *Ein Frankfurter Rechtsanwalt wird Kaffeepflanzer im Urwald Brasiliens. Bericht eines Emigranten 1938–1975* (Frankfurt am Main: Josef Knecht Verlag 1975), p. 54.

29 See also Ruth Kaphan cited in Gudrun Fischer, *'Unser Land spie uns aus'*, p. 95; Marco Antonio Neves Soares, *Da Alemanha aos Trópicos. Identidades judaicas na terra vermelha (1933–2003)* (Londrina: Editora da Universidade Estadual de Londrina 2012), p. 162.
30 Mathilde Maier, *Alle Gärten meines Lebens* (Frankfurt am Main: Josef Knecht Verlag 1978), p. 88.
31 Hans Rosenthal cited in Gross Breesen Letter 10, Virginia, May 1941, pp. 446–7, http://www.docstoc.com/docs/150584735/Brief-Gross-Breesen-Silesia (accessed 21 November 2013).
32 For more information regarding Inge and Hans Rosenthal's lives, see Maria Luiza Tucci Carneiro, *Weltbürger. Brasilien und die jüdischen Flüchtlinge (1933–1948)* (Vienna: LIT Verlag 2014), pp. 331–3 and Gudrun Fischer, *'Unser Land spie uns aus'*, pp. 51–66.
33 Karin Schauff, *Brasilianischer Garten*, pp. 181–2.
34 Michael Traumann in *Flucht in den Dschungel*, film by Michael Juncker.
35 Hans Stern cited in Maria Luiza Tucci Carneiro, *Weltbürger*, p. 258.
36 Paula J. Van Regenmorter, *Brazilian Music for Saxophone: A Survey of Solo and Small Chamber Works* (Ann Arbor: Proquest, Umi Dissertation Publishing 2009), p. 82.
37 See Bruno Kiefer, *História da Música Brasileira* (Porto Alegre: Editora Movimento 1976).
38 *Mosaico na TV* is continued successfully today by Francisco Gotthilf's son and grandson. For more information about the history of *Mosaico na TV*, see Roney Cytrynowicz, *Senhor Mosaico. Francisco Gotthilf e o programa Mosaico na TV* (São Paulo: Editora Narrativa-Um 2008).
39 Alice Brill Czapski, *Da arte e da linguagem* (São Paulo: Editora Perspectiva 1988), p. 12.
40 The Santa Helena group was a loose fraternity of artists of predominantly Italian descent, named for their meeting place, the Palacete Santa Helena. Several of the most influential Brazilian artists of the twentieth century came out of this group.
41 Eleonore Koch in Fernanda Pitta, 'Chronology', in *Lore Koch*, ed. by Ana Carolina Ramos and Charles Cosac (São Paulo: Cosac Naify 2013), pp. 232–3, here p. 243.
42 In 1948, Gisela married Francisco Eichbaum, a reputed physician and researcher who immigrated to Brazil in 1940. His sister, the distinguished linguist Gerda Bell, fled the Nazis to New Zealand where she became an important cultural mediator between Germany and New Zealand. Among other things, she was a lecturer at Victoria University of Wellington.
43 Enock Sacramento cited in Antonio Carlos Suster Abdalla and Alvaro Machado, *Gisela Eichbaum. Canções sem palavras. Songs without Words* (São Paulo: Cult. Arte e Comunicação 2013), p. 130.
44 See Pietro Maria Bardi cited in *Gisela Eichbaum. 40 anos de pintura e desenho / 40 Years of Painting and Drawing*, n. pag.

45 Alice Brill Czapski's parents had divorced shortly after her birth. Her mother Martha had gone on ahead to Brazil several months before. Erich Brill was to bring his daughter Alice to Brazil later when Martha Brill was in a position to care for herself and the child.

46 Alice Brill Czapski, 'Das waren bittere Jahre ...', in '... *auf brasilianischem Boden fand ich eine neue Heimat*', pp. 149–63, here p. 163. Heedless of all warning, Erich Brill returned to Europe in 1936 and was murdered in 1942. Martha Brill, who had worked as a publicist before emigrating, was unable to take up her work in journalism again in Brazil. However, with her autobiographical roman-à-clef *Der Schmelztiegel*, she became a literary chronicler of the German-speaking exile in Brazil.

47 See Bill Hinchberger, 'Brazil Photos: Alice Brill and the History of Brazilian Photography', http://www.brazilmax.com/news.cfm/tborigem/fe_artcultmus/id/37 (accessed 28 November 2013).

48 'Verticalization' refers in this context to the rapid increase in high-rise buildings and property development, usually requiring small houses to be torn down. The city spread not only outwards in these years but also upwards.

49 See Gabriele Stiller-Kern, ' "Warum ist Lots Frau zu Salz erstarrt?" Eine Begegnung mit Hans Günter Flieg', in *Hans Günter Flieg. Dokumentarfotografie aus Brasilien (1940–1970)*, ed. by Ingrid Mössinger and Katharina Metz (Leipzig, Bielefeld: Kerber Verlag 2008), pp. 24–5, here p. 24; Marcia Mello and Mauricio Lissovsky, *Refúgio do olhar. A fotografia de Kurt Klagsbrunn no Brasil dos anos 1940* (Rio de Janeiro: Editora Casa da Palavra 2013), p. 15.

50 See Klaus Honnef, 'Kurt Klagsbrunn – Spezialist und Pionier der Gesellschaftsfotografie', in *Kurt Klagsbrunn. Fotograf im Land der Zukunft*, ed. by Ursula Seeber and Barbara Weidle (Bonn: Weidle Verlag 2013), pp. 27–35.

CHAPTER FOUR

A Distant Sanctuary:

Australia and Child Holocaust Survivors

Suzanne D. Rutland

In November 1948, eighteen-year-old Peter Rossler arrived in Brisbane as a 'Welfare Guardian Boy' with his older brother, Honza (later Henry). They were the only survivors of his immediate family. Peter was sent to the Lodz Ghetto at the age of eleven. There, he witnessed the death of his father, aged forty-six, and later his mother, aged thirty-six. Luckily, he and Honza were transferred to an orphanage in the ghetto, where they received better treatment due to Head of the Jewish Council Chaim Rumkowski's concern for orphans. In August 1944, when the ghetto was liquidated, the two teenage boys were transported to Auschwitz where they faced the selections. Peter Rossler later described his lucky experience when they faced the inspection at the selection table that meant death or life:

> The moment arrived, and it was my brother's turn. He was asked his age – he was 16 at the time – and was briefly inspected by the uniformed man. He was directed to proceed to the right. Next it was my turn. I said I was 14. That could have been fatal. The man, who I later found out may have been the notorious Dr Mengele, the 'Angel of Death', looked at my underdeveloped, starved body, and pointed me to the left. Without hesitation, I turned around and followed my brother to the right . . . and nobody stopped me.[1]

This was just one of Peter's lucky escapes which enabled him to survive. The two boys were sent out of Auschwitz to the Kaufering labour camp in

Bavaria, and here again luck was on his side, when a kind Czech Jewish doctor helped him. After surviving a death march to Camp Allach near Dachau, the two brothers were liberated there. Honza and Peter returned to Prague, where one uncle with his wife had survived in Theresienstadt, but they then decided to accept the offer to be sponsored as 'Welfare Guardian Boys' to Australia. Peter and his brother found a new life in Australia, with Honza becoming an architect and Peter a research scientist.[2]

This chapter seeks to explore the experiences of Jewish orphans from the Holocaust, such as Peter Rossler, and their migration to Australia. While Glen Palmer[3] and Wolf Matsdorf[4] have researched the prewar children schemes, less has been written about the story of Jewish orphan survivors and their sponsorship to Australia between 1946 and 1950. Drawing on research from the National Archives of Australia, the *Jewish Welfare Societies*, the Archives of the *American Joint Distribution Committee* (JDC) and the *Hebrew Immigrant Aid Society* (HIAS), this chapter seeks to fill this void. It addresses several aspects of the sponsorship programme: (1) the fundraising efforts of the children and guardian schemes, both during and after the war; (2) the difficulties these schemes experienced in locating suitable child candidates; (3) the initial correspondence with the JDC; (4) the eventual cooperation with the Russian–French *Organization to Save the Children* (*Oeuvre de Secours aux Enfants*, OSE); and (5) the reception and care offered to those who arrived on these shores. It will look at the different policies in place in both Melbourne and Sydney, examining the facilities for the children at the *Frances Barkman Home* in Melbourne and the *Montefiore Home* in Hunters' Hill, Sydney, as well as the special reception given to the group of 'Buchenwald Boys' provided by Mina Fink at *HIAS House* in Melbourne.

In 1945, after the Holocaust, the majority of surviving Jews wished to leave the European continent and start a new life far from the scene that had become for them a mass graveyard. Most wished to emigrate either to Palestine or to the United States, but for some, distant Australia seemed a hopeful refuge. In the period between 1945 and 1961 approximately 25,000 Jewish Displaced Persons (DPs) established a new life at 'the edge of the Diaspora', continuing a trend that had begun in the late 1930s when the first refugees fleeing Nazism arrived in Australia.[5] In 1933, there were only 23,000 Jews in Australia, according to official census figures. Between 1938 and 1961, the community almost tripled in size to 61,000.[6] The Holocaust survivors of this period who found refuge in Australia completely changed the nature of the Jewish community. However, as a result of prewar anti-Jewish refugee hysteria,[7] the Australian government, both Labor and Liberal, insisted that the reception and integration of the refugees was the responsibility of the Jewish community. No government funds were to be expended on Jews because of the fear of a political backlash and this included child survivors. Sponsors of the refugees, including children, were responsible for accommodating the newcomers and helping those in need find their feet in a new land. Two organizations, the *Save the Children's Scheme* (also called the *Rescue the Children Scheme*) and the *Jewish Welfare Guardian Scheme*, became involved in this task of rescuing child survivors.

In response to a government request, the *Federation of Australian Jewish Welfare Societies* (FAJWS) was formed in the late 1930s to be responsible for the reception and integration of Jewish refugees. While most Jewish refugees and survivors arrived sponsored by family members, the FAJWS did directly sponsor some of the refugees and acted as a backup service for those sponsored privately but requiring assistance. Boats were met and immigrants were helped with finding employment or setting up in business through interest-free loans. Other activities included taking care of the child survivors who arrived after the war, assisted by the *Save the Children's Scheme* and the *Welfare Guardians*.

A key aspect of the welfare societies' work in the pre- and postwar era was the sponsorship of child migrants, both refugees and orphan survivors of the Holocaust, who hoped to create a new life in Australia. Indeed, from the beginning of the crisis of German Jewry in the 1930s, the *Australian Jewish Welfare Society* (AJWS) expressed its greatest concern for the survival of Jewish children. In December 1938, part of the quota promised by the Minister for the Interior, John McEwen, was an allocation of permits for 1,500 children aged between seven and twelve at the rate of 500 a year over the three years of the quota, which totalled 15,000.[8] With the outbreak of war in 1939 this agreement lapsed and only seventeen German-Jewish children arrived. They were cared for by the AJWS at the *Larino Children's Home* in Melbourne.[9] During the war years, the *Welfare Society* made a number of different proposals to bring out small groups of children.[10] In December 1939, approval was granted for the admission of fifty Jewish orphans of German and Austrian background, and in 1940 further approval was given for another hundred Dutch and Belgian Jewish orphans, but the *Society* was not able to bring these children out due to transport problems.[11] In 1943 the government agreed to a quota of 150 Jewish orphans entering Australia and an appeal for the *Rescue the Children Scheme* raised £50,000.[12] In 1944 this quota was doubled to 300 orphans[13] and in Sydney the *Save the Children's Scheme Committee* was formed to administer the funds collected in 1943 and to organize reception and accommodation for the Jewish children when they arrived.[14]

However, no Jewish children were brought to Australia during the war because, as was commonly known, there was almost no shipping for civilians and troopships had to be made available. Interestingly, New Zealand was able to provide sanctuary to almost 750 non-Jewish Polish children (as discussed later in Ann Beaglehole's chapter in this volume). An undated Australian departmental memo noted that:

> It may be mentioned that the AJWS are very disappointed that no ship has been made available to bring their contingent of children from France

or Switzerland, and they have drawn attention to the success of the authorities concerned in arranging for the Polish children to be taken to NZ.[15]

Negotiations for a similar transfer of Polish children to Australia took place, but the war ended before an agreement could be reached.[16]

By January 1945 it was clear that the war was drawing to a close and the Australian-Jewish community prepared to receive its quota of 300 children, aged between seven and fourteen years.[17] A further appeal was launched in Sydney, Melbourne, Adelaide and Perth and it was stressed that the campaign must have a quick response as in March 1945 the government wished to launch the *Victory Loan Appeal* and to concentrate all financial energies on that appeal. As a result of this request by the government, there was a great debate at a special meeting in Melbourne as to whether the appeal should be launched at the time. Representatives of the more conservative Jewish establishment such as Rabbi Jacob Danglow and Peter Isaacson argued against the appeal, while other 'seasoned' campaigners such as Sam Wynn supported it. After much discussion, Alec Masel proposed a motion for the formation of an *Appeal Committee for the Rescue the Children Campaign* and this was passed by the meeting.[18] The combined total raised between 1943 and 1945 was approximately £70,000, with New South Wales' contribution being £23,000, Victoria £32,000, Western Australia £12,000 and South Australia £2,500.[19] It was hoped that more Jewish children would arrive through the planned government sponsored scheme to transplant 5,000 orphans from Europe to Australia and that some of the funds could be used to assist them, but this scheme did not eventuate.[20]

Initially, it appeared that the tremendous effort required to raise £70,000 was to no avail as the Australian-Jewish community had great difficulty in finding suitable Jewish orphans. There was a large number of surviving Jewish orphans in Europe, but most wished to settle in Palestine. The situation was summed up in the following way by a *Sunday Telegraph* journalist:

> Thousands of Jewish children in eastern and central Europe are on the move in an attempt to reach Palestine ... The mass movement is the result of appalling living conditions, starvation, increasing anti-Semitism, and the search for lost parents ... more than 100,000 Jewish children have not yet been traced in Europe. It projects the imagination into a world utterly foreign to our own, hostile and hideous.[21]

As a result of this tragic situation, Vera Weizmann wrote in 1945 to the *Welfare Society* asking it to transfer funds raised for the *Rescue the Children Appeal* to *Youth Aliyah*, to help these children reach Palestine.[22] This request could not be met since the funds raised could not be used for any other purpose because the government had granted the FAJWS tax exemption for the appeal.[23]

General Secretary of the AJWS (Sydney) and the FAJWS, Walter Brand, was one of the strongest advocates for bringing Jewish orphans to Australia. London born, Brand immigrated to Australia in 1920 after serving in the British Army during the First World War, and in 1940 he was appointed to the position of AJWS General Secretary, serving in that role until 1964. While Brand was dedicated to his clients' needs, he was hampered by his officious manner and his lack of Yiddish or any other European language. As a result, his clientele often perceived him as being insensitive to their needs, and many survivors criticized his leadership.[24]

With the end of the war, Brand began an intense correspondence with the leaders of the JDC to support the migration of child survivors to Australia, so that they could fill the quota of 300, which the government had agreed to. In May 1945, Brand wrote a long, emotive letter to Moses (Mo) Leavitt, who became executive vice-chairman of the JDC in 1947, requesting assistance with bringing orphan children to Australia. He wrote that the initial permits had been issued in 1943 and although 'much water has flowed under the bridge . . . we find ourselves in somewhat the same position as the day the permits were issued'.[25] He complained that the authorities at Australia House, London, which was in charge of all immigration to Australia, were 'not very co-operative', and that they were also faced with transportation problems. He stressed that even with the assistance of *Youth Aliyah*, not all the surviving children could be settled in Palestine, and so some should be sent to Australia.[26] These arguments were to become an ongoing theme in his correspondence with the JDC officials in both New York and Paris. As he wrote later in the year:

> That is why I cannot understand why certain organizations are adversed [*sic*] to handing over a couple of hundred children so that they can be taken immediately from the horrors of Europe and given succour in a democratic Jewish community. I have always maintained that irrespective from what the outcome of Palestine will be, Jewish Communities elsewhere must be built up so that they can always help to finance the needs of Palestine. This is my personal opinion and I am not prepared to discuss the matter by letter. What I am concerned about is that we honour our promise to the Commonwealth Government to bring Jewish children to Australia, and the first is 300 being given to me. As I have already told Mr ROSEN when this quota has been completed, I have not the intention to tell my Community that they have completed this task.

Brand also approached Lewis Neikrug, asking for help from HIAS, in August 1946.[27] From Brand's perspective, bringing orphans to Australia was offering them a new life in a wonderful country on the other side of the world far from the horrors of Nazi Europe.

However, the availability of young Jewish orphans for migration to Australia, and other English-speaking countries was very limited. The various JDC officials presented a range of arguments for the limited number of Jewish orphans up to the age of fourteen suitable and available for migrating to Australia. Firstly, those children who did survive were already teenagers, since most of the children under the age of ten perished. Of those who survived, many wished to emigrate to Palestine, and were preparing for their *Aliyah*. Others wished to stay in their host European countries, such as France, where they were learning the language and beginning to feel some sense of security.

The officials of the JDC were frustrated with Brand's insistence on finding suitable orphans for filling the Australian quota. After enumerating the reasons why it was difficult to locate suitable children, Robert Pilpel writing from New York requested Amelia Igel, the JDC child consultant in Paris, to write to Brand and, as he expressed it: 'as I think social workers used to say, you might wish to interpret this information to Mr Brand'.[28] Igel was very diplomatic in her correspondence with Brand, stressing:

> Although one hears of the many orphan children in Germany and throughout Europe there are actually very few full orphans whom we consider for emigration. Many of the children have one parent and most have family ties and look forward to reunion with relatives at the earliest possible time. The orphan children who have been cared for in groups are for the most part planning to go to Palestine, and the JDC is not in a position to influence these plans. I do want to assure you however that the AJDC is alert to identify those children who might be eligible and available for emigration . . . .[29]

Negotiations continued with Otto Schiff who suggested that the age limit of fourteen be increased because it was very difficult to find suitable orphans for Australia in the younger age groups. The *Melbourne Welfare Society*, however, initially opposed this suggestion and insisted that only very young children should be brought out.[30] Barkman responded strongly in the negative, writing:

> From experience, we find we have been most successful with the children we brought from Germany more than seven years ago, and part of that success was due in no small measure because the children were young enough to become acclimatised to Australian life and conditions. We are very proud of our children who have had the best education and attention and principally too because they are so happy and a credit to our Jewish community. What we have done for these children we will do for others but we must get them when they are still young enough to go to our Australian Schools and become part of the Australian and Jewish community.[31]

A rift also developed between the AJWS and *Bloomsbury House* over funding and contacts with other Jewish welfare organizations were sought.

Australian-Jewish leaders such as Rabbi Dr Israel Porush and John Lewinnek, while overseas, investigated the situation to try and find suitable orphans for Australia.[32] In Melbourne, until the arrival of Jewish orphans, funds raised by the *Appeal* were used to board children of recently arrived immigrants at *Larino Home*. This policy greatly assisted working mothers.[33] Until mid-1948 the Sydney branch turned down requests for similar assistance even though some Jewish children were being placed in Catholic institutions.[34]

After the Holocaust, the British government continued to maintain the strict quota system for Jewish immigrants to Palestine, introduced by the MacDonald White Paper in 1939. Any survivors who attempted to arrive in Palestine illegally and were caught by the British mandatory authorities were either interned in Cyprus, or sent back to Europe. Eventually, as a result of these problems, the AJWS came to an agreement with the French Union OSE in 1947, which was established for child care, health and hygiene among Jewish children and selected the orphans for Australia.[35] The original group of orphans selected for Australia in 1943–4 had already emigrated to Palestine or the United States and the youths selected were mainly from concentration camp survivors who were wandering around Europe. The age limit was raised to sixteen and in 1950 extended to twenty-one.[36] Since most of the applicants did not have any reliable documentation, and at times had to lie about their age in order to survive during the war, they once again faced the same problems, only this time they claimed to be younger than their actual age.[37] The arrangements were made through OSE in Switzerland. Both OSE and the JDC gave the orphans a choice of countries, and once they had made their selection, the sponsored youth came out in batches with a migrating couple on their boat appointed as their chaperones. For example, in January 1948 the first group of ten children (with a further sixteen youths sponsored by the *Welfare Guardian Scheme*) arrived on the *SS Radnick* under the care of Dr David Szeps and his wife.[38] Dr Szeps survived the war on forged non-Jewish papers organized by a sympathetic Greek Orthodox Ukrainian priest.[39]

One of the largest groups of orphans arrived on the *SS Derna*, looked after by Dr Henryk Frant and his wife, Zofia. Having studied medicine in Vilna and specialized as an obstetrician and gynaecologist in Vienna, Dr Frant accepted a position in Poland. After serving in the Polish army in 1939, he was sent to the Warsaw ghetto, but managed to survive with his wife. Their young daughter was hidden on the non-Jewish side and they managed to retrieve her after the war. With the increasing Cold War Tensions, they decided to emigrate and were sent to Sydney by the JDC, with sixty-one orphans under their care, travelling on the *SS Derna*.[40] Diane Armstrong, an Australian-Jewish novelist who also travelled on the *SS Derna* with her parents after the war, described the group as they boarded the ship:

> As the boys stepped onto the gangplank, the doctor ticked them off his list one by one, as if on a school outing. Dr Henryk Frant and his wife

Zofia were already wondering whether they had taken on too much in accepting the job of chaperoning this large, unwieldy group whose ages ranged from nine to twenty . . .[41]

Indeed, the voyage proved very difficult, with a fire breaking out on the ship, which was forced to dock in India and undertake repairs, so that the trip between Marseilles and Australia took ten weeks. A Sydney Jewish newspaper reported that if it had not been for Dr Frant:

> [t]he lives of the passengers would have been unbearable. He performed operations, distributed medicines out of his private medicine case and gave consultations day and night. Dr Frant also assisted in the birth of a daughter to a Jewish woman aboard. All his services were free to all aboard.[42]

Brand was also concerned about covering the transportation costs for bringing the children to Australia. The funds raised for both the children's and guardian schemes received tax deductibility, on the basis that the money would only be spent in Australia, which meant that no funds could be transferred to Europe for transportation. He corresponded with the JDC and OSE, expressing the hope that the *Intergovernmental Committee on Refugees* (IGCR) would provide the required funding. The JDC office in Paris pointed out that while the IGCR would be approached, the JDC and HIAS would cover the costs in the first instance. Each case would then be presented to the IGCR for approval, but only after emigration had been completed and it could be proved that there was no private funding available. It was estimated that they would not be able to recover more than 30 per cent of their claims.[43]

Australian Jewry was not the only Anglo-Saxon community which wished to sponsor Holocaust child survivors. Canadian and South African Jewry had raised funds for similar schemes. The Canadian Scheme was most liberal, allowing for up to 1,000 children. In the end, 1,120 were sponsored under the *War Orphans Project* in the period from 1947 to 1952, and brought in under the auspices of the *Canadian Jewish Congress*.[44] Initially, the Canadians sought younger orphans, but then lifted the age to eighteen, and the majority who were sponsored were in their late teens, with a higher proportion being male. The South African Jewish community wanted to sponsor 400 full orphan children from two to twelve years, and was able to cover all costs including land costs in Europe and transportation costs. In a report on the various schemes, Herbert Katzki, a key JDC official, noted that the South African scheme was very desirable, since there was a 'closely integrated Jewish community, which can provide many advantages for the children'.[45] However, their age criteria made it very difficult for them to find suitable children to bring to South Africa, as was noted in a number of letters to Brand. During the immediate postwar period, there was competition between these Diaspora centres in finding suitable orphans from the younger age groups. Manfred Saalheimer, who supervized the Canadian project from the JDC offices in Paris, informed the Canadian Jewish leadership that he was 'just another fellow who had come for another children's project which had come to be considered one of many'.[46] As a result, the Canadian social works depicted 'much more grandiose future perspectives then reality could ever have afforded, all means being valid in order to convince reluctant candidates'.[47]

In all, 317 children were assisted to settle in Australia in the immediate postwar period under both the *Rescue the Child Fund* and the *Welfare Guardian Scheme*. Bringing them to Australia involved different challenges of accommodating and taking care of them. When the children arrived, they were distributed between the various states, with most being settled in Sydney and Melbourne. As with Peter and Honza Rossler, a few of the children went to Brisbane where they were cared for at the *Welfare Society* hostel, while some Jewish families in Adelaide took in few. The Perth Jewish community felt that it was not in the position to accept responsibility for any of the children so that the £12,000 that they had raised was distributed between Sydney and Melbourne.[48]

The majority of Jewish orphans who were sponsored to Australia were boys. The community policy was to house them in a Jewish hostel until they found employment and could become independent. The smaller number of girls was placed in foster homes. In Sydney the majority of the Jewish boys were cared for at the *Isabella Lazarus Home*, which had been built in conjunction with the *Montefiore Home* in the 1930s at Hunter's Hill, in Sydney's north. Although the *Home* was opened in 1939 it was requisitioned by the army for the duration of the war and only returned to the Jewish community at the end of the war. In 1945, the *Jewish Welfare Society* at first considered building a children's home at Chelsea Park, a former agricultural training farm in Sydney's western suburbs. Architectural plans were drawn up, but the scheme was found to be too expensive[49] and the *Isabella Lazarus Home* was renovated instead. Some of the large dormitories, each with eight beds, were converted for the needs of the Welfare sponsored boys who lived there for the first two months.

With the imminent arrival of the first orphans in 1946, the original committee established in Sydney in 1944 was divided into: an executive committee headed initially by Great Synagogue stalwart, Israel Green, and Walter Brand, General Secretary of the AJWS; and a House Committee, headed by Dr Fanny Reading with Bertha Porush, wife of Rabbi Dr Israel Porush, senior minister of the Great Synagogue, a very active and devoted member. The House Committee attended to the children's needs, including providing clothing and schooling and assisting with employment.[50] Schneider, a German Jew who arrived in Australia in the 1920s, acted as English instructor and mentor. Zoltan Schwartz, one of his charges, commented that 'we all knew a better man for the job could not have been found'.[51] There was also a panel of doctors and dentists who attended to the children's health needs. In 1948, Sydney David Einfeld was placed in charge of the boys and girls and the Einfelds established a close relationship with many of the youth.[52] Employment was found as quickly as possible for the youths and many were helped to train for a trade at Technical Colleges. The limitations of finance meant that the committee could not assist many who wished to study at tertiary level.

By 1949 the number of Jewish children arriving under the scheme had declined and it was decided in 1950 to disband the *Children's Committee*.[53] After protracted negotiations with the *Welfare Society*, the chairman of the *Children's Committee*, Jack Davis, was co-opted onto the *Welfare Society Board*[54] and in 1952 the child migration finances were brought under the control of the AJWS in Sydney.[55]

In Melbourne, the Jewish children were cared for at the *Larino Children's Home* at the Balwyn estate. In 1939, Frances Barkman, a Jewish teacher and welfare worker, was instrumental in establishing *Larino* to receive Jewish child refugees from Nazi Germany, with an initial group of seventeen children managing to arrive before war broke out. Barkman was a child refugee, who had been born in Kiev, Russia, and whose family had fled the Russian pogroms and arrived in Melbourne in 1891, when she was aged six.[56] During the war, she dedicated herself to the 'Larino children', as Glen Palmer called them. The property had initially been owned privately and in 1946–7 there was much discussion as to its continuing role. In June 1947, the Executive of the *Australian Jewish Welfare & Relief Society* (AJW&RS) decided to purchase the Home[57] and in April 1948 the *Rescue the Children Appeal* agreed that their funds could be used for the upkeep of the property.[58] At the same time, the name was changed to *Frances Barkman Home*, acknowledging the devoted services of Frances Barkman, the *Welfare Society*'s honorary secretary until her death in late 1946.[59] The property had been leased, but in October 1947 it was purchased in the name of the AJWS and the necessary repairs were undertaken.[60]

As in Sydney, a separate House Committee, initially under chairperson Leah Frieze (1948–57) administered the *Frances Barkman House*.[61] The Home remained full, with an average compliment of thirty-three to thirty-four children[62] until by 1957 it was in such a state of disrepair that a new property was bought at Malvern.[63] In 1958, a special *Children's Appeal Committee* was formed under the leadership of Walter Lippmann.[64] Under Lippmann's able direction, this appeal was very successful and Lippmann subsequently assumed the leadership of the AJW&RS from Leo Fink in 1960.[65] The original property was sold in 1965, and two more children's homes were established in the name of Frances Barkman.

In both Sydney and Melbourne, the women who volunteered to be members of the House Committees were very dedicated to attending to the needs of their young clients. They provided clothes for the children, bought birthday presents, organized parties as well as functions for those celebrating their *bar/bat mitzvahs*, and took the children out to cultural events and picnics.[66]

Care of the children and youths in both Sydney and Melbourne posed many problems and challenges from the point of view of their psychological and emotional development. It had been hoped to bring out younger children but most of those sponsored were in the older age bracket, with the average age being between fifteen and seventeen. The *Jewish Welfare Society* in both Melbourne and Sydney provided English instruction to assist in the youths' integration into Australian society. As noted above, Schneider, the English instructor of the Sydney 'Guardian Boys' was much loved. However, for older youths learning a new language was challenging, especially as they had all missed out on their normal schooling during the war years. There was also the problem of the gap between the Anglo-Jews and the challenge of establishing themselves in a new and alien society, as well as the 'anti-reffo' feeling that had already manifest itself in the general society before the war.[67]

There were great controversies over their religious education and in each city there were complaints at the lack of support of the rabbinate. The Sydney committee commented that Rev. William Katz, a prewar refugee from Germany, was the only minister to regularly visit the *Isabella Lazarus Home*.[68] In 1948, there was a stormy session at the *New South Wales Jewish Board of Deputies* at which Rabbi Dr Eliezer Berkovits of the Central Synagogue walked out, angered by comments of the Board's president, Saul Symonds.[69] In Melbourne, Susie Hertz, later to become the founding Jewish Studies teacher at *Beth Rivkah*, provided sterling service for the Jewish education of the children at *Larino* from 1939 until the mid-1950s.[70]

In addition to the *Children's Scheme*, older boys and girls in the age group fourteen to nineteen were brought out under the auspices of the *Jewish Welfare Guardian Society*, which copied the pattern of the *Big Brother Movement*. Jewish families in Australia agreed to act as guardians for a boy or girl until they reached the age of twenty-one. Guardians were allocated to their charges through a ballot system. These youths did not necessarily live with their guardians, but the guardian accepted the responsibility of providing for their charge's material and spiritual well-being, including equipment and clothing. The scheme was introduced by John Wars before the war and about twenty youths came out in 1938–9, most of them later serving in various branches of the forces.[71] A number of youths also came out in the same period from the Gross Breesen agricultural training farm in Germany, and most of these were given work on the land by the *Welfare Society*.[72] After the war, John Wars, who had moved to Sydney, continued to work for the *Guardian* scheme. The government agreed initially to admit 100 girls and boys under the scheme and a *Federation of Jewish Welfare Guardian Societies* was formed so that the youth could be distributed throughout Australia, and in March 1945 Wars was elected as the federal president.[73]

The first youth to arrive after the war under the *Welfare Guardian Society* was Tom Keleman, whose guardian was Julian Rose. Keleman came out in 1947 and worked for three years as part of the *Sydney Welfare Society* staff.

John Wars stressed that the *Welfare Guardian Society* could not function successfully with large numbers because each new arrival was a personal responsibility for a family and suitable guardians were not easy to find. By 1951, sixty-seven Jewish youths, all victims of the Nazi regime, had been brought to Australia under this scheme. Some required total support, some just needed help in establishing themselves in a job and finding accommodation while a few had problems of mental health and one had tuberculosis.[74]

As with the *Children's Scheme*, difficulties were encountered, especially with the initial language barriers, until the youth managed to master some English, with the assistance of the English classes offered by Jewish Welfare as discussed above, and the problem of compatibility between the guardians and their charges. The youth, many of whom were survivors of concentration camps such as Buchenwald and Belsen, needed 'much warmth and understanding'.[75] In a letter published in the *Sydney Jewish News*, Albert Halm who had arrived under the auspices of the *Children's Scheme*, summed up the problems, stressing:

> In some cases misunderstandings may have occurred between guardians and boys. This was probably due to the lack of understanding and patience to cure those who were not used to normal family life, and to the new life in the guardian's family. This new life was especially difficult to a foreign orphan, who had lost his parents before he realised what parents mean, who was a slave of the higher German race while he should have been studying and who neither enjoyed childhood nor parents' love.[76]

Despite these problems, Halm stressed the gratitude felt by the 'Guardian Boys' and girls on 'whose faces a smile had not appeared for many years'[77] and who were surprised by the kindness with which they were received.

Most of the guardians were very caring and became involved in the boys' lives, trying to assist wherever possible. One of the guardians, Hans Vidor, himself a refugee from Austria who had arrived in Sydney in the 1930s, even wrote to Igel to ask if he should send some pocket money while his charge was waiting in Paris for transportation to Australia. Igel advised that was not advisable, as they had organized temporary employment for the boys, who had previously shown signs of restlessness. She informed Vidor that the boy he was sponsoring was 'a fine appearing youngster almost six foot tall, strong and healthy and neatly dressed. He has completed an apprenticeship as an electrician and is eagerly looking forward to his new life in Australia'.[78]

Separate committees administered the *Children's Scheme* and *Guardian Society*,[79] but there was an overlapping of personnel and facilities so that they were not entirely separate. Most of the 'Guardian Boys' in Sydney also spent their first few months at the *Isabella Lazarus Home*, as did the boys who came out under the *Children's Scheme*. The weekends were usually spent in the home of an Australian-Jewish family to enable the youth to become acquainted with the general Jewish community. It was resolved that these weekend hosts and hostesses had to be members of a synagogue.[80] Walter Brand, himself, was not only passionate in his support of the schemes at an official level but also at a personal level. He sponsored three 'Guardian Boys', and he and his wife, Vera, formed a very close parental relationship with William Markovicz (Bill Marr), one of the boys he sponsored, who married another Jewish orphan. They both could not speak highly enough of the Brands, who they felt were very lovely and treated them so warmly as part of the family.

The Marrs presented a very different face to Walter Brand, than the testimonies of the *Dunera* internees and other survivors who were critical of his British officiousness and lack of sympathy. In 1940, a total of 2,500 male internees arrived in Sydney on the *Dunera*, including 1,750 Jewish refugees, largely from Germany and Austria, but also including some from Czechoslovakia and other parts of Europe. They were immediately sent to an internment camp at Hay, on the border of New South Wales and South Australia, literally in the middle of nowhere, and felt that Australian Jewry had deserted them. It took six months before Brand visited the Hay internment camp with Rabbi Leib A. Falk in March 1941. In March 1943, Rabbi Elchanan Blumenthal, who arrived on the *Dunera* and became the founding headmaster of the *North Bondi Jewish Day School* (later *Moriah War Memorial College*), declared: 'To our great disappointment the officials of the Australian Jewry have exemplified themselves like a bad step-mother, as if they have no hearts'.[81]

The experiences of Jenine Cibulka were more typical in terms of the reception survivors received from Brand. She had survived in a Catholic orphanage and left Paris in September, travelling on the *Napoli* from Italy. As with many of the young survivors, she really enjoyed the trip out to Australia, despite the dormitory accommodation and food, and having to wash herself in salt water. However, as she described it:

> When we arrived in Sydney on 28 October 1948, I had no idea what town or family awaited me. To make matters worse, we were greeted by an official from the Jewish [W]elfare [S]ociety who spoke entirely in English. I had learned some English at school, but I couldn't understand a word he said.[82]

Jenine described that she was allocated to a 'Mr Brent'. He seemed elderly (although he was only thirty-seven at the time) and also only spoke English. She recalled that she was terrified, fearing that she would have to live alone with him and sobbed uncontrollably as he drove her to her new home. However, when they arrived, they were met by his wife, Ellen, who greeted her with a bunch of flowers and spoke to her in perfect French. After this terrible start to life in Australia, she settled into her new family, noting that they were very good to her.[83]

One of the most dedicated workers for the *Guardian Scheme* in Sydney was Isadore (John) Lewinnek, a prewar refugee from Germany, who had married into the Blashki family but was himself childless. Each year Lewinnek, together with Kurt Wollstein, organized a Chanukah party at the Maccabean Hall for the youth sponsored by the two schemes. In 1954, over 1,000 people attended the party where tribute was paid to Lewinnek for his role in assisting in the readjustment of this group.[84]

Mina Fink was deeply involved in the rehabilitation of a group of forty-five boys, who were survivors of Buchenwald concentration camp aged between fourteen and nineteen at liberation on 11 April 1945, most of whom were resettled in Melbourne. She found that at first there was tension with these survivors who were living as a group of forty at *Camberwell House* (later renamed *HIAS House*) and had lost their trust in human beings. After counselling and assistance in finding employment, they gradually regained their confidence and their belief that there were people who cared for them.[85]

Reminiscing about his experience of travelling to Australia as one of the Buchenwald group, Max Zilberman recalled how they arrived by train to Melbourne after disembarking from their ship in Sydney, and Mina was waiting at the station to welcome them with three limousines to take them to *Camberwell House*. Thus, his first impressions of his new life in Australia were very positive. Zilberman and his Buchenwald friends found 'beds, warmth, food, community and kindness in Camberwell House'.[86]

As well as providing the basic needs of shelter and food, *Camberwell House* also provided an important social network. After they had moved out, previous residents frequently came back to the house to socialize. Dances and events were held at the house and the 'Buchenwald Boys' were frequently taken on outings with the Fink family. The approach of the *Australian Jewish Welfare Societies* was very different from the *Canadian Scheme*, which was based on the concept that the family was the best way of reconstructing the orphan's life and sought Jewish foster families. Often placements were unsuccessful, and the child could have to move from one home to another. As time progressed, it also became much more difficult to find suitable volunteers, so that the Canadian social workers tried to make the descriptions of the children as positive as possible. In contrast, the Australian programmes largely followed the collective systems favoured by the continental organizations, such as OSE in France and *Aide aux Israelites Victimes de la Guerre* in Belgium. Most of the children arrived in groups and were based in the Melbourne *Frances Barkman* and Sydney *Isabella Lazarus* children's homes. Ernst Papanek, an Austrian-born child psychologist, argues that in relation to a refugee child 'more than any other child, he must gain anew the feeling that he is accepted, that he is a member of a group'.[87] The story of the 'Buchenwald Boys' illustrates the importance of the development of a group spirit in the rebuilding of shattered lives after the Holocaust.[88] The support provided through this group identification is seen with the annual Buchenwald Boys Ball. Each year these Jewish survivors would dress up and take their wives to both commemorate and celebrate their liberation from Buchenwald on 11 April 1945. The homes and hostels also provided a safe place, where the orphans could return if needed. Thus, Zilberman found a job as an electrician and moved out of *Camberwell House* within a month. He discovered that his twin sister had survived and sponsored both her and her husband to come to Melbourne. However, when she died shortly after of stomach cancer, he was devastated and returned for a period to *Camberwell House* to grieve. In this way, most of the young orphans who came out to Australia were able to adjust to their new world and rebuild their lives.

One of those boys who came under the *Children's Scheme*, reminiscing on this period, stressed that:

> One thing we all agreed on, though, was the kindness and welcome we had each received from our hosts. We were impressed that even after they had collected the money for our fares [to Australia] they continued to fund our living in the Home, have us taught the language and when they were finished with one lot of us, got on with the next. It seemed as if they were an army opposed to that other – the destroyers who had spent every bit of their energy on annihilation – and were a part of the second nation I had come across that was willing to give refuge, the second set of people dedicated to building up, to restoring life.[89]

Under the *Save the Children* and *Welfare Guardian Schemes*, 317 Jewish children and youths were helped in this way to recreate a new life in Australia, their faith and trust in human nature gradually being restored. The Australian approach of housing the boys in hostels, rather than in foster homes, proved successful. It meant that the group lived together with other young people who had experienced the same traumas and difficulties during the Holocaust. They had all gone through the same, almost unimaginable experiences and could understand each other, as well as providing group support. At the same time, caring members of the Jewish community tried their best to provide them with additional care and support. This was seen most clearly with the 'Buchenwald Boys', and the close relationship they established with Mina Fink, but also with Sydney Einfeld's activities in Sydney. Their roles demonstrated that a warm, caring person is able to assist in the rehabilitation of a traumatized youngster. A number of these young survivors later repaid their debt to the community by active involvement in communal leadership. In addition, child survivor groups were formed in Sydney and Melbourne to enable the recording of their stories to ensure that their legacy lives on for future generations. Above all, the fact that most of these young people made a successful transition into life in Australia demonstrates the resilience of human nature, an essential component in the Jewish experience, and the importance of not being controlled by one's past victim status.

Notes

1. Peter Rossler, *The Words to Remember It: Memoirs of Child Holocaust Survivors* (Melbourne: Scribe 2009), p. 38.
2. Ibid., p. 45.
3. See Glen Palmer, *Reluctant Refuge: Unaccompanied Refugee and Evacuee Children in Australia, 1933–1945* (East Roseville: Kangaroo Press 1997).
4. Wolf Simon Matsdorf, *No Time to Grow: The Story of the Gross-Breeseners in Australia* (Sydney: Mandelbaum Publishing 1994).
5. For this characterization of the Australian Jewish community, see Suzanne D. Rutland, *Edge of the Diaspora: Two Centuries of Jewish Settlement in Australia*, 2nd edition (New York: Holmes & Meier 2001).
6. These population figures come from the official government census conducted every five years. There has been significant debate about the census figures among various demographers of Australian Jewry, largely because of the significant under-enumeration, which most scholars estimate at 20 per cent. On this controversy, see Suzanne D. Rutland, *Edge of the Diaspora*, p. 287.
7. Suzanne D. Rutland, 'Postwar Anti-Jewish Refugee Hysteria: A Case of Racial or Religious Bigotry?', *Journal of Australian Studies* 77 (2003), pp. 69–79.
8. Brand to Symonds, 5 July 1946, Box E18, ECAJ Corres. Files, February 1946–October 1946, Archive of Australian Judaica (AAJ). For a discussion of the New South Wales war orphans scheme see Anne Andgel, *Fifty Years of Caring: The History of the Australian Jewish Welfare Society, 1939–98* (Sydney: AJWS and Australian Jewish Historical Society 1988), pp. 46–7 and pp. 97–105.
9. Interview with Ingrid Naumburger (née Ehrlich) a member of this group, Sydney, December 1985. See also Glen Palmer, *Reluctant Refuge*, and Rodney Benjamin, *A Serious Influx of Jews: A History of Jewish Welfare in Victoria* (St Leonards, NSW: Allen & Unwin 1998).
10. NAA (National Archives of Australia): A434, 49/3/3, 'A.J.W.S. Scheme for Admission of 300 Refugee Children, Part I', Department of Immigration, Memo No 39/7975, 15 October 1940.
11. NAA: A434, 49/3/3, J.S. Collings, 'Jewish Refugee Children', 25 February 1943.
12. NAA: A434, 49/3/3, Memo No. 43/2/216 and Memo from Brand to the Minister for the Interior, 10 March 1943, and *Hebrew Standard of Australasia* (*HS*), 15 April 1943.
13. NAA: A434, 49/3/3, Memo No 43/2/216, 18 January 1944, signed J. Horgan, and Memo for Cabinet, 28 January 1944, Minister for the Interior. When the government granted approval for the 300 orphans it was noted that 'the AJWS, which will accept responsibility for the children if admitted to Australia, is well able to undertake this work and there is no likelihood of any of the children becoming a public burden'.
14. Minutes, Children's Scheme Committee, 16 August 1944. On 28 August the name was changed to AJWS Child Migrants' Committee.

15 NAA: A433, 1944/2/5976, Undated departmental memo, 'Polish Refugee Children in Iran. Question of Admission to Australia for the duration of the war'.
16 NAA: A433, 1944/2/5976, Memo, 9 January 1945.
17 *Sydney Jewish News* (*SJN*), 5 and 19 January 1945.
18 Ibid., 9 February 1945.
19 *YMHA News*, 5 September 1946.
20 *SJN*, 12 January 1945. It was discovered that European governments were not prepared to lose their children.
21 *Sunday Telegraph*, 26 May 1946.
22 AJWS Ex. Council Minutes, Sydney, 30 September 1946.
23 Ibid., 18 April 1946.
24 Suzanne D. Rutland, 'Brand, Walter Levi (1893–1964)', *Australian Dictionary of Biography*, National Centre of Biography, Australian National University, http://adb.anu.edu.au/biography/brand-walter-levi-9572/text16865 (accessed 10 January 2013). This article was first published in hardcopy in *Australian Dictionary of Biography*, ed. by John Ritchie et al., vol. 13 (Melbourne: Melbourne University Press 1993).
25 Walter Brand to Moses Leavitt, 15 May 1945, 'Australia, Immigration of Children, 1946–1949', JDC AR 45/54 #98 [Formerly AR 45/64 #147], American Joint Distribution Committee Archives, New York (JDCA-NY).
26 Walter Brand to Moses Leavitt, 15 May 1945, 'Australia, Immigration of Children, 1946–1949', JDC AR 45/54 #98 [Formerly AR 45/64 #147], JDCA-NY.
27 Walter Brand to Lewis Neikrug, 6 August 1946, MKM 46.19, HIAS Archives, Centre for Jewish History, New York (HIASA-NY).
28 Robert Pilpel to Amelia Igel, 22 August 1947, 'Australia, Immigration of Children, 1946–1949', JDC AR 45/54 #98 [Formerly AR 45/64 #147], JDCA-NY.
29 Amelia Igel to Walter Brand, 11 July 1947, 'Australia, Immigration of Children, 1946–1949', JDC AR 45/54 #98 [Formerly AR 45/64 #147], JDCA-NY.
30 Ibid.
31 Frances Barkman to Lewis Neikrug, 25 September 1946, MKM 19.46, HIASA-NY.
32 See for example *SJN*, 20 September 1946 and Symonds to Heyes, re Isadore (John) Lewinnek in Europe, 19 April 1948, 'Immigration', Box E30, ECAJ Corres. Files, AAJ.
33 Wynn to Einfeld, 27 April 1948, Box E17, ECAJ Corres, Files, 1948–1949, T-Z, AAJ.
34 AJWS Ex. Council Minutes, Sydney, 21 June 1948.
35 Ibid., 30 January 1947.
36 Anne Andgel, *Fifty Years of Caring*, p. 97.

37 In relation to the Canadian Scheme, there was one case of a child who impersonated the identity of another child. Antoine Burgard, '"A new life in a new country": Trajectories of Holocaust Orphans to Canada (1945–1952)', paper presented at the Second International Multidisciplinary Conference, 'Children and War: Past and Present', 10–12 July 2013, University of Salzburg, p. 7.

38 AJWS Ex. Council Minutes, Sydney, 22 January 1948.

39 At one stage, the Nazis imprisoned Dr Szeps and whilst he was being whipped he had to call out Hail Mary, not to give way to his false identity. Interview with Dr Szeps, Sydney 1983. Suzanne D. Rutland, *Take Heart Again: The Story of a Fellowship of Jewish Doctors* (Sydney: Australian Jewish Historical Society 1983), p. 31.

40 Interview with Zofia Frant, Sydney 1983.

41 Diane Armstrong, *The Voyage of their Life: The Story of the SS Derna and its Passengers* (Pymble, NSW: Flamingo 2002), p. 9.

42 *SJN*, 19 November 1948.

43 Aaron Rosen to Walter Brand, 5 June 1947, 'Australia, Immigration of Children, 1946–1949', JDC AR 45/54 #98 [Formerly AR 45/64 #147], JDCA-NY.

44 Antoine Burgard, '"A new life in a new country": Trajectories of Holocaust Orphans to Canada (1945–1952)', paper delivered at 'Children and War: Past and Present', 2nd Conference, Salzburg, 10–12 July 2013, Conference Papers (CD), p. 1.

45 Report prepared by Herbert Katzki, Paris office, 'Australia, Immigration of Children, 1946–1949', JDC AR 45/54 #98 [Formerly AR 45/64 #147], JDCA-NY.

46 Letter from Manfred Saalheimer to Saul Hayes, CJC Chairman, as reported by Hayes to the CJC staff meeting, Montreal, 29 August 1947, cited in Burgard, 'Trajectories of Holocaust Orphans to Canada (1945–1952)', p. 4.

47 Ibid., p. 6.

48 AJWS Ex. Council Minutes, 21 June 1949 and AJW&RS, 2 August and 11 October 1950.

49 Children's Scheme Committee Minutes, 4 October and 26 November 1944.

50 Children's Scheme Committee Minutes, AJWS, 18 February 1948.

51 Edi Schwarz and Zoltan Schwartz, *The Army-Cap Boy: The Story of a Teenage Boy's Survival in Hitler's Europe* (Melbourne: Macmillan 1983), p. 169.

52 Interview with Sydney Einfeld and AJWS Ex. Council Minutes, 15 March 1948.

53 Ibid., 5 June 1950.

54 Ibid., 13 November 1950.

55 Ibid., 22 April 1952.

56 See Paul R. Bartrop, 'Barkman, Frances (1885–1946)', *Australian Dictionary of Biography*, National Centre of Biography, Australian National University, http://adb.anu.edu.au/biography/barkman-frances-9434/text16585 (accessed

9 January 2013). This article was first published in hardcopy in *Australian Dictionary of Biography*, vol. 13 (MUP 1993).
57 AJW&RS Minutes, Melbourne Jewish-Care, 5 June 1947.
58 Ibid., 18 March and 14 April 1948.
59 AJW&RS Minutes, 9 June 1948. See Paul R. Bartrop, 'Barkman, Frances (1885–1946)', Australian Dictionary of Biography, National Centre of Biography, Australian National University, http://adb.anu.edu.au/biography/barkman-frances-9434/text16585 (accessed 9 January 2013). This article was first published in hardcopy in *Australian Dictionary of Biography*, vol. 13 (MUP 1993).
60 Rodney Benjamin, *A Serious Influx of Jews*, p. 148.
61 AJW&RS Minutes, 27 June 1957. For more detail on the Frances Barkman House, see Rodney Benjamin, *A Serious Influx of Jews*, pp. 247–64.
62 See AJW&RS Annual Reports, 1947–60.
63 AJW&RS Minutes, 26 June and 28 August 1958.
64 Ibid., 8 September 1958.
65 Interview with Walter Lippmann, Sydney and Melbourne, 1984.
66 Rodney Benjamin, *A Serious Influx*, pp. 256–9.
67 Konrad Kwiet, 'The Second Time Around: Re-Acculturation of German-Jewish Refugees in Australia', *The Journal of Holocaust Education* 10/1 (2001), p. 39.
68 AJWS Ex. Council Minutes, Sydney 18 February 1952.
69 *SJN*, 30 April 1948.
70 Interview with Ingrid Naumburger and AJW&RS Annual Reports, Melbourne, 1953–4.
71 *YMHA News*, 2 September 1948.
72 See Wolf Simon Matsdorf, *No Time to Grow*.
73 *SJN*, 16 December 1949.
74 Ibid., 19 January 1951.
75 Ibid., 7 December 1948, comment by Dr H. Frant who accompanied a group of Welfare boys on the *SS Derna*.
76 *YMHA News*, 28 October 1948.
77 Ibid.
78 Hans Vidor to Amelia Igel, 25 November 1947, 'Australia C – 15.002: Australian Children Project', Geneva II, Box No 322B, File No 25, JDCA-Jerusalem.
79 Children's Scheme Committee Minutes, AJWS, 18 February 1948.
80 Ibid., 25 February 1948.
81 As quoted in Konrad Kwiet, '"Be patient and reasonable": The Internment of German-Jewish Refugees in Australia', in *Jews in the Sixth Continent*, ed. by W. D. Rubinstein (Sydney: Allen & Unwin 1987), p. 71.
82 Jenine Cibulka, *The Words to Remember It*, p. 325.

83 Ibid., p. 326.
84 See Annual Report AJWS, Sydney, 1955.
85 Interview with Mina Fink, Melbourne, 1984.
86 Suzanne D. Rutland and Sarah Rood, *Nationality Stateless, Destination Australia: JDC and the Australian Survivor Community* (Melbourne: American Joint Distribution Committee 2008), p. 90.
87 As cited in Burgard, 'Trajectories of Holocaust Orphans in Canada (1945–1952)', p. 10, from Tara Zahra, *The Lost Children: Reconstructing Europe's Families after World War II* (Cambridge/London: Harvard University Press 2011), p. 100.
88 Professor Danny Ben-Moshe, Kinderblock 66, http://www.youtube.com/watch?v-8__0LWXpM8 (accessed 7 June 2015).
89 Edi Schwarz and Zoltan Schwartz, *The Army-Cap Boy*, p. 173.

CHAPTER FIVE

'The children are a triumph':

New Zealand's Response to Europe's Children and Youth, 1933–49

Ann Beaglehole

'The children are a triumph' wrote senior public servant Reuel Lochore in his 1951 book *From Europe to New Zealand: An Account of our Continental European Settlers*. He was referring to the children of Jewish refugees escaping from Nazi Europe who had settled in New Zealand in the 1930s. Lochore thought that the children, showing 'real genius of adaptation', were 'the real success of this migration of people who were wholly unsuited to our conditions'.[1] In 1944, the journal of the *New Zealand Manufacturers Association* had published an article on child immigration whose author claimed:

> Children are the best type of immigrants. They are fresh and eager; willing to accept their adopted country as their own; to adopt its ways and to be in every way except by birth citizens of that country. Coming as children they have no great language problems to overcome and no foreign background to forget.[2]

This chapter examines New Zealand's response to refugee children and youth from Europe in the years 1933–49. Several million children and youth were persecuted and displaced during those years and 1.5 million are estimated to have died in the Holocaust. New Zealand admitted around

1,000 juvenile refugees. The figure comprises the following groups: twenty Jewish orphans, mainly from Białystok in Poland ('Deckston orphans') who arrived in two groups in 1935 and in 1937;[3] an estimated 300 Jewish children and youth who came alone, or with their families, in the years between the rise of Hitler and the outbreak of the Second World War;[4] five Kindertransportees who emigrated from Britain to New Zealand in 1939–40, and in 1946;[5] 732 Polish children (mainly Catholic) who were given refuge, initially on a temporary basis, by the New Zealand government in 1944;[6] a small number of young Holocaust survivors who arrived in the years 1946–8; and lastly, the small number of young people who came as part of New Zealand's postwar Displaced Persons (DP) intake from 1949.

The discussion focuses primarily on immigration policy. During the 1930s and 1940s, New Zealand preferred British settlers and placed strict controls on non-British immigration, particularly on the admission of 'racial minorities', such as Slavs, Jews and Chinese people.[7] The policies of virtual exclusion of adult 'racial minority' refugees, however, existed alongside a widely held perception that children, regardless of their ethnicity, and especially orphans and other children removed from parental influence, made the most suitable migrants. The chapter considers the relatively warm welcome given to children and asks whether young people with different ethnic or religious backgrounds had different experiences. The New Zealand to which they came was markedly culturally homogeneous, with Anglo-Celtic culture predominating. The chapter touches on the responses of children and youth to their new social and cultural environment and includes comments from their school teachers.[8]

During the 1930s, New Zealand did not accept applicants for entry because they were refugees. Rather, like other migrants, refugees were subject to the restrictions of the 1931 Immigration Restriction Amendment Act. The Act, which gave the Minister of Customs the discretion to decide who was suitable to enter New Zealand, prevented non-British subjects (so-called 'aliens') from entering New Zealand unless they had guaranteed employment, a considerable amount of capital or 'possessed knowledge or skills which would enable them to rehabilitate readily, but without detriment to any resident of New Zealand'.[9] Jewish refugees who inquired about migration to New Zealand in the years 1933–9 were told by the New Zealand High Commissioner's Office in London that it was hardly worthwhile making an application:

> The New Zealand Government is not at present encouraging immigration ... In the case of persons not of British birth and parentage, it is necessary for such persons to obtain permits from the Minister of Customs at Wellington before they may proceed to the Dominion. The High Commissioner has received advice from his Government that it has recently been found necessary to discontinue the issuing of such permits except in very special cases.[10]

The immigration authorities' first and foremost consideration was whether an applicant could be readily absorbed into the Dominion's population. Edwin Dudley Good, Comptroller of Customs in the mid-1930s, was explicit: 'Non-Jewish applicants are regarded as a more suitable type of immigrant'.[11] Thousands of applications from Jewish refugees trying to flee Nazi Europe were declined. Of the around 1,100 Jewish refugees admitted by New Zealand in the years between the rise of Hitler and the outbreak of the Second World War were a few hundred children and young people.[12]

Sonny was born in 1928 in Karlsruhe, Germany, and was eleven years old when she arrived in New Zealand before the outbreak of the Second World War. Her father had been imprisoned in Dachau after 'Kristallnacht' (the burning of the synagogues in November 1938) and later released. Sonny and her parents reached New Zealand in 1939. When interviewed fifty years later, she said that she was not herself 'deprived or beaten up by anybody', yet had clear memories of 'the atmosphere of fear' at her parents' house.[13] She was afraid of Hitler's 'fanatical voice on the radio', and of 'Goebbels' voice, screaming'.[14] At her German school, when the propaganda about Jews being an 'inferior race' was being propounded by slogans such as 'we must rid ourselves of Jews and purify the German race', she had been 'stood out in front of the class' and pointed to 'as an example'.[15] Once in New Zealand, Sonny set about becoming a New Zealand child as quickly as possible. 'I was young enough to adapt very quickly. My sister who was seventeen had a much more difficult time. I was just at an age when it was easy for me to accept the way New Zealand kids were. I tried to be like them. I wanted to belong'.[16] Sonny finished her schooling in New Zealand. She went on to university and also trained as a teacher.[17]

Gerty (born 1923, Brno, Czechoslovakia) was sixteen when she arrived with her brother in New Zealand in 1939. Her parents, unable to get visas and entry permits, stayed behind and perished in a concentration camp. Fifty years later, Gerty recalled the desperate search for a country to escape to:

> You had to be very clever and to have contacts of an important sort to be able to get out and to get in anywhere. People tried desperately hard. For us, it was a mixture of luck, coincidences and a fair amount of machinations and skill. You also had to have a certain amount of money. It was my mother who was determined to get us out. 'The sooner the better', she said. New Zealand was one of the prize places to go to, but it was incredibly difficult to get in. New Zealand didn't want us; nor did anyone else really.[18]

As a young girl from a protected middle-class background, without the support of parents, Gerty faced a tough transition to life in Wellington. Her introduction to the cultural and social environment in the late 1930s was at a nursery for children of working mothers run by two 'very strict', 'aged Presbyterian nurses'.[19]

> The job . . . had to be one that gave me a roof over my head. What sort of job are you fit for when you are sixteen? I didn't know any English; I had never swept a room, in fact I had never held a broom in my hand.[20]

The nursery was a tough, grim place, 'run on a shoe string'.[21] Gerty recalled that 'if you were on duty to look after the children, pre-schoolers, twenty-six of them, it meant that at the same time you were expected to do the mending'.[22] Hardest of all was 'the cultural and intellectual isolation'.[23]

> [N]othing, absolutely nothing I had read, did anybody else know anything about. The greatest difficulty was the realization that when you start to communicate and to understand the language, if something wells up in your mind, an analogy, or a reference, or a comparison . . ., you've got to swallow it down again because the person you are speaking to knows nothing of it. I came to realize that it is not only the people you have known, not only the family friends and relatives and others who know you and what you are and what you are talking about, not only are they gone, but also everything you have read and thought is suddenly nil, is nil. You are nothing. You know nothing, because everything you have known is irrelevant. What do people mean by being homesick? What is it? Is it missing a particular food, or people or what? The isolation, the total rootlessness, I experienced was very much deeper than a hankering for home. To me, it was the ideas, the thoughts, the conversations I suddenly couldn't share. I learned to wall myself off and to think: 'that's of no interest to anybody else, that's just my own. It cannot be shared'.[24]

Gerty felt that she had 'to transplant' for there was 'no way back'.[25] She was 'damn lucky to have got away' and had no choice but to make 'conscious efforts to become a New Zealander':

> I worked at it, for example by trying to learn English as quickly as possible. I associated with other refugees as little as I could. I tried hard to adapt and understand New Zealanders' point of view. I didn't expect New Zealanders to accept me. By the end of the war, I felt like a New Zealander. At this stage my background seemed irrelevant. I didn't look back. I was too busy learning new things. There was no point in being self-indulgent. Living in the present was the right thing to do. It is only since getting older that I have started to look back – a bit.[26]

In sharp contrast with the thousands of Jewish adults declined permits to enter New Zealand in the years between the rise of Hitler and the outbreak of the Second World War, two small groups of Polish-Jewish orphaned children succeeded in gaining admittance. The sought-after visas to enable the children to enter New Zealand were obtained by Max and Annie Deckston, immigrants from Poland who had settled in Wellington in 1900.[27]

In 1932, on a visit back to Poland, they were reported to have been shocked by the plight of some Jewish children in orphanages in Białystok. Poland was badly affected by the Depression and evidence of poverty was widespread. With anti-Semitism growing in Europe, they decided to bring orphaned children to New Zealand. The President of the New Zealand Jewish community lobbied the government on their behalf. Annie Deckston 'called on officials and thumped their desks until she got what she wanted'.[28] While the Deckstons' motives for bringing the children to New Zealand are unclear,[29] they certainly saved the lives of the children for they escaped the fate of most of the Jews of the Białystok ghetto who were subsequently killed in the Nazi extermination camp of Treblinka.

Twenty children came in two groups between 1935 and 1937. 'Little victims of European savagery find refuge in New Zealand', reported the *New Zealand Radio Record*.[30] 'Arrangements are now being made to bring eight more friendless, homeless little sufferers from Europe'.[31] However, the Deckstons' attempt to bring a third group failed. The New Zealand government 'placed insurmountable obstacles in their way and these children were left to their fate in Poland'.[32]

In New Zealand, the children 'sorely missed the homes they came from'; teenagers 'felt out of depth and bewildered'.[33] Some 'resented that they were rescued' while the rest of their families 'were abandoned'.[34] Subject to strict discipline at the *Deckston Home*, some experienced 'depolonization'. An example of this was being allowed to speak only English and Yiddish, not Polish.[35] The banning of Polish contrasts with the experiences of the Polish children who came in 1944, discussed below, whose Polish identity was fostered. However, it is similar to the forbidding of the use of the German language within some German and Austrian-Jewish refugee families.[36] In contrast, too, with the Polish children who came in 1944, the 'Deckston children' attended local primary schools. They were split up and placed in different classes and experienced some bullying from their classmates.[37]

One of the 'Deckston children', Chaim (not his real name),[38] was born in 1927 in a village on the border of Poland and Russia (unlike most of the other 'Deckston children', he was not from Białystok). Although he experienced a certain amount of 'solidarity'[39] with the other children in the *Deckston Home*, he also felt the isolation and abrupt severance from roots that Gerty had faced. When interviewed almost fifty years after his arrival in New Zealand, he groped for clear memories of his Polish childhood. Although the details continued to elude him, he had a strong sense, he said, that those years had remained part of him: particularly the music, the gestures of the people, and the smells of the food. He recalled that, at a dinner long after he had left the *Deckston Home* for Israel, he had tasted some jellied marrow and other foods that he had never had in New Zealand, and tears had come into his eyes 'because this was what my mother used to make'.[40]

Chaim's maternal grandfather had been a rabbi; his mother's brothers had become 'strong communists'.[41] Pervasive anti-Semitism had made his life difficult as a young boy in a strongly Jewish family in the 1930s. 'Then a most unusual thing happened. A man, a Jew, came from New Zealand, looking for children to bring out to his country'.[42] The New Zealander was looking for orphans but because one of the boys supposed to go, could not, Chaim was offered his place.

> My mother said: 'I want you to go. This is an opportunity'. She saw the situation in Poland. I remember kneeling down before my grandfather and him placing his hands on my head, blessing me. Then I was on the boat with eleven or twelve other children. I was ten years old.[43]

Chaim received only two letters from his family once he was in New Zealand. 'Then the war came and I never heard from my family again. My mother, my father and my sister were killed'.[44] At the age of fifteen, Chaim left school and the *Deckston Home* and became apprenticed as a toolmaker.[45]

Jewish welfare societies in the main centres were available to help the new arrivals from Europe settle, including by offering English-language classes and information about schools for the children. Some refugees were grateful for the help offered; others, including some refugees with previously tenuous connections to Judaism, did not wish to form links with members of the established New Zealand Jewish community which during the 1930s and 1940s was 'fairly rigid in adhering to Jewish rituals and traditions'.[46] Gerty recalled feeling that members of the refugee committee who looked after her were 'disappointed' at her not being 'more religious'. She was 'agnostic' and in New Zealand went only once to the synagogue.[47] Sometimes Zionism provided a bond when religion could not do so and some children became involved in the Zionist youth movement and felt accepted and formed friendships. In addition to religious differences, cultural differences between the newly arrived young people and the established community could be a barrier to good relationships. While some members of the established Jewish community were keen to help and befriend the newcomers, others were ambivalent about the arrivals from Europe and found them 'too strange to be comfortable with socially'.[48]

The acceptance of 732 (mainly Catholic) Polish children in 1944 is the most prominent instance in which New Zealand took a generous approach to refugee children. New Zealand's formal refugee resettlement programme has often been considered to have begun with the admission of the children, most of them orphaned in the war, and their caregivers for the duration of the war.

After 1939, when Poland was invaded by both Germany and the Soviet Union, between 1.5 and 2 million Poles were deported to the Soviet Union. Many children were orphaned or became lost or separated from their families. Following the German invasion of the Soviet Union in 1941, an amnesty was declared for captive Poles, in return for the formation of a Polish army to fight the Germans. Unable to return home because of the war, thousands of Polish children were given refuge in orphanages set up in the southern Soviet Union by the Polish army. In 1942, about 20,000 Polish women and children, many of them orphans, were evacuated from the Soviet Union. Some reached Iran where they spent the next three years in refugee camps.[49]

The idea to give asylum in New Zealand to the Polish children came from Countess Wodzicka, the *Polish Red Cross* delegate in New Zealand and wife of Poland's Honorary Consul, who suggested it to her friend Janet Fraser, the wife of Labour Prime Minister Peter Fraser. Fraser wrote to the Polish Honorary Consul – Count Kazimierz Wodzicki – on 23 December 1943, offering the 'hospitality' of the New Zealand government to between 500 and 700 Polish refugees. 'Our whole conception of the scheme is that it should cater for the largest number of children' he wrote.[50] The *Auckland Star* quoted him as saying: 'It would be an act of Christian philanthropy and kindness, in which New Zealanders should be pleased to participate, to welcome these children, a few of their parents and attendants, giving them a chance to recuperate'.[51]

Sister Stella (Józefa Wrotniak) was sixteen when, with her family, she was deported to a forced labour camp in northern Siberia.[52] As she recalled over sixty years later:

> [O]n 10 February 1940, on a bitterly cold night at 1.30 am, we heard loud knocking on our door. These uninvited guests were armed Russian secret police and a few local Ukrainians. Some of them behaved arrogantly and noisily, and one of them told us to be packed and ready to depart in 30 minutes.[53]

The journey by sleigh to the 'nearest railhead', 'a time of terror and uncertainty' has been 'erased' from Sister Stella's memory.[54] But she recalled the 'cattle trucks and locomotives' . . . 'already waiting for us at the railway station':

> [W]e were loaded into a carriage with four other families from our village. The doors were bolted and padlocked from the outside. . . . The carriage had small barred windows and a hole in the wooden floor was the toilet. . . . We were packed like sardines, having to lie close together. One could only sit in a crouching position.[55]

The journey, the first of many, took several weeks. The last leg, from Bombay to New Zealand, was on board the American troopship the *General Randall* which was also carrying about 3,000 soldiers on their way back from the battlefront to have leave in Australia and New Zealand.[56] In her 1974 book, *The Invited: The Story of 733 Polish Children who grew up in New Zealand*, Krystyna Skwarko writes that the *General Randall* struck them as 'almost a luxury vessel in comparison with the merchant ship'[57] that had transported them from Basra on the first part of their sea journey to New Zealand.

On the *General Randall* were canvas bunks, plenty of wash basins and showers, excellent food and above all the kindness of the soldiers to the children. Few will forget 'Uncle New Zealand' and many others whose names the children did not know but 'whose kindness they remember to this day'.[58]

The adults in the group (the children's caregivers) were mainly women, many of them widows. 'Some of the children were so young and so traumatized by harrowing experiences of exile and war – including loss of their families – that they did not know who or how old they were, or where they came from'.[59] When they had disembarked, the refugees travelled as a group to a former internment camp at Pahiatua which became known as the *Polish Children's Camp*.[60] 'After the dry, barren and yellow countryside of Persia, New Zealand appeared a real fairyland'.[61] Thirty years later, one of the children[62] recalled the arrival:

> After a month of sea travel we sailed into Wellington Harbour . . . There were hundreds of smiling Wellington school children waving New Zealand and Polish flags as a gesture of welcome on the platform from which we were to leave for Pahiatua. The singing of the national anthems and gifts and flowers made the occasion even more moving.[63]

Six decades after his arrival, another of the children, Jan Wojciechowski also recalled the warmth of that initial welcome. As he climbed 'up the narrow steps into his assigned carriage' at Wellington Railway Station, he was handed a bottle of milk, a carton of ice-cream, and a boxed lunch, prepared by the *Red Cross*.

> That first sweet taste of the creamy New Zealand ice-cream would stay with Jan and his sisters for many years; clothing and possessions were meaningless to a boy whose life had become conditioned by food and survival. The concept of New Zealand as a physical space, a nation, was similarly of no consequence to him. Life and home for him had become 'here', like his ancestors of the eastern Poland borderlands, whose image of homeland was simply where they were, rather than some country with ever-shifting borders and rulers. Ice-cream, though, was real. It was food. It was nice. It was survival, the only reality he needed to know.[64]

Due to the political situation in Poland after 1945 the majority of the Polish refugees did not want to return to Poland. They were then accepted for permanent settlement in New Zealand.[65] The *Polish Children's Camp* was gradually closed down. The children, who had completed a Polish primary education at the camp, were sent away in small groups to receive their secondary education at Catholic boarding schools in different parts of New Zealand. The children and their caregivers did not want to be split up and would have preferred the security and familiarity of their Polish world at the camp to continue but, from the government's point of view, the camp was untenable on a permanent basis because it was an 'alien enclave', as the settlement of migrants and refugees in ethnic clusters was known in the mid-twentieth century. Since the children were going to stay permanently in New Zealand they had to be prepared for life in their new country.[66]

After visiting Majdanek death camp in Poland, New Zealand diplomat and intelligence officer Paddy Costello, in a detailed report to Prime Minister Peter Fraser and the External Affairs Department on 26 March 1945 (six weeks before the end of the war in Europe) provided details of the gas chambers and other facts about the way the extermination was carried out.[67] From mid-April 1945, New Zealand newspapers began to publish photographs and eyewitness accounts of the concentration camps. In mid-May 1945, the newspapers published accounts by New Zealanders who served with the British Army and had visited the camps and were able to verify that earlier accounts had not been exaggerated.[68] The fact that the New Zealand government and New Zealanders were well aware of the atrocities is significant in the light of the country's restrictive postwar Jewish immigration policy.

When the war in Europe was over, the *Jewish Welfare Society* set up a search bureau to help Jews living in New Zealand trace missing family members[69] and an immigration office to 'assist people who are settled here to bring out their relatives'.[70] The immigration project soon encountered major obstacles.[71] To some extent, shipping problems and the priority given to servicemen and to other New Zealanders in the United Kingdom who had applied to return home accounted for the delays and the reluctance to bring Holocaust survivors to New Zealand.[72] But the main impediment was 'the question of policy'.[73] A statement by the New Zealand Delegation to the *United Nations Special Committee on Refugees and Displaced Persons* on 10 May 1946 made the point that the New Zealand government 'does not favour mass or group immigration of refugees' and that the immigration of 'aliens' would continue to be restricted under the Immigration Act.[74] New Zealand's policy on the survivors of the Holocaust was to continue the restrictions practised before the war. R. M. Campbell, Official Secretary to the New Zealand High Commission in London, told the *Intergovernmental Committee on Refugees* that each case was dealt with 'in a sympathetic manner'.[75] Yet, only 120 permits were granted out of 588 requests from close relatives, with a further 200 issued subsequently.[76]

New Zealand's restrictive policy needs to be seen in the context of the growing national consensus that the country needed more people.[77] In December 1945, a parliamentary select committee was set up 'to consider the ways and means of increasing the population of the Dominion', with immigration one of the issues to be considered.[78] The four New Zealand Jewish communities submitted a memorandum to the committee. The reasons they offered in support of the migration of the relatives of New Zealand Jews included: 'the saving of the remnants of European Jewry' and 'the stabilizing effect' that the reunion of families would have on the lives of those already here.⁷⁹ The Jewish communities gave detailed information on the applicants they wished to bring to New Zealand: 340 were close relatives of New Zealand Jews; many were young people with the trade and technical skills needed by New Zealand.⁸⁰ While the select committee's report contained a measure of sympathy for Jews, it did not recommend lifting the restrictions on Jewish immigration. The committee favoured the admission of migrants of 'British stock', and, if sufficient numbers of this type of immigrant were not available, then immigrants from Northern European countries.⁸¹

Among the small number of Holocaust survivors accepted by New Zealand in the 1946–8 years were some children and youth. Mary (born 1935), and her brother (born in 1938 presumably; I did not interview him), from Hungary, arrived in 1947. Aged eleven and eight, they were among the first immigrants permitted to enter New Zealand after the war. Their mother had been killed in a concentration camp; their father had died when deported to the Soviet Union as a slave labourer. Deportations to the death camps began in Hungary in 1944. Fifty years later, Mary recalled:

> In November 1944 there was a dawn raid. All women under forty in our building had to go down into the courtyard where they were told: 'you're all coming with us'. 'You have ten minutes to pack'. I can remember my mother coming up, taking a few things and saying goodbye. That is the last we ever saw of her.⁸²

Mary and her brother were placed for a while in a *Red Cross* home, but were eventually removed from there by a former housekeeper and friend of the family who cared for the children while Budapest was under siege. 'We were supposedly her illegitimate children'.⁸³ Mary recalled that, when the war ended and the survivors started to return: 'the worst things were kept from us children'.

> Nobody really told us about concentration camps. Nobody said what happened there or that people had died. People dying was very seldom mentioned. . . . I never actually mourned my mother because it was always that she might yet come back. And people did. Other people. It took years and years to accept that she was actually dead. My father was 'officially' dead in 1943 – we received a telegram. Yet, later on, I would dream that they both came back . . . and that the 'official' information had been wrong.⁸⁴

After the war, the friend who had cared for Mary and her brother 'moved heaven and earth' to arrange for the children to join their remaining family in New Zealand. They left Hungary in late 1946 aboard a military plane.⁸⁵

New Zealand, initially reluctant to accept survivors living in the Displaced Persons camps in Europe, eventually admitted more than 4,500 of them between 1949 and 1952.[86] They were selected by a New Zealand mission in Europe and brought to New Zealand by chartered ships of the *International Refugee Organization* (IRO).[87] Included among them were some children and youth, though not as many as New Zealand wanted.

Not unlike other Commonwealth countries such as Australia, the government favoured youthful DPs, willing to work on farms, on hydro schemes, on logging operations, as domestic workers and in hospitals.[88] 'What was wanted was the type of man who could rough it and do a day's work', said the prominent Labour politician and former Minister of Public Works Bob Semple, expressing his concern in Parliament that the wrong refugees were being selected. 'The country wanted the type of men who built the Empire', he said.[89] Young workers suited New Zealand best but those not quite of working age were sought after too, with 'unaccompanied youth' aged fifteen to seventeen wanted for placement as trainees in various trades.[90]

Single people were preferred to family groups because they would not compete with New Zealand families for housing.[91] But, as the Director of Employment noted in his report to the Minister, children not attached to family groups were New Zealand's first priority.[92] Orphans between the ages of five and twelve years were greatly desired, because 'from the point of view of assimilation, children present the least problems', wrote the Director of Employment to the Minister of Employment.[93] The Selection Mission was instructed to select 200 orphans and unaccompanied children.[94] The process of DP selection shows that New Zealand considered some young people more acceptable than others on the basis of their ethnicity. A significant factor in the selection of the DPs was bias in favour of Northern Europeans and against Jews and 'Slavs'. This was justified by the assumption that a small community such as New Zealand could not afford to have 'alien groups who are not at one with ourselves'.[95] The Director of Employment's advice to the Minister was that:

> Preference should be given to racial types which are likely to be easily assimilated into New Zealand industries . . . It is considered that the most suitable types are likely to be found amongst races other than Jews or Slavs.[96]

Official papers suggest that New Zealand supported proposals to enable Jewish refugees to go to Palestine (about to become Israel) as a way of addressing the problem of the large number of unwanted Jewish DPs.[97] Foss Shanahan, the Acting Permanent Head of the Prime Minister's Department, wrote to the Prime Minister in 1946 that: 'The proposals for the future of Palestine provided *inter alia* for the immediate entry of some 100,000 Jews, and for continuing Jewish immigration after these are absorbed'.[98] After 1948, restrictions on Jewish DPs could more easily be justified on the grounds that the applicants of Jewish origin had in Israel a national home to go to.[99]

'Balts', as people of Baltic origin from Estonia, Lithuania and Latvia were then termed, were regarded as the most desirable of the displaced persons because they were thought to be the easiest to assimilate.[100] There was, however, a stumbling block to New Zealand selecting DPs on the basis of their ethnicity. This was an IRO requirement that DP selection be carried out without discrimination against specific groups.[101] A paper written by the Department of External Affairs for the guidance of the officers selecting the DPs suggested ways by which New Zealand could circumvent IRO stipulations:

> It is usual to require receiving countries to agree that selection will be carried out without discrimination to race and religion. The final responsibility for selection rests, however, with the receiving countries and any difficulties that might present themselves in this respect can be overcome by selection officers taking care to ensure that the people selected can reasonably be assimilated into the life of the community. In this respect, Jewish refugees are likely to be difficult to assimilate. Nationals of the Baltic States would be most suitable for settlement in New Zealand and should be given preference.[102]

New Zealand's selection preferences had to be eventually disregarded to some extent as there was a shortage of youthful Balts and orphans and unaccompanied children were particularly scarce. In order to fill the quota some flexibility was permitted to selectors.[103] An article about the arrival of the first group of DPs that appeared in the June 1949 issue of the Department of Labour's *Monthly Review of Employment* reassured readers that the 928 'European settlers' on board the ship had been 'specially selected in Europe by a New Zealand Mission'.[104] It went on to say:

> Looking back, it is hard to know just what we did expect. Certainly not a rabble, but on the other hand neither did we expect ... people so courteous and intelligent, so well-ordered, clean and quiet. Nor people so ready to laugh and be jolly. Nor such lovely children.[105]

George, born during the German occupation in 1944 in Przemysl, Poland, to a Greek Orthodox father and a Jewish mother, arrived with his parents as part of one of the later DP intakes. His father had saved his mother and a number of other Jews from deportation to a concentration camp. After the war, when the family fled to Vienna to escape the Russians' advance, George was two or three years old. Fifty years later, he recalled the displaced persons camp in Austria where the family had lived for three years and the local school he attended outside the camp.

Eight years old when he arrived in New Zealand, George began his new life in yet another camp – at Pahiatua – where the Polish children had been accommodated. In answer to the question: 'What was it like to be a refugee child?', he said: 'If you are brought up in a refugee camp that is all you know. You don't know you are a refugee, you don't know the meaning of the word. You think living in a camp is the most normal thing in the world'.[106]

At New Zealand schools, George, as with many of the other refugee children, achieved academic success but encountered teasing and bullying. Bewildered, anxious children, struggling to fit in, were devastated by instances of such behaviour. 'It is this feeling of total vulnerability, when there isn't a spot that isn't open to attack, which cuts all ground from beneath your feet. You feel you are completely defenceless and completely impotent', recalled Lucie (born 1931 in Sumperk, Czechoslovakia), eight when she arrived in New Zealand from Czechoslovakia.[107] Name calling – 'Bloody German Jew', or 'Hungarian rat', and others in a similar vein – was more often directed at boys. Boys were also more often the target of physical violence.[108]

The views of five teachers, interviewed in the late 1980s, contribute to a picture of refugee children at New Zealand schools between the 1930s and the late 1940s. The teachers were asked to look back forty years and comment on the behaviour of refugee, immigrant and Jewish pupils in their classrooms and on the attitudes of local children towards their culturally different classmates.[109]

The teachers said that the 'foreign' children had usually fitted into the school system with considerable ease. The role of teachers was confined to facilitating that process by treating foreign children no differently from anyone else. One teacher commented that 'the refugee children were not a significant matter in the teaching world'[110] partly because they were small in number, scattered over many schools and also because they adapted so readily. The children were expected to 'fit into the mould' as quickly as possible.[111] One of the teachers observed that teachers at that time were 'not tuned in to minorities, their rights, or what we should be doing for them. The foreign kids were just expected to conform and mostly they were clever enough to do just that'.[112]

While it was 'ingrained in liberal teachers'[113] not to notice cultural differences, when pressed, some teachers made the following comments: 'He was very un-English', or 'He was Jewish-looking'.[114] Other observations related to different clothes worn by the children and to the foreign students' seriousness and intensity about their work and 'their earnest desire to succeed'.[115]

The teachers were divided over how well the children were accepted by other children. Bullying was unacceptable but out-of-sight behaviour was hard to control. They acknowledged that instances of anti-Semitism, along the lines of taunts such as: 'Hitler didn't do the job properly', had occurred from time to time.[116] But all agreed that, on the whole, the children were 'no problem in the classroom'.[117]

In 2003, New Zealand's then refugee settlement agency, the *Refugee and Migrant Service* (RMS), commissioned a survey on the settlement success of refugee children. The RMS was interested in finding out what had happened to some of the children who had arrived as refugees. They were particularly interested in the academic and vocational qualifications obtained by the former refugee children. The highest number of questionnaire returns (eighty-six) was from the most numerous group – the Polish refugee children who had arrived in 1944. The survey concluded that the refugee children who had settled in New Zealand had made successful 'adjustment', 'can be found in all walks of life', and were making 'a valuable contribution to New Zealand's multicultural society'.[118] The survey report acknowledged that some of the findings were inconclusive because the study had a low rate of response and relied on the 'voluntary responses of former refugee children', which meant that responses were 'likely to be biased in favour of high achievers who were more likely to be interested in contributing and more willing to respond'.[119] However, the survey's findings in relation to the Polish children who came in 1944 are nonetheless of interest. The survey noted that despite their length of displacement and disrupted schooling, and the emphasis given to learning Polish, not English, at the children's camp, with the medium of instruction being Polish (because the children had been expected to return to Poland at the end of the war), the children had 'overcome considerable barriers to learning' and had 'some remarkable successes', with 'high levels of educational and occupational achievement'.[120]

During the 1930s and 1940s, New Zealanders assumed that the most desirable immigrants would be British. Yet, New Zealand responded relatively generously (for a small country)[121] to refugee children and youth from Nazi-occupied Europe, particularly to the Polish children given asylum during the Second World War. Before and during the war, immigration policy was less restrictive in respect of children and youth than towards the many thousands of adult (mainly Jewish) refugees who sought to enter New Zealand during that period. In the immediate postwar years, Holocaust survivors, including young people, encountered severe restrictions in gaining admittance. In 1949, New Zealand wanted more children and young people to fill its DP quota than were available in the camps. Bias against Jews and Poles was also an aspect of the selection process.

What is one to make of New Zealand's eagerness to accept children and youth, particularly orphaned ones? A mix of motives and considerations can be seen. They include: the humanitarian impulse of helping poor children in need (it is easier for many people to feel compassion for orphaned children than for adults); and the belief that New Zealand has something special to offer as the best place in the world to raise children. It is likely that the view that orphaned children, whatever their cultural and ethnic backgrounds, unlike adults or children who migrate with their own families, can most easily be moulded into 'assimilated' and useful citizens, also explains the desirability of orphaned refugee children.

Undoubtedly children and youth of different ethnicities had different experiences. The Polish children who came in 1944, regarded as desired 'invited guests' and sought-after orphans, accepted initially on a temporary basis, did not face the struggle for admission and acceptance experienced by the Jewish children and young people who reached New Zealand before and after the war. There were differences in the responses of the children and young people to their new environment. The Polish children were accommodated together at the *Polish Children's Camp* at Pahiatua. Their recreated Polish world shielded them from direct encounter with the New Zealand social and cultural environment, at least until after the war when they embarked on their secondary education at Catholic boarding schools. The Polish children were lucky in having a period of time at the *Polish Children's Camp*, a place where their Polish identity was nurtured. This period of transition between their old world and the new strengthened them for their exposure to the New Zealand environment of the mid-twentieth century in which children faced strong pressures to conform.

By contrast, the much smaller number of Jewish children – the 'Deckston orphans' and the children and youth who came alone or with their families before and after the war – experienced a more abrupt encounter with New Zealand society. Gerty, on her own at age sixteen, was straightaway flung into a harsh alien world of work for which she was unprepared and in which her previous education and experiences were irrelevant. Most of the Jewish children attended local schools and some experienced bullying. Their first languages and cultures having become identified with the perpetrators of the Holocaust, they faced conflicts of identity. The 'Deckston children' were forbidden to speak Polish at the *Deckston Home* and allowed to speak only Yiddish or English. Some children from Germany and Austria were forbidden to speak German, 'the enemy language' in their homes.[122]

Do children and youth adapt easily to new environments as the two writers quoted at the start of this essay, and the teachers interviewed, believed? Certainly, most children learn new languages more easily than adults and some appear to fit in with relative ease. But adjusting to a new country may not be as quick and painless for children and youth as some adults have supposed. Children and youth typically confront issues of belonging and identity not faced by adults. Furthermore, for some young people, as this chapter has shown, the fear, powerlessness and losses they had endured before their arrival, had wrenching, and probably long-term consequences, however young they were at the time the traumatic events took place and regardless of circumstances after their arrival.

Notes

1 Reuel A. Lochore, *From Europe to New Zealand: An Account of our Continental European Settlers* (Wellington: A.H. & A.W. Reed, in conjunction with New Zealand Institute of International Affairs 1951), p. 88.
2 'Providing for Child Immigrants', *New Zealand National Review* (15 June 1944), pp. 13–14.

3   Steven Sedley, *The Deckston Story: The Story of Annie and Max Deckston, Jewish Philanthropists, who Saved Twenty Polish Children from the Holocaust* (Wellington: Holocaust Centre of New Zealand 2012), back cover; Simone Gigliotti and Monica Tempian, 'From Europe to the Antipodes: Acculturation and Identity of Deckston Children and Kindertransport Children in New Zealand', in *The Kindertransport to Britain 1938/39: New Perspectives*, ed. by Andrea Hammel and Bea Lowkowicz, *Yearbook of the Research Centre for German and Austrian Exile Studies*, vol. 13 (Amsterdam: Rodopi 2012), p. 103.

4   The figure of 300 is based on a table of refugees' occupations in 1945, given by Reuel A. Lochore, which states that thirty-five of the refugees were 'full-time students' and that 251 of the women were 'engaged mainly in domestic duties'. Lochore states that this latter category included women who were working part-time in their husbands' businesses. Some of these women would also have been caring for children. See Reuel A. Lochore, *From Europe to New Zealand*, pp. 77–8.

5   The Kindertranportees are discussed in Simone Gigliotti and Monica Tempian, 'From Europe to the Antipodes', pp. 110–16.

6   The figure is cited in Adam Manterys, Stefania Zawada, Stanislaw Manterys and Jozef Zawada (eds), *New Zealand's First Refugees: Pahiatua's Polish Children* (Wellington: Polish Children's Reunion Committee 2004), p. 355.

7   Ann Beaglehole, *A Small Price to Pay: Refugees from Hitler in New Zealand, 1936–1946* (Wellington: Allen & Unwin, with Historical Branch 1988), pp. 4–6.

8   The chapter is based on the author's current and past work about refugees in New Zealand, including interviews with former Jewish child refugees and their teachers undertaken in the late 1980s. It also draws on recent work on the 'Deckston Children', on the Kindertransportees and on the Polish children who came in 1944. Some of the material on immigration policy before and after the Second World War has appeared most recently in Ann Beaglehole, *Refuge New Zealand: A Nation's Response to Refugees and Asylum Seekers* (Dunedin: Otago University Press 2013).

9   Comptroller to Minister, 16 August 1937, in F. A. Ponton, 'Immigration Restriction in New Zealand: A Study of Policy, 1908–1939', University of New Zealand (Victoria) MA thesis in History, Wellington, 1946, p. 91.

10 New Zealand High Commissioners Office, London to Dr Siegfried Rothmann, 9 September 1938, cited in Ann Beaglehole, *A Small Price to Pay*, p. 15.

11 Archives New Zealand (ANZ), IC 20/86, Part 1, Skilled labour and tradesmen, E.D. Good to New Zealand Trade and Tourist Commissioner, 3 March 1939, p.1.

12 Reuel A. Lochore, *From Europe to New Zealand*, p. 71.

13 Quoted from interview with Sonny, 'Facing the Past: Looking Back at Refugee Childhood in New Zealand', PhD thesis in History, Victoria University of Wellington, Wellington, 1990, pp. 295–6. Hereafter 'Facing the Past'. Interviews with thirty-two child refugees and children of survivors growing up in New Zealand were completed by Ann Beaglehole between August 1987 and

February 1988 for the PhD thesis referred to and for the subsequent publication of the same name. The first names used in this chapter are actual first names of interviewees except for 'Chaim'. Biographical details given are the actual ones of the interviewees. Family names of the interviewees are not disclosed to respect the wishes of some of the participants for confidentiality.

14 Quoted from interview in Ann Beaglehole, 'Facing the Past', PhD Thesis, 1990, p. 296.
15 Ibid.
16 Ibid., p. 297.
17 Ibid.
18 Quoted from interview in Ann Beaglehole, 'A Small Price to Pay; Refugees from Hitler in New Zealand, 1936–1946', Victoria University of Wellington MA thesis in History, Wellington, 1986, p. 149. Thirty-two former refugees were interviewed by Ann Beaglehole in 1984–6 for the MA thesis and subsequent publication of the same name. The first names and biographical details given in this chapter are actual. Family names of the interviewees are not disclosed to respect the wishes of some of the participants for confidentiality.
19 Quoted from interview in Beaglehole, 'A Small Price to Pay', p. 150.
20 Ibid.
21 Ibid.
22 Ibid.
23 Ibid., p. 151.
24 Ibid., pp. 151–2.
25 Ibid., p. 152.
26 Ibid.
27 Steven Sedley, *The Deckston Story*, p. 8.
28 Ibid., pp. 20–1.
29 The Deckstons' motivation is raised in Simone Gigliotti and Monica Tempian, 'From Europe to the Antipodes', pp. 104–5.
30 *New Zealand Radio Record*, Vol. xii, No. 50 (26 May 1939), p. 2.
31 Quoted in Stephen Levine (ed.), *A Standard for the People* (Christchurch: Hazard Press 1994), pp. 207–8.
32 Steven Sedley, *The Deckston Story*, p. 21.
33 Ibid., p. 22.
34 Ibid.
35 Simone Gigliotti and Monica Tempian, 'From Europe to the Antipodes', p. 107.
36 Ann Beaglehole, *Facing the Past: Looking Back at Refugee Childhood in New Zealand, 1940s–1960s* (Wellington: Allen & Unwin 1990), pp. 92–100.
37 Simone Gigliotti and Monica Tempian, 'From Europe to the Antipodes', p. 107.

38 Chaim's actual name is not disclosed for confidentiality reasons.
39 Simone Gigliotti and Monica Tempian, 'From Europe to the Antipodes', p. 107.
40 Quoted from interview in Beaglehole, 'Facing the Past', p. 286.
41 Ibid.
42 Ibid.
43 Ibid.
44 Ibid., p. 287.
45 Ibid.
46 Quoted from interview with Gerty in Ann Beaglehole, *A Small Price to Pay*, p. 64.
47 Ibid.
48 Quoted from interview in Ann Beaglehole, *A Small Price to Pay*, pp. 62–5.
49 Adam Manterys et al., *New Zealand's First Refugees*, back cover, pp. 20–3, p. 27, p. 351.
50 Peter Fraser cited in Adam Manterys et al., *New Zealand's First Refugees*, pp. 27–8.
51 'Polish Children', *Auckland Star*, 8 August 1944, p. 2.
52 She tells her story in Adam Manterys et al., *New Zealand's First Refugees*, pp. 44–59.
53 Cited in Adam Manterys et al., *New Zealand's First Refugees*, p. 45.
54 Ibid.
55 Ibid., pp. 45–6.
56 Krystyna Skwarko, *The Invited: The Story of 733 Polish Children who Grew Up in New Zealand* (Wellington: Millwood Press 1974), Part 3, without page number.
57 Ibid.
58 Ibid.
59 Ibid.
60 Department of Labour, New Zealand Immigration Service, *Refugee Women: The New Zealand Refugee Quota Programme* (Wellington, 1994), p. 16.
61 Krystyna Skwarko, *The Invited*, Part 3, page numbers not given.
62 By the time they arrived in New Zealand in 1944, the children were mostly in the six to ten years or eleven to fourteen years age groups, though there were also some pre-schoolers among them. See Gordon Campbell, 'The Intergenerational Settlement of Refugee Children in New Zealand', cited in Adam Manterys et al., *New Zealand's First Refugees*, pp. 344–6.
63 Cited in Krystyna Skwarko, *The Invited*, without page number.
64 John Roy-Wojciechowski and Allan Parker, *A Strange Outcome: The Remarkable Survival Story of a Polish Child* (Auckland: Penguin Books 2004), p. 121. Jan or John Roy-Wojciechowski was probably born on 25 September

1933 in Ostrowki, Poland. John Roy does not know his exact birth date, see *A Strange Outcome*, p. 33, p. 37. Please note that in *A Strange Outcome*, the spelling of the author's name is: John Roy-Wojciechowski, i.e., the hyphen is not between John and Roy but between Roy and Wojciechowski.

65   Krystyna Skwarko, *The Invited*, Part 3, page numbers not given.

66   Ann Beaglehole's conversation with Theresa Sawicka, 30 August 2007, about the findings in her thesis: Theresa Sawicka-Brockie, 'Forsaken Journeys: The Polish Experience and Identity of the Pahiatua children in New Zealand', PhD thesis in Anthropology, University of Auckland, Auckland, 1987; Krystyna Skwarko, *The Invited*, Part 3, page numbers not given.

67   James McNeish, *The Sixth Man: The Extraordinary Life of Paddy Costello* (Auckland: Random House 2007), pp. 164–6; James McNeish, *Dance of the Peacocks: New Zealanders in Exile in the Time of Hitler and Mao Tse Tung* (Auckland: Random House 2003), pp. 352–3.

68   Nancy M. Taylor, *The New Zealand People at War; the Home Front: Official History of New Zealand in the Second World War, 1939–1945*, vol. 2 (Wellington: V.R. Ward, Government Printer 1986), pp. 1246–50.

69   *New Zealand Jewish Chronicle* (April–May 1945), p. 190.

70   *New Zealand Jewish Chronicle* (November 1945), p. 69.

71   Ibid.

72   ANZ, EA 108/4/4, Part 1, R. M. Campbell, Official Secretary, New Zealand High Commission, London to Sir Herbert Emerson, Director, Intergovernmental Committee on Refugees, 25 January 1946, summarized from Ann Beaglehole, *A Small Price to Pay*, pp. 119–20, p. 163, fn. 24.

73   ANZ, EA 108/4/4, Part 1, Sir Herbert Emerson, Director of Intergovernmental Committee on Refugees to R.M. Campbell, Official Secretary, New Zealand High Commission, London, 14 January 1946, summarized from Beaglehole, *A Small Price to Pay*, p. 119.

74   ANZ, EA 108/4/4, Part 1, R. M. Campbell to Sir Herbert Emerson, 25 January 1946; ANZ, L1 22/1/27, Part 1, International Refugee Organization, Immigration, General, from 1946, Statement by the New Zealand Delegation to the United Nations Special Committee on Refugees and Displaced Persons, 10 May 1946, summarized from Ann Beaglehole, *A Small Price to Pay*, pp. 119–20, p. 164, fn 26. See also ANZ, Nash Papers 1597/0918 and 1597/11. These papers refer to the period 1945–7 and are concerned with the many applications from refugees in Europe to join their relatives in New Zealand.

75   ANZ, EA 108/4/4, Part 1, R. M. Campbell to Sir Herbert Emerson, 25 January 1946, cited in Ann Beaglehole, *A Small Price to Pay*, p. 119.

76   Lazarus M. Goldman, *The History of the Jews in New Zealand* (Wellington: A.H and A.W. Reed 1958), p. 234. Goldman derived this figure from a report to the Interchurch Council of New Zealand by Mrs O. S. Heymann, undated.

77   The reasons for this trend are discussed in Department of Labour, 'Immigration', *Monthly Review of Employment* (March 1947), pp. 1–5.

78 Department of Labour, 'Immigration', *Monthly Review of Employment* (March 1947), p. 1.
79 Jewish Communities of New Zealand, 'Memorandum to the Select Committee on Dominion Population', April 1946, cited in Ann Beaglehole, *A Small Price to Pay*, p. 120.
80 ANZ, Ll 22/1/27, Part 1, International Refugee Organization, Immigration, General, from 1946, 'Report on Data Received from the Jewish Communities of New Zealand Regarding Relatives who Desire to Come to This Country', July 1946, enclosed with a memorandum for Acting Minister of Customs, from Permanent Head, Prime Minister's Department, 25 March 1947, cited in Ann Beaglehole, *A Small Price to Pay*, p. 164, fn. 39.
81 *Appendix to the Journals of the House of Representatives (AJHR)*, Vol. 5, I-17 (1946), 'Report of the Select Committee on Dominion Population', p. 44, p. 99, pp. 116–17.
82 Quoted from interview in Ann Beaglehole, *Facing the Past*, p. 294.
83 Ibid.
84 Ibid.
85 Ibid.
86 Department of Statistics, *New Zealand Yearbook*, 1965, p. 75.
87 Anton Binzegger, *New Zealand's Policy on Refugees* (Wellington: New Zealand Institute of International Affairs 1980), p. 13.
88 Ann Beaglehole, 'A Small Price to Pay', p. 124.
89 *New Zealand Parliamentary Debates*, vol. 292, 1 November 1950, p. 3906.
90 ANZ, CAB 66/1/1 Part 1, Individual immigration of Aliens, Minister of Immigration to Cabinet, 'Resettlement of Displaced Persons through International Refugee Organisation', 15 December 1950, p. 2, (contained within EA series on International Refugee Organization).
91 ANZ, LI 22/1/27, Part 1, International Refugee Organization, Immigration, general, from 1946, Director of Employment to Minister of Employment, 23 December 1947; Department of Labour, *Monthly Review of Employment*, 'Immigration' (March 1947), p. 5, summarized from Ann Beaglehole, 'A Small Price to Pay', p. 125.
92 ANZ, L1, 22/1/27, Part 1, International Refugee Organization, Immigration, general, from 1946, Director of Employment to Minister of Employment, 23 December 1947, p. 2, summarized from Ann Beaglehole, 'A Small Price to Pay', p. 125.
93 ANZ, LI 22/1/27, Part 1, Director of Employment to Minister of Employment, 23 December 1947, cited in Ann Beaglehole, 'A Small Price to Pay', p. 125.
94 ANZ, LI 22/1/27, International Refugee Organization, Part 3, 'Report of the New Zealand Selection Team of the *Dunbalk Bay* draft', circa April 1949, p. 3.
95 ANZ, LI 22/1/27, Part 5, Displaced Persons from Europe, Assistant Under-Secretary, Department of Internal Affairs to Director of Employment,

Department of Labour and Employment, 'Immigration', 16 May 1950, p. 1, cited in Ann Beaglehole, 'A Small Price to Pay', p. 125.

96 ANZ, LI 22/1/27, Part 1, Displaced Persons from Europe, International Refugee Organization, Immigration, General, from 1946, Director of Employment to Minister of Employment, 23 December 1947, cited in Ann Beaglehole, 'A Small Price to Pay', p. 125.

97 ANZ, External Affairs, 108/4/1, Parts 3 and 4, or EA2, 1949, 15c and EA2, 1948, 14b.

98 ANZ, External Affairs, EA 108/4/1 Part 2, Foss Shanahan, Acting Permanent Head of Prime Minister's Department, to the Prime Minister, 20 September 1946.

99 Lazarus M. Goldman, *The History of the Jews in New Zealand*, pp. 235–6.

100 ANZ, LI 22/1/27, Part 1, International Refugee Organization, Immigration, General, from 1946, Director of Employment to Minister of Immigration, 15 April 1948, summarized from Ann Beaglehole, 'A Small Price to Pay', p. 125.

101 ANZ, L1 22/1/27, Part 2, Displaced Persons from Europe, Acceptance of Displaced Persons, Official Secretary, New Zealand High Commission to Secretary of External Affairs, 17 December 1948.

102 ANZ, LI 22/1/27, Part 2, Displaced Persons from Europe, Acceptance of Displaced Persons, Department of External Affairs to the Official Secretary, Office of the High Commissioner for New Zealand, 'Immigration: Acceptance of Displaced Persons', undated, quoted in Ann Beaglehole, 'A Small Price to Pay', p. 126.

103 Ann Beaglehole, 'A Small Price to Pay', p. 126.

104 Department of Labour, *Monthly Review of Employment*, 4/8 (June 1949), p. 4.

105 Ibid., pp. 4–5.

106 Quoted from interview in Ann Beaglehole, 'Facing the Past', p. 288.

107 Ann Beaglehole, *A Small Price to Pay*, 1988, p. 135.

108 Quoted from interview in Ann Beaglehole, 'Facing the Past', p. 135.

109 Ibid., Appendix 1b, p. 309.

110 Ibid., p. 113.

111 Ibid.

112 Ibid.

113 Ibid., p. 114.

114 Ibid.

115 Ibid., pp. 114–15.

116 Ibid., p. 115.

117 Ibid., p. 116. The section is summarized from 'Teachers' views' in ibid., pp. 113–16.

118 Gordon Campbell, 'The Intergenerational Settlement of Refugee Children', in Adam Manterys et al., *New Zealand's First Refugees*, Appendix B, p. 344.

119 Gordon Campbell, cited in Adam Manterys et al., *New Zealand's First Refugees*, Appendix B, p. 349.
120 Ibid., pp. 345–9.
121 New Zealand's population was around 1.5 million (exclusive of Maori) in 1944.
122 Ann Beaglehole, 'Facing the Past', pp. 181–2.

CHAPTER SIX

'No common mother tongue or fatherland':

Jewish Refugee Children in British Kenya

Jennifer Reeve

Jewish refugees from Central Europe looking to escape Nazi persecution sought refuge all over the world. With destinations ranging from Britain, the USA and Canada to much further afield in Australia, Argentina and Shanghai, people boarded ships hoping that these places, some more unusual than others, would offer the safety that their homelands in Europe no longer could. Much of the scholarship on the international reaction to the Jewish refugee crisis of the 1930s has highlighted the closed doors that these Jewish men, women and children faced and important work has been carried out on the limited nature of the American and British domestic responses to the Jewish refugee crisis.

The crisis, however, also impacted Britain's Empire. As well as the infamous struggles in and over Palestine, other parts of the Empire felt international pressure to act. Studies of the action taken by the British Dominions including Canada, Australia and South Africa have demonstrated the restrictive policies adopted by these countries.[1] However, many contemporaries believed it was Britain's tropical colonies that offered the best potential contribution to the refugee problem. While some of the plans and actions taken in the colonies have received scholarly attention, generally little has been written about the movement of refugees to Britain's tropical colonies including, but not limited to, territories in Africa and the West Indies.[2]

Likewise, distinctions have not always been made between child and adult experiences of the Holocaust. Although immediate postwar attempts were made to collect child testimony (especially in Eastern Europe) many child survivors did not necessarily distinguish their experiences from survivors of different ages.[3] Furthermore, Holocaust scholarship initially focused on the actions of the perpetrators, while victims were encouraged to remain silent.[4] However, there clearly was a difference in the experiences of children and adults. This is evidenced by children's low survival rate. Approximately 1.5 million Jewish and non-Jewish children died during the Holocaust; a survival rate of 6–11 per cent, compared to 33 per cent for adults.[5]

The experience of Jewish children who survived the Holocaust as refugees differs from those children who survived in camps or ghettos and children who were born after the war in Displaced Persons camps.[6] This chapter focuses on the experiences of children who survived the Holocaust as refugees in British colonial territory. Although these groups experienced the Holocaust in very different ways, some similarities and connections are also evident. In all situations, children were forced to 'grow up' very quickly, often adopting adult roles as their families fragmented and circumstances changed. Schooling was difficult and disrupted. Jewish identity was heightened, challenged and changed.[7] In the context of exile, journeys across continents and oceans were done so with no preparation; children had to function in family groups completely uprooted from the familiar. The transition to places so culturally, climatically and linguistically diverse was a difficult experience for adult refugees; the response of children was no less complex but ultimately different.

This chapter will examine Jewish refugee children's unique perspectives on the path and place of refuge in the British Empire. It will utilize hitherto unused British Colonial Office files and both published and unpublished refugee testimony. Published sources will include Stefanie Zweig's autobiographical novel *Nowhere in Africa* (*Nirgendwo in Afrika*, 1998). In June 1938, Stefanie Zweig, aged five, and her mother, Jettel, left the Silesian city of Breslau (now Wroclaw) for Kenya. They were reunited with Walter Zweig, Stefanie's father, who had travelled to Kenya some months previously to establish a home for them there. The family struggled through wartime Kenya, where Walter, a judge in Germany, had little skill in the agricultural work he was set to upon arrival. Most of Stefanie Zweig's immediate family (both sets of grandparents and her aunts and uncles) died in the Holocaust. At the end of the war, Stefanie's father was keen to return to Germany and took up a judicial role in Frankfurt. *Nowhere in Africa* recounts Zweig's childhood in Kenya and, although it is classified as an 'autobiographical novel', contains recollections and information corroborated by later interviews, other refugees and Colonial Office files.

This chapter is based on unpublished material that includes the recollections of the Berg sisters and Heinz Bauer, whose memoirs, interview testimonies, family papers and photographs are housed at the United States Holocaust Memorial Museum (USHMM). In May 1939, Jill Pauly (born Gisella Berg) and Inge Katzenstein (née Berg), two Jewish sisters from a small village just outside Cologne, fled Nazi-controlled Europe for Kenya. Jill was six years old and Inge was ten. The Bergs' close-knit, observant Jewish family managed to escape almost intact. Having secured twenty-one visas for Kenya, seventeen members of the Berg family eventually found safety there.[8] After some initial difficulties, the family established a relatively successful cattle farming business and stayed until after the war, when they departed for the United States, where they sought to resettle within an Orthodox community. Although other destinations, including Palestine and South Africa, would have provided the Orthodox Jewish life that the Bergs desired, after the challenges of the previous eight years neither of these locations were deemed by their father to be stable enough in which to create a new life. In Palestine, the state of Israel had not yet been declared, and the girls' father believed moving to South Africa would be 'jumping from the frying pan into the fire' because of the treatment of black people in the territory.[9]

The experiences of Heinz Bauer, an Austrian Jew, who was studying medicine at the University of Vienna at the time of the 'Anschluss', will also be examined. His father, a government-appointed dentist, knew that he would lose his job after the Nazi invasion of Austria, and the family immediately decided that they had to leave. Despite much difficulty, Heinz and his brother made their way to Kenya via Paris and London, with the help of an English patient of their father's. The family were eventually reunited in Kenya, where they enjoyed a relatively settled life, with Heinz taking work as a farmer, his brother, as a dentist and his mother teaching piano. After the war, the whole family settled in the US, where Heinz went on to became a professor of pathology.[10]

In comparison to the sovereign nations which offered refuge, British colonial territory had a more complex and diverse social and racial system. Jewish refugees, a persecuted minority in Central Europe, entered British territory on more similar terms with the white European colonizers than with the black African or Indian subjects, further complicating racial identity for refugee children. This chapter, therefore, offers the starting point for an examination of these wide-ranging concerns and gives voice to some of the Empire's refugee children.

From these official sources and personal stories come several key themes: the importance of language; notions of 'homeland'; the nature of racial/cultural relations; and the children's self-perception as 'other'.[11] These factors were also all connected, and an exploration of them serves to highlight the specificity of the experience of refugee children in the colonial Empire, but also its widespread relevance to the study of young people and their experiences of displacement and persecution during the Holocaust.

Studies of both British and American domestic policy towards Jewish refugees have outlined the limited nature of action taken by these two major powers before and during the Second World War. While there were many similarities between Britain's and America's policies, Britain's action towards child refugees is generally considered to be more generous. Britain established the *Kindertransport*, an initiative which facilitated escape from Nazi-controlled Europe for thousands of children. Between 2 December 1938 and 31 August 1939, Britain welcomed 9,354 children. Of this number, 7,482 were Jewish.[12] The generous nature of this policy was, in part, based on the assumption that Jewish children were less dangerous than Jewish adults, largely because the young were believed to be more 'assimilable'. Criticism remains over the longer-term impact on parents and family networks this policy caused, but it nonetheless is credited with saving the lives of many children.[13]

In contrast, scholars have generally lamented the lack of American action on the behalf of children, specifically focusing on the failure of the Wagner–Rogers Bill as evidence of this. In February 1939, a bi-partisan bill outlined a plan to settle 20,000 refugee children in the United States over two years, in addition to the existing immigration quotas for this period. The plan, however, was very unpopular, and even after significant amendment, it did not pass.[14] The failure of the Wagner–Rogers Bill is viewed as evidence of anti-immigration and anti-Semitic attitudes in the American government.[15]

In the colonial context, British officials both in Whitehall and in the colonies generated a specific but limited policy towards refugees, attempting to combine colonial concerns of development with refugee land settlement. However, in the British Empire, a specific policy towards the settlement of Jewish children was never adopted. Instead, children arrived, almost always with family, and had to adjust to colonial life immediately, with very little assistance or thought from the government.

At the Évian Refugee Conference, an international meeting on refugees called by the United States and held in July 1938, Kenya was considered to be the most likely place of large-scale refugee settlement in the British Empire. Kenya attracted particular interest because there was historical precedent for the idea. In 1903, Joseph Chamberlain, the Secretary of State for the Colonies, offered to Theodor Herzl, the leader of the World Zionist Organization, Kenya as an alternative homeland to Palestine. Upon Herzl's death in 1905, the offer was rejected, and the World Zionist Organization continued to press for settlement in Palestine alone.[16]

Small-scale settlement nevertheless continued, and those Jews who had escaped Imperial Russian persecution by settling in Africa at the turn of the century were joined by a slow but steady movement of other Jewish settlers from lands ruled by the Tsar. Between 1933 and 1945, Kenya admitted between 650 and 1,000 Jewish refugees. Despite debate over these figures, it remained the second largest influx of Jewish refugees in Africa, after South Africa which admitted between 6,000 and 7,000 refugees.[17]

The movement of Jewish refugees to Kenya in the 1930s followed a general pattern, repeated in statistics from across Europe. Small numbers arrived in 1933 after Hitler gained power, and numbers increased again after the Nuremberg Laws of 1935. The peak of refugee entry occurred after 'Kristallnacht', the violent attacks on Jewish people and property which took place in November 1938.[18] The narratives of the families studied in this chapter also follow this general trend. Although the families took different routes, all the journeys were complex and fraught with danger and some element of distress. Another common experience was that they all travelled on German vessels. Stefanie and Jettel Zweig travelled from Hamburg, stopping at various ports including Nice and Tangiers, before travelling around Africa and arriving at Mombassa. The Berg family departed Cologne by train for Genoa, Italy. A two-week journey took them through the Mediterranean and Red Sea and then around and down the coast of Africa, where they landed in Mombassa. Bauer sailed from Southampton via ports including Los Palmas in the Canary Islands, Cape Town, Durban, three unnamed ports in Mozambique, Dar-es-Salaam in Tanganyika and finally Mombassa.[19]

Government responses to the movement of Jewish refugees also followed a general pattern; entry into countries and territories of refuge was continuously restricted. Refugees needed a £50 deposit per person to enter Kenya. Officially, this was to act as a kind of security bond should they not be able to find employment. Unofficially, this large sum of money essentially closed the colony as a potential route of escape for many Jewish refugees, especially as their possessions were increasingly confiscated by the German state.

For those Jewish refugees who managed to enter the colony, the outbreak of war in September 1939 meant another profound change. After an initial arrest of 'enemy aliens' at the outbreak of war, general internment was instigated in May 1940 across the Empire, mirroring action taken in Britain. Men were taken first, but the internment of women and children shortly followed. Although this was a brief interlude, and, as in Britain, refugees were released quickly, they nonetheless remained classed as 'enemy aliens' for the duration of the war. This limited possibilities of employment, and it was not until after December 1943 that 'enemy aliens' were able to join the British army.

In addition to the consequences of war, Jewish refugees arriving in Kenya were also affected by (and interacted with) British colonialism. Kenya was a racially diverse colony, and British colonial policy was made in the context of a politically powerful white settler community, a vocal Indian settler community, and the indigenous African population. European refugees caused unrest amongst the first two groups, and British officials were concerned about the impact of European settlers on their African colonial subjects both economically and culturally. As Governor Brooke-Popham put it to the Secretary of State for the Colonies Malcolm MacDonald: '[t]he real benefit which the African derives from his association with the European farmer lies not so much in the financial return but rather in the education and experience gained'. However, Brooke-Popham was keen to highlight, specifically in relation to growing Jewish settlement, that the British nature of this influence was key, arguing: '[t]his can best be done by forming in their midst a British settlement where British principles may not only be preserved but also extended'.[20]

British concerns were further complicated by their perceptions of the Jewish refugee. Poor refugees were particularly problematic as they threatened the image of the powerful 'white man' to indigenous populations. The deposit of £50 required to enter the colony was there also to ensure refugees possessed enough financial standing to function within the bounds of acceptable 'white' behaviour in Kenya's social structure.

There was also the assumption amongst the policymaking elite that Jewish refugees were not suited to agricultural labour (despite the obvious successes of kibbutzim in Palestine). It was widely believed that the only sustainable solution to the Jewish refugee crisis was urban settlement.[21] In Kenya, this threatened Indian interests, as this community had successfully established themselves as artisans and shopkeepers. Given the pro-Arab sentiment at the Foreign Office as well as Colonial Office concerns over Arab relations throughout the Empire (notably in India), strict rules were applied to refugees which effectively limited them to agricultural work. In the case of organized settlement, refugees were directed to specific farms. More generally, refugees were expected to assume roles that reflected the racial hierarchies in the colonies. This meant that many of them took roles on farms in the highlands. Over questions of settlement, policymakers always weighed the needs of refugees against the higher priority of maintaining stability (and thereby British interests) in the colony. Those refugees who successfully entered the colony therefore found it necessary to adopt a specific position within the social structure. They were expected to adopt the roles assigned to white settlers, such as farm managers, and to take on black help in their homes and with their children. Colonial officials both in London and in the colonies reiterated the importance of 'the assimilation of the emigrants into the general social structure of the Colony' as it was upon a rigid and racially defined social hierarchy that British imperial power (at least in the minds of colonial officials) was maintained.[22]

It was into this complex and conflicted environment that young refugees arrived. In this milieu of difference, certain themes emerged that defined young people's experience of refuge in tropical colonial territories. Through examples from their arrival, their school experience, internment and finally the end of the war, the themes of language, 'home', inter-cultural and race relations, and 'otherness' highlight the specificity of refugee childhood experiences within the colonial context and arguably in exile more broadly.

Upon arrival in a new country, Jewish refugees of all ages were faced with the challenge of learning a new language. In the case of colonial Kenya, there were two languages: English and Swahili. Children often learned foreign languages more quickly than their parents and thus became the cultural ears and mouths of the family, what Huyck and Fields describe as 'cultural intermediaries'.[23] Not only did this affect family relationships, but the choice of language (be it English, Swahili and/or native German) had significant consequences on identity, perceptions of 'otherness' and conceptions of 'home'.

Stefanie Zweig, for example, recalls the divisive nature of language: 'In my childhood my father and I, who loved each other so dearly ... had one mutual grief. We had neither a common mother tongue nor a common fatherland. Hitler had seen to that'.[24] The negative effect of such difficulties has been noted by Susanne Heim, who explains that 'the failures and helplessness of the parents' in relation to language acquisition 'reduced the respect of their children'.[25] Stefanie meanwhile learned Swahili 'with the speed and eagerness of a child' and quickly learned English when she was made to attend an English school. While she did not settle particularly well at school, her love of the English language soon developed. She recalls that:

> I had an unforgettable teacher who fed the insatiable 11-year-old with Dickens, Thackeray and Shakespeare. Hamlet was the second man of my life. To this day I read Shelley, Keats and Robert Browning. To quote Rupert Brooke, one of my first idols: there is some far corner of a foreign field that is forever England.[26]

The love of the English language and literature evident in Stefanie's memoirs is in marked contrast to the recollections of Inge Katzenstein, who recalls her own 'demoralizing' experience of learning English. As well as the degradation she felt from being put into kindergarten at the age of ten, she has particularly negative memories of being required to memorize a British poem, 'The Daffodils' by William Wordsworth, when her English was not adequate enough to read the poem. In a *First Person* interview given at the USHMM in 2003, she mentions how upset she was at the time and that she still hates the poem today.[27] The humiliation and trauma of the event have clearly had a lasting effect on Inge, pointing to the importance of language and the early experiences of child refugees. However, contrary to some findings which suggest that trauma caused by exile is more damaging for younger children, Inge's memories of her experiences as an older child are more negative than those of Zweig, who was only five when she arrived in the colony.[28]

For Stefanie, language was also tied up very closely with her perceptions of 'home'. In *Nowhere in Africa*, Stefanie recalls being upset at her father's decision to return the family to Germany after the war. She describes her sadness at the decision in terms of language, referring to the preparation she needed to make 'for the familiar unloved sounds'.[29] Specifically, she associated great emotion with the word 'home', writing that '[s]he said the word a few times to herself, first happily in English, then reluctantly in German. In both languages, the syllables hummed like a bee filled with anger'.[30] In 2003, reflecting on her return to Germany and the 'shock' it caused, Zweig again returned to the place of language, recalling that learning a new language at fifteen years of age was much harder than it had been when she was five. Although she did so within a couple of months, Zweig wrote that '[n]ow it was I who had to give up home and language, tradition, loyalty and love'.[31]

Conceptions of a 'homeland' and 'mother tongue' were evidently deeply interconnected for many Jewish refugee children. For some, the colonies where they found safety became home, and English, their mother tongue. For others, the experience left more ambivalent memories of a place of refuge but not of a homeland. Jill Pauly's recollections of her time in Kenya are mixed. While she has happy memories of childhood, she describes two lives: one at school and one on the farm. For Jill, there seems to have been a cultural distinction between life in Africa and life in colonial Africa.

Nonetheless, Pauly describes that, for sometime after moving to the USA, Kenya remained 'home'. In an interview given in 1999, she recalls the initial difficulty the family had settling in the USA. Jill and Inge arrived at about fourteen and eighteen years old respectively. Both girls took some time to adjust to the new life, and they faced different challenges because of their ages. Jill recalls the practical challenges her family faced when trying to establish a chicken farming business in New Jersey. She also laments that neither she nor her sister went to college. This was, in part, down to her father's views, but generally the transition to American life, especially in regard to education, employment and Orthodox Jewish living took some time. It seems that with both their marriages, the sisters began to settle into American life. Moreover, the welcome they received in the USA and the perceived lack of anti-Semitism there are frequent themes in the interviews given by Pauly.[32] These also helped establish the USA as 'home'.

The attachment and the extent to which the Berg family ultimately connected with their new home in America is made clear by the donation they made of a Sefer Torah to a synagogue in Silver Spring, Washington DC. The Torah was of great sentimental value to the family. It was purchased by a great-uncle who later died in the Holocaust and given to the family as they left for Kenya in order to help them maintain the Orthodox religious practices they had observed in Germany. It was then carried by one of the last family members to escape Germany, an uncle, to Kenya. There it was used in religious services and formed a central part of the small Jewish community that grew up around the Berg family farm. Its donation for safe-keeping to a synagogue in America is suggestive of the way that both Jill Pauly and Inge Katzenstein have adopted America as their new 'homeland'.[33]

In contrast, Stefanie Zweig's attachment to Kenya was much stronger and has remained so. Despite certain difficulties with school and internment (as discussed below), Zweig fell in love with Africa and the people she met there. Her lingering attachment to Kenya and her feelings of belonging were again expressed by reference to language. In 2003, the writer explained that 'the assessment as to which is my mother-language is still going on. I count in English, adore Alice in Wonderland, am best friends with Winnie-the-Pooh and I am still hunting for the humour in German jokes'.[34] This highlights not only a detachment from German culture, but also the strength of her continuing affinity to Kenya and the language and culture she adopted there.

Heinz Bauer's adoption of Kenya as 'home' was based on his feeling of safety in the colony. In his unpublished memoir, he wrote that:

> [c]onsciously, my past may be dead, but it is not forgotten. It lies lurking in the back of my mind, the fear that it could all happen to me again. Even now . . . free from those fears and a free man again, it comes back to me in my dreams, when the unwanted subconscious reigns supreme. But there is always the precious awakening, the beautiful reality of a new day to be lived in full. I shall always cherish my freedom because I have known what life is like without it.[35]

Slightly older than the other refugee children discussed, Bauer was a medical student in Vienna at the time of the 'Anschluss', and, having been exposed to Nazi persecution, his feeling of relief at having reached the safety of Kenya was particularly strong. After arriving in Kenya, both Heinz and his brother found unpaid work on a farm, where they were initially hosted by an old Jewish couple. While his brother soon found work in dentistry, Heinz remained, undertaking tasks including dairy farming as well as harvesting. Within a year of his arrival, both Heinz's parents and his girlfriend, Lisal, had arrived safely in Kenya. Heniz and Lisal quickly married and took up work as a farmer and governess respectively, before eventually settling on a farm together.

Bauer's feelings towards Kenya were mostly positive, especially in comparison to Austria. As Bauer explained in the 1940s, while still in Kenya:

> I am often asked here whether I intend to go back 'home' after the war and it is hard to make these friendly Britishers, themselves often homesick, understand that for me it is all dead. To feel at home again can not be brought about by reliving memories of happy times gone by, or through piecing together the fragments of a life broken by a cruel fate. None of it can ever be restored to its former splendor. It is all gone and nothing can bring it back.[36]

Nonetheless, the opportunities he left behind in Austria did play on his mind. He described his connection to Kenya in the following way: 'In truth, even I was not immersed wholeheartedly, mainly because I could not forget that the culmination of my hopes and dreams was to become a physician'.[37] He further explained:

> I rarely spoke of it, but I knew that the pain was always there and nothing could make it go away. My enjoyment of Kenya and and [sic] the thrill of farming were not capable of restoring my full peace of mind. So even I, dear Kenya, am a Brutus, but there are goals within me that even you can not supplant![38]

Arriving in a new country was particularly daunting for young refugees. As well as questions of language and 'home', children were confronted with cultural differences and a social and racial structure that was hitherto unknown to them.

On departure, children had little or no knowledge of the places to which they were going. Jill Pauly recalls how, before they left Germany, her mother took her to the library to look at books about Kenya, perhaps aware of just how different the children would find the British colony.[39] Displaying a similar concern, Walter Zweig suggested to his wife that 'you will have to explain to [Stefanie] that not all people are white'.[40] However, this proved to be little preparation for the changes, and Stefanie describes herself on arrival in Kenya as a 'stunned, frightened little girl – who until then had thought all people were white-skinned and everybody talked German'.[41] These childlike memories of new racial encounters reflected the particularity of experience for young people who fled to the colonies, whose journey abroad was often as thrilling as it was terrifying.

Moreover, on arrival, young refugees had to learn quickly to function in colonial Kenya, where racial hierarchies dictated life. They recall a racially stratified society: the dominance of the white community, the middle position of the Indian settlers, and that black Africans occupied the very lowest status in the racial hierarchy of the colony. Many of the refugees adopted the language and the racial discourse of colonial Kenya. Heinz Bauer, for example, repeated such attitudes in his memoir, giving instructions as to the 'best' way to interact with the African people:

> They were certainly not like children, a popular and patronizing misconception, but they were also not, at least in an employer–employee relationship, quite like our idea of a typical adult. They needed the consideration one gave an adult, but coupled with the firmness and understanding so essential in any successful parent. Like children, they had a keen sense of justice, and like intelligent individuals of any age, they could be persuaded by discussion ... To be accepted and respected as a person in authority, an order had to be firm, clear, consistent, and,

except in rare and special circumstances, irrevocable ... keeping a certain distance on a personal level ... grievances and requests had to be transmitted through the foreman. I learned this time-tested colonial and diplomatic attitude quickly.[42]

Another indication of the adoption of racial discourse by refugees is the use of the word 'boy' as a common denominator for African men. Heinz Bauer noted that '[t]he only strange thing was that these men were always called "boys", which seemed peculiar at first, but we soon got used to it'. Likewise, both Jill and Inge recall their daily walk to school during which they were accompanied by Kenyan men who worked for their family. Jill explained that 'white children were not walking alone, so there was always an African boy that accompanied us'. However, Inge reminds her sister that 'they weren't boys, they were men'. Nonetheless, Jill goes on to say that the 'black boys', who were 'so protective' when they accompanied them, 'took pride in walking [them] and bringing [them] home'.[43]

Stefanie Zweig also engaged with the colonial hierarchies and explores these in relation to Indian settlers. In *Nowhere in Africa*, she writes that 'Patel, the Indian who owned the shop, was a rich and dreaded man', who 'had discovered very quickly that people from Europe were as avid about their letters and newspapers as his compatriots were about their rice, of which he never had a sufficient supply anyway'.[44] This idea is elaborated further in relation to the hiring of black help. Stefanie notes that their Indian landlord's 'cleverly thought-out psychological coup' ensured that his white European tenants were 'still able to afford help, which an unwritten law required for the white upper classes'.[45] This not only served the purpose of the British, who wanted to ensure strong racial boundaries, but it also maintained for the refugees 'the illusion that they were on their way to integration and had the same standard of living as the English in the houses at the edge of the town'.[46]

Zweig's experiences are perhaps those that transgress the colonial racial hierarchy the most, seen clearly in her relationship with Owuor, the African farmhand who not only saved her father's life before she and her mother arrived in Kenya, but who also became the family's essential guide. In the account of her first meeting with Owuor, Zweig writes:

> Owuor was wearing a long, white shirt over his trousers, just like the cheerful angels in the picture books for good children. Owuor had a flat nose and thick lips, and his head looked like a black moon. As soon as the sun shone on the droplets of sweat on his forehead, the droplets changed into multicoloured beads ... Owuor's skin smelled of delightful light honey, chased away any fear, and made a big person out of a little girl.[47]

With regard to the novel's reception, Zweig laments that the contemporary German public's interest was mainly centred on the figure of Owuor, commenting that '[t]o most German readers Owuor, the man with the mighty hands and witty tongue, was of far greater interest than the refugees'.[48] However, even within its portrayal of the close relationship between Zweig and Owuor, *Nowhere in Africa*, as Natalie Eppelsheimer argues, displays 'an internalized colonial mentality' and a romanticization of colonial Africa.[49] In fact, Eppelsheimer has placed Zweig's memoirs in the context of Germany's contemporary perceptions of Africa, suggesting that a romanticized image of the country and its people plays a significant role in Zweig's popularity.[50]

The use of language, the attachment to Africa and perceptions of race were all connected in how the young refugees conceptualized their own identities, both during their stay in Kenya and after. Refugee identity in colonial Kenya was connected with feelings of 'otherness', despite the adoption, at least in part, of the racial hierarchies encountered. These feelings certainly started even before the moment of departure from Europe. Even very young children understood that their Jewishness led to discrimination by the Nazis, and both Jill and Inge recall their feelings of fear as they left Europe.[51] While many refugee children have positive memories of their time in Kenyan exile, a sense of 'otherness' also permeates their recollections. This relates specifically to the British school system and the experience of internment.

Schooling was very important for Jewish families, and re-establishing education became a priority for many as soon as they arrived in Kenya. Many families sent their children to British-run boarding schools, which was standard practice in the colony. However, the foreign boarding school system separated refugee children from the educational and cultural traditions of their parents and threatened the religious life of Jewish families. For most children, schools became sites of inter-cultural tensions. The boarding schools made no provisions for practising Jews; Sabbath was not observed, and kosher food was not provided.

The Bergs countered these challenges by enrolling their children as day students, but this only highlighted their sense of 'otherness', something both Jill and Inge refer to in their *First Person* interview. Moreover, Jill specifically recalls anti-Semitic responses from teachers and pupils in her school. For example, a teacher told her class that there was a 'Little German Jewish spy in our midst'. Another incident involved outright violence from a member of staff, who used a ruler to beat her on the legs.[52]

Zweig's encounters were no less mixed. She recalls in her autobiographical novel some of the areas of tension, including the type of uniform refugee children were likely to wear. She writes that '[t]heir school uniforms were made from inexpensive material and had certainly not been purchased at the appropriate store for school supplies in Nairobi: instead they were sewn by Indian tailors. Almost none of the children wore the school insignia'.[53]

Zweig speculates that the differences between the Jewish and English students must have been observable to the head teacher at her school. Refugee children, she writes:

[h]ardly ever laughed, always looked older than they really were, and were driven by excessive ambition when measured by English standards. These serious, uncomfortably precocious creatures had barely mastered the language, and that had happened surprisingly fast, when, through their curiosity and drive, which even to devoted teachers could be annoying, they became outsiders in a community in which only success in sports counted.[54]

These concerns regarding how she was perceived by others is suggestive of the feelings of 'otherness' and outsiderness.

Internment also highlighted to the young refugees their precarious role in colonial society. Zweig recalls that:

[t]he war brought new challenges. The only important thing now was to protect the country from people who by birth, language, education, and loyalty might be linked more closely to the enemy than to the host country ... Within three days, all enemy nationals from the towns and even those from the remote farms had been handed over to the military forces in Nairobi and informed that their status had been changed from 'refugee' to 'enemy alien'.[55]

This identity change particularly affected Jill Pauly, who speaks passionately about the subject: 'nobody there was bright enough to figure out that the Jews were being persecuted by the Nazis, that they were not spies for Germany'.[56]

Zweig also recalls how internment was a severe lesson to the refugees who had adopted specific roles in Kenya's racial structure. Internment raised difficult questions for the British who, according to Zweig, considered it 'immoral as it was tasteless to put whites into the same clothes as black inmates', especially as '[t]here was not a single European in any of the country's jails'.[57] So, when the Jewish refugees were interned, the British dressed them differently. However, 'the fact that the interned men were now wearing the same kind of khaki uniforms as their guards' meant that, especially for military personnel, 'the unwanted but necessary similarity in appearance between the defenders of the homeland and their potential aggressors created a lot of annoyance'.[58]

The place of the Jewish refugee in the colonial mindset was made clear in these debates. Being forced to be part of the colonial community, yet always set apart from it, was a reality of which many of the young refugees became sharply aware. The British policy of internment was based clearly on their perceptions of race and national identity. John E. Shuckburgh, an undersecretary of state at the Colonial Office, was

[s]ceptical about the 'anti-Nazi' German, whether in this country or elsewhere. Germans are first and foremost Germans. Some of them may

dislike the Nazi regime, but I would not trust a single individual among them not to help the German government ... when it is fighting for its life.⁵⁹

However much refugees adopted their designated roles in Kenya, many also perceived themselves as 'other'. This fact stayed with these refugees long after their families left various colonial refuges. In contrast, for Bauer, who did not experience school in the colony and whose views on internment appear more benign, the sense of 'otherness' is not so pervasive. On this occasion, Bauer's age and the particular good fortune he had in his experiences might have impacted his views. Nonetheless, it once more points to the complexity of the exile experience and the way in which factors such as age, family and good luck impacted it.

Refugee journeys across continents and oceans were done so with no or little preparation. Arrival and survival relied on the family but were restricted by internment policies and British education. Children had to function in family groups completely uprooted from the familiar. The impact of this at the time and later in life was significant. Lauren Levine Enzie states that '[y]ears later, some [Jewish refugees] remain inextricably bound to the country and/or language of their birth, while others feel permanently exiled from their former linguistic and cultural community'.⁶⁰ Furthermore, recent studies of the impact of resettlement on young refugees argue that '[t]he ease or difficulty of resettlement is affected by the size of the refugee group, the timing of arrival, the size and maintenance of the same ethnic group in the host country, and cultural continuity'.⁶¹ Eppelsheimer explains that this was indeed the case in colonial Kenya:

> [t]he status of the refugees and their lives in the colony depended on several factors, among them the date of arrival in Kenya, their financial situation, their contacts (or the absence thereof) to the established Anglo-Jewry, government officials, or influential members of the British settler elite, and sometimes mere coincidence and luck in finding people who were spontaneously willing to help strangers from the continent.⁶²

These aspects certainly did alter young refugees' engagement with languages and conceptions of 'home'. Just as importantly was the specificity of the British colonial context in which they lived, particularly the racial hierarchy that shaped how Jewish refugees were supposed to fit into the rigid social life of the colony.

Jill Pauly and Inge Katzenstein's experiences were deeply influenced by the fact that they were able to maintain a strong Jewish identity, largely because their extended family escaped with them and provided this.

Although the loss of German nationality at the point of departure (i.e. when they became 'stateless') was difficult and is referred to in several interviews, their Jewishness appears to have dominated their sense of self. Postwar America welcomed the Berg family's Jewishness, and the sisters eventually adopted the USA as 'home'. Zweig had a much more limited continuity in her family life and Jewish culture, both because the family was not strictly Orthodox and because of her parents' own difficulties in adjusting to African life. Lacking both a connection to Germany and a strong sense of Jewishness, Stefanie was more open to adopting the colony in both language and conceptions of 'home'.

It is ironic that the Bergs, who as successful agriculturalists were the type of settlers that were tolerable for the British, had girls who never fully adjusted to life in British colonial Kenya. The Zweigs on the other hand were the kind of problematic settlers the British feared. Walter Zweig was poorly suited to agricultural settlement; yet, for his young daughter, Kenya and the English language became and continue to be a central part of her identity.

Heinz Bauer's age and the good fortune he had in receiving help at the most desperate of times impacted the way he adjusted to life in Kenya. He writes fondly of the British, even defending the way refugees were treated. For example, he argues that '[o]nce a refugee was a legal resident of Kenya ... no distinction was made between [him or her] and any other immigrant'.[63] He also says: 'We were all given an equal and fair chance which is much to the credit of the British'.[64] Even over the question of the financial requirements necessary for entry, he summarizes: '[b]ut, to be quite fair, without their knowing what kind of people we were, such misgivings were somewhat understandable'.[65]

British refugee and immigration policies never sought to provide a 'home'. Colonial refugee policy, like British policy generally, was, as Louise London suggests, not about those seeking safety but about protecting the country the refugees wished to enter.[66] That any refugee found safety in Kenya or ultimately settled there was more about the choices and specific circumstances of those people than the intention of British policy. Nonetheless, refuge in Kenya clearly impacted the Jewish identity of those child refugees who found safety in the colonies in complex and lingering ways. An assessment of some of these experiences, using the testimony of the children who found, however fleeting, a 'home' in British colonial Africa, offers an insight into exile stories of children more broadly, expanding the geography of refugee Diasporas. Moreover, these refugees interacted with British attitudes towards race and 'otherness' – of Jewish refugees themselves, African colonial populations and Indian imperial subjects – and therefore the fate of these refugees not only adds to Holocaust and Diaspora history, but also to the wider international response to fundamental crises of citizenship and homeland during the 1930s and 1940s in Europe and its colonies.

Notes

1. For a good general overview of the Dominions' response, see Paul R. Bartrop (ed.), *False Havens: The British Empire and the Holocaust* (Lanham, MD: University Press of America 1995).
2. For example, see Paul Bartrop, 'From Lisbon to Jamaica: A Study of British Refugees Rescue during the Second World War', *Immigrants and Minorities* 13/1 (March 1994), pp. 48–64; Anne Hugon, 'Les Colonies, un Refuge pour les Juifs? Le Cas de la Gold Coast (1938–1945)', *Vingtieme Siecle* 84 (2004), pp. 23–41; Hugh MacMillan and Frank Shapiro, *Zion in Africa: The Jews of Zambia* (London: I.B. Tauris 1999); Geneviève Pitot, *The Maritian Shekel: The Story of the Jewish Detainees in Mauritius 1940–1945*, translated by Donna Edouard (Lanham, MD: Rowman and Littlefield 2000); Frank Shapiro, *Haven in Africa* (Jerusalem: Gefen 2002); Robert G. Weisbrod, *African Zion: The Attempt to Establish a Jewish Colony in the East Africa Protectorate 1903–1905* (Philadelphia, PA: The Jewish Publication Society of America 1968).
3. See Boaz Cohen, 'The Children's Voice: Postwar Collection of Testimonies from Child Survivors of the Holocaust', *Holocaust and Genocide Studies* 21/1 (Spring 2007), pp. 73–95. For a different perspective on the specificity of child experiences, see Robert Krell, 'Psychological Reverberations of the Holocaust in the Lives of Child Survivors', *Monna and Otto Weinmann Lecture Series* (Washington D.C.: USHMM 1997).
4. See Robert Krell, 'Psychological Reverberations'.
5. Paul A. Shapiro, 'Foreword', *Children and the Holocaust: Symposium Presentations* (Washington D.C.: USHMM 2004), p. i.
6. Hagit Lavsky, 'The Role of Children in the Rehabilitation Process of Survivors: The Case of Bergen-Belsen', *Children and the Holocaust: Symposium Presentations* (Washington D.C.: USHMM 2004), p. 104.
7. For a more detailed discussion of the consequences of emigration on Jewish identity in both children and adults, see Susanne Heim, 'Emigration and Jewish Identity: "An Enormous Heartbreak"', *The Journal for Holocaust Education* 10/1 (Summer 2001), pp. 21–33.
8. Jill Pauly and Inge Katzenstein, Interview, *First Person* series, 2003, http://www.ushmm.org/remember/office-of-survivor-affairs/survivor-volunteer/jill-pauly (accessed 30 October 2013); Jill Pauly, 'Oral History Interview with Jill Pauly', 27 February 1998, RG-50.106*0092, USHMM Permanent Collection, http://collections.ushmm.org/search/catalog/irn506657 (accessed 30 October 2013).
9. Jill Pauly, 'Oral History Interview with Jill Pauly'.
10. Heinz Bauer, *Memoir* (unpublished, 1940), RG-02.083, USHMM Permanent Collection; Walter Lacquer, *Generation Exodus: The Fate of Young Jewish Refugees from Nazi Germany* (Hanover, NH: Brandeis University 2001), p. 14.
11. Similar observations have been made in Natalie Eppelsheimer, 'Homecomings and Homemakings: Stefanie Zweig and the Exile Experience In, Out of, and Nowhere in Africa, 1902–2002', PhD thesis, University of California, Irvine,

2008. However, the issues are approached from a literary point of view (with a major emphasis on all of Zweig's written work), and a particular focus on Africa and reception in Germany. Here the issues are placed more explicitly in a British colonial context, with an emphasis on the way that British colonial culture (and child refugee policy) impacted young refugees.

12 Martin Gilbert, *Kristallnacht: Prelude to Destruction* (London, New York: HarperCollins 2006), p. 227.

13 Louise London, *Whitehall and the Jews 1938–1948. British Immigration Policy and the Holocaust* (Cambridge: Cambridge University Press 2001), pp. 118–21.

14 For details of the bill, see Richard D. Breitman and Alan M. Kraut, *American Refugee Policy and European Jewry* (Bloomington, IN: Indiana University Press 1987), p. 73.

15 David S. Wyman claims that 'nativism, anti-Semitism, and economic insecurity' were central factors in the failure of the Wagner–Rogers Bill. David S. Wyman, *Paper Walls: America and the Refugee Crisis 1938–1941* (Amherst, MA: University of Massachusetts Press 1968), p. 94.

16 For more details on the history of the association between Jewish settlement and East Africa, see Robert G. Weisbrod, *African Zion*.

17 Natalie Eppelsheimer, 'Homecomings and Homemakings', p. 140.

18 Peter Mwangi Kagwanja, 'Unwanted in the "White Highlands": The Politics of Civil Society and the Making of a Refugee in Kenya', PhD thesis, University of Illinois at Urbana-Champaign, Urbana-Champaign, 2003, p. 107.

19 Heinz Bauer, *Memoir*; Inge Katzenstein, Interview, *First Person*; Jill Pauly, 'Oral History Interview with Jill Pauly'; Jill Pauly and Inge Katzenstein, Interview, *First Person*; Stefanie Zweig, *Nowhere in Africa: An Autobiographical Novel*, translated by Marlies Comjean (Madison, WI: University of Wisconsin Press 2004), pp. 3–18.

20 Brooke-Popham, letter, 6 April 1939, CO533/511/6, The National Archives of the United Kingdom (hereafter TNA).

21 For example, see J. G. Hibbert, minute, 30 January 1939, CO 323/1688/1, TNA.

22 Draft letter, MacDonald to Brooke-Popham, 17 August 1938; Paskin to Secretary, Central British Fund for German Jewry, 2 November 1938, CO533/497/8, TNA.

23 Earl E. Huyck and Rona Fields, 'Impact of Resettlement on Refugee Children', *International Migration Review* 15/1 (Spring–Summer 1981), p. 246.

24 Stefanie Zweig, *Nowhere in Africa*, p. vii.

25 Susanne Heim, 'Emigration and Jewish Identity', pp. 21–33.

26 Stefanie Zweig, 'Strangers in a Strange Land', *The Guardian* (UK), 21 March 2003, http://www.guardian.co.uk/culture/2003/mar/21/artsfeatures (accessed 30 October 2013).

27 Jill Pauly and Inge Katzenstein, Interview, *First Person*.

28 Marianne Kröger argues that '[a]dolescents, by virtue of their level of cognitive and psychological development, had by contrast a better chance of surviving

exile relatively unscathed'. Marianne Kröger, 'Child Exiles: A New Research Area?', *Shofar* 23/1 (Fall 2004), p. 11.
29. Stefanie Zweig, *Nowhere in Africa*, pp. 261–2.
30. Ibid.
31. Natalie Eppelsheimer, 'Homecomings and Homemakings', p. 223.
32. Jill Pauly, 'Oral History Interview with Jill Pauly'.
33. Jill Pauly and Inge Katzenstein, Interview, *First Person*.
34. Stefanie Zweig, 'Strangers in a Strange Land'.
35. See Heinz Bauer, *Memoir*.
36. Ibid.
37. Ibid.
38. Ibid.
39. Jill Pauly, interview by author, Washington D.C.: USHMM, 30 July 2012.
40. Stefanie Zweig, *Nowhere in Africa*, p. 5.
41. Stefanie Zweig, 'Strangers in a Strange Land'.
42. Heinz Bauer, *Memoir*.
43. Natalie Eppelsheimer, 'Homecomings and Homemakings', p. 199 and p. 205.
44. Stefanie Zweig, *Nowhere in Africa*, p. 63.
45. Ibid, p. 64.
46. Ibid., pp. 163–4.
47. Ibid., p. 19.
48. Ibid., p. viii.
49. Natalie Eppelsheimer, 'Homecomings and Homemakings', p. 12.
50. Ibid., pp. 28–33.
51. Jill Pauly and Inge Katzenstein, Interview, *First Person*.
52. Ibid.
53. Stefanie Zweig, *Nowhere in Africa*, pp. 72–4.
54. Ibid.
55. Ibid., pp. 43–4.
56. Jill Pauly and Inge Katzenstein, Interview, *First Person*.
57. Stefanie Zweig, *Nowhere in Africa*, pp. 44–5.
58. Ibid.
59. Shuckbrugh, minute, 9 June 1941, CO 968/33/13, TNA.
60. Lauren Levine Enzie (ed.), *Exile and Displacement: Survivors of the Nazi Persecution Remember the Emigration Experience* (Oxford/New York: Peter Lang 2001), p. xvi.
61. Earl E. Huyck and Rona Fields, 'Impact of Resettlement', p. 248.
62. Natalie Eppelsheimer, 'Homecomings and Homemakings', p. 171.
63. Heinz Bauer, *Memoir*.

64 Ibid.
65 Ibid.
66 Louise London, 'British Refugee Policy and the Anglo-American Relationship, 1933–1945', *The Forty Years' Crisis: Refugees in Europe 1919–1959*, Birkbeck College, University of London, 14 September 2010.

PART TWO

The Holocaust:
Ghetto and Camp Battlegrounds: Imprisonment, Activism and Forced Labour

CHAPTER SEVEN

Polish and Soviet Child Forced Labourers in National Socialist Germany and German-Occupied Eastern Europe, 1939–45

Johannes-Dieter Steinert

International research has widely neglected the fact that a great number of the forced labourers in National Socialist Germany and German-occupied Eastern Europe were children. They worked in all branches of industry, in agriculture and as domestics in German households. The *Wehrmacht* and SS deployed children in construction work on fortifications, bridges, roads and airfields.

Based on a wide range of official documents from German, Polish, Ukrainian, Belorussian, American and Israeli archives as well as hundreds of published and unpublished testimonies, this chapter provides an overview of research carried out during recent years.[1] It focuses on Polish and Soviet child forced labourers, who – apart from Jewish forced labourers – had to endure the worst working and living conditions in Germany. Moreover, German occupation policies in Poland and the Soviet Union were far more brutal than in any other occupied country, and German deportation practices were the most inhumane. While the emphasis of the research has been on the victims and their experiences, these have been placed within the broad and crucial context of the political and ideological imperatives of the National Socialist perpetrators.

Two areas of research have been of particular interest: firstly, there is the participation of German military and civil institutions in deportations and in employing forced labourers as well as the various interdependencies between child forced labour, deportation practices and Germanization policies, in particular in occupied Poland. Secondly, there is the experience of deportation and forced labour as constructed and narrated in former child forced labourers' testimonies.

For the purpose of this article, the term forced labour 'shall mean all work or service which is exacted from any person under the menace of any penalty and for which the said person has not offered himself voluntarily'.[2] This definition, introduced by the *International Labour Organization* in its 1930 Forced Labour Convention,[3] allows an historical analysis of forced labour in both Germany and in German-occupied areas, whereas deportation is not a necessary condition for forced labour. Furthermore, while the 1930 Convention does not ban all forms of forced and compulsory labour, Article 11(1) clearly states that 'only adult able-bodied males who are of an apparent age of not less than 18 and not more than 45 years may be called upon for forced or compulsory labour'.[4]

Due to a lack of contemporary statistics on child forced labourers, it is most difficult to give any exact numbers. However, based on postwar repatriation figures, it can be estimated that at least 1 million forced labourers under the age of eighteen years were deported from German occupied areas of the Soviet Union, mainly from Ukraine and Belarus to Germany, as well as at least 500,000 from Poland. As the latest known official German statistics show a figure of nearly 3.8 million 'foreign civil workers' (*Ausländische Zivilarbeiter*) from the Soviet Union and Poland employed in August 1944,[5] it is safe to say that the German war economy relied on child forced labour. Even more difficult to estimate is the number of children forced to work in German-occupied Eastern Europe. This has mainly to do with the fact that the total number of forced labourers in these areas is still unknown. Some historians name a total of 20–22 million, but do not provide any information about the criteria for inclusion.[6] Following the definition given by the *International Labour Organization* in 1930, however, the majority of workers in German-occupied territories can be regarded as forced labourers, including the minors among them.

In the course of the research it became obvious that the age of child deportees abducted by German civilian and military authorities decreased during the war. In short: the longer the war lasted, the younger the deportees were. Although there is no statistical proof possible, the tendency can be seen, for example, in official regulations about age limits as well as in documents on the registration and mass deportation of age groups both in occupied Poland and the Soviet Union. Moreover, in 1944, thousands of Belorussian boys and girls aged ten years, and even younger, were deported to Germany by military units of Army Group Centre.

The deportations took place according to general orders given by Berlin, whereas the translation of these orders into practice was determined by a variety of regional and local factors, among them competition between the Reich and occupied areas as well as competition between civil and military authorities within the occupied areas. Additionally, German occupation policies tried to solve self-imposed social problems by deportation. Polish and Soviet children were, for example, victims of a German policy that in many areas allowed them to go to school until the age of twelve years only. As many of them, in particular in urban areas, could not find employment immediately, German authorities often perceived these children as a 'social problem' that should be solved by deportations to Germany.[7] The inclusion of children in groups of forced labourers also helped to fulfil the quotas given by Fritz Sauckel's labour deployment administration, and allowed the keeping of skilled adult workers within the occupied areas. Additionally, social problems, described in some German documents as the 'decline of the youth' (*Jugendverwahrlosung*),[8] were caused by ruthless deportations of parents and other family members, as well as by the enormous displacements of the population at the beginning of the war, by the transfer of workers and production plants to the eastern parts of the Soviet Union, by conscriptions to the Red Army, and by joining the partisans. The remaining population was dominated by a high proportion of women, children, the elderly, and persons unfit for work. Thus, children often found themselves isolated, without intact family structures and social networks. These factors all help to explain the high proportion of women and children amongst the so-called *Ostarbeiter* (civilian workers from the Soviet Union).

Nearly all deportations were carried out using an enormous amount of both physical violence and mental pressure. Methods included street raids, round-ups at schools, churches, cinemas, villages and even beaches by police and military forces, the selection of age groups and examinations by enforced collaboration of local Polish and Soviet administrations. The latter were important in filling the quotas, and it also put enormous pressure onto individual villages and families, who often had to name family members for deportation. This opened the doors for local authorities to settle old scores and to get rid of unpopular members of the community as well as for bribery, extortion and abuse.[9] When families had to name one or two members for deportation to Germany, the decision-making process would often include even younger children, when, for example, the father was with the Red Army, the mother had to care for siblings, the elder brother was with the partisans, and the elder sister was pregnant.

Apart from such mass deportations, there were interdependencies between deportation and German racist occupation policies. Well known is the Germanization programme, which was carried out mainly in the Polish annexed territories, where the so-called *Eindeutschungsfähigkeit* – the physical and mental ability to become German – of families and individuals, among them children, was checked by using pseudo-scientific criteria. As a number of children who had fulfilled these racist criteria and had been given to German families were used as cheap labour in agriculture, small businesses and as domestics, the links between Germanization and forced labour became visible. In this context, it should also be stressed that Heinrich Himmler, who for ideological reasons was strictly against employing East European workers in Germany, intended to fill gaps on the German labour market by Germanizations, and, at some time, intended to develop his own ideologically anchored supply structures for the German labour market.[10]

Similar links can be seen between forced labour and the *Deutsche Volksliste* – a register of ethnic Germans screened for naturalization. Although without any doubt most of the adults signed up for the *Volksliste* and thereby applied for German citizenship voluntarily, some documents and testimonies refer to a high degree of pressure.[11] Families and individuals who were regarded as being ethnic German but refused to change nationality were deported to the General Government, to forced labour camps, and as forced labourers to Germany. On the other hand, there were child forced labourers who were allowed to return home after their parents agreed to become German nationals.[12] Finally, there were children who did not agree with their parents' decision to change nationality, but regarded themselves as victims and returned to Poland after the war. Some of them had spent years of the war in Germany, where they were often been treated as badly as Eastern European forced labourers by their German employers.

Also part of the Germanization programme was the eviction of Polish farmers and their replacement by ethnic Germans who had been transferred from the Soviet Union according to the 1939 Ribbentrop–Molotov agreement. Until January 1943, around 400,000 Polish citizens had been deported to the General Government, while 220,000 had been displaced within the annexed areas.[13] Their fate was often forced labour carried out locally, but deportations also took place to the so-called *Altreich* (Germany in its prewar boundaries) and to special camps.[14]

In 1942, however, the Germanization programme was extended to the General Government, when the *Generalplan Ost* – the Masterplan East – was translated into practice. Well known are the expulsions of Polish families from the Zamość area.[15] Little is known, however, about the accompanying selections of children for both Germanization and for forced labour.[16] According to historian Kiryl Sosnowski, there were 30,000 children among the 110,000 expellees; 4,454 of them were selected for Germanization.[17] Additionally, an unknown number of children were selected for forced labour, while others regarded unsuitable for work were murdered in the gas chambers of Majdanek and Auschwitz or by phenol injections.[18]

A strong link between forced labour and the Germanization programme can also be seen in the deportation of Polish and Soviet domestics for German households in the Reich, among them children aged fifteen years and younger. One of the conditions for selection and deportation was that these female workers met German racist criteria, with the aim of naturalizing them after a probation period.[19] Official German statistics from May 1944 show a total of 32,715 Soviet and 9,519 Polish domestics working in German households.[20]

Other child forced labourers were deported from Belarus with the support of the *Weißruthenisches Jugendwerk*, a youth organization created by the German civil authorities to secure collaboration among the minors.[21] It can be estimated that around 10,000 Belorussian child forced labourers with an official minimum age of fourteen years were deported by the German military and civil authorities to Germany with the support of this youth organization, half of them to the Junkers plants (*Junkerswerke*) in Dessau and Crimmitschau.[22]

Military units also deported children and adults in the course of anti-partisan warfare. At an early stage of such military operations, workers were selected to supply Himmler's concentration camps with forced labourers; later, however, they were distributed by the Sauckel administration to workplaces in Germany.[23] Finally, selections and deportations of child forced labourers took place during the German retreat from Eastern Europe as part of the German scorched earth strategy,[24] as well as in May and June 1944 by units of Army Group Centre under the code name *HEU-Aktion*. While German propaganda stressed the point that *HEU* abbreviated *Heimatlos – Elternlos – Unterkunftslos* (uprooted, orphaned, homeless),[25] research has shown that many children did not fit into these categories but were systematically seized by German military units who even surrounded villages for this very purpose.[26] According to a German military report for June and July 1944, 3,000 boys and girls aged ten to fourteen were captured by the 9th Army alone,[27] while the number of children imprisoned by the 2nd and the 4th Army remains unknown. These children were initially taken as hostages to ensure the loyalty of their parents forced into fortification work for the German Army, and were finally transported to Germany, the majority of them again to the *Junkerswerke*.[28]

Although memory and testimony are individual and not collective phenomena, influenced not at least by later life experiences and the contexts in which such narratives are constructed, the following section identifies a selection of patterns of experience and typical elements in the testimonies of Polish and Soviet former child forced labourers.

The analysis of hundreds of testimonies[29] has shown that former child forced labourers talked in detail and often with great emotion both about the process of separation from their families and about their deportation to Germany. Due to the context in which testimonies were constructed and to the age of the children at the time of deportation, there are more or less comprehensive accounts of prewar life. More important, however, were the personal experiences of a round-up, the notification by the local labour office, the appearance of policemen and soldiers in the village and on the farm, and the pressure put onto the family by German and local authorities, etc. Some children remembered the process of decision making within the family, after the order had been given that one of its members had to go to Germany. They reported, for example, the absence of the father, and the fact that the mother had to care for other children as well, so that she could hardly leave. Many interviewees mentioned that they had successfully avoided deportation for a while, and that it was bad luck that finally led to deportation after they had tried to escape to a nearby forest, or had accidently faced a policeman after leaving their hiding place. Particularly emotional were reports of the act of separation from parents, other members of the family, relatives, friends and neighbours: how parents reacted, what the children took with them to Germany – if there was a chance to do so – how family members accompanied them to the train, and visited them in the transit camp. All this indicates the importance of these events within the children's biographies. Similar statements cannot be found to this extent in testimonies of adult forced labourers.

Belorussian Olga Andreewna Djatschenko's story contained many examples of the generalizations made above. She was sixteen years old when she and her family had 'agreed' to send her to Germany, after German officials had threatened to send her parents to a concentration camp. In October 1942, her father brought her by carriage to the nearby town of Stolin, where a transit camp had been established in the buildings of the former ghetto. During the following week, her mother and one of her sisters went to see her in the camp, before she was brought to the railway station. Interviewed seventy years later, Olga could not control her emotions:

> Such weeping, dejection, as if we were prisoners, we are not human beings any longer, when they drove us somewhere. And we had no idea where to, it was war, and we were children from deep in the countryside, who had not seen anything in their life. And suddenly it is war, and we were taken from our parents.[30]

Like Olga, many children recollected the pain of parting, some told in lyrical phases about a 'cry in the air that tore the soul to pieces', that the 'dearest mother cried' and 'the whole earth and heaven as well as the birds'.[31] Olga's goods train faced a delay of three days because partisans had blown up the track in the countryside, while other child forced labourers remembered that their trains went extremely fast because of partisans, or that partisans had followed the train and had fired at the carriage with the guards.[32] Food, recalled Olga, was not distributed before Brest, where they had a short stop only, before continuing the journey to Gdynia. Here the group was accommodated in huts, and Olga had to endure the greatest humiliation of her young life, when she had to undress in front of 'young men dressed in white coats' before disinfection took place and her head and her private parts were shaved. She felt 'embarrassed' and 'humiliated'.[33] Afterwards, a medical examination took place, before the train went on to Elbing, where Olga's group was housed in a former prisoner of war camp: 'There, we sat down on our baggage, we cried and cried, and prayed for strength, mind, resilience and so on. We got caught in something and punished by war. [cried] I remember but I cannot, cannot speak about it. [talks in tears] It was such a – one cannot tell'.[34]

Soviet children also described in detail their journeys to Germany, which often took more than a week. The length of the transports and the disastrous conditions on the cattle and goods trains must be the reason why they remember it so well, while Polish children, who had a much shorter way, did not so often talk about how they went to Germany. Soviet children, however, recalled the narrowness in the cramped wagons; how cold or hot it was; that there was no possibility to sit and lay down properly; that there were no toilet and washing facilities but permanent hunger and thirst. Although adult forced labourers talk about the length of and the conditions in the transports too, there are some typical age and gender-related memories in children's testimonies. In particular, girls stressed the fact that they could not relieve themselves on the train, but had to wait long hours for a stop, and that they finally had to do it together with boys and men on a field. Similar were the descriptions of delousing, which took place both on the way to Germany and then again after arriving. Even after many decades, the narratives transmit an idea of the humiliating situation, in particular when the girls had to undress completely in front of uniformed men, who watched them having a shower and carried out the delousing procedure.

There were also detailed reports about arriving in Germany – 'we feared for our lives and had terrible fear what would happen to us', Stanislawa wrote in a letter[35] – and the feeling of being sold on a slave or cattle market, when employers chose their forced labourers in public. Galina (born 1927), for example, recollected that the farmer had inspected her carefully, including her teeth.[36] Typical of children's testimonies are emotional remarks about the continuous pain of parting, homesickness and endless tears at night, accompanied by deep concerns about parents, siblings and other members of the family. 'We could not make ourselves understood, were desperate and yearned for our families', so said 1925-born Stanislawa;[37] while Galina, aged fourteen years when deported to Germany, remembered: 'Oh, I was so homesick. I cried day and night. I wanted to be home again. I always wanted to be home. I cannot describe how terrible and difficult it was for me'.[38] Tears and homesickness have become engraved so deeply into Galina's memory, that even decades after her deportation, she did not want to read anything about the war or to watch movies about it.[39]

Like their adult counterparts, children talked about the more than miserable accommodation, the barbed wire enclosed camps, the meagre supplies and the never ending hunger. Striking were the complaints about the scanty sanitary and laundry facilities as well as the lack of soap. Alina Radłowska (born 1928), from Lodz, talked in a positive way about her working conditions at *Telefunken* in Berlin, and how she was treated. Her accommodation, however, was dreadful, full of bedbugs. And it did not even help to knot the bed linen together under her chin at night. These creatures were disgusting and more terrible than the permanent hunger.[40] Children who recollected lice, fleas and bedbugs, often talked about the impossibility of maintaining any degree of personal hygiene. Cold water from a tap was not at all sufficient,[41] and despite intensive hunting of vermin at night, the whole situation was hopeless. Even a special disinfection commando that had been called in brought only temporary relief, according to fourteen-year-old Julian Oleg Nowak, who spent many sleepless nights in Bremen.[42]

Most striking was the hunger that nearly all children employed in industry had to endure. 'We were so hungry', Galyna Burenko said in her interview:

> In the morning we got water with flour. This we drank, and we had two tiny pieces of bread, and those who cut the bread for us managed to make our pieces smaller so that there was more left for themselves. We went hungry to work. At lunchtime we had soup with a few pieces of fish, including their heads, white turnip and cabbage. Like hogwash, perhaps even worse. In the evening water with flour again. That was our food. Only on Sundays they gave us a few potatoes and that cooked blood. At first, I could not eat it, it was sickening. But then I learnt to swallow it because I was so hungry.[43]

Soviet children remembered their daily humiliation when they were escorted from the camp to the factory, and in this context they occasionally compared their situation with Polish forced labourers who after a while were allowed to walk on their own from the camp to the workplace or to take a bus or a tram. Galyna Burenko, who had been deported from occupied Russia, talked about the 'long ordeal' she had to get through twice a day when she was sixteen years old. She had to get up at 4.00 am in the morning, followed by the march through the town to arrive at 6.00 am at the *Bush* plant for optical instruments in Rathenow. After a twelve hour shift her group was escorted back to the camp.[44] 'It hurt', Ludmilla Grischajewa from Kursk remarked briefly and concisely in this context,[45] while Olga Djatschenko from Stolin recalled policemen with torches at the front and the rear of her column as well as the noises her group produced with their wooden soles, 'like Belgian horses'.[46] Her feet hurt from the wooden soles, and she was always in great fear,[47] while Kazimiera Kalińska from Lodz felt like a criminal when escorted by the armed guards.[48] Dressed insufficiently against the weather, hungry and freezing, many children felt exposed. Some were beaten by the guards with whips, when they were hardly able to walk fast enough after a long day's work on their tired legs and excoriated feet.[49]

Age-specific differences can be identified when children spoke about their working conditions, although most stressed the point that work was much too hard and exhausting for them, and that they could hardly stay awake during night shifts. However, most interviewers, who obviously saw only the elderly person behind the microphone in front of them, ignored such statements and did not ask for further details. Julian Oleg Nowak (born 1927), for example, reported about his twelve hour shift in the Bremer wool combing work: a 'murderous ordeal', without any inhalation protection against the dense dust. He remembered the permanent coughing, and that

German workers did not enter the most dangerous shop floors at all.⁵⁰ Some children had to fill sacks with lime without any protection; others had to carry out blast operations and to handle the rock masses; many suffered rashes and abscesses.⁵¹ The night shifts were worst for Julian but like some other children, he combined his complaints with the positive experience that against all rules, one of the German foremen allowed him occasionally some hours of sleep in the changing room or in the hall with the wool fibres.⁵² This, however, did not apply to Larisa, who found no sleep at all during the night shift week, except some minutes on the toilet or while walking.⁵³ Like Jan, who worked in an accumulator factory in Hanover, she had to stay after the night shift in the camp where she found no privacy during the day, and where she had to carry out additional work in the afternoons, before she had to leave for the factory at 7.00 pm in the evening again.⁵⁴ When tiredness became overwhelming, some children fell asleep during work or passed out, Daniela Adamiak remembered from her time at a *Telefunken* plant. When foreman Petz was in charge, said Daniela, the children were woken up by beating, while foreman Lindych allowed some rest, blanketed the children and monitored that all had their turn.⁵⁵

Interviewers also often ignored what children said about being beaten. In this context it is safe to say that child forced labourers were beaten more often than adults: They were beaten because they were children and because they were East European forced labourers – often at the same time insulted as Polish or Russian pigs (*Polenschwein, Russenschwein*) and subhumans (*Untermensch*). According to many testimonies, such abuse was regarded as most painful when conducted by German children in the streets. 'When they drove us from the railway station to the camp, a group of small children accompanied us; they spat at us, threw stones and dirt and called us dogs, oxen and pigs',⁵⁶ reported 1927-born Nikolai Nikitovitsch from the Dnjepropetrovsk area. 'At that time we didn't know the meaning of these words, which we only understood later. But worst was that our guards did not react in any way'.⁵⁷ Such statements mirrored a situation children often had to experience during their time in Germany. Although only a few of them were able to understand when arriving in Germany what these German children were shouting, the nonverbal communication was obvious. Jadwiga (born 1931) had to endure a similar experience, when children in Breslau spat at her, while the adults again did not intervene.⁵⁸ German children echoed what they had heard from their parents, at school and in the Hitler Youth. Katharina, a twelve-year-old Polish girl, forced to work in a German household, remembered that the five-year-old daughter of her employers called her racist names and spat into her face.⁵⁹

The often catastrophic living and working conditions provoked disobedience, resistance and sabotage, followed by severe punishment, torture by the Gestapo and transfer to so-called labour education camps (*Arbeitserziehungslager*) or concentration camps. In the latter, the number of young prisoners increased during the final years of the war. At the end of

May 1944, 22.9 per cent of all foreign civil workers (*ausländische Zivilarbeiter*) kept in Mauthausen concentration camp, for example, were younger than twenty years old, while in March 1945 this figure had risen to 34.5 per cent. Of interest also are statistics from March 1943 showing that 11.2 per cent of all prisoners in Mauthausen were younger than twenty years old, while at the same time 54 per cent of so-called *Zivilrussen* (civilian Russian workers) belonged to this age group. This indicates that young Soviet forced labourers were imprisoned at a much higher percentage than older workers, probably due to their greater resistance and higher rates of escape from employment.[60] Furthermore, nearly all children talked about the punishments they had to endure and those they had to witness, including executions. In some testimonies there is also information on the long-lasting physical and mental consequences resulting from such violence, such as continuous sleep disorder and nightmares.

Remarks about Germans were predominantly negative, as far as they were not characterized by strong relativisms, possibly caused by the context in which many interviews have been conducted during the time when German compensation payments have been discussed. Some of the oral history projects were even linked to German institutions. Positive statements were often made about elderly persons, with grandparents on the farms, elderly colleagues in the firms, who occasionally placed a sandwich somewhere or slipped it into the child's pocket, unseen by other Germans.

The testimonies of children forced to work in the occupied areas were in many respects very similar to those from children deported to Germany. Although most of the children could stay in their towns and villages or nearby, and although a number could even sleep at home, it is obvious that these children remember forced labour as a turning point in their biographies too. All were pulled out of school; and some had to work for the ethnic German settlers, who had taken over their parents' farms. Zofia Sobczak, for example, was just ten years old, when a blonde German lady turned up in her classroom in Poznań. All the children had to stand up and were inspected by this woman. Finally, she pointed at Zofia and said 'she'. With that, Zofia's school days ended and her time as a forced labourer in a German household began.[61] Kazimierz Trzasalski from Zagaj was the same age, when an ethnic German farmer who had taken over a farm in the neighbourhood, made him his shepherd. Kazimierz's parents did not dare to object.[62] Similar remarks can be found in an interview with Zofia Cieślak from Gołocin, who remembered that one day a German settler gathered the families of her village to let them know via an interpreter that from now on all children had to work for him.[63]

Older children learned that work for a German employer at home protected them from being deported to Germany. Such jobs were arranged by parents, friends and neighbours, sometimes with the help of bribes. Nearly all of these children recalled the permanent fear of being deported to Germany at the end of the day. Just like the deported minors, child forced labourers in the occupied areas had to endure mistreatment by their German employers. Some remembered that they resigned themselves to their fate, because they feared being sent to a forced labour camp or to Germany. 'Just one telephone call, and you will go where your father is', this sentence repeatedly said by her employer, Franziska has never forgotten. Her father, an active member of the Polish resistance, was imprisoned in Żabikowo concentration camp.[64] Some testimonies indicate that staying at home was not always perceived as an advantage. While children deported to Germany were homesick and worried about their loved ones at home, those who stayed at home had to endure the effects of German occupation policies, and often found themselves in the roles of adults, who had to care for their families. In these interviews, many complain that until now neither the German nor the Polish governments have acknowledged them officially as forced labourers and treat them in the same way as their deported fellow contemporaries. Characteristic are detailed recollections about disrupted childhoods under German occupation. This includes memories about expulsion and displacement, the loss of relatives, and changes in social relations. Children had to learn that their parents could not protect them any longer, and that they were at the mercy of Germans. Former friends quickly mutated to enemies in Hitler Youth uniforms. Although some children remember proudly that they did not avoid any confrontation with members of the Hitler Youth, they were aware that this could end in prisons and camps.

The research on how children remembered liberation made obvious some further differences between their testimonies and those of adults. According to historian Gelinada Grinchenko, children recalled their liberation by the Red Army in a cheerful and enthusiastic way. Most of them could not wait to go home.[65] Soviet statistics show that 5.2 million Soviet citizens were repatriated in 1944–5, followed by 246,000 between 1946 and 1949. Children who had grown up during forced labour in Germany were often integrated into Red Army Reserve Units, where they rubbed shoulders with a total of 1 million other repatriates. Some even served in the Red Army during the final stages of the war.[66] So far, little is known about the treatment of children in the Soviet filtration camps, and whether they were screened in the same way as adults were. According to historian Tetjana Pastuschenko, children who returned to Ukraine were treated more indulgently than adult returnees.[67]

Historians from the former Soviet Union agree that in general former forced labourers did not talk openly about their experiences in Germany until 1990. Forced labour was regarded as a blot on the biography.[68] The fact that millions of Soviet citizens had worked in Germany did not fit into the official Soviet war history that celebrated mass heroism and patriotism.[69] Avgustina (born 1927), for example, had been arrested by the Gestapo because she had helped a Soviet prisoner of war to escape. She was not hanged but imprisoned temporarily in one of the notorious so-called labour education camps (*Arbeitserziehungslager*). When liberated by the Red Army, she was eighteen years old, so that Soviet repatriation officers, who did not believe her story because she was not sentenced to death by the Gestapo, did not treat her as a child. She had to endure insults and abuses when staying in a Soviet repatriation camp in Brandenburg, where she was called a traitor and a whore. Finally, in October 1945, she was allowed to return home, where her father greeted her with the question in his eyes why she had not stayed in the West, while the *Narodnij Komissariat Wnutrennych Del* (NKWD, People's Office for the Interior; Soviet Secret Service) over many years suspected her of having been a spy for the Germans. When getting married to a Red Army officer, the NKWD warned her fiancé not to spoil his career. However, they got married, moved to the Caucasus and finally returned to Charkow in 1962; but, it was only after the end of the Soviet Union that Avgustina told her sons about her time as a child forced labourer in Germany.[70]

In contrast to the repatriation of Soviet citizens which was organized via filtration camps, Polish forced labourers had a much shorter journey home, and many of them left Germany and Austria without any assistance. While enforced repatriation of Soviet Displaced Persons had been agreed in Yalta, a high percentage of Polish Displaced Persons (DPs) were reluctant to go back to a Poland which was now under Soviet influence. At the end of 1946 there were still nearly 300,000 Polish DPs in the Western Zones of occupation in Germany, compared to 20,000 Soviet DPs.[71]

A special group among the DP population were the so-called unaccompanied children, who came to Germany and Austria mainly under the Germanization programme. According to German sources, at least 20,000 Polish children had been kidnapped during the war, compared to 200,000 children named in Polish sources.[72] While those taken as babies and toddlers could not remember their original home at all, many of the older children made their way home on their own or they went into one of the DP camps for repatriation. Others, like adults, refused to go home; they stayed in Germany and Austria, or went to a third country. However, it was only when the large waves of repatriation ebbed away, that the problem of unaccompanied children became obvious in the DP camps.[73]

The analysis has shed some light on both the history of Polish and Soviet child forced labour and on their testimonies. By changing the focus of historical research from forced labour in general to child forced labour in particular and by using age and gender as central categories for analysis, a whole range of desiderata became obvious. While a study on Jewish child forced labourers is currently in preparation, research on other groups of children from all occupied areas is lacking. Such research should focus not only on children deported to Germany but also on children forced to work under German civilian and military command in their homelands and in third countries. A second area of future research can be seen in regional and local studies as well in economic sectors and branches of industry. Widely neglected so far are non-Jewish children who had to work in concentration, labour and other camps. The same applies to the postwar history of most groups of child survivors. Such studies would open the field for historical comparisons and a better understanding of child testimonies. Finally, there is still time to conduct interviews with former child forced labourers, carried out by interviewers who should be much more sensitive to the fact that the interviewees talk about their childhood experiences and not about forced labour in general.

Notes

1 The research project has been generously supported by the Gerda Henkel Stiftung, the British Academy, the Stiftung 'Erinnerung, Verantwortung und Zukunft', and the Arts & Humanities Research Council.
2 International Labour Organization, C029 – Forced Labour Convention, 1930 (No. 29), Article 2(1).
3 Ibid.
4 Ibid., Article 11(1).
5 Ulrich Herbert, *Fremdarbeiter. Politik und Praxis des 'Ausländer-Einsatzes' in der Kriegswirtschaft des Dritten Reiches* (Berlin/Bonn: Dietz 1985), p. 271.
6 Rolf-Dieter Müller, 'Die Zwangsrekrutierung von "Ostarbeitern" 1941–1944', in *Der Zweite Weltkrieg*, ed. by Wolfgang Michalka (Munich/Zurich: Seehamer 1989), pp. 772–83, here p. 774; Jens-Christian Wagner, 'Zwangsarbeit im Nationalsozialismus – Ein Überblick', in *Zwangsarbeit. Die Deutschen, die Zwangsarbeiter und der Krieg. Begleitband zur Ausstellung*, ed. by Volkhard Knigge, Rikola-Gunnar Lüttgenau and Jens-Christian Wagner (Essen: Klartext 2010), pp. 180–93, here p. 180.
7 Federal Archives, Berlin, R 58 / 184, Meldungen aus dem Reich, no. 90, 23.5.1940.
8 Central State Archives of Supreme Bodies of Power and Government of Ukraine, Kiev, 3676-4-105, Der Chef der Sicherheitspolizei und des SD, Meldungen aus den besetzten Ostgebieten [1942].
9 Ulrich Herbert, *Fremdarbeiter. Politik und Praxis*, p. 86; Rolf-Dieter Müller, 'Die Zwangsrekrutierung von "Ostarbeitern" 1941–1944', in *Der Zweite Weltkrieg*, ed. by Wolfgang Michalka, pp. 772–83, here p. 777; Christian Gerlach, *Kalkulierte Morde. Die deutsche Wirtschafts- und Vernichtungspolitik in Weißrußland 1941 bis 1944* (Hamburg: Hamburger Edition 1999), p. 450–1.
10 Mark Mazower, *Hitler's Empire. Nazi Rule in Occupied Europe* (London: Allen Lane 2009), p. 297; Federal Archives, Berlin, R 49 / 5, RFSS. Reichskommissar für die Festigung deutschen Volkstums, gez. H. Himmler, Anordnung – Nr. 17/II, 9.5.1940.
11 Kiryl Sosnowski, *The Tragedy of Children under Nazi Rule* (Poznan, Warsaw: Zachodnia Agencja Prasowa 1962), p. 48; Peter Longerich, *Heinrich Himmler.*

Biographie (Munich: Pantheon 2010), p. 616; United Nations – Archives and Records Management Section, New York, S-0437-0016-22, Kreishauptman des Kreises Debica to Josef Schwakopf, 26.6.1942.

12 Christoph U. Schminck-Gustavus, *Hungern für Hitler. Erinnerungen polnischer Zwangsarbeiter im Deutschen Reich 1940–1945* (Reinbek bei Hamburg: Rowohlt 1984), p. 42.

13 Isabel Heinemann, *'Rasse, Siedlung, deutsches Blut'. Das Rasse- und Siedlungshauptamt der SS und die rassenpolitische Neuordnung Europas* (Göttingen: Wallstein 2003), pp. 227–8.

14 *Obozy hitlerowskie na ziemiach polskich 1939–1945*, ed. by Główna Komisja Badania Hitlerowskich w Polsce – Rada Ochrony Pomników Walki i Męczeństwa (Warsaw: Panstwowe Wydawnictwo Naukowe 1979), p. 673.

15 Dieter Pohl, *Von der 'Judenpolitik' zum Judenmord. Der Distrikt Lublin des Generalgouvernements 1934–1944* (Frankfurt am Main: Peter Lang Verlag 1993), p. 153.

16 Isabel Heinemann, *'Rasse, Siedlung, deutsches Blut'. Das Rasse- und Siedlungshauptamt der SS und die rassenpolitische Neuordnung Europas* (Göttingen: Wallstein 2003), pp. 410–12.

17 Kiryl Sosnowski, *The Tragedy of Children under Nazi Rule* (Poznan/Warsaw: Zachodnia Agencja Prasowa 1962), p. 63.

18 Barbara Distel, 'Kinder und Jugendliche im nationalsozialistischen Verfolgungssystem', in *Kinder und Jugendliche als Opfer des Holocaust. Dokumentation einer Internationalen Tagung in der Gedenkstätte Haus der Wannseekonferenz 12. bis 14. Dezember 1994*, ed. by Edgar Bamberger and Annegret Ehmann (Heidelberg: Dokumentationszentrum deutscher Sinti und Roma 1995), pp. 53–67, here p. 61; Helena Kubica, 'Children and Adolescents in Auschwitz', in *Auschwitz 1940–1945. Central Issues in the History of the Camp, vol. II: The Prisoners – Their Life and Work*, ed. by Wacław Długoborski and Franciszek Piper (Oświęcim: Auschwitz-Birkenau State Museum 2000), pp. 201–90, here pp. 208–9; Federal Archives, Ludwigsburg, B 162 / 1029, Untersuchungsrichter Jozef Skorzynski, Hauptkommission für die Untersuchung deutscher Verbrechen in Polen, Protokoll über die Einsichtnahme in die Akten der Staatsanwaltschaft beim Landgericht in Zamosc, 14.-25.5.1949, Aussage Jan Szczepanowski, 37 Jahre alt, wohnhaft in Kol. Stary Hyza Zamosc, pp. 215–16.

19 Federal Archives, Berlin, R 58 / 1030, Reichsführer SS to Höhere SS- und Polizeiführer, 10.9.1942.

20 Federal Archives, Berlin, R 59 / 48, Kaltenbrunner to Himmler, 13.8.1944.

21 Christian Gerlach, *Kalkulierte Morde. Die deutsche Wirtschafts- und Vernichtungspolitik in Weißrußland 1941 bis 1944* (Hamburg: Hamburger Edition 1999), p. 1084; Alexander Brakel, *Unter Rotem Stern und Hakenkreuz. Baranowicze 1939 bis 1944. Das westliche Weißrußland unter sowjetischer und deutscher Besatzung* (Paderborn: Schöningh 2009), p. 214.

22 National Historical Archives of Belarus, Minsk, 385/2/56, List of camps in Germany, end 1944; Babette Quinkert, 'Terror und Propaganda. Die

"Ostarbeiteranwerbung" im Generalkommissariat Weißruthenien', *Zeitschrift für Geschichtswissenschaft* 47/8 (1999), pp. 700–21, here p. 717.

23 'Himmler to Höhere SS- und Polizeiführer in Rußland et al., SS-Befehl, 6.1.1943', in *Deutschland im zweiten Weltkrieg*, vol. 3: *Der grundlegende Umschwung im Kriegsverlauf, November 1942 bis September 1943*, (Cologne: Pahl-Rugenstein 1977), p. 354; Federal Archives, Berlin, NS 19 / 1432, RFSS, Persönlicher Stab, to Chef SS-Hauptamt et al., 28.6.1943. BA NS 19 / 1436, Himmler to Chef Bandenkampf-Verbände et al., 10.7.1943.

24 Johannes-Dieter Steinert, *Deportation und Zwangsarbeit. Polnische und sowjetische Kinder im nationalsozialistischen Deutschland und im besetzten Osteuropa 1939–1945* (Essen: Klartext 2013), pp. 125–34.

25 Federal Archives, Freiburg, RH 20-9 / 198, AOK 9, Qu. 2, Erfassung von Arbeitskräften; Rückführung von Jugendlichen ins Reich (Deckname: 'Heuaktion'), 28 May 1944.

26 National Historical Archives of Belarus, Minsk, 1363/1/597, Declaration handwritten by Kurt Merettig, 16 August 1947.

27 Federal Archives, Freiburg, RW 46 / 17, Heeresgruppenwirtschaftsführer Mitte, Abt. Arbeit, Beitrag zum KTB für die Zeit vom 26.6. bis 2.7.1944, 11.9.1944.

28 Johannes-Dieter Steinert, *Deportation und Zwangsarbeit*, pp. 134–42.

29 See the collections of unpublished interviews Vertrieben aus Warschau 1944 – Kinderschicksale. Historisches Museum und Staatsarchiv Warschau in Zusammenarbeit mit der Stiftung niedersächsische Gedenkstätten, http://http://www.banwar1944.eu/?ml_id=2 (accessed 8 June 2015); (2) Forced Labor 1939–1945. Memory and History. Stiftung Erinnerung, Verantwortung und Zukunft, Freie Universität Berlin und Deutsches Historisches Museum, http://www.zwangsarbeit-archiv.de/en/index.html (accessed 8 June 2015); International Forced Labourers Documentation Project. Archive, Fernuniversität Hagen; Child Forced Labourers in Occupied Poland. Author's collection, University of Wolverhampton.

30 International Forced Labourers Documentation Project, Fernuniversität Hagen, Olga Andreewna Djatschenko, born 1925 in David-Gorodok.

31 Anna Borisowna N., born 1925 in Belgorod, in *Die Sprache der Opfer. Briefzeugnisse aus Rußland und der Ukraine zur Zwangsarbeit als Quelle der Geschichtsschreibung*, ed. by Gisela Schwarze (Essen: Klartext 2005), p. 71; Maria Pawlowna S., born 1926 in Charkow, ibid., p. 130.

32 International Forced Labourers Documentation Project, Fernuniversität Hagen, Galina Fedorovna Agranovskaja, born 1928 in Moskau. Maria J., born 1925 in Rostow area, in *Die Sprache der Opfer*, ed. by Gisela Schwarze, p. 139.

33 International Forced Labourers Documentation Project, Fernuniversität Hagen, Olga Andreewna Djatschenko, born 1925 in David-Gorodok.

34 Ibid.

35 Stanislawa R., born 1925 in Poland, in Janet Anschütz and Irmtraud Heike, *Feinde im eigenen Land. Zwangsarbeit in Hannover im Zweiten Weltkrieg* (Bielefeld: Verlag für Regionalgeschichte 2000), p. 63.

36 Galina, born 1927 in Crimean area, in Susanne Kraatz, (ed.), *Verschleppt und vergessen. Schicksale jugendlicher 'OstarbeiterInnen' von der Krim im Zweiten Weltkrieg und danach. Begleitbuch zur Ausstellung im Rathaus der Stadt Heidelberg, 5.-20. Oktober 1995* (Heidelberg: Freundeskreis Heidelberg-Simferopol 1995), p. 129.

37 Stanisława R., born 1925 in Poland, in Janet Anschütz and Irmtraud Heike, *Feinde im eigenen Land*, p. 65.

38 Galina, born 1927 in Crimean area, in *Verschleppt und vergessen*, ed. by Susanne Kraatz, p. 129.

39 Galina, born 1927 in Crimean area, in *Verschleppt und vergessen*, ed. by Susanne Kraatz, p. 129.

40 Alina Radłowska, born 1928 in Lodz, in *Schönes, schreckliches Ulm. 130 Berichte ehemaliger polnischer Zwangsarbeiterinnen und Zwangsarbeiter, die in den Jahren 1940 bis 1945 in die Region Ulm / Neu-Ulm verschleppt worden waren*, ed. by Silvester Lechner (Ulm: DZOK 1997), p. 284.

41 Jadwiga Krolik, born 1929, in ibid., p. 284.

42 Christoph U. Schminck-Gustavus, *Hungern für Hitler. Erinnerungen polnischer Zwangsarbeiter im Deutschen Reich 1940–1945* (Reinbek bei Hamburg: Rowohlt 1984), p. 40.

43 International Forced Labourers Documentation Project, Fernuniversität Hagen, Galyna Burenko, born 1925 in Jenissejsk.

44 Ibid.

45 International Forced Labourers Documentation Project, Fernuniversität Hagen, Ludmilla Timofejewna Grischajewa, born 1927 in Kursk.

46 International Forced Labourers Documentation Project, Fernuniversität Hagen, Olga Andreewna Djatschenko, born 1925 in David-Gorodok.

47 Ibid.

48 Kazimiera Kalińska, born 1927 in Lodz, in *Schönes, schreckliches Ulm*, ed. by Silvester Lechner, p. 189.

49 Marija Petrowna Moisejewna, fifteen years old, born in Charkow (deported in August 1942), in Jana Müller, *'Ich weiß nicht, wie wir alles überlebt haben, vielleicht, weil wir jung waren'. Zwangsarbeit in Dessau im Spiegel biografischer Skizzen* (Dessau: Geschichtswerkstatt 2004), p. 18.

50 Julian Oleg Nowak, born 1927, in Christoph U. Schminck-Gustavus, *Hungern für Hitler*, p. 51.

51 Lynn H. Nicholas, *Cruel World. The Children of Europe in the Nazi Web* (New York: Alfred A. Knopf 2005), pp. 344–5; Margarethe Ruff, *'Um ihre Jugend betrogen'. Ukrainische Zwangsarbeiter/innen in Vorarlberg 1942–1945* (Bregenz: Vorarlberger Autoren Gemeinschaft 1997), p. 59; Vertrieben aus Warschau 1944 – Kinderschicksale http://www.banwar1944.eu/?ml_id=2 (accessed 8 June 2015), Interview Halina Paszkowska, born 1932 in Warschau.

52 Julian Oleg Nowak, born 1927, in Christoph U. Schminck-Gustavus, *Hungern für Hitler. Erinnerungen polnischer Zwangsarbeiter im Deutschen Reich 1940–1945* (Reinbek bei Hamburg: Rowohlt 1984), p. 46.

53 Larisa St., born 1928 in Leningrad, in *Die Sprache der Opfer*, ed. by Gisela Schwarze, p. 106.
54 Jan S., born 1925 in Polen, in Janet Anschütz and Irmtraud Heike, *Feinde im eigenen Land*, p. 60.
55 Daniela Adamiak, born 1927 in Lodz, in *Schönes, schreckliches Ulm*, ed. by Silvester Lechner, p. 86.
56 Nikolai Nikitovitsch D., born 1927 in Dnjepropetrovsk area, in Eginhard Scharf, *'Man machte mit uns was man wollte'. Ausländische Zwangsarbeiter in Ludwigshafen am Rhein 1939–1945* (Heidelberg: Verlag Regionalkultur 2004), p. 293.
57 Ibid.
58 Vertrieben aus Warschau 1944 – Kinderschicksale http://www.banwar1944.eu/?ml_id=2 (accessed 8 June 2015), Report Jadwiga Kołodziejska-Jedynak, born 1931 in Warschau.
59 Katharina P., born 1931, in Annekatrein Mendel, *Zwangsarbeit im Kinderzimmer. 'Ostarbeiterinnen' in deutschen Familien von 1939 bis 1945. Gespräche mit Polinnen und Deutschen* (Frankfurt/Main: Dipa 1994), p. 59.
60 Bertrand Perz, 'Kinder und Jugendliche im Konzentrationslager Mauthausen und seinen Außenlagern', *Dachauer Hefte* 9 (1993), pp. 71–90, here pp. 76–9.
61 Zofia Sobczak, born 1934 in Poznań, in Johannes-Dieter Steinert, *Deportation und Zwangsarbeit*, p. 209.
62 Kazimierz Trzasalski, born 1930 in Zagaj, in ibid., p. 209.
63 Zofia Cieślak, born 1930 in Gołocin, in ibid., p. 209.
64 Franziska E., born 1924, in Annekatrein Mendel, *Zwangsarbeit im Kinderzimmer. 'Ostarbeiterinnen' in deutschen Familien von 1939 bis 1945. Gespräche mit Polinnen und Deutschen* (Frankfurt/Main: Dipa 1994), pp. 40–1.
65 Gelinada Grinchenko, 'Ehemalige "Ostarbeiter" berichten. Erste Auswertung eines Oral-History-Projektes aus der Ostukraine', in *Hitlers Sklaven. Lebensgeschichtliche Analysen zur Zwangsarbeit im internationalen Vergleich*, ed. by Alexander von Plato, Almut Leh and Christoph Thonfeld (Vienna, Cologne, Weimar: Böhlau 2008), pp. 230–40, here p. 236.
66 Ulrike Goeken-Haidl, *Der Weg zurück. Die Repatriierung sowjetischer Kriegsgefangener und Zwangsarbeiter während und nach dem Zweiten Weltkrieg* (Essen: Klartext 2006), pp. 545–6.
67 Tetjana Pastuschenko, *Das Niederlassen von Repatriierten ist verboten ... Die Lage von ehemaligen Zwangsarbeiter/innen und Kriegsgefangenen in der Ukraine nach dem Krieg* (Kiev: Institut für Geschichte der Ukraine 2011), p. 130.
68 Irina Scherbakowa, 'Mündliche Zeugnisse zur Zwangsarbeit aus Rußland', in *Hitlers Sklaven*, ed. by Alexander von Plato, Almut Leh and Christoph Thonfeld, pp. 241–54, here p. 253.
69 Gelinada Grinchenko, 'Ehemalige "Ostarbeiter" berichten. Erste Auswertung eines Oral-History-Projektes aus der Ostukraine', in *Hitlers Sklaven*, ed. by Alexander von Plato, Almut Leh and Christoph Thonfeld, pp. 230–40, here p. 232.

70 Avgustina V., born 1927 in Ukraine, in Janet Anschütz and Irmtraud Heike, *Feinde im eigenen Land*, p. 173.
71 Wolfgang Jacobmeyer, *Vom Zwangsarbeiter zum Heimatlosen Ausländer. Die Displaced Persons in Westdeutschland 1945–1951* (Göttingen: Vandenhoeck & Ruprecht 1985), p. 85, p. 122, p. 139.
72 Ines Hopfer, Geraubte Identität. *Die gewaltsame 'Eindeutschung' von polnischen Kindern in der NS-Zeit* (Vienna, Cologne, Weimar: Böhlau 2010), p. 61; Mark Wyman, *DPs. Europe's Displaced Persons, 1945–1951* (Ithaca, London: Cornell University Press 1989), p. 93.
73 Johannes-Dieter Steinert, *Nach Holocaust und Zwangsarbeit. Britische humanitäre Hilfe in Deutschland. Die Helfer, die Befreiten und die Deutschen* (Osnabrück: Secolo 2007), pp. 140–3.

CHAPTER EIGHT

The Forced Relocation to the Krakow Ghetto as Remembered by Child Survivors

Joanna Sliwa

'Nothing that I remember was changing, except that the parents were ... talking about the gathering of the Jewish people to one place. But we, as children, have never paid any attention to it. Until it happened. When it came in 1941'.[1] That is how Paul Fajnwaks, a nine-year-old boy at the time, began his recollections of learning about a planned move from his apartment to another place in Krakow that was allotted specifically for Jews. Paul's parents did not explain anything to him nor to his eleven-year-old brother Jerzy and seven-year-old sister Frania. Paul did not even recall how they reached the ghetto. All he could remember some fifty years after the events was what happened once he entered it. 'We were gathered to a ghetto, which was totally surrounded by barbed wire poles, and some brick and cement blocks that were separating [us] from the total population of Krakow',[2] Paul continued his description of the new environment in which he was thrust together with his family. He explained how the physically confined space affected his emotional state at the time. 'And that's when I felt that we were put in a cage. And as a child at that time, I was very not comfortable.'[3] Paul had lived in German-occupied Krakow for a year and a half, and thus he and his family had already experienced numerous hardships imposed by the German regime against all Krakovians, and Jews in particular. Yet, it was the ghetto that for Paul signified the onset of persecution. Paul's testimony illuminates how children like him remembered and experienced the passage from a heavily regulated – yet still possessing some vestiges of normality – life in the city to their segregated existence in the closed Jewish district. This transition marked a major rupture in the youngsters' lives. The ghetto itself was a concept utterly foreign to children old enough to understand the changes. And for many, the ghetto embodied the defining moment of their wartime existence. This chapter explores children's recollections of their forced relocation into the ghetto of Krakow and examines the impact that such territorial shift exerted on young people's lives.[4] In doing so, the chapter also elucidates how the Krakow ghetto came into being and how it was organized spatially. The main focus is on the beginning stages of the ghetto's formation, from March to October 1941, and the ghettoization experience of Jewish children in German-occupied Poland in general, and in Krakow in particular.[5]

According to National Socialist law, Jewish children up to the age of fourteen were individuals unable to work, and racially inferior. Their young age, however, did not preclude them from participating in events as they unfolded; observing their surroundings; having their own memories and feelings; formulating their own interpretations of events; and responding to the conditions imposed on them, all while wielding very limited agency. Interestingly, children represent a group that is still under-researched.[6] Although children under the age of fourteen numbered nearly 1 million out of Poland's prewar Jewish population of more than 3 million, their wartime fate has long been relegated to the margins of scholarship.[7] An exploration of their experiences and recollections, however, yields much information about how the Holocaust progressed geographically and administratively; in Eastern Europe, the General Government, the Krakow District, and in its capital – the city of Krakow (where Jews numbered 56,000 among its 250,000 inhabitants).[8] By focusing on the situation of children in the Krakow ghetto, this chapter detaches itself from the overarching narrative that places the Warsaw and the Lodz ghettos at the epicentre of children's collective experience of ghettoization during the Holocaust. Indeed, those two ghettos were the largest in the General Government, and in the Warthegau, respectively, and are the best known, most documented and widely studied. However, they are not emblematic of what happened to the millions of other Jews, including children, in medium- and small-sized ghettos throughout German-occupied Poland.[9] While children in the Warsaw and Lodz ghettos shared certain experiences with their peers elsewhere, these also differed, due to the particular (prewar and wartime) life conditions, historical factors, demographic composition, as well as Jews' self-identity in various areas of occupied Poland.

Writing a history of Jewish children during the Second World War is fraught with its own challenges. Numerically, few child witnesses survived to tell their wartime stories, and many were too young to remember concrete occurrences. Chronicling the details of their lives during the war could expose children and their rescuers to danger, including death. Then too, what mattered to the Germans was the fact of eliminating Jewish children, not documenting their existence. Thus written and oral testimonies of child survivors are indispensable.¹⁰ The memories, feelings, thoughts, behaviour and actions can be ultimately recalled only by those who experienced it. Historian Joanna Michlic studied children's accounts in depth. She noted the durability and integrity of child survivors' recollections over time.¹¹ Used in conjunction with other evidence, such testimonies illuminate aspects of children's wartime lives that would otherwise pass unnoticed.

The present chapter draws upon accounts submitted by child survivors.¹² Their breadth and content depend on the time period when the testimony was collected and the agency that commissioned the project. For example, the *Central Committee of Jews in Poland* (*Centralny Komitet Żydów w Polsce*) collected written accounts from both adults and children in the immediate postwar years.¹³ Survivors' memories were then relatively unaffected by secondary knowledge.¹⁴ Later testimonials, although they contain subsequently acquired information, are nevertheless essential to glean from how child survivors have understood their wartime experiences over time. They often reveal memories of events and experiences that, for a multitude of reasons, had not been previously referenced.¹⁵ In particular, testimonies from the *Shoah Foundation Visual History Archive*, recorded over fifty years after the war, and critically examined in this chapter, offer a wealth of information about how child survivors remembered their wartime experiences, and how they processed them mentally.¹⁶ Any serious study of children's wartime experiences must take into account the children's own voices, and not only rely on adult recollections and official documentation written about them.

Paul Fajnwaks, whose personal story opened this chapter, probed the depths of his memory to summon his emotions, thoughts and actions when he lived in German-occupied Krakow. Although he had experienced what he called 'incidents' from his Polish Gentile peers, who pointed out his Jewishness already in the prewar years, the moment of moving into the ghetto was a formative event in his life. It stigmatized him as being different. Paul explained: 'It first went into me when we went into the ghetto, when we were gathered in the ghetto, and my parents had to wear – and everybody who was Jewish – the yellow stars'.¹⁷ Prior to that, Paul's identities as a youngster, Krakovian and Pole defined who he was in relation to others. The actual enclosure in the ghetto was an unexpected and shocking development for young Jewish Krakovians, like Paul.

Without access to timely and reliable information, Krakovian Jews depended on rumours. One such speculation concerned the creation of a closed Jewish district, similar to isolated living areas for Jews that the Germans established throughout the General Government. The order of the Governor of the Krakow District, Dr Otto Wächter, promulgated the opening of what the Germans called a *Jüdischer Wohnbezirk* (Jewish residential district) on 3 March 1941.¹⁸ The news spread with lightning speed. The announcement was published in newspapers and pasted throughout the city. This law explained that health and security reasons necessitated the separation of Jews from Krakow's non-Jewish population. In fact, the decree was also designed to solve the housing crisis that German officers encountered upon arriving in the city. Contemporary documents suggest that the ghetto fell under the jurisdiction of different authorities – such as the Office of the District Governor, City Commissar of Krakow and the Gestapo – possibly to disperse responsibility and avoid concentration of power. Despite its official name and legal rationalization, the 'Jewish residential district' in Krakow was nothing but a ghetto; an enclosed and guarded area, in which Jews were forcibly concentrated and secluded. This was a new notion for Jewish children.

'Mommy found out that there will be a ghetto in Krakow'.[19] With these words ten-year-old Dawid Wulf began his testimony for the postwar *Central Committee of Jews in Poland*. The formation of the ghetto marked a major shift in his life. Although he was unaware of what exactly a ghetto meant, he sensed its negative connotation, and before he could learn its meaning, he fled the city together with his parents. 'I was very young at the time, and I did not really understand what it meant, but I was very happy that instead of to the ghetto my mommy, daddy, and I went to Wiśnicz Nowy', a town located some fifty kilometres away from Krakow.[20] Dawid's story points to the different trajectories of Krakovian Jewish families in the wake of the creation of a ghetto in Krakow.

The recollections of children who entered the ghetto offer a glimpse of how the move progressed and what youngsters encountered in their new environment. Marcel Baral, a nine-year-old boy at the time, began his description of the next stage in his life: 'There was a decree that all Jews had to leave town and go to Podgórze across the river, the Vistula River, and that's where the Jews would be able to live freely. In fact, they would be protected against Polish antisemites'.[21] Presented this way, the ghetto ostensibly shielded Jews against their Gentile neighbours and allowed for the existence of a Jewish enclave. 'That was the official story'.[22] The Germans couched the creation of the ghetto as a sort of privilege for select Jews. Only Jews in possession of identity cards and work papers – as well as their spouses and children under fourteen years of age – were allowed to settle there.[23] Overall, 16,036 Jews applied for such permission.[24] Yet, not even 11,000 received it. The rest were either expelled, or, like Dawid Wulf and his parents, left the city without applying for entry permits to seek places where they could still live relatively freely, meaning outside the confines of a formal ghetto.

At the time of the ghetto's creation, the city's Jews knew of similar structures in other parts of the General Government.[25] While Krakow's ghetto fit into that process, it was also different than most other ghettos in German-occupied Poland. In Krakow, Jews were driven out of the historically Jewish quarter of Kazimierz, which was considered to be located too close to the headquarters of Hans Frank, Governor-General of occupied Poland, in the Wawel Castle.[26] To Frank, it was unfathomable to concentrate those whom he – and the ideology he subscribed to – deemed subhuman in proximity to the most representative sections of the city and to his stately residence. Frank also held grand plans for 'his' city. Motivated by 'aesthetic' reasons, Frank wanted to clear the city, considered Germanic in origin, of Jews.[27] Thus, the ghetto was located in a more remote section of Krakow, which was nevertheless close to Kazimierz and connected to it by two bridges. Podgórze, itself a mysterious place to a number of Jewish children, consisted of an area in which not too many Jews had lived before the war.[28] Such a location, on the outskirts of the city, abruptly removed Jews, including youngsters, from their homes, communal and religious institutions, and familiar surroundings, as well as their Gentile neighbours. Barbed wire and a brick wall that resembled Jewish tombstones marked the borders of the ghetto, as did bricked entranceways, doors, and windows that overlooked the 'Aryan side'. Four gates, on Plac Zgody, Traugutta Street, Limanowskiego –Lwowska Streets and Limanowskiego Street–Rynek Podgórski regulated human and vehicle traffic, and contact between Jews and Gentiles. The main entrance on Limanowskiego Street–Rynek Podgórski, the Germans labelled with a sign in Yiddish to further marginalize the city's Jewish inhabitants.[29] Bordered by the Vistula River to the north, Krzemionki (flint mines) to the south, railway tracks to the east, and the non-Jewish section of Podgórze to the west, the Germans had designated an area in which Jews were isolated and removed from the city centre.

In preparation for the forced relocation the German administration introduced a number of laws and new procedures. They limited Jewish presence beyond the ghetto walls to individuals with identity cards approved by the Krakow District Office. Wielding control over the number and type of the ghetto population, the *Arbeitsamt* (German Labour Office) became the new issuer of such documents.[30] In addition, tram stops were discontinued in the planned ghetto.[31] Also, Jews were ordered to obtain permits from the *Treuhand-Aussenstelle* (External Trust Agency) to transport their belongings.[32] Podgórze was divided into sections 'A' and 'B', with section 'A' consisting of some fifteen streets designated as a Jewish area and covering about twenty hectares.[33] The Germans transferred Gentile Poles from their former residencies in section 'A' to the formerly Jewish (*pożydowskie*) dwellings in Kazimierz. Jews were required to apply for apartments through the *Jewish Housing Office*. Those who failed to move into the ghetto by 20 March 1941 (the same deadline applied to Gentiles moving out of Podgórze) risked eviction and restriction to only twenty-five kilograms of their personal property. Gentiles complained about the German decision to move all the city's Jews to Podgórze due to logistical obstacles. The rector of St Joseph's parish deplored losing his followers.[34] Such objections went unanswered.

Only seventeen days were given for entry permit recipients to prepare for the move, pack their belongings, arrange for carts, and settle any business and personal matters in the city. Child survivors recalled that with experience living under German occupation for almost two years, some adults had acted with forethought. They sold their valuables to other Poles, thereby resisting the German policy of submitting household items and valuables, and entrusted other precious articles with Gentile acquaintances. What they loaded onto carts were the few items of daily use and furniture they were allowed or managed to take with them. Children took a couple of their prized possessions, like books and toys, although such things did not rank highly among parents' priorities. While a number of Jews made their own arrangements, the *Jewish Social Self-Help* (*Żydowska Samopomoc Społeczna*) provided assistance to the needy for transporting their belongings.[35] Caught in the midst of the moving fever, children experienced a profound loss, the full consequences of which they would understand only later. Certainly, with some household items confiscated and parts of (or entire) apartments requisitioned by the Germans in the beginning stages of the occupation, Jewish children had already experienced a sense of loss. Their physical move into another section of the city and into a new living place without the possibility of bringing all their possessions exacerbated children's feeling of privation. They were uprooted from their familiar environments and beloved homes, and stripped of their cherished items.

Predictably, the busiest time for the move occurred just before the decreed deadline. According to *Gazeta Żydowska*, the only Jewish newspaper the Germans allowed to be published in the General Government, despite the commotion, consternation and terror, 'Everywhere the moving proceeded in the greatest order, without rush or hampering traffic'.[36] Marcel Baral confirmed the newspaper's statement. He recalled how well the Jewish Council (which the Jews continued to call by the prewar name for the organized Jewish Community – *Gmina*) planned housing assignments: 'Everybody knew which room, which building, which street is allocated for them. It was in very orderly fashion. At least initially'.[37] Photographs and recordings of the Jews' expulsion reveal a string of people of all ages carrying things, pushing carts, and riding on horse-drawn wagons. Although the images do not portray actual responses of Gentile neighbours, some negative reactions were carved deeply into children's memories. Rena Ferber, who was twelve years old at the time, observed: 'We just walked, and the Polish people stood on the sidewalk and they were yelling "Good riddance!" "Go! Don't come back!"'[38] Verbal assaults were one response that the children remembered. Another was the profiteering opportunity that the move presented for peasants from the vicinity of Krakow. Janek Jablon, then ten years old, recalled that peasants came to the city to buy things from Jews for low prices, knowing Jews could not cart everything with them.[39]

While some children experienced the move to the ghetto as another act of discrimination accentuating their earlier experiences of social distance, others became now for the first time aware of the implications of discrimination and segregation. As Paul Fajnwaks acknowledged: 'That was the first time that I realized that we are different people from the others'.[40]

Geographically and physically isolated, Jewish youngsters recognized the limits of the circumscribed space they now inhabited. Left without any explanation, yet having learned not to ask questions, they had to cope with their confinement on their own. Restrained to the few streets and the clearly defined boundaries of the ghetto, Jewish children were disconnected from 'the other side of the wall' and the freedom they ascribed to it.[41] This confinement exacerbated their feeling of alienation from the outside world and instilled fear and anxiety. Paul Fajnwaks explained: 'And being surrounded by barbed wire, and not being able to go out to the other side of the street . . . all of a sudden it hit me that we are Jewish and that we are getting persecuted by the Germans, and I was very afraid of it'.[42]

Fajnwaks's feeling of Jewishness as a negative trait was common. While some children practised Judaism to maintain a familiar structure to their life, others began to question their faith, or the faith that seemed to isolate them from the rest of society. For example, during Passover, when Jews are forbidden to eat leavened food, Stella Müller, who was eleven or twelve years old at the time, mocked observant Jews by ostentatiously holding and pretending to be devouring a slice of bread.[43] She despised the Yiddish that she heard on the streets (and the language she was not familiar with), and was annoyed by Orthodox boys who showed their identity by keeping their *peyes* (side-curls). She distanced herself from the religion she perceived as having contributed to her isolation from the larger society, and seemed to warrant an inferior status. That way, Stella persuaded herself that she really did not deserve to be there. She was not like those religious people at all; she was different.

Children experienced estrangement in yet other ways. Upon entering the ghetto, youngsters were struck by their harsh living conditions. The crowded apartments and the congested, smelly and noisy streets were part of an alienating existence. They often did not resemble the orderly and pleasant appearance of streets where children's former homes were located, or which they frequented with their parents or guardians. The new living quarters were suffocating compared to the sometimes comfortable prewar homes that a number of children had lived in. Even for children who had been raised in the relatively small Jewish section of the city, with all its distinct sounds and smells, and in modest apartments, the ghetto felt like a foreign space.

With the exception of a few children who had either lived in Podgórze before the war, or whose relatives had lived there, youngsters and their families moved into a completely new area, where they had to share the space with strangers. The Germans crammed Jews into 288 residential buildings with 2,273 apartments and 3,148 rooms.[44] On average, forty-one people lived in each building, approximately five in every apartment, and about three people per each window.[45] Based on the Jewish Council's estimates of 1 May 1941, there were 10,873 Jews in the ghetto; 5,034 men (including 870 boys up to the age of twelve) and 5,839 women (including

912 girls up to the age of twelve).[46] Living conditions became even more unbearable when the Germans incorporated twenty-seven communes and parts of two municipalities into Krakow on 1 June 1941. Hans Frank was doing everything to concentrate the Jews in the few already active ghettos, and to avoid establishing new ones. On 21 October 1941, Frank officially prohibited the creation of new ghettos, thereby straining the limits of the Krakow ghetto.[47]

As of 14 October 1941, the official number of Krakow ghetto inhabitants reached 15,288.[48] At this point, the ghetto was bursting at its seams. To accommodate new arrivals, one-room dwellings now housed seven inhabitants, one-room apartments with kitchens housed ten people, two-room apartments housed fifteen to sixteen people, and three-room apartments housed twenty individuals.[49] To carve out some privacy, families partitioned rooms with sheets. Janina Fischler, who was eleven or twelve years old at the time, recalled the loss of privacy in every aspect of ghetto existence. In the dilapidated house without running water or a toilet that she lived in, the outhouse and communal water tap became sources of friction. Residents struggled for privacy amidst the hurried atmosphere and constant quarrels. The courtyard and the line to satisfying basic human needs also acquired a new function. It emerged as a place of exchanging information; a social sphere actually.[50]

Private and public matters became intertwined. The loss of basic human need for privacy exposed youngsters to adult behaviour and life situations that they would not have had witnessed in times of peace. The experience of ghettoization shocked children old enough to understand the changes. And it resulted in feelings that destroyed their childhood. For nine-year-old Celina Karp, the move into the ghetto shattered her sense of rootedness and violated her safety. 'Life changed completely. You lost, not that you ever had, a feeling of security, but as a child I did. And at that point I no longer had that sense of security. It was totally replaced by the beginnings of fear'.[51] The debilitating new surroundings – as well as the prevailing uncertainty and insecurity – instilled anxiety.

The harsh restrictions demanded that youngsters tread carefully within the space of the ghetto. Thus, many young children were confined to spending their days indoors. In essence, they became twice separated; from their non-Jewish peers on the 'Aryan side' and from their peers inside the ghetto. Parents, who performed forced labour during the day feared for their unattended offspring. Not every parent had the advantage of leaving their child with another adult, an older child, or in a care institution. Many among those children retreated into hiding. A 'hiding place', as defined by sociologist Marta Cobel-Tokarska in her study of hiding during the Holocaust in Poland, was 'a place which was assumed to be safer than the outside world, and in which an individual was supposed to remain invisible to the people who posed a threat to him or her'.[52] In the ghetto, many Jews created spaces within the spatially confined and legally restricted area to hide from the Germans' wrath. Hiding was a constant in the lives of many children in the Krakow ghetto and finding hiding places was an achievement in its own right. For some, their own dwellings in the ghetto served as short-term hiding places. They stayed in rooms until their parents returned from work. Then too, places throughout the apartment, and even the building itself, served as 'safe' nooks in case of sudden danger. Both adults and children thought of sometimes quite outrageous shelters, hoping that hiding in them would offer a chance for survival: behind cupboards, inside ovens, under tables, in attics and cellars, under heaps of potatoes or in laundry baskets. Parents instructed their children to remain silent and hide in case of commotion. Children, for their part, quickly understood that their lives depended on staying invisible. They knew, as did nine-year-old Luiza Gruner, that 'My job was to hide, not to be seen'.[53]

Instructed to remain invisible within the ghetto, children had few options for spending their time. Some were either allowed to go outdoors during the day, or forced by circumstances to spend the days in the street, or did so against their parents' warnings. Before the district was sealed, a number of children ventured to Krzemionki (which became part of the ghetto in April 1941), a site of flint stone mines. With practically no green areas in the ghetto, Krzemionki became a meeting place for young people, where they could experience relative freedom. As a former dumping ground, Krzemionki was hardly appropriate as a recreational space. But the Jewish Council described it as 'the only place where one can relax and enjoy the air away from the dusty streets'.[54] Yet, left without supervision during the day, children were sometimes exposed to danger; hence the Council looked unfavourably upon the children's presence there.

To the ghetto administration, children were a nuisance in the public sphere. One article in *Gazeta Żydowska* blamed youngsters for devastating the precious few green areas in the ghetto, and deplored that 'Unfortunately, some people, especially children, do not appreciate the useful green areas, and, crossing diagonally, they trample on the green areas and destroy the grass'.[55] The Jewish Council appealed to ghetto inhabitants to respect every inch of green. Outdoor play, associated with children's freedom and expression, might be a marker of childhood in times of peace. However, the few spots of public greenery in the ghetto served not to restore childhood by offering a place to play, but rather a way to beautify the ghetto.[56] In principal a common space; in practice it was off-limits particularly to children. Although the Council and the ghetto's sole media outlet, *Gazeta Żydowska*, focused on the negative aspects of children's use of public spaces, their concern might have resulted from the need to protect children against accidental dangers. It appears that to the Jewish Council, the children were better protected if hidden from the public purview (meaning from the Germans' sight), sheltered at home, or entrusted into the care of institutions created specifically for them.[57]

Despite the concerns of the ghetto's Jewish administration, youngsters continued to arrive to the ghetto. Not all children entered at the same time or in the same way. Exposed to life-threatening situations when hiding or passing as Gentiles on the 'Aryan side', many Jews paradoxically perceived the ghetto as the safest place to live. They reasoned that it was the only area the Germans formally (and specifically) sanctioned as a 'Jewish space' within the city.[58] Thus, many youngsters without official permits to live in the Krakow ghetto were either smuggled in or they sneaked in by themselves and joined their parents or relatives already there. With or without the help of a German guard, member of the Polish Blue Police, or Jewish policemen who guarded the perimeter of the ghetto, youngsters entered through an unguarded passageway, a hole in the ghetto wall, one of the ghetto gates, or under a barbed wire. The existence of those who sneaked in was rarely, if ever, recorded. Hence, their entire existence in the ghetto was clandestine. While some children sneaked in for an indefinite period of time, others entered temporarily because it appeared a safer alternative to other ghettos in the vicinity. Ironically, for a number of youngsters, the Krakow ghetto served as a refuge.

However, the ghetto was certainly no safe haven for Jewish children or any Jew for that matter. That became clear as it developed into a site of exploitation, persecution and killing. With the Germans' escalating capricious and organized violence, the ghetto's spatial structure acquired new meanings, too. Streets became sites of daily misery; courtyards turned into inconspicuous social spaces; particular buildings and their immediate surroundings emerged as coveted hiding places (such as the building of the Jewish Police); apartments lost their veneer of relative safety; the main square (Plac Zgody) assumed the role of a collection point for deportation; and the decreasing borders of the ghetto tightened the noose. If children experienced isolation, congestion, confusion, inferiority and terror upon entering the ghetto and in the beginning stages of the ghetto's existence, those feelings were exacerbated later. For many youngsters, the forced passage from the freedom of their homes into the confines of the ghetto signalled an end to their childhood and the onset of persecution. It also raised their awareness of being different.

Once inside the ghetto, children's lives changed completely. The most obvious change was the new reality of life in a spatially restricted area. Adults rarely, if ever, explained the circumstances to youngsters. Yet, young children sensed the pervading danger, and older ones soon experienced it. Children devised survival strategies on their own, or were prompted by their guardians to employ them. Their physical survival depended on staying invisible, hidden from public view. On the other hand, the survival of the Jewish people depended on recognizing the plight of its youngest members, thereby addressing the visibility of children in the landscape of the ghetto. This took various forms, from organizing daytime activities to assuring shelter. Physical survival was one mechanism; emotional survival was another. Once children realized their different status vis-à-vis other Poles, they either reconciled with and embraced their Jewish identity, or tried to reject it. Although these strategies did not guarantee children's survival, they sometimes offered an opportunity for temporary physical and psychological refuge.

This chapter examined how Jewish child survivors remembered and experienced their forced relocation into the Krakow ghetto. An analysis of that physical and emotional transition allows us to probe into the defining moment of many a Jewish child's Holocaust experience. Doing so elucidates a key, if often overlooked, aspect of ghettoization. In fact, it was not until many years after the events that child survivors were given a chance to ponder the meaning of one of the major shifts in their wartime lives. Those who were in the position to explain were few. According to the official reports prepared by Jewish organizations inside the Krakow ghetto, there were 2,500 children at the peak of the ghetto's existence, in December 1941.[59] In May 1945, the *Krakow Voivodship Commission* (*Wojewódzka Komisja Żydowska*) registered merely 500 child survivors under its care.[60] Not all of them endured the ghetto or even survived the war in Krakow. Therefore, the accounts of those few who experienced life in the Krakow ghetto are an invaluable source on how children like them remembered and interpreted not only their entry into the ghetto, but also their entire ghetto experience.

Notes

1 Faynwachs (Fajnwaks), Paul. Interview 14951. *Visual History Archive*. USC Shoah Foundation. 2013. Web. https://sfi.usc.edu/ (accessed 8 June 2015).

2 Ibid.

3 Ibid.

4 On how spatial dimension of a ghetto influenced behaviour during the Holocaust see: Barbara Engelking, *Holocaust and Memory. The Experience of the Holocaust and Its Consequences: An Investigation Based on Personal Narratives* (London/New York: Leicester University Press in association with the European Jewish Publication Society 2001), pp. 81–214.

5 The scholarship on the lives of Jewish children during the Holocaust has narrowed on two issues. On the one hand, scholars have focused on rescue of children and their fate in hiding: Ewa Kurek-Lesik, *Your Life is Worth Mine. How Polish Nuns Saved Hundreds of Jewish Children in German-Occupied Poland, 1939–1945* (New York: Hippocrene Books 1997); Nahum Bogner, *At the Mercy of Strangers. The Rescue of Jewish Children with Assumed Identities in Poland* (Jerusalem: Yad Vashem 2009). On the other hand, studies have centred on compiling documents about children and on the analysis of their accounts: *Archiwum Ringelbluma. Tom 2. Dzieci. Tajne Nauczanie w Getcie Warszawskim*, ed. by Ruta Sakowska (Warsaw: Wydawn, Naukowe PWN, Żydowski Instytut Historyczny 2001); Joanna B. Michlic, 'Jewish Children in Nazi-Occupied Poland. Early Post-War Recollections of Survival and Polish-Jewish Relations During the Holocaust', in *Yad Vashem's Search and Research Lectures and Papers* (Jerusalem: Yad Vashem 2008); Justyna

Kowalska-Leder, *Doświadczenie Zagłady z Pespektywy Dziecka w Polskiej Literaturze Dokumentu Osobistego* (Wrocław: Wydawn. Uniwersytetu Wrocławskiego 2009); Joanna B. Michlic, 'The Raw Memory of War. The Reading of Early Postwar Testimonies of Children in Dom Dziecka in Otwock', in *Yad Vashem Studies* (Jerusalem: Yad Vashem 2009); and the series *The Last Eyewitnesses: Children of the Holocaust Speak*. Jewish child life during the Holocaust in Poland emerges, too, in works on the postwar period: Emunah Nachmany Gafny, *Dividing Hearts. The Removal of Jewish Children from Gentile Families in Poland in the Immediate Post Holocaust Years* (Jerusalem: Yad Vashem 2009); Noemi Bażanowska, *To był mój dom. Zydowski Dom Dziecka w Krakowie w latach 1945–1957* (Krakow: Żydowski Instytut Historyczny 2011); Tara Zahra, *The Lost Children: Reconstructing Europe's Families after World War II* (Cambridge, MA: Harvard University Press 2011). Recent scholarship has examined children's wartime experiences based on case studies. Examples include: Hanna Schmidt-Holländer, 'Reinstating Normality: The Stabilizing Function of School in Jewish Ghettos in German-Occupied Poland', in *Zeitschrift für Genozidforschung. Alltag im Ghetto: Struturen, Ordnungen, Lebenswelt(en) im Blick neuer Forschung*, ed. by Stephan Lehnstaedt and Kristin Platt, vol. 1/2 (Issue 13, 2012), pp. 82–101; Martyna Grądzka, *Przerwane dzieciństwo. Losy dzieci Żydowskiego Domu Sierot przy ul. Dietla 64 w Krakowie podczas okupacji niemieckiej / A Broken Childhood. The Fate of the Children from the Jewish Orphanage at 64 Dietla Street in Cracow during the German Occupation* (Krakow: Wydawnictwo Wysoki Zamek 2012).

6 Such analytic works include: Debórah Dwork, *Children With A Star. Jewish Youth in Nazi Europe* (New Haven, CT: Yale University Press 1991); Lynn Nicholas, *Cruel World. The Children of Europe in the Nazi Web* (New York: A.A. Knopf 2005); Nicholas Stargardt, *Witnesses of War. Children's Lives Under the Nazis* (New York: Knopf 2006); Suzanne Vromen, *Hidden Children of the Holocaust. Belgian Nuns and Their Daring Rescue of Young Jews from the Nazis* (Oxford, New York: Oxford University Press 2008); Patricia Heberer, *Children During the Holocaust* (Lanham, MD: Alta Mira Press 2011).

7 Jacob Lestschinsky, *Crisis, Catastrophe and Survival* (New York: Institute of Jewish Affairs of the World Jewish Congress 1948), p. 60.

8 Little has been written about Jews in wartime Krakow. Aleksander Biberstein, *Zagłada żydów w Krakowie* (Krakow: Wydawn. Literackie 1985); Yael Peled, *Krakow ha-yehudit 1939–1943. Amidah, mahteret, ma'avaq* (Tel Aviv: Hakibbutz Hameuchdad 1992); Katarzyna Zimmerer, *Zamordowany Świat. Losy Żydów w Krakowie 1939–1945* (Krakow: Wydawn. Literackie 2004); Arin Sharif-Nassab, *Über-Lebensgeschichten: Der Holocaust in Krakau. Biographische Studien* (Innsbruck: Studienverlag 2005); Monika Bednarek, Edyta Gawron, Grzegorz Jeżowski, Barbara Zbroja and Katarzyna Zimmerer (eds), *Kraków: Czas okupacji 1939–1945* (Krakow: Muzeum Historyczne Miasta Krakowa 2010); Andrea Löw and Markus Roth, *Juden in Krakau unter deutscher Besatzung 1939–1945* (Göttingen: Wallstein 2011); Andrzej Chwalba, *Okupacyjny Kraków w latach 1939–1945* (Krakow: Wydawn. Literackie 2011); Anna Czocher, *W Okupowanym Krakowie. Codzienność*

polskich mieszkańców miasta 1939–1945 (Gdańsk: Wydawn. Oskar, Muzeum II Wojny Światowej 2011).

9   Recent studies on ghettoization include: Barbara Engelking and Jacek Leociak, *The Warsaw Ghetto. A Guide to the Perished City* (New Haven, CT: Yale University Press 2009); Guy Miron and Shlomit Shulhani (eds), *The Yad Vashem Encyclopedia of the Ghettos During the Holocaust* (Jerusalem: Yad Vashem 2010); Dan Michman, *The Emergence of Jewish Ghettos During the Holocaust* (New York: Cambridge University Press 2011); Martin Dean and Mel Hecker (eds), *The United States Holocaust Memorial Museum Encyclopedia of Camps and Ghettos 1939–1945*, vol. 2, *Ghettos in German-Occupied Eastern Europe* (Bloomington, IN: Indiana University Press in association with the US Holocaust Memorial Museum 2012).

10 Debórah Dwork, *Children With A Star,* pp. xvii–xlii.

11 Joanna B. Michlic, 'The Aftermath and After: Memories of Child Survivors of the Holocaust', in *Lessons and Legacies X. Back to the Sources: Reexamining Perpetrators, Victims, and Bystanders,* ed. by Sara R. Horowitz (Evanston, IL: Northwestern University Press 2012), pp. 141–89.

12 For studies on the use of oral testimonies see: Lawrence Langer, *Holocaust Testimonies: The Ruins of Memory* (New Haven, CT: Yale University Press 1991); Shoshana Felman and Dori Laub, *Testimony: Crises of Witnessing in Literature, Psychoanalysis, and History* (New York: Routledge 1991); Suzanne Kaplan, *Children in the Holocaust: Dealing with Affects and Memory Images in Trauma and Generational Linking* (Uppsala: Uppsala Programme for Holocaust and Genocide Studies, Uppsala University 2002); Daniel Baranowski, *Ich bin die Stimme der sechs Millionen: Das Videoarchiv im Ort der Information* (Berlin: Stiftung Denkmal für die Ermordeten Juden Europas 2009).

13 See Maria Hochberg-Mariańska and Noe Gruss (eds), *The Children Accuse* (Portland, OR: Vallentine Mitchell 1996); Feliks Tych, Alfons Kenkmann, Elisabeth Kohlhaas and Andreas Eberhardt (eds), *Kinder über den Holocaust: Frühe Zeugnisse 1944–1948* (Berlin: Metropol Verlag 2008); Laura Jockusch, *Collect and Record! Jewish Holocaust Documentation in Early Postwar Europe* (New York: Oxford University Press 2012).

14 With regard to immediate postwar testimonies see Joanna B. Michlic, 'The Raw Memory of War'; Alan Rosen, *The Wonder of Their Voices: The 1946 Holocaust Interviews of David Boder* (New York: Oxford University Press 2010).

15 Here I refer to the work of Dr Sharon Kangisser-Cohen at the Institute of Contemporary Jewry, Division of Oral History at the Hebrew University of Jerusalem, and especially to her study, *Testimony & Time: Holocaust Survivors Remember* (Jerusalem: Yad Vashem 2014).

16 For information about the Shoah Foundation collection, see Michael Berenbaum, 'Video History of the Holocaust: The Case of the Shoah Foundation', in *Humanity at the Limit: The Impact of the Holocaust Experience on Jews and Christians,* ed. by Michael A. Signer (Bloomington, IN: Indiana University Press 2000), pp. 348–54; Annette Wieviorka, *The Era of the Witness* (Ithaca, London: Cornell University Press 2006); Noah Shenker,

'Embodied Memory: The Formation of Archived Audiovisual Holocaust Testimony in the United States', Dissertation (University of Southern California 2009); Rachel Einwohner, 'Ethical Considerations on the Use of Archived Testimonies in Holocaust Research: Beyond the IRB Exemption', *Qualitative Sociology* 34/3 (2011), pp. 415–30.

17 Faynwachs, Paul. Interview 14951. *Visual History Archive*. USC Shoah Foundation. 2013. Web. Paul's statement serves as an example of how child survivors' recollections – when they concern technical details – can be corroborated with official documents. In Krakow, Jews over the age of twelve wore white armbands with a blue Star of David. 'Des Distriktchef von Krakau Wächter; Rozporządzenie o znamionowaniu żydów w okręgu Krakowa. 18. XI. 1939.' APKr [Archiwum Państwowe w Krakowie] J13922. Despite Paul's slip, the fact that Jews had to wear an external marking that identified them as such was true and stuck in his memory.

18 'Zarządzenie: utworzenie dzielnicy mieszkaniowej dla żydów w Krakowie', 3.III.1941. APKr J13922.

19 Relacje: Zeznania Ocalałych Żydów: Wulf Dawid. AŻIH [Archiwum Żydowskiego Instytutu Historycznego] 301/2314, p. 1.

20 Relacje: Zeznania Ocalałych Żydów: Wulf Dawid. AŻIH 301/2314, p. 1.

21 Baral, Martin (Marcel). Interview 1663. *Visual History Archive*. USC Shoah Foundation. 2013. Web.

22 Ibid.

23 As of 25 April 1941, the Germans halted issuing identity cards for Jews in Krakow altogether, thereby making their stay in the city illegal. 'Obwieszczenie Stadthauptmanna dotyczy: kart rozpoznawczych dla nie niemieckiej ludności. 25.IV.1941. Pavlu'. APKr. SMKr reel J13913, p. 599.

24 'Karty Żydów ubiegających się o pozostanie w getcie krakowskim, 1941'. AŻIH 218.III.

25 Lacking a central and firm ghettoization policy, the Krakow ghetto came into being relatively late. It comprised one of the 342 ghettos in the General Government, and one of the 71 ghettos in the Krakow District. These numbers are based on the path-breaking research done for the *USHMM Encyclopedia of Camps and Ghettos*. The Krakow ghetto was part of the second wave of ghettoization that occurred in the wake of German invasion of the Soviet Union on 22 June 1941.

26 Kazimierz was established as a town for both Jews and Gentiles in 1335. In 1800, it was incorporated as a district of Krakow. It was considered a 'Jewish district' due to the size of its Jewish population, and the Jewish character of businesses, sacral buildings and communal institutions.

27 David Silberklang, 'Ghettos: Establishment of Ghettos', *The YIVO Encyclopedia of Jews in Eastern Europe*. http://www.yivoencyclopedia.org/article.aspx/Ghettos/Establishment_of_Ghettos (accessed 19 August 2014).

28 Formerly a town, Podgórze was incorporated into Krakow in 1915. A separate Jewish community (*gmina*) existed in Podgórze until 1937, when it joined the main Krakow Jewish Community.

29 The Germans associated a ghetto with the image of *Ostjuden* (East European Jews) and their language, Yiddish. To unify the written language in the ghetto and to complicate life for Jews who were unfamiliar with Yiddish, the Germans ordered that beginning on 4 April 1941, all business signs in the ghetto be written in Yiddish, and Polish signs be removed by 10 May 1941. See 'Wiadomości z Krakowa: szyldy na przedsiębiorstwach żydowskich', *Gazeta Żydowska*, Nr 28, 8.IV.1941, p. 4. USHMM ITS [United States Holocaust Memorial Museum Archive] 1.2.7.2.8233100.0128; 'Wiadomości z Krakowa: Usunięcie szyldów i napisów polskich', *Gazeta Żydowska*, Nr 36, 6.V.1941, p. 3.

30 'Zarządzenie o wysiedleniu Żydów z obrębu miasta Krakowa. Wächter. 25.II.1941' and 'Obwieszczenie do zamieszkałych w Krakowie posiadaczy żydowskich kart rozpoznawczych', *Gazeta Żydowska*, Nr 17, 28.II.1941, p. 4. This switch signified a new role for the ghetto – as a pool of forced labour.

31 'Obwieszczenie dotyczące przystanków tramwajowych w dzielnicy Podgórze', handwritten note. APKr, PNN 41, p. 1593. Throughout the existence of the ghetto, locked trams for 'Aryans' ran through the area, stopping only outside of the ghetto perimeter.

32 'Przewóz rzeczy żydowskich w Krakowie', *Gazeta Żydowska*, Nr 17, 28.II.1941, p. 4.

33 'Wiadomości z Krakowa: Przydział mieszkań w dzielnicy żydowskiej', *Gazeta Żydowska*, Nr 20, 11.III.1941.

34 Biberstein, *Zagłada Żydów w Krakowie*, pp. 45–6; Taduesz Pankiewicz, *The Cracow Ghetto Pharmacy* (Washington, D.C.: USHMM 2000), p. 2. It is unclear if Christian Poles opposed the creation of a ghetto altogether and expressed their stance indirectly through the complaints mentioned above, or whether they were simply dissatisfied with the impediments the Germans hurled at them.

35 'Korespondencja Prezydium Ż.S.S z Komitetem Powiatowym Ż.S.S. w Krakowie', 13.III.1941. AŻIH 211/585.

36 'Wiadomości z Krakowa: Zakończenie akcji przesiedleńczej', *Gazeta Żydowska*, Nr 23, 21.III.1941, p. 4. USHMM ITS 1.2.7.2.8233100.0080.

37 Baral, Martin (Marcel). Interview 1663. *Visual History Archive*. USC Shoah Foundation. 2013. Web.

38 Finder (Ferber), Rena. Interview 21482. *Visual History Archive*. USC Shoah Foundation. 2013. Web.

39 Jablon, Ephroim (Janek). Interview 43451. *Visual History Archive*. USC Shoah Foundation. 2013. Web.

40 Faynwachs, Paul. Interview 14951. *Visual History Archive*. USC Shoah Foundation. 2013. Web.

41 A number of youngsters ventured out of the ghetto out of curiosity, to see familiar places on the 'Aryan side'. Others sneaked out to buy or barter for goods on the 'Aryan side' and smuggle them into the ghetto.

42 Faynwachs, Paul. Interview 14951. *Visual History Archive*. USC Shoah Foundation. 2013. Web.

43 Stella Müller-Madej, *Oczami Dziecka: wspomnienia z dzieciństwa w getcie i obozach koncentracyjnych* (Krakow: Nakład Autora 1991), p. 47.

44 Ten other buildings were allotted for non-residential purposes.

45 'Vermerk I: Betr.: Wohnungs- und Gesundheitsverhaeltnisse im Abschnitt "A" des juedischen Wohnbezirkes in Krakau'. 20.IX.1941. USHMM RG 15-245, pp. 39–97.0148-0150; 'Wiadomości z Krakowa: Zarządzenie. Przedmiot: Utworzenie dzielnicy mieszkaniowej dla żydów w Krakowie', *Gazeta Żydowska,* Nr 19, 7.III.1941; 'Wiadomości z Krakowa: Przydział mieszkań w dzielnicy żydowskiej', *Gazeta Żydowska*, Nr 20, 11.III.1941.

46 'Ludność Dzielnicy Żydowskiej w Krakowie według płci i wieku. Stan z 1.V.1941,' Gmina Żydowska Kraków, Biuro Ewidencji Ludności. APKr J13871, p. 1.

47 Werner Prag and Wolfgang Jacobmeyer (eds), *Das Diensttagebuch des deutschen Generalgouverneur in Polen, 1939–1945* (Stuttgart: Deutsche Verlags-Anstalt 1975), p. 386, p. 436; Dan Michman, *The Emergence of Jewish Ghettos*, p. 124.

48 'Prozentuales Verhaltniss der Wohnstubenzahl zur Einwohnerzahl im Judenwohnbezirk'. APKr reel J13871, p. 19; 'Die Belegung von Wohnstatten im Judenwohnbezirk. Stand vom 14 Oktober 1941'. APKr reel J13871, p. 21.

49 'Vermerk II: Betr.: Auffüllung des Abschnittes "A" des jüdischen Wohnbezirks in Krakau,' 13.X.1941. USHMM RG 15-245, pp. 39–97.0157-0158.

50 Janina Fischler-Martinho, *Have You Seen My Little Sister?* (London; Portland, OR: Vallentine Mitchell 1997), pp. 133–5.

51 Karp Biniaz, Celina. Interview 11133. *Visual History Archive*. USC Shoah Foundation. 2013. Web.

52 Marta Cobel-Tokarska, *Bezludna wyspa, nora, grób* (Warsaw: IPN 2012), p. 14.

53 Gruner Gans, Louise (Luiza). Interview 40851. *Visual History Archive*. USC Shoah Foundation. 2013.Web.

54 'Wiadomości z Krakowa: Szanujcie przyrodę!' *Gazeta Żydowska*, Nr 47, 13.VI.1941, p. 4. USHMM ITS 1.2.7.2.8233200.0019.

55 Ibid.

56 Among the issues that Zahra discusses in her book, *The Lost Children*, is the potential of play and various pedagogical approaches for restoring childhood in the postwar period (p. 9, pp. 88–117). For an in-depth discussion of play and the Holocaust, see George Eisen, *Children and Play in the Holocaust: Games among the Shadows* (Amherst, MA: The University of Massachusetts Press 1988).

57 The Department for Care for Children and Orphans (*Towarzystwo Opieki nad Dziećmi i Sierotami dawniej Centos*), the Jewish Orphanage, the Jewish Council, the Jewish Welfare Committee (*Żydowski Komitet Opiekuńczy Miejski w Krakowie*), and the Jewish Social Self-Help (*Żydowska Samopomoc Społeczna*) addressed the children's plight and dedicated spaces where youngsters could spend their days.

58 'Trzecie rozporządzenie o ograniczeniach pobytu w Generalnym Gubernatorstwie', *Verordnungsblatt für das Generalgovernement*. Nr. 99. 25 October 1941. With the imposition of Hans Frank's 'Third decree about limiting Jews' presence in the General Government' of 15 October 1941, Jews who left the ghetto without a permit risked the death penalty, as did Gentiles who assisted them.

59 Żydowska Samopomoc Społeczna, 'Protokół spotkania Żydowskiego Miejskiego Komitetu Opiekuńczego w dniu 17 grudnia 1941 r'. USHMM 1997 A.0124, reel 31.

60 Noemi Bażanowska, *To był mój dom*, p. 29.

CHAPTER NINE

The Fate of Children at the Majdanek Concentration Camp[1]

Marta Grudzińska (translated from the Polish by Małgorzata Paprota)[2]

This chapter examines the experiences of Jewish and non-Jewish children at the Majdanek concentration and extermination camp. It addresses the establishment, functions and operational scope of the camp, its confined environment from the perspective of children, their social relations with adult inmates, and chances for survival in the camp through labour, protection and humanitarian aid.

Konzentrationslager Lublin (KL Lublin), commonly referred to as Majdanek,[3] was established in the autumn of 1941 on the orders of Heinrich Himmler. The camp was constructed to the east of Lublin, in the immediate vicinity of the Lublin–Zamość road.[4] Its position and the surrounding flat terrain made the camp visible from almost all directions. The concept and layout of the camp were modified several times.[5] It eventually occupied an area of 270 hectares (2.7 square kilometres), comprising three parts: the SS sector, the administrative area and the prisoner area; this was divided into five compounds known as 'prisoner fields', with twenty-two barracks in each to house the prisoners.

Over the nearly four years of its existence, Majdanek changed its character several times. Established as a prisoner of war (POW) camp, it soon became a concentration camp while also serving as a penal camp, transit camp, labour camp and an extermination camp for Jews. Jews constituted the most numerous ethnic group among the prisoners, followed by Poles, Soviet Union nationals and Western Europeans.[6] Around 150,000 persons are estimated to have entered the camp; 78,000 of them are believed to have perished there.[7] There were four autonomous camps within Majdanek: a women's camp, a field hospital for disabled POWs, a camp for hostages and a *Wehrmacht* labour camp. Men were held in prisoner fields I, II, III and IV; women and children in field V. In September 1943, women were transferred from field V to field I, with men and the infirmary moved to field V.

Yet, throughout its operation, Majdanek retained the features of a provisional concentration camp. This is evidenced by the wooden stable-type barracks, easy to dismantle or destroy, and the lack of sanitation facilities for prisoners. It was only in late 1943 that most barracks were connected to water mains and a sanitary sewage system, with washing facilities and latrines installed.[8] The construction works were never completed, although they continued up until the evacuation of the camp in July 1944. The prisoners were held in the most rudimentary conditions throughout the existence of the camp. Jan Nowak, a Polish political prisoner, recalls: 'The conditions in that camp – there was mud, hunger. Mud I'd never seen before. Lice, bedbugs, fleas and near-death starvation. I have not seen similar conditions in any other camp, and I have been to as many as four'.[9]

In the first year of its operation, Majdanek was solely a men's camp; women were not interned there until October 1942.[10] The decision to establish a separate camp for female prisoners was taken by the second commandant of Majdanek, Otto Koegel,[11] but it was only on the order of the subsequent commandant, Arthur Hermann Florstedt, issued on 22 July 1943, that the women's camp (*Frauenkonzentrationslager*, or FKL) became a separate unit operating in one of the prisoner fields.[12] It was not, however, an independent body; it remained under the control of the camp's Command and was structurally interconnected with other units. The camp was staffed by female overseers trained at KL Ravensbrück.[13] The senior overseer (*Oberaufseherin*) of the women's camp throughout its operation was Elsa Ehrich.[14] Directly subordinate to the commandant, she was accountable to him for all issues concerning the female compound.[15] Hermine Braunsteiner was head of office[16] and other duties were performed by female overseers.[17] The so-called prisoner self-administration functioned alongside the SS guards.[18] Women prisoners were assigned a separate set of numbers. Their files were stored separately in the main camp office, although they were archived along the same rules as other files.[19]

When the FKL was at its planning stage and its exact location was being decided, a proposal was mooted in the *SS Main Economic and Administrative Department* (*Wirtschafts- und Verwaltungshauptamt*, WVHA) to create another camp in Majdanek's field V. This camp would house children from the Soviet Union who lost homes and families as a result of warfare or pacification operations.[20] The final decision on what would become of 'the children of bandits from the East' was taken by Himmler on 6 January 1943.[21] His order issued on that day stipulates that entire families be transported en masse from the Soviet Union to KL Lublin or Auschwitz, where 'racially worthless youngsters, both male and female', would be transferred to workshops or factories operating at the camps, where the children would not only work, but also be 'educated' and trained.[22] The education, according to the order, would instil in the children 'obedience, diligence, unconditional submission and honesty towards their German masters'.[23] Boys would learn the trade of a farm labourer, toolmaker, stonemason, carpenter or similar; girls, apart from farm labour, would be taught weaving, spinning and knitting; the children would also learn to count to 100 and recognize road signs.[24] On 21 January 1943, Himmler entrusted Oswald Pohl, head of WVHA, with the task of organizing such a camp.[25] Pohl ordered a children's camp to be established in Majdanek's field V,[26] most likely because this would not necessitate a separate camp to be organized, saving the trouble of another construction site. It was decided that the view from field V onto other fields should be blocked and the construction of teaching facilities should commence. These plans were, however, never implemented. As early as on 13 March 1943, the Concentration Camp Authority announced that 'the construction of a camp for children and minors at the Lublin concentration camp has been postponed owing to the need to carry out construction work'.[27] No steps were taken to establish a camp for these children elsewhere on Polish territory.

In the middle of May 1943, *Einsatzgruppe B*, operating in the middle part of the Eastern Front, proposed that children should not be separated from their mothers, because mothers would not decide to escape if this would mean leaving their children in the camp.[28] There are, however, no guidelines concerning Majdanek, where Belarusian children with their parents were interned starting from March 1943. They were placed in field V, although the separate section for minors had not materialized.

KL Lublin was an extermination camp for Jewish children and a transit camp for Polish and Belarusian ones.[29] At no time did the camp provide even minimally appropriate accommodation, sanitation or nutrition for its youngest inmates. The mass mortality of children, many of whom died as a result of illness either in the camp or shortly after leaving it, is therefore not surprising. One example of extreme malnutrition is Stanisław Kukiełka, a six-year-old boy deported from the Zamość region, who after several weeks in the camp weighed six kilograms, the average weight of a healthy three-month-old.[30]

Jewish children were transferred to KL Lublin after successive ghettos were liquidated;[31] Belarusian children were interned as part of punitive measures exacted on some regions of Belarus in retaliation for cooperation with partisans;[32] and Polish children were transported to the camp from areas where mass evictions or pacification operations took place, mainly from the Zamość region. There were also transports of people, including children, who were placed in the camp directly after being arrested. Prisoners were usually transported to Lublin by rail, in freight cattle wagons, while smaller groups were carried by lorries. Entire families of Poles from the Zamość region and of Jews from the liquidated ghettos were transported together in order to prevent escapes during the journey.³³ The dearth of source materials makes it difficult to establish with certainty the number of children arriving with each transport. Jewish children were often not recorded at all and killed directly after arriving at Majdanek; Polish and Belarusian children were entered only into their mother's clothing file, where the number of children was recorded, sometimes along with their names and ages.³⁴

The first families with children to arrive at Majdanek were Belarusians, who were interned as part of reprisals against the partisans operating in the area.³⁵ This was in accordance with Himmler's 6 January 1943 order, which stated that 'during actions against bandits ... men, women and children suspected of associating with bands [are] to be rounded up and transported to the camp in Lublin or Oświęcim ...'.³⁶ Belarusians, most of whom were children and women, were transported to Majdanek between spring 1943 and January 1944. They were moved from transit camps or prisons in Vitebsk, Minsk, Borisov, Kovel and Grodno.³⁷ The first group from Vitebsk, 769 women and children, aged between fifteen and sixty, was registered in the camp on 20 March 1943. The last group from the area which included children arrived from the prisons in Borisov and Minsk on 3 January 1944; eighteen children with their mothers were in the group.³⁸ Beata Siwek-Ciupak has established that between these dates, the camp received at least sixteen transports, in which children constituted some 11 per cent of arrivals, or almost 1,000 persons in a total of 8,000.³⁹

Jewish children were transported to Majdanek from successively liquidated ghettos. The first group of arrivals came from the Majdan Tatarski ghetto on 20 April 1942.⁴⁰ Wiesław Dobrowolski, a Jewish inmate at Majdanek at the time, recalls that around 1,200 persons were brought to the camp on that date; men, women and children, including some twenty infants.⁴¹ Those incapable of work, including children, were at the time taken to a forest in Krępiec, several kilometres away from the camp, and shot.⁴² A female Jewish prisoner who survived gives her account:

> In the camp they stuffed us all into several shacks, where we were so crowded that everyone was literally suspended in the air. ... I stood with my eight-year-old girl, I held her in my arms. ... The next day lorries arrived and the Nazis told people to get on them. Many rushed to get out of the stuffy shack as soon as possible. ... I saw the cars leave full and then, in a short time, come back empty. I saw the bodies of those who suffocated or died of exhaustion or heart attack also loaded on the lorries. The German counted quickly and added the living to the dead. That made me think, I realised all were being killed.⁴³

The surviving children from the Majdan Tatarski ghetto were brought to Majdanek and killed in its gas chambers on 9 November 1942.⁴⁴ The highest number of transports with Jewish children were sent to Majdanek in May 1943, after the liquidation of the Warsaw ghetto.⁴⁵ Between April and late

June 1943, the camp received Jews from the ghettos in Międzyrzec, Rejowiec, and from the so-called secondary ghettos in other towns of the Lublin region.[46] The last arrivals of Jewish children took place in August 1943, following the liquidation of the Białystok ghetto.[47]

Polish children with their families were placed at Majdanek as part of evictions and pacification operations, which aimed to clear the Zamość area of Polish families and make it available for resettlement by German farmers.[48] Before being deported, the families were held at transit camps in Zwierzyniec and Zamość.[49] Janina Buczek-Różańska, eleven years old at the time, recalls being transported to the camp:

> We were taken to wagons and carried to Biłgoraj. In the village of Puszcza Solska we were told to move over to trucks. After a two-hour drive we got off in a forest next to barracks fenced with barbed wire. We stayed there for a few days. One night we were taken out of the barracks and marched down the road. Shots kept being fired, there was constantly someone left behind. To this day I cannot fathom how elderly women could have walked ... or sick people, or children. We were loaded onto a freight train and locked. We were driven all day and not unloaded until Lublin. And again we walked, with the last of our strength. Many were killed and left on the road leading from Lublin to Majdanek.[50]

Eugenia Deskur-Dunin-Marcinkiewicz, a Polish political prisoner, reports that the people from the Zamość region were informed that:

> [t]hey were only at Majdanek temporarily ... on their way to their destination, which was land in a peaceful area of the country, promised to them by Germans. They were all to obtain land in return for the farms they abandoned. They were told the Russian is drawing in, burning everything, so Germans had to evacuate them ... They were told to take everything they had and could carry. They dragged heavy bundles with them all the way. They walked ... They took different roads, hiding from airplanes by day and walking by night ... That's how they reached Majdanek. All of them, although many left their homes already ill. Children down with fever ... Scarlet fever and typhus ... There were no medicines. They ate what they carried with them ... They shared their food with soldiers, with their guards ... Now they've been told to leave their bundles in the field, behind the wire fences.[51]

Some 9,000 persons, many of them children, were interned at Majdanek as a result of this operation.

Between late December 1943 and late March 1944, the so-called 'death transports' arrived in the camp from the Lublin Castle prison. There could be as many as forty persons, including children, in these groups; they were shot next to the crematorium. The last transport with children before the planned liquidation of the women's field at Majdanek which preceded the evacuation of the camp arrived on 24 February 1944 from the village of Huszlew in the Łosice poviate.[52] Persons from the Zamość region were interned at Majdanek as late as in June 1944.[53]

The survival of children was far more precarious than any other victim group. Many of them did not remain in Majdanek for longer than six months. They were removed for a number of reasons: they could not be deployed in factories, mines or munitions plants, nor were they a valuable asset for the German industry. In accordance with German policy, however, they could be used to increase the population of the Reich; therefore minors were usually transferred to Germanization camps. This was the case especially with Belarusian children, who were removed from their mothers at Majdanek, placed in separate barracks, and then transported to Konstantynów or other Germanization camps near Lodz. It is estimated that as many as three-quarters of families removed from the Zamość region who arrived in Majdanek were, after several weeks in the camp, sent to the Reich as forced labour. A small group among those removed from the camp were minors transferred to other camps and freed Polish children. For Jewish children, there was no way out of the camp, although there were some exceptions: a group of young children hidden among Belarusian children by women working in the camp hospital survived and were transferred to a camp near Lodz.[54] Minors who were considered adults and capable of work managed to leave the camp, as did two infants born in the camp in the winter of 1943, who remained in the camp in hiding; these were sent along with their mothers to KL Auschwitz-Birkenau in April 1944 when Majdanek was about to be evacuated. On 18 April 1944, two days after their arrival in Auschwitz-Birkenau, the Jewish women and their children perished in a gas chamber.[55]

Like all others arriving in Majdanek, children went through a 'rite' of induction into prisoner life: their personal effects along with luggage were taken away, they showered, and were then entered into the camp register. If a transport had a particularly high number of deportees, the inmates-to-be would wait to be formally admitted into the camp for as long as several days. They were held waiting in the selection square next to the bathhouse and the gas chambers or in an area between prisoner fields, with no regard for weather conditions and no food or drink.[56] With large transports of Jews, this was where initial selection took place, with men and children over fourteen separated from women and younger children. The elderly, the infirm and most of the children were sent to their deaths.[57] Children over fourteen or those who were able to pass off as such were counted amongst adults. To the author's knowledge the youngest Jewish child who passed the initial selection was Pinchas Gutter, aged eleven at the time, who was transported with his parents and twin sister from the Warsaw ghetto.[58] On occasion, women and children transferred from other camps or prisons were directly placed in a prisoner field and only later put through selection, after which they would shower, change into camp uniform and have prisoner badges attached.[59]

The induction into camp life continued through a type of 'cleansing'. Before bathing, the prisoners' hair was shaved off and the whole body was dipped in a concrete vat filled with a disinfectant. Piotr Kiriszczenko from Belarus, a child at the time, remembers women and girls crying as their hair was being shaved off. A former prisoner from Belarus, a young girl at the time, has similar memories:

> And I had two very long braids. I remember, Mrs Wrońska took me in her arms, held me, and I just [held onto – M.G.] these braids and wouldn't let them go. . . . Mrs Wrońska begged, said I had not a single insect in my head and she tells them 'Leave it'. But no, they cut the hair . . . but in that bathhouse they cut off my hair, I remember, I was sitting in the corner and they cut off my hair like that, and I cried so much, because I'd had two such long, beautiful braids.[60]

The bath was nothing more than a sprinkle in the showers. 'At bathing time, they hurried us, naked, into the room, pouring water which was scalding hot and then ice-cold', recalls Stanisław Kukiełka, a former prisoner who was six at the time: 'when this happened, there was terrible squealing and crying, and Germans looked in through the window and laughed'.[61] After the bath, the prisoners were marched to their barracks, where they were given clothing. Children did not wear the striped uniforms – they were allowed to wear their own clothes or given civilian garments left by other prisoners. Starting from October 1942, women and children were placed in field V, with the exception of some families from the Zamość region, who were placed in field III due to the overcrowding of the women's camp in the summer of 1943. In September 1943, the entire women's camp, along with children, was transported to field I, where it remained until Majdanek was liberated.[62]

As soon as prisoners entered the gate of their field for the first time, they became subjected to the regime of camp regulations. No exceptions were made for children. The wake-up call was at 3.00 am or 4.00 a.m during the spring and summer, and 5.00 a.m between September and April.[63] The prisoners had to dress quickly, make the plank beds, and have a quick breakfast, which was a mug of black, unsweetened ersatz coffee or a drink brewed from weeds. Occasionally, this was replaced by soup, which was water thickened with wholemeal flour.[64] The meals were ladled into rusty, battered tins, or tin mugs and bowls;[65] no spoons, forks, knives, or bottles for babies were issued. The tins, mugs and bowls not only served as tableware, but were also used for washing and laundry. The morning roll call started at 5.00 am between April and September and at 6.00 am in other months; no one, even the children, was exempt from it regardless of the season or weather. The prisoners were made to line up in neat rows on the roll call yard next to their barracks. One female barracks leader, writing about prisoners from the Zamość region, recalls:

> How do I 'make' these people, who have never been in a similar situation, line up? How do I explain to the elderly that it is absolutely impossible for anyone to stay in the barracks for the roll call? How do I 'make' parents take sick, feverish children to the yard in this weather? How???[66]

If any children, woken up too early and taken outdoors in the cold, rain or snow, started crying, they and their mothers would be beaten up by female overseers.[67] Daily life in the camp was extremely difficult for prisoners and even more so for children. After the roll call, prisoners formed work gangs and were marched to work. Many children worked within the camp, carrying or crushing stones.[68] To ensure extra food rations and care for Belarusian children, Helena Kurcyusz, a Polish political prisoner, organized work details for them: they cut lawns next to the SS barracks, carried sand, or cut turf from field IV and placed it on the slopes near field V blocks.[69] In the autumn of 1943, several dozen children were deployed at the broom and brush factory, part of the German industrial enterprise *Ostindustrie*.[70] Two hundred Jewish boys were placed with a work detail peeling potatoes and other vegetables. Children from the Zamość area were employed fertilizing the vegetable patch with ashes from the crematoria.[71]

The meal break started at 11.45 am. The inmates were issued a ladleful soup with no salt or fat, made from kale or pigweed in the summer and rotten swede in the winter. Work resumed at around 1.00 pm. The evening roll call commenced around 6.00 pm in the summer and 4.30 pm in the autumn and winter; it took two to three hours but could go on all night if a prisoner was missing or the camp regulations had been infringed.[72] After roll call, the evening meal consisted of a piece of sawdust bread and the same drink that accompanied breakfast. Twice a week this was supplemented with a slice of horse sausage, a little sugar beet marmalade or some margarine; occasionally the bread was replaced with unpeeled potatoes.[73]

Food was scarce, and entirely deficient in nutritional value. It was harmful not just for infants, but also for older children, who experienced stomach pains and bloody diarrhoea after eating. The desperate mothers would feed anything available to their babies, more often than not hastening their demise. Alina Paradowska, a Pole, testifies: 'I witnessed a barely alive mother from a Zamość area transport feed cabbage soup to a baby that was several months old, as there was nothing else for the baby to eat. Sadly, the baby did not survive this kind of food'.[74] Desperate youngsters rummaged in rubbish bins in search of mouldy bread or vegetable peel.[75] 'I knew all the rubbish bins, I knew where something to eat could be found', the then ten-year-old boy goes on to say.[76]

Children also looked for food in the dirt around the kitchen, picking out grains of cooked buckwheat or small leaves of cabbage left on the ground after soup had been spilled.[77] They were often punished by the SS guards for acquiring extra food: a boy who was found in the possession of a tomato was thrown by a guard into a cesspit and was not allowed to climb out.[78] In the winter of 1943, two boys were found to have obtained some carrots; they were punished with twenty-five lashes each and were made to stand at attention, holding carrots in their mouths, between the inner and outer barbed wire fence surrounding the prisoner fields until late at night.[79] Persistent hunger distorted the psychology of the children. Kiriszczenko recalls:

> After two months in the camp I became a completely different person. The tears disappeared. You wake up in the morning, you wake up your mate, and he's dead and you're not afraid of the dead body. If he had any bread, you'll take it and eat it, looking him in the face, and you're not afraid of anything.[80]

Ongoing malnutrition also affected how children were perceived in terms of gender and age. Henryka Ostrowska testifies:

> I can't [tell], because these children did not wear clothes. These children wore rags and that's why I can't tell you whether it was a girl or a boy, whether these were girls or boys. The kids' hair was closely shorn. They wore some dirty rags...[81]

Clothing gave the children no protection against the elements.[82] Wearing extra garments, or even paper underneath the clothes, evoked a sharp reaction from the SS guards.[83] The barracks in field V, where women and children were housed, were for the most part unsuited for their function as dwellings.[84] The temperature indoors was the same as outside. In February 1943 two small iron stoves were installed in each barrack; the fuel for these stoves was scarce.[85] The construction of wooden floors and three-level bunk beds started at the end of February and the beginning of March 1943.[86] Women and children slept on the floor before the bunk beds were installed, and when the barracks were overcrowded.[87] Pallets, filled with wood chips or chopped straw mixed with sand and soil, and blankets were distributed to prisoners several days or even weeks after they arrived in the camp.[88] In later years, the bunk beds were equipped with dirty pallets, blankets and bolsters, soiled with excrement and discharge from wounds and infested with vermin. The barracks were not connected to a sewage system and had no sanitation facilities whatsoever until the spring of 1943.[89] The lack of water made it impossible to wash or bathe babies or to launder their clothes or nappies.[90]

In terms of personal hygiene, the prisoners were not allowed any cleaning or grooming products like soap, toothbrushes, combs, towels or even toilet paper.[91] The women's field did not have even the most rudimentary toilet.[92]

By day, the prisoners used the cesspits, which were not shielded in any way; by night, when the prisoners were not allowed to leave the barracks, large wooden containers performed the function of a latrine. These containers, usually overflowing with excrement, exuded a noxious stench, compounded by the fact that the windows remained shut even in a heatwave.[93] It was only after the women's camp was transferred to field I in October 1943 that hygiene improved. The field was equipped with toilets and washbasins, enabling the prisoners to wash, launder clothing and fight insects.[94]

The sordid conditions and the insects, in particular an infestation of lice which spread infections, contributed to the propagation of scabies and other skin diseases.[95] Young children also suffered from other childhood diseases: whooping cough, chickenpox, measles and mumps.[96] To contain epidemics, separate barracks were organized for children ill with contagious diseases.[97] The women who looked after the young patients were usually Polish volunteers or Jewish nurses and doctors.[98] Apart from administering what treatments were available and looking after the sick, the female prisoners working at the camp hospital delivered babies and cared for them and their mothers after the birth.[99] There were no nappies or blankets for infants; they were wrapped in cellulose wrapping or paper bandages after bathing.[100]

The conditions in the barracks were at their worst when the camp was severely overcrowded, which was between May and July 1943. In field V barracks, bunk beds were pushed together by twos; five or six women and children slept in each. Due to overcrowding, some families from the Zamość region were moved to eleven barracks in field III,[101] but this did not alleviate the chaos in the camp. A block leader describes what went on:

> I tell the policewoman, who is bringing new people again, to pass onto the Office the message that there ARE NO MORE places in block 19. Not only are all the bunk beds occupied (by 3 people in each), but the rest, above the planned capacity of 600 people, are sleeping on the floor alongside the beds. I ask the Office to withhold any further people . . . In response, the Office sends me a large group . . .[102]

Thus, barracks intended for 600 persons had to house 1,575.[103] These were the conditions in which mothers and children from the Zamość region and some Belarusian mothers and children were held. The situation of the children from the Zamość region was more favourable in that they were not separated from their mothers.[104] Most Belarusian children were placed in separate barracks, where they were cared for by designated women; their mothers were allowed to contact them for one hour on Sundays.[105]

Particularly desperate was the plight of the Jewish children who were placed for brief periods in isolated barracks in field V at the time when transports from the liquidated ghettos were at their most frequent.[106] Stefania Błońska, a Pole, recalls:

It's hard to describe this, in the heat, in the stench, on the floor and what few beds there were, a crowd of women and tiny babies. I won't forget a mother ... who held her child, an infant, in her arms: the mother's forearm, the back and the bottom of the baby was one big wound. The most difficult kind, a laceration – a burn, from a shrapnel shell. . . . Filthy, undressed for days . . ., festering wounds.[107]

The barracks where the children were held at the end of August and beginning of September 1943 had no beds, blankets or water.[108] The children were not allowed to go to the latrines, so older ones would use the floor to defecate, while younger ones were constantly soiled with their own excrement.[109] These children were also hungry, for, according to the testimony of Krystyna Tarasiewicz, a Pole:

[Y]oung, starving, frightened kids – spent hours queuing in front of the soup pot, to get half a bowl of stinking cabbage soup or a swede. The handing out of soup was accompanied by squeals and crying. Younger, weak children were pushed to the end of the queue by older and stronger children, who stormed their way to the soup pot.[110]

Some very young children were incapable of eating the soup by themselves.[111] Mothers, realizing how bad the children's situation was, tried to provide some food to their children, risking their own lives, as recalled by Tarasiewicz:

Sometimes, after the evening roll call, when the *Lagerpolizei* were having their dinner, a mother managed to come closer to the fence to throw her child a piece of bread she procured, hear the child's desperate complaint, and see hopelessness in a feverish little face, pale and tearful.[112]

The children, knowing what fate awaited them, complained: 'Mum, I beg you, take me away from here wherever you want, I can't make it any longer', or warned their mothers: 'Mum, run away, here it's death, here it's death, run away quickly!'[113] These children were sent to gas chambers after a short stay in the camp. Marcin Gryta, a Polish political prisoner, remembers a transport he witnessed:

Suddenly from field V came a lorry, packed with girls aged 10 to 15. . . . These children were taken to the gas chamber. The children's crying and wailing filled the camp with such despair that many of us, who had seen ordeal before could not bear this. . . . I watched, breathless, the car of death stop before the bathhouse barracks. As the back of the lorry was emptied, the children were pushed off and viciously beaten; some were thrown to the ground like timber. The lorry went back to get another load of victims. When it passed by us again, a girl, having recognised her father among the onlookers frozen with horror, shouted: 'Daddy, save me!' The father collapsed.[114]

The primary form of immediate death was execution. Executions continued throughout the functioning of the camp, and were performed on minors who were earmarked for death during the pre-entry selection process as well as some of those who were admitted into the camp and entered into its records. Up until the autumn of 1942, when gas chambers started functioning, direct extermination was mostly achieved by shooting. Most children perished this way in April 1942, when the Jews from the Lublin ghetto were transported to the camp. The process of selection which preceded the execution is thus described by Dobrowolski:

> We stood in front of the main gate. Some high-ranking SS man ordered all the women and children, and men below 18 or over 45 years of age, to the left side of the road, and all other men to the right. The latter will be examined by a doctor and admitted to a labour camp; the former, along with women and children, will be transferred to another, lighter-regime camp, where work will be less hard. . . . Many claimed to be ill only in order not to be parted from their families, whatever fate awaited them. . . . Some 30 metres away from us there was a large group of a thousand persons, and every few moments somebody from my group ran over to the side of women and children.[115]

Instead of a 'lighter-regime' camp, that group was taken to the Krępiec forest and shot. In April 1942, around 1,500 women and children were shot in the forest.[116] Tadeusz Drabik, a resident of the village of Krępiec, witnessed the killings. He recalls that 'the shootings were done on groups or individual people over enormous ditches'.[117] Hidden in the thicket, he heard and saw the massacre: 'children and women, in particular women with babes in arms, fell into the ditch out of fear, even before shots rang out. . . . The German murderers threw grenades into the ditches to kill off any victims who remained alive'.[118]

The largest mass execution in the history of Majdanek took place on 3 November 1943, when around 18,000 prisoners of Jewish origin were shot.[119] Music was played from loudspeakers to drown out the sounds of the shooting.[120] The execution started around 6.00 am or 7.00 am in the morning, after all Jews from the camp and the Lublin sub-camps were gathered in field V. Feliks Siejwa, a Polish political prisoner, remembers:

> The hellish concert went on for eight hours without a pause, for eight hours death beat out a grim staccato. The Jewish masses marched to the rhythm of a devilish symphony from the sub-camps, from outside of the mother camp. The airstrip, the tailoring workshops, men, women, children. Jewish women and children were led out of field I. . .[121]

The supervisor of the crematorium, who watched from a distance of several dozen metres, testified:

> Part of the Jews gathered in field V were rushed into a single barracks, where they had to strip naked.... A row of armed policemen was positioned on either side of the way from the passage to the ditch. Naked Jews were made to run between these columns to the ditches. There, a Sonderkommando SS-man pushed 10 men into each ditch.... They had to lie down, and then Sonderkommando SS-men standing at the edge of the ditch shot them. Subsequent groups were made to run to the end of the ditch and there lie down on the bodies of those shot before them, so that the ditch would gradually fill up almost to the edge.[122]

The killing lasted until 5.00 pm. The SS personnel who operated the guns changed; the loudspeakers placed in cars continued to play music throughout.[123] According to many accounts of former prisoners and testimonies of Germans, all the Jewish children were killed on that day.[124] *SS-Hauptscharführer* Rieger, chief officer of the automobile workshops, describes the killings of children on that day:

> The worst happened when a group of mothers with small children had to lie down on the, still twitching, bodies in the ditch. The wretched women begged their murderers for mercy for the babies, not wanting them to drown in the blood pooling in the ditches, they held the babies up in the air, extending their lives by brief moments. SS-men put an end to their futile efforts with machine-gun bullets.[125]

This was not the only execution to take place near the crematorium behind field V. Since late 1943, the already mentioned 'death transports' arrived in Majdanek. There were also cases of SS personnel shooting people, including children, of their own accord.[126]

Once the gas chambers were in operation, asphyxiation with carbon monoxide or Zyklon B became the main form of exterminating Jews: pregnant women, children, elderly, and those incapable of work.[127] Prisoners were selected for gassing by camp commanders and doctors. Estera Gurfinkel, a Jewish woman, recalls:

> I had no idea what was going on with me. They started separating people again. The young here, the elderly and children there. I stayed alive only because my mother-in-law was there, she took them. ... I did not believe then and I could not believe that they were murdering children.[128]

Fathers, who could not take the children with them after the selection, left them in the care of the women in the family.[129] Those mothers who would not part with their children had them forcibly taken.[130] Lucina Domb, a former prisoner, testifies: 'What mother would surrender her child? Braunsteiner, Knoblich, Brigitte, the Bloody Brigitte, took them away with the help of dogs.

There were others. Children were torn from their mothers and thrown like stones'.[131] Jerzy Kwiatkowski, a Polish political prisoner, reports: 'A mother who will not surrender her child to be gassed may go to her death with the child. Many women decide to do that themselves – they choose to die with their child'.[132] Wanda Ossowska, a Polish woman, recalls the wife of Mosiek Kacenelebegen, who was gassed along with their three daughters because she and her husband promised to each other that they would not leave the children.[133] This was also the choice of Pfeffer's wife, who preferred to die with their child rather than have the privilege of living.[134] Every selection caused a dejected atmosphere in the camp. Kwiatkowski writes: 'I can still hear the crying and the laments – mothers are crying after their children; adult women are mourning their infirm, elderly mothers and fathers; husbands, whose wives would not part with their children, despair'.[135] There were cases of mothers driven mad, and fathers committing suicides, after having their children taken from them.[136]

After they were brought to the doors of the gas chambers, children were stripped naked, and then herded inside.[137] Kwiatkowski reports:

> [T]hey let in many more persons that the number of showers would indicate, so that a shower in these conditions was all but impossible. Despite that, they keep letting more and more people in; it's getting more and more crowded, finally, they are packed so tightly you can barely shut the door behind the last one. But water does not start flowing from the sprinklers; instead, small vents positioned in the ceiling leak the 'cyclone' gas. The SS-man looks through a peephole in the door and waits for the tangle of bodies to stop moving; then he shuts off the gas vents and switches the ventilators on.[138]

After the gas chambers were opened, the corpses were removed and transported to a site where they were burnt:

> They are taking out the bodies. . . . There is no force that could separate these two. . . . Oh, and those arms you won't open up. The arms of the mother embrace the child too tightly. Maybe she gave her breath to the tiny lips to make the child's life longer?[139]

There were cases of children being burnt alive, hanged, beaten to death, having their head smashed against walls or trees.[140] Several minors were murdered in the old crematorium.[141] Igor Newerly, a collaborator of Janusz Korczak from the Warsaw ghetto, recalls a group of Jewish boys, barely sane, who witnessed their colleagues being killed: 'The drunk SS-men started hanging them, just like that, for fun or for practice; several boys were hanged on wooden beams, others trembled, looking on from their bunk beds'.[142] Particularly cruel was the orderly G. Konietzny, as reported by a Polish female prisoner working at the hospital:

I remember a young woman in labour brought to the hospital by Konietzny, the orderly, a man devoid of any human feelings. Konietzny assisted in the labour, comforting the woman and sympathising with her suffering. After the baby was born and bathed, he took it in its arms and showed to the mother: 'look what a beautiful baby you bore'. When she asked to hold it in her arms, he gave it to her, and then brutally snatched it away, put it into a bag, naked, and cycled straight to the crematorium.[143]

The same man, while intoxicated with alcohol, explained to female prisoners that 'children were best burnt alive, because they suffer longer in the gas than adults', as reported by Ossowska.[144]

Hunger, as examined previously, was the most acute problem for children in the camp. Other prisoners responded to their famine by giving them food. Edward Dolecki, a Pole, recalls:

Poor mothers had to feed and raise these children with no drop of milk, in the most humiliating sanitary conditions. Unthinkable, so the prisoners come up with an idea: we must give up some of our food rations to save children and women. Each block runs a collection of donations.[145]

Another prisoner reported that: 'All my sugar, hardtack, eggs, etc., I gave away in five minutes to mothers with infants. My colleagues are doing the same'.[146] Similar situations occurred in the women's field. Kiriszczenko recalls: 'We would often run to the barracks where Polish people lived. You ask for bread, you burst in tears, you tell them about your despair. And so you get a tiny piece of bread, the size of a matchbox, so dear and tasty'.[147] After work, prisoners at Majdanek organized games for children and made toys for them out of rags and concrete; children were taught to read and write.[148] Female inmates employed at tailoring workshops made clothes for children born in the camp; they sewed shirts and nappies, and used offcuts of thick textiles to make shoes.[149]

The worst was the plight of Jewish children. Some were isolated from other prisoners, making it almost impossible to help them. Despite this, Polish women incarcerated in the camp came to their aid, risking their own lives. Brzosko-Mędryk writes:

Polish women, those who have left their children at home, and Polish girls, who do not yet know the challenge of motherhood, come up – despite the prohibition – to the fence of this children's ghetto to bring help. They introduce a little order, they pick the hungry ones, the shy ones, the ones too weak to push their way in front of the rest – so they all can have their share of the watery soup which deceives hunger. Then they sneak out children to their own blocks to wash and feed them.[150]

This account echoes her witness report, where she testifies:

> When the Jewish transport intensified . . . Jewish children were isolated in a separate block. Women prisoners acted to 'sneak out' the children and hide them from transports to gas chambers. . . . The leaders of these drives were Matylda Woliniewska, Stefania Błońska, Ewa Piwińska, Janina Bartosik and many others.[151]

Children received invaluable help from the women who worked at the camp infirmary. Risking their lives, these women hid orphaned children in the hospital to care for them there.[152] Women prisoners volunteered to work with the Belarusian children placed in the typhus barracks.[153] When the hospital became overcrowded and mothers had to take their children back to their barracks, the volunteers taught them how to administer treatments such as compresses or poultices and cupping therapy.

Despite their efforts and sacrifices, prisoners were unable to feed or clothe the hundreds, and sometimes even thousands, of children who passed through Majdanek. But an assessment of the help the children received can be found in the account of a boy from Belarus, who wrote: 'I owe my life to Monika. A loaf of bread was worth a gold ring in the camp. Just to think how much good she did for me . . ., to be precise – she saved my life and those of my friends'.[154] The people of the Lublin region, as well as charities, especially the *Polish Red Cross* and the *Central Welfare Council*, also rallied to help the children. Owing to their efforts, the German authorities allowed extra food to be collected and distributed among prisoners and released from the camp 2,196 Poles from the Zamość region in August 1943.[155] Those in good health were directed to villages near Lublin, while the sick were sent for treatment to the John of God and the Infant Jesus hospitals in Lublin.[156] Hospital records show that the children suffered chiefly from marasmus, acute enteritis, measles, chickenpox, scarlet fever and dysentery.[157] A nurse at the John of God hospital recalls: 'I remember one of the girls, nine-year-old Marysia, who, wrapped in a blanket, looked like a small bundle. She was too weak to stand or sit, she was unable to eat on her own'.[158] The extreme emaciation of the children hindered medical treatment. It was not only doctors who cared for the children; the people of the Lublin region also offered their assistance.[159] Food and clothing was brought to the hospitals daily; chemists donated medicines and nutrition supplements. Despite this, the mortality rate in the hospitals was very high.

Incarceration in the camp affected the mentality of those children who managed to survive. Henryk Wujec, who was two years old at the time of his internment in the camp, remembers that, after leaving the camp, he experienced fits of hysteria at the sight of a uniform.[160] Buczek-Różańska reports:

> I have had an acute fear of gunshots since then. Today, I can't, I can't, if someone was in this room, and took out a gun and took a shot at the

window, or in the air, then I, I don't think I could take it [emotion]. There's something left. I'm embarrassed to talk about it, but it's true. This fear. Then, I am sorry I'm crying, but I said I am this little girl, I am experiencing it all, I can see.[161]

Anna Brzezińska was unable to learn German at university because she associated the language with fear and commands in the camp.[162] In addition to these long-term psychological effects of imprisonment in Majdanek, there were many examples of families torn apart. Families separated during the war spent years after liberation searching for missing members. This was the experience of Włodzimierz Bułachow of Vitebsk in Belarus, who was separated from his mother and four siblings and sent to Konstantynów. The family was reunited only twenty-five years after the war.[163]

Since its beginning, the Majdanek concentration camp fulfilled many tasks which had not been planned for. The women's field, which functioned as part of the camp starting from October 1942, was inextricably connected with the history of children incarcerated there. The plan to create an autonomous children's camp was never implemented. No orders exist concerning transportation of minors to Majdanek or guidelines on their treatment. It is difficult to establish the basis on which they were brought to the camp or detained there. Children were placed in field V along with women; they were subjected to the same camp authorities as the women, and shared the same camp hospital and kitchen. The meals they received were devoid of nutrients; the clothes they were issued were suited neither for the season nor the children's ages. The most rudimentary living conditions, hunger and epidemics claimed the lives of many children. Jewish children under fourteen years of age were condemned to death immediately; those who managed to be admitted into the camp, also by lying about their age, were constantly under the threat of being selected for death.

Through the aid of other prisoners and the efforts of the *Polish Red Cross* and the *Central Welfare Council*, attempts were made to improve the plight of children in the camp. Regrettably, even those released from the camp in the summer of 1943 died of emaciation either immediately or not long after leaving the camp. As with many other victims of Nazi concentration camps, those who survived Majdanek were deeply affected by their experiences in the camp, and endured a long road to recovery well into their adult lives.

Notes

1   This chapter is a version of the author's Master's thesis in History, which has been updated with new research and reference material, shortened, and verified with respect to historical facts. The thesis was defended at the Catholic University of Lublin in 2001. See Archiwum Państwowego Muzeum na Majdanku (Archives of the State Museum at Majdanek, hereafter APMM),

Opracowania (Monographs), shelfmark XIV-6, v. 5, M. Grudzińska, *Losy dzieci w obozie koncentracyjnym na Majdanku 1942–1944* (*The Plight of Children at the Majdanek Concentration Camp 1942–1944*).

2 The editors acknowledge the generous support of the School of History, Philosophy, Political Science and International Relations at Victoria University of Wellington for funding Małgorzata Paprota to complete the translation of the chapter. We are also grateful to Karolina Piwowarczyk from the agency, Biuro Tłumaczeń Alpha, who handled the translation's logistics, and to Krystyna Duszniak who recommended the company.

3 The name Majdanek was only occasionally used in German records but was commonly utilized by the prisoners, the residents of the Lublin region and charities helping the inmates. The name derives from a district of Lublin adjacent to the camp. The formal name of the camp was 'Kriegsgefangenenlager der Waffen SS in Lublin' (KGL Lublin) until March 1943, and later 'Konzentrationslager der Waffen SS Lublin' (KL Lublin).

4 Józef Marszałek, 'Geneza i budowa obozu' ('The Establishment and Construction of the Camp'), in *Majdanek, 1941–1944*, ed. by Tadeusz Mencel (Lublin: Wydawnictwo Lubelskie 1991), p. 39; Józef Marszałek, *Majdanek, obóz koncentracyjny w Lublinie* (*Majdanek, the Concentration Camp in Lublin*) (Lublin: Interpress 1987), p. 17.

5 Józef Marszałek, 'Geneza i budowa obozu', in *Majdanek, 1941–1944*, ed. by Tadeusz Mencel, pp. 31–49; Tadeusz Mencel, 'Konzentrations i Vernichtungslager Lublin (1941–1944) – charakterystyka ogólna' ('Concentration and Extermination Camp Lublin 1941–1944 – General Description'), in ibid., p. 411.

6 Italian, German, French and Dutch nationals constituted a small percentage of the inmates.

7 Tomasz Kranz, 'Ewidencja zgonów i śmiertelność więźniów KL Lublin' ('Register of Deaths and Mortality Rates of KL Lublin Inmates'), *Zeszyty Majdanka* (*Majdanek Notebooks*) XXIII (2005), p. 45. The number of Jewish victims is estimated to be 59,000.

8 Tadeusz Mencel, 'Konzentrations i Vernichtungslager Lublin (1941–1944)', in *Majdanek, 1941–1944*, ed. by Tadeusz Mencel, p. 419.

9 Józef Musioł, *Świadkowie* (*Witnesses*) (Katowice: Śląsk 1979), p. 13.

10 Zofia Murawska, 'Kobiety w obozie koncentracyjnym na Majdanku' ('Women at the Majdanek Concentration Camp'), *Zeszyty Majdanka* IV (1969), p. 94.

11 Ibid., p. 93.

12 Zofia Murawska, 'Organizacja' ('Organization'), in *Majdanek 1941–1944*, ed. by Tadeusz Mencel, p. 85.

13 Zofia Murawska, 'Kobiety w obozie koncentracyjnym na Majdanku', p. 98.

14 Ibid., p. 99.

15 Ibid. She was a ruthless woman who abused prisoners. She usually carried a whip or a cane, and used them on female inmates for the slightest reason. She was eager to select women and children inmates for the gas chambers.

'Zbrodniarze z Majdanka przed sądem' ('Majdanek Criminals on Trial'), in *Majdanek 1941–1944*, ed. by Tadeusz Mencel, p. 427; Elsa Ehrich was the only member of the female personnel to be sentenced to death in 1948.

16 After the war, Hermine Braunsteiner left for New York, where she married and changed her surname to Ryan. In 1973 she was stripped of American citizenship, arrested and deported to the Federal Republic of Germany. She was released on bail in 1976. In 1981, a court in Düsseldorf sentenced her to life imprisonment. Braunsteiner's activity was not limited to office work; she willingly took part in selections, whipped prisoners, and even set dogs on them. Zofia Murawska, 'Kobiety w obozie koncentracyjnym na Majdanku', p. 102.

17 A particularly sadistic overseer was Hildegarde Lächert, known as 'Bloody Birgitte'. She beat prisoners with a stick, wooden boards, a whip and an iron pipe; she would throw bricks at them; she also participated in selections. Other cruel overseers included Marthe Ulbricht, dubbed 'Ny-ny'; Charlotte Weber, 'the Ant'; Luize Danz; Alice Orlowski; and another overseer known as 'Rosmari'. Out of twenty-five female overseers, three who worked at Majdanek were convicted in the trial of Auschwitz-Birkenau staff in 1947: Danz was sentenced to life imprisonment, while Orlowski and Lächert received terms of fifteen years in prison. Orlowski and Lächert were released from prison in 1956, Danz a year later. Four overseers were tried in Polish courts in 1948–9 for crimes committed at KL Lublin; the highest sentence handed by that court was twelve years' imprisonment. A court in Düsseldorf sentenced Lächert to twelve years in prison and acquitted three other overseers: Hermina Boettcher, Charlotte Meyer and Rosa Süs; Orlowski died before the end of the trial. Appendix: 'Funkcjonariusze obozu przed sądami' ('Camp Personnel on Trial'), in *Majdanek 1941–1944*, ed. by Tadeusz Mencel, pp. 463–9; Zofia Murawska, 'Organizacja', in *Majdanek 1941–1944*, ed. by Tadeusz Mencel, p. 86.

18 Zofia Murawska, 'Kobiety w obozie koncentracyjnym na Majdanku', p. 103.

19 Ibid., p. 99. The numbers received by the prisoners did not exceed 20,000. The numbers of prisoners who died, were released or transferred were reused for new arrivals. Zofia Leszczyńska, 'Sposoby ewidencji więźniów w obozie koncentracyjnym na Majdanku' ('Ways of Registering Prisoners at the Majdanek Concentration Camp'), *Zeszyty Majdanka* VIII (1975), pp. 38–9.

20 Zofia Murawska, 'Dzieci w obozie koncentracyjnym na Majdanku' ('Children at the Majdanek Concentration Camp'), *Zeszyty Majdanka* vol. V (1971), p. 141; Zofia Murawska, 'Organizacja', in *Majdanek 1941–1944*, ed. by Tadeusz Mencel, p. 87.

21 Ibid.; Rozkaz Himmlera z dn. 6.01.1943 r. dotyczący wychowania tzw. 'dzieci band' (Order of Heinrich Himmler from 6.01.1943 concerning the education of the so-called 'children of bands'), in Roman Hrabar, *Na rozkaz i bez rozkazu. Sto i jeden wybranych dowodów hitlerowskiego ludobójstwa na dzieciach* (*Following Orders, Acting Without Orders. 101 Selected Pieces of Evidence to Nazi Genocide on Children*) (Katowice: Śląsk 1968), p. 117.

22 Ibid.

23 Ibid.
24 Ibid.
25 Zofia Murawska, 'Organizacja', in *Majdanek 1941–1944*, ed. by Tadeusz Mencel, p. 87.
26 Dowód nr 14 (Evidence 14), in Roman Hrabar, *Na rozkaz i bez rozkazu*, p. 129; Zofia Murawska, 'Organizacja', in *Majdanek 1941–1944*, ed. by Tadeusz Mencel, p. 87.
27 Dowód nr 14, ibid.; Zofia Murawska, 'Organizacja', in *Majdanek 1941–1944*, ed. by Tadeusz Mencel, p. 88.
28 Ibid.
29 Zofia Murawska, 'Dzieci w obozie koncentracyjnym na Majdanku' ('Children at the Majdanek Concentration Camp'), in *Zbrodnie hitlerowskie na dzieciach i młodzieży polskiej 1939–1945* (*Nazi Crimes on Polish Children and Youths 1939–1945*) (Warsaw: Wydawn. Prawnicze 1969), p. 43; Tomasz Kranz, 'Eksterminacja Żydów na Majdanku i rola obozu w realizacji "Akcji Reinhardt"' ('Extermination of Jews at Majdanek and the Role of the Camp in the Implementation of "Operation Reinhard"'), *Zeszyty Majdanka* vol. XXII (2003); Tomasz Kranz, *Extermination of Jews at the Majdanek Concentration Camp* (Lublin: Państwowe Muzeum na Majdanku 2007), pp. 32–9.
30 APMM, Pamiętniki, relacje, ankiety byłych więźniów (Memoirs, Reports, Interviews of Former Prisoners), shelfmark VII/M-380, S. Kukiełka, p. 1.
31 On Jewish children, see Barbara Schwindt, 'Dzieci żydowskie w obozie koncentracyjnym na Majdanku' ('Jewish Children at the Majdanek Concentration Camp'), *Zeszyty Majdanka* XXII (2003), pp. 57–76.
32 Beata Siwek-Ciupak, 'Więźniowie białoruscy w obozie koncentracyjnym na Majdanku' ('Belarusian Prisoners at the Majdanek Concentration Camp'), *Zeszyty Majdanka* XXII (2005), pp. 197–227.
33 Zofia Leszczyńska, 'Transporty więźniów do obozu na Majdanku' ('Transports of Prisoners to the Majdanek Concentration Camp'), *Zeszyty Majdanka* IV (1969), p. 178; Zofia Murawska, 'System strzeżenia i sposoby izolacji więźniów w obozie koncentracyjnym na Majdanku' ('The System of Guarding Prisoners and Ways of Isolating them at the Majdanek Concentration Camp'), *Zeszyty Majdanka* I (1965), p. 97.
34 See APMM, Administracja KL Lublin 1941–1944, shelfmark Id6, Wykazy rzeczy odebranych więźniom (Registers of Items Sequestered from Prisoners) – Effektenkammerverzeichnis, 27, pp. 37, 48.
35 For more on this issue see Beata Siwek-Ciupak, 'Więźniowie białoruscy w obozie koncentracyjnym na Majdanku', pp. 197–227.
36 Rozkaz Himmlera z dn. 6.01.1943 r. dotyczący wychowania tzw. 'dzieci band', in Roman Hrabar, *Na rozkaz i bez rozkazu*, p. 117. The town of Oświęcim was incorporated into the Reich during the Second World War; Auschwitz was its name in German.
37 Danuta Brzosko-Mędryk, *Matylda* (Warsaw: Wydawn. Ministerstwa Obrony Narodowej 1970), p. 27; Zofia Pawłowska, 'Pole kobiet' ('The Women's Field'), in *Przeżyli Majdanek. Wspomnienia byłych więźniów obozu koncentracyjnego na*

Majdanku (*Memories of Former Inmates of the Majdanek Concentration Camp*), ed. by Rajca Czesław and Anna Wiśniewska (Lublin: Państwowe Muzeum na Majdanku 1980), p. 172; Piotr Kiriszczenko, 'Transporty z Białorusi' ('Transports from Belarus'), ibid., p. 199; Matylda Woliniewska, 'Przeciw przemocy' ('Against Violence'), in *My z Majdanka. Wspomnienia byłych więźniarek* (*We of Majdanek. Recollections of Women, Former Prisoners*), ed. by Krystyna Tarasiewicz (Lublin: Wydawn. Lubelskie 1988), p. 16; Helena Kurcyusz, 'Komando dziecięce' ('The Children's Commando'), ibid., p. 189.

38   See APMM, Administracja KL Lublin 1941–1944, shelfmark Id 16, Doniesienia obozu kobiecego o nowych transportach więźniarek (Reports of the Female Camp on New Transports of Prisoners), pp. 2–9; APMM, Centralna Opieka Podziemna OPUS (Central Underground Care Division, hereafter OPUS), shelfmark XII-11, Notatki Marii Rosner z pobytu na Majdanku (Maria Rosner's Notes from her Time at Majdanek). 1943–1944, p. 7; APMM: Zbiór fotokopii i kserokopii (Collection of Photocopies and Xerox Copies), shelfmark XIX-597, Zawiadomienia oddziału Politycznego do Magazynu Odzieżowego z 13.5.1943 r. (The Memos of the Political Division to the Clothing Warehouse), p. 17, p. 23; Stefania Perzanowska, *Gdy myśli do Majdanka wracają* (Lublin: Wydawnictwo Lubelskie 1970), pp. 64–5. Maria Pych, 'Fluchtverdächtig', in *Jesteśmy świadkami. Pamiętniki więźniów Majdanka* (*We are Witnesses. The Memoirs of Majdanek Prisoners*), ed. by Rajca Czesław, Anna Wiśniewska and Elżbieta Rosiak (Lublin: Wydawnictwo lubelskie 1969), p. 267; Zofia Leszczyńska, 'Transporty więźniów do obozu na Majdanku', p. 228; Zofia Murawska, 'Kobiety w obozie koncentracyjnym na Majdanku', p. 116; Zofia Murawska-Gryń, 'Dzieci w hitlerowskich obozach koncentracyjnych' ('Children at Nazi Concentration Camps'), *Zeszyty Majdanka* vol. X (1980), p. 6; Zofia Leszczyńska, 'Transporty i stany liczbowe obozu', in *Majdanek 1941–1944*, ed. by Tadeusz Mencel, p. 113; Zofia Leszczyńska, 'Transporty więźniów do obozu na Majdanku', p. 228.

39   Beata Siwek-Ciupak, 'Więźniowie białoruscy w obozie koncentracyjnym na Majdanku', p. 207.

40   'Zeznania szefa krematorium Ericha Muhsfeldta na temat byłego obozu koncentracyjnego w Lublinie' ('The Testimony of the Head Officer of the Crematorium, Erich Musfeld, on the Former Concentration Camp in Lublin'), ed. by A. Żmijewska-Wiśniewska, *Zeszyty Majdanka* I (1965), p. 139.

41   Ibid.

42   APMM, Zbiór nagrań audio (Collection of Audio Recordings), shelfmark VIII-559, Jerzy Gągoł; Robert Kuwałek, 'Żydzi lubelscy w obozie koncentracyjnym na Majdanku' ('Lublin Jews at the Majdanek Concentration Camp'), *Zeszyty Majdanka* XXII (2003), p. 82; 'Zbrodnie w lesie Krępieckim w świetle zeznań świadków' ('The Crimes in the Krępiec Forest in Witness Statements'), ibid., pp. 277–306.

43   Anna Bach, 'Żydzi z Lublina na Majdanku' ('Lublin Jews at Majdanek'), in *Majdanek. Obóz koncentracyjny w relacjach więźniów i świadków* (*Majdanek. The Concentration Camp in the Accounts of Prisoners and Witnesses*), ed. by Marta Grudzińska (Lublin: Państwowe Muzeum na Majdanku 2011), pp. 21–3. Owing to the efforts of the Head of the *Judenrat*, Dr Marek Alten,

she was released from the camp after several days as an employee of the *Judenrat*. She lost her parents and two sisters at Majdanek. She managed to escape from the ghetto with her daughter before it was liquidated. She hid in Lublin and then in Warsaw using 'Aryan' documents.

44 Julia Celińska, 'Opowiadania kucharza' ('The Cook's Tales'), ibid. The author describes her first moments at Majdanek: 'Just after we arrived at Majdanek, segregation took place in the field. The old, the young and children were separated. Three of the women at the square would not give up their children. One was the former wife of my current husband, Cukierman Fela, who would not let go of the hand of her four-year-old boy, the second was Bromberg Dora, who would not part with her six-year-old boy, and the third was the wife of a furrier from Lublin, whose name I can't remember and who would not be parted from her child at any cost. All these women were removed to one side, given a beating as others looked on and battered to death. Their children, forcibly taken from them, shared the fate of all the others'. See also Symcha Turkieltaub, 'Uśmiercanie w komorze gazowej' ('Killing in the Gas Chamber'), ibid., p. 36.

45 These transports arrived daily in groups which could reach several hundred persons each. It is estimated that around 20,000 persons arrived in Majdanek in this way. Tomasz Kranz, *Extermination of Jews at the Majdanek Concentration Camp*, p. 29; Jerzy Kwiatkowski, *485 dni na Majdanku (485 days at Majdanek)* (Lublin: Wydawnictwo Lubelskie 1966), p. 110; Tamary Szapiro, 'Samobójstwa, Selekcje' ('Suicides, Selections'), in *Dokumenty zbrodni i męczeństwa (Testimony to Crime and Martyrdom)*, ed. by Michał Borwicz (Kraków: Centralny Komitet Żydów Polskich 1945), p. 71.

46 Zofia Leszczyńska, 'Transporty więźniów do obozu na Majdanku', p. 106.

47 It has been established that 6,500 persons were interned at Majdanek as a result. Tomasz Kranz, *Extermination of Jews at the Majdanek Concentration Camp*, p. 29.

48 For more on this, see Janina Kiełboń, *Wysiedleńcy z Zamojszczyzny w obozie koncentracyjnym na Majdanku 1943 (Exiles from the Zamość Region at the Majdanek Concentration Camp 1943)* (Lublin: Państwowe Muzeum na Majdanku 2006).

49 APMM, Pamiętniki, relacje, ankiety byłych więźniów, shelfmark VII-135, Ankiety byłych więźniów Majdanka (Questionnaires of Former Majdanek Prisoners); ibid., np. B-424 Brodziak Kazimierz, B-483 Borowiec Władysław.

50 Janina Buczek-Różańska, 'Wysiedleni z Zamojszczyzny' ('Exiles from the Zamość Region'), in *Majdanek. Obóz koncentracyjny*, ed. by Marta Grudzińska, p. 28.

51 APMM, Pamiętniki, relacje, ankiety byłych więźniów, shelfmark VII/M-688, Eugenia Deskur-Dunin-Marcinkiewicz, *Kandydat do wspólnego stołu wolnych demokratycznych narodów (A Candidate to Sit at the Table of Free Democratic Nations)*, p. 59.

52 Zofia Leszczyńska, 'Transporty więźniów do obozu na Majdanku', p. 230; Zofia Murawska-Gryń, 'Dzieci w hitlerowskich obozach koncentracyjnych', p. 7.

53 APMM holds 129 questionnaires completed by persons born after 1930 and interned in the camp at the time. See APMM, Pamiętniki, relacje, ankiety byłych więźniów, shelfmark VII-135.

54 'In the morning, overseer Ehrich came to the infirmary with a few SS-men. She summoned the block leader and asked how many Jewish children we had. Hania Fularska, the then block leader, was ill and running a high fever, and, befuddled, gave her a number.... We immediately realised that Hania either gave her a lower than true number, or made a mistake. We were bewildered: what should we do? We wouldn't give up the several unaccounted-for children, because there really were a few more. We had a frantic discussion about which ones would be easiest to hide and how to organise it.... The Russian children in the infirmary did not breathe a word, although they knew perfectly well what was happening. The Jewish children hidden amongst them shared their fate – they were all transported to the children's camp near Lodz', recalls Wiesława Grzegorzewska-Nowosławska. Wiesława Grzegorzewska-Nowosławska, 'Poczucie wspólnoty' ('A Sense of Community'), in *My z Majdanka*, ed. by Krystyna Tarasiewicz, p. 83.

55 Zofia Murawska, 'Kobiety w obozie koncentracyjnym na Majdanku', p. 164.

56 Ibid., p. 124.

57 Zofia Murawska-Gryń, 'Dzieci w hitlerowskich obozach koncentracyjnych', p. 143; Barbara Schwindt, 'Dzieci żydowskie w obozie koncentracyjnym na Majdanku', p. 62–3.

58 APMM, Zbiór nagrań video (Video Recordings), shelfmark XXII-530, Pinchas Gutter. See also Holocaust Survivor Pinchas Gutter Testimony: http://www.youtube.com/watch?v=H1mfybmZxgI (accessed 24 October 2013). He lost his closest family in the preliminary selection in the camp.

59 APMM, Pamiętniki, relacje, ankiety byłych więźniów, shelfmark VII/M-688, Eugenia Deskur-Dunin-Marcinkiewicz, *Kandydat do wspólnego stołu wolnych demokratycznych narodów*, p. 32; Jerzy Kwiatkowski, *485 dni na Majdanku*, p. 164.

60 APMM, Zbiór nagrań video, shelfmark XXII-202, Mieszkańcy Bidaczowa, Julia Strzałka.

61 APMM, Pamiętniki, relacje, ankiety byłych więźniów, shelfmark VII/M-380, S. Kukiełka, p. 1.

62 Zofia Murawska, 'Kobiety w obozie koncentracyjnym na Majdanku', p. 98.

63 Zofia Murawska-Gryń, 'Warunki egzystencji więźniów' ('The Living Conditions of Prisoners'), in *Majdanek 1941–1944*, ed. by Tadeusz Mencel, p. 145.

64 Józef Marszałek, *Majdanek, obóz koncentracyjny w Lublinie*, p. 90.

65 APMM, Pamiętniki, relacje, ankiety byłych więźniów, shelfmark VII/M-380, S. Kukiełka, p. 1.

66 APMM, Pamiętniki, relacje, ankiety byłych więźniów, shelfmark VII/M-688, Eugenia Deskur-Dunin-Marcinkiewicz, *Kandydat do wspólnego stołu wolnych demokratycznych narodów*, p. 59.

67 APMM, Pamiętniki, relacje, ankiety byłych więźniów, shelfmark VII/M-380, S. Kukiełka, p. 1; Edward Dolecki, 'Schutzpolizeikommando', in *Przeżyli Majdanek*, ed. by Rajca Czesław and Anna Wiśniewska, p. 184.

68 APMM, Pamiętniki, relacje, ankiety byłych więźniów, shelfmark VII/M-380, S. Kukiełka, p. 1; Danuta Brzosko-Mędryk, *Matylda*, p. 27.

69 Helena Kurcyusz, 'Komando dziecięce' ('The Children's Commando'), in *My z Majdanka*, ed. by Krystyna Tarasiewicz, p. 49; APMM, Pamiętniki, relacje, ankiety byłych więźniów, shelfmark VII/M-108, Korespondencja od białoruskich więźniów Majdanka z 1967–68 r. (Letters from the Belarusian Prisoners at Majdanek from 1967–68); APMM, Pamiętniki, relacje, ankiety byłych więźniów, shelfmark VII/M-109, Helena Kurcyusz, Spis dzieci białoruskich; APMM, dokumenty prywatne więźniów (Private Documents of the Inmates), shelfmark IV-46, Zeszyt Helena Kurcyusz (The Notebook of Helena Kurcyusz); Zofia Murawska, 'Dzieci w obozie koncentracyjnym na Majdanku', p. 151.

70 APMM, Administracja KL Lublin 1941–1944, shelfmark I.c.4, Raporty dzienne o zatrudnieniu więźniów w przedsiębiorstwach 'Ostindustrie', listy imienne zatrudnionych w 1943 r. (Daily Reports on the Employment of Inmates in *Ostindustrie* Enterprises; List of Names of those Employed in 1943), pages 7, 39, 41, 51, 53, 55 contain information on the employment of children at the broom and brush factory. Exact dates cannot be recovered owing to the poor condition of the paper; the number of the children employed is not stated.

71 Zofia Murawska, 'Dzieci w obozie koncentracyjnym na Majdanku', p. 151.

72 Ibid., p. 145; Józef Marszałek, *Majdanek, obóz koncentracyjny w Lublinie*, p. 84.

73 Zofia Murawska, 'Dzieci w obozie koncentracyjnym na Majdanku', p. 129; Zofia Murawska-Gryń, 'Warunki egzystencji więźniów', p. 153.

74 APMM, Pamiętniki, relacje, ankiety byłych więźniów, shelfmark VII-135-161, Protokół przesłuchania świadka (Witness Interview Report): Alina Paradowska, p. 9.

75 Piotr Kiriszczenko, 'Transporty z Białorusi', in *Przeżyli Majdanek*, ed. by Rajca Czesław and Anna Wiśniewska, p. 197.

76 Ibid., p. 198.

77 Maria Bielicka-Szczepańska, *Piętnaście miesięcy na Majdanku* (*Fifteen Months at Majdanek*), APMM, VII/M-212, p. 5.

78 Ibid.

79 Ibid, p. 163.

80 Piotr Kiriszczenko, 'Transporty z Białorusi', in *Przeżyli Majdanek*, ed. by Rajca Czesław and Anna Wiśniewska, p. 197.

81 Józef Musioł, *Świadkowie*, p. 71. This description is consistent with the appearance of the children from the Zamość region in photographs. The children were taken to Lublin hospitals in August 1943. APMM, Zbiór fotografii (Collection of photographs), shelfmark XVII.

82 APMM, Pamiętniki, relacje, ankiety byłych więźniów, shelfmark VII/M-139, Janina Buczek-Różańska, Relacje, p. 6.

83 Zofia Murawska-Gryń, 'Warunki egzystencji więźniów', p. 144.
84 In early 1943, new arrivals were placed in unfinished buildings, with no windows, doors, floors or furniture.
85 Zofia Murawska-Gryń, 'Warunki egzystencji więźniów', p. 144. A single bucket of coal per day had to heat a barracks of 40.80m × 9.60m.
86 Ibid.
87 Ibid., p. 130; Halina Birenbaum, *Nadzieja umiera ostatnia* (Warsaw: Czytelnik 1988), pp. 87–8.
88 Zofia Murawska-Gryń, 'Warunki egzystencji więźniów', p. 130; Józef Marszałek, *Majdanek, obóz koncentracyjny w Lublinie*, p. 86.
89 Zofia Murawska, 'Kobiety w obozie koncentracyjnym na Majdanku', p. 128.
90 Women prisoners experienced this particularly acutely in the summer of 1943, when Commandant H. Florsted issued a ban on using the water wells, threatening anyone who approached them with death. The ban lasted four weeks. Jerzy Kwiatkowski, *485 dni na Majdanku*, p. 166, p. 303; Zofia Murawska-Gryń, 'Warunki egzystencji więźniów', p. 138.
91 Wanda Kiedrzyńska and Zofia Murawska, *Kobieta w obozie koncentracyjnym* (*The Woman at the Concentration Camp*) (Lublin: Państwowe Muzeum na Majdanku 1972), p. 54.
92 Ibid.
93 Ibid.; Halina Birenbaum, *Nadzieja umiera ostatnia*, pp. 87–8.
94 Józef Marszałek, *Majdanek, obóz koncentracyjny w Lublinie*, p. 89.
95 Wanda Ślusarczyk-Burakiewicz, 'Sonia i Luba' ('Sonia and Luba'), in *My z Majdanka*, ed. by Krystyna Tarasiewicz, p. 176; Zofia Polubiec, *By nie odeszły w mrok zapomnienia. Udział kobiet polskich w II wojnie światowej* (*So That They are Not Forgotten. The Participation of Polish Women in World War II*), ed. by Kazimierz Sobczyk (Warsaw: Książka i Wiedza 1976), p. 417.
96 Zofia Pawłowska, 'Pole kobiet', in *Przeżyli Majdanek*, ed. by Rajca Czesław and Anna Wiśniewska, p. 170.
97 Wanda Ślusarczyk-Burakiewicz, 'Sonia i Luba', in *My z Majdanka*, ed. by Krystyna Tarasiewicz, p. 176; Zofia Pawłowska, 'Pole kobiet', in *Przeżyli Majdanek*, ed. by Rajca Czesław and Anna Wiśniewska, p. 172; Józef Marszałek, *Majdanek, obóz koncentracyjny w Lublinie*, p. 109.
98 Wanda Ślusarczyk-Burakiewicz, ibid.; Zofia Pawłowska, ibid.
99 APMM, Pamiętniki, relacje, ankiety byłych więźniów, shelfmark VII/M-70, S. Perzanowska, Gdy myśli do Majdanka powracają, p. 89; APMM, Zbiór opracowań (Collection of Monographs), shelfmark XIV-2, v. 46, Dzieci urodzone w obozie na Majdanku (Children Born at the Majdanek Camp).
100 APMM, Pamiętniki, relacje, ankiety byłych więźniów, shelfmark VII/M-70, S. Perzanowska, Gdy myśli do Majdanka powracają, p. 90.
101 Zofia Murawska-Gryń, 'Warunki egzystencji więźniów', p. 132; Zofia Murawska, 'Dzieci w obozie koncentracyjnym na Majdanku', p. 147.

102 APMM, Pamiętniki, relacje, ankiety byłych więźniów, shelfmark VII/M-688, Eugenia Deskur-Dunin-Marcinkiewicz, *Kandydat do wspólnego stołu wolnych demokratycznych narodów*, p. 57.

103 Ibid.

104 Wanda Kiedrzyńska and Zofia Murawska, *Kobieta w obozie koncentracyjnym*, p. 44.

105 APMM, Centralna Opieka Podziemia (OPUS), shelfmark XII/10, part I, Raporty o sytuacji na Majdanku 1943–1944 (Reports Concerning the Situation at Majdanek 1943–1944), p. 339; Wanda Ślusarczyk-Burakiewicz, 'Sonia i Luba', in *My z Majdanka*, ed. by Krystyna Tarasiewicz, pp. 176–8; Jozef Wnuk, *Losy dzieci polskich w okresie okupacji hitlerowskiej* (*The Fate of Polish Children under Nazi Occupation*) (Warsaw: Młodzieżowa Agencja Wydawnicza 1980), p. 76; Helena Kurcyusz, 'Komando dziecięce', in *My z Majdanka*, ed. by Krystyna Tarasiewicz, p. 189.

106 Danuta Brzosko-Mędryk, *Czy świadek szuka zemsty* (*Does the Witness Seek Revenge?*) (Warsaw: Wydwanictwo Ministerstwa Obrony Narodowej 1976), p. 57.

107 Stefania Błońska, 'Pół roku' ('Half a Year'), in *My z Majdanka*, ed. by Krystyna Tarasiewicz, p. 151.

108 Ibid; Krystyna Tarasiewicz, 'Nasze zmagania o przetrwanie' ('Our Struggle to Survive'), in *My z Majdanka*, ed. by Krystyna Tarasiewicz, p. 31; Zofia Murawska, 'Dzieci w obozie koncentracyjnym na Majdanku', p. 144.

109 APMM, Pamiętniki, relacje, ankiety byłych więźniów, shelfmark VII/M-186, Danuta Brzosko-Mędryk, *Dlaczego?!*, p. 155.

110 Krystyna Tarasiewicz, 'Nasze zmagania o przetrwanie', in *My z Majdanka*, ed. by Krystyna Tarasiewicz, p. 31.

111 Ibid.

112 Ibid.

113 Ibid., p. 32.

114 Marcin Gryta, *Byłem numerem* (*I was a Number*) (Lublin: Wydawnictwo Lubelskie 1962), pp. 77–8.

115 Wiesław Dobrowolski, *Pięć lat na muszce, wspomnienia więźnia Majdanka* (*Five Years at Gunpoint. Reminiscences of a Majdanek Prisoner*) (Lublin: Wydawn. Paweł Skokowski 1994), pp. 33–4.

116 *Zeznania szefa krematorium Ericha Muhsfeldta*, ed. by A. Żmijewska-Wiśniewska, p. 139; Zofia Murawska, 'Kobiety w obozie koncentracyjnym na Majdanku', p. 154.

117 Ludwik Christians, *Piekło XX wieku. Zbrodnia, hart ducha i miłosierdzie* (*A 20th-century Hell: Crime, Strength of Spirit and Mercy*) (Warsaw: Katolickie Tow. Wydawn. 'Rodzina Polska' 1946), p. 294.

118 Ibid. If those condemned to death did not undress to their underwear by themselves, this was done by commandos of prisoners employed specifically for that purpose. They were also tasked with searching the clothes for valuables, sorting these valuables, and burying the bodies. APMM, Zbiór mikrofilmów (Collection of Microfilms), shelfmark XX-123, Komisja

Powiatowa Badania Zbrodni Niemieckich w Lublinie. Zeznania świadków (The Poviate Commission for Investigating Nazi Crimes in Lublin. Witness Testimonies), p. 27.

119 Rajca Czesław, 'Eksterminacja bezpośrednia' ('Direct Extermination'), in *Majdanek, 1941–1944*, ed. by Tadeusz Mencel, p. 258; *Zeznania szefa krematorium Ericha Muhsfeldta*, ed. by A. Żmijewska-Wiśniewska, p. 143; *Erntefest 3–4 listopada 1943 – zapomniany epizod Zagłady* (*Erntefest 3–4 November 1943 – A Forgotten Episode of the Holocaust*), ed. by Wojciech Lenarczyk and Dariusz Libionka (Lublin: Państwowe Muzeum na Majdanku 2009); Tomasz Kranz, *Extermination of Jews at the Majdanek Concentration Camp*, pp. 63–9.

120 Feliks Siejwa, 'Była to największa egzekucja w dziejach obozu koncentracyjnego' ('It was the Biggest Execution in the History of the Concentration Camps'), in *Masowe egzekucje Żydów 3 listopada 1943 r., Majdanek, Poniatowa, Trawniki. Wspomnienia* (*Mass Executions of Jews on 3 November 1943, Majdanek, Poniatowa, Trawniki. Recollections*), ed. by Edward Dziadosz (Lublin: Państwowe Muzeum na Majdanku 1988), p. 12.

121 Ibid.

122 *Zeznania szefa krematorium Ericha Muhsfeldta*, ed. by A. Żmijewska-Wiśniewska, p. 143. The person referred to here is Anton Thumann, leader of Division III.

123 Ibid.

124 APMM, Zbiór nagrań video, shelfmark. XXII-1, Maria Gancarz; Akta w sprawie zbrodni hitlerowskich na Lubelszczyźnie (Files on Nazi Crimes in the Lublin Region), vol. III/Przeciwko J. Sporrenbergowi i Moserowi (Against J. Sporrenberg and Moser), APMM, Zbiór mikrofilmów, shelfmark XVIII-168, kl. 662; Feliks Siejwa, 'Była to największa egzekucja w dziejach obozu koncentracyjnego', p. 12; Maria Pych, 'Fluchtverdächtig', in *Jesteśmy świadkami*, ed. by Rajca Czesław, Anna Wiśniewska and Elżbieta Rosiak, p. 274.

125 Jacek E. Wilczur, Roman Hrabar and Zofia Tokarz, *Czas niewoli czas śmierci* (*The Time of Captivity, the Time to Die*) (Warsaw: Interpress 1979), p. 215. After all the Jews had been shot, the ditches were covered with a thin layer of soil. Out of several thousand persons destined to die on that day, 300 Jewish women and 300 men were left alive to sort the belongings of those murdered and to cover up the traces of the crime. *Zeznania szefa krematorium Ericha Muhsfeldta*, ed. by A. Żmijewska-Wiśniewska, pp. 143–4.

126 The orderly Günter Konietzny, nicknamed 'Rooster', killed ten persons when admitting a transport from the Soviet Union, claiming this was in revenge for the death of his brother on the Eastern Front. On another occasion, he shot at Jewish children aged two to ten. Józef Musioł, *Świadkowie*, p. 122; Zofia Murawska, 'Kobiety w obozie koncentracyjnym na Majdanku', p. 155.

127 Zyklon B (prussic acid, hydrogen cyanide) was obtained by infusing diatomaceous earth with liquid hydrogen cyanide. Its form can be liquid or gaseous. It was normally used as a disinfectant and for pest control. In humans, it causes death by interfering with cellular respiration and the asphyxiation of some nerve centres. Death follows breathing problems,

vomiting and convulsions. Carbon monoxide (CO) is a gas and was delivered to the camps in cylinders. Strongly poisonous, it blocks the transport of oxygen to tissues. Early symptoms of CO poisoning include strong headache and vomiting; a longer exposure is lethal. Tomasz Kranz, *Extermination of Jews at the Majdanek Concentration Camp*, pp. 41–8.

128 Estera Gurfynkel, 'Zeznania matki' ('A Mother's Testimony'), in *Dokumenty zbrodni i męczeństwa*, ed. by Michał Borwicz, p. 70.

129 APMM, Pamiętniki, relacje, ankiety byłych więźniów, shelfmark VII/M-764, Abraham Zalchendler, Cztery lata w obozach koncentracyjnych (Four Years in Concentration Camps), p. 2.

130 Jozef Wnuk, *Dzieci polskie oskarżają (Polish Children Accuse)* (Lublin: Wydawn. Lubelskie 1975), p. 119; Zofia Murawska-Gryń, 'Dzieci w hitlerowskich obozach koncentracyjnych', p. 43.

131 Eberhard Fechner, *Proces. Obóz na Majdanku w świetle wypowiedzi uczestników rozprawy przed sądem w Düsseldorfie* (Lublin: Państwowe Muzeum na Majdanku 1996), p. 59.

132 Jerzy Kwiatkowski, *485 dni na Majdanku*, p. 113.

133 Wanda Ossowska, *Przeżyłam . . . Lwów-Warszawa 1939–1946 (I Survived . . . Lvov-Warsaw 1939–1946)* (Warsaw: Oficyna Przeglądu Powszechnego 1990), p. 270.

134 Jerzy Pfeffer, *Jak uciekłem z Majdanka (How I Escaped from Majdanek)* (Wrocław: Tom 1990), p. 30.

135 Jerzy Kwiatkowski, *485 dni na Majdanku*. The mental state of mothers after the gassing of their children is reflected in 'Matka' (Mother), a poem written in the camp by Pola Braun, in *Pieśni zza drutów. Wiersze, pieśni i piosenki powstałe w obozie koncentracyjnym na Majdanku (Songs from Behind the Barbed Wire. Poems, Songs and Ditties Written at Majdanek Concentration Camp)*, ed. by Zofia Murawska-Gryń (Lublin: Towarzystwo Opieki nad Majdankiem 1985), p. 22.

136 Jerzy Pfeffer, *Jak uciekłem z Majdanka*, p. 34; Józef Musioł, *Świadkowie*, p. 43.

137 Józef Musioł, *Świadkowie*, p. 33.

138 Jerzy Kwiatkowski, *485 dni na Majdanku*, p. 110.

139 APMM, Pamiętniki, relacje, ankiety byłych więźniów, shelfmark VII/M-186, Danuta Brzosko-Mędryk, *Dlaczego?!*, p. 97.

140 APMM, Pamiętniki, relacje, ankiety byłych więźniów, shelfmark VII-135-204, Protokół przesłuchania świadka (Witness Interview Report): Joanna Chylińska-Józefaciuk, p. 2; ibid., shelfmark VII/M-178, Symcha Turkieltaub, *51 tygodni na Majdanku (51 Weeks at Majdanek)*, p. 9; ibid., Komisja Powiatowa . . ., *Prawda o Majdanku. Z zeznań świadków (The Truth about Majdanek: From the Testimonies of Witnesses)* (Lublin 1944), p. 9.

141 APMM, Pamiętniki, relacje, ankiety byłych więźniów, shelfmark VII-135-161, Protokół przesłuchania świadka (Witness Interview Report): Alina-Maria Paradowska, p. 4; APMM, Pamiętniki, relacje, ankiety byłych więźniów, shelfmark VII/M-186, Danuta Brzosko-Mędryk, *Dlaczego?!*, p. 98.

142 Igor Newerly, 'Nas w nocy wieszali' ('They would Hang us at Night'), in *Męczeństwo i zagłada Żydów w zapisach literatury polskiej* (*Martyrdom and Extermination of Jews in Polish Literature*), ed. by Irena Maciejewska (Warsaw: Krajowa Agencja Wydawnicza 1988), p. 269.

143 Jadwiga Lipska-Węgrzycka, 'Byłam szrajberką rewiru' ('I was Head of Office at the Infirmary'), in *My z Majdanka*, ed. by Krystyna Tarasiewicz, pp. 118–19.

144 Wanda Ossowska, *Przeżyłam . . . Lwów-Warszawa 1939–1946*, p. 274.

145 Edward Dolecki, 'Schutzpolizeikommando', in *Przeżyli Majdanek*, ed. by Rajca Czesław and Anna Wiśniewska, p. 184.

146 Jerzy Kwiatkowski, *485 dni na Majdanku*, pp. 164, 338.

147 Piotr Kiriszczenko, 'Transporty z Białorusi', in *Przeżyli Majdanek*, ed. by Rajca Czesław and Anna Wiśniewska, p. 197.

148 Zofia Murawska-Gryń, 'Dzieci w hitlerowskich obozach koncentracyjnych', p. 18.

149 APMM, Pamiętniki, relacje, ankiety byłych więźniów, shelfmark VII/M-70, S. Perzanowska, Gdy myśli do Majdanka powracają, p. 90; Zofia Pawłowska, 'Pole kobiet', in *Przeżyli Majdanek*, ed. by Rajca Czesław and Anna Wiśniewska, p. 171; Wanda Ossowska, *Przeżyłam . . . Lwów-Warszawa 1939–1946*, p. 273.

150 APMM, Pamiętniki, relacje, ankiety byłych więźniów, shelfmark VII/M-186, Danuta Brzosko-Mędryk, *Dlaczego?!*, p. 155.

151 APMM, Pamiętniki, relacje, ankiety byłych więźniów, shelfmark VII-135-160, Protokół przesłuchania świadka (Witness Interview Report), Danuta Brzosko-Mędryk, *Dlaczego?!*, p. 11.

152 Wanda Ślusarczyk-Burakiewicz, 'Sonia i Luba', in *My z Majdanka*, ed. by Krystyna Tarasiewicz, pp. 176–8.

153 Zofia Pawłowska, 'Pole kobiet', in *Przeżyli Majdanek*, ed. by Rajca Czesław and Anna Wiśniewska, p. 172.

154 Piotr Kiriszczenko, 'Transporty z Białorusi', p. 200.

155 APMM, Zbiór fotokopii i kserokopii, shelfmark XIX-139, *Wykazy wysiedleńców z Zamojszczyzny zwalnianych z Majdanka w sierpniu 1943* (*The List of Displaced Persons from the Zamość Region Released from Majdanek in August 1943*).

156 Zofia Leszczyńska, *Kronika obozu na Majdanku* (*The Chronicle of the Majdanek Camp*) (Lublin: Wydawnictwo Lubelskie 1980), pp. 197–218; APMM, Opracowania, shelfmark XIV-2, v. 57, Jozef Wnuk, *Wykaz dzieci i dorosłych chorych przewiezionych w lipcu i sierpniu do szpitala Jana Bożego w Lublinie* (*A List of Children and Sick Adults Transferred in July and August to the John of God Hospital in Lublin*); Janina Kiełboń, *Wysiedleńcy z Zamojszczyzny*, p. 77.

157 Jozef Wnuk, *Losy dzieci polskich w okresie okupacji hitlerowskiej*, p. 120.

158 Zofia Murawska-Gryń, 'Dzieci w obozie koncentracyjnym na Majdanku', p. 149.

159 APMM, Pamiętniki, relacje, ankiety byłych więźniów, shelfmark VII/M-402, T. Rybak, Wspomnienia dotyczące pomocy i ratunku dzieci w czasie okupacji (Recollections Concerning Aid to Children and their Rescue during the Occupation); Zofia Murawska-Gryń, 'Dzieci w obozie koncentracyjnym na Majdanku', p. 149.

160 APMM, Zbiór nagrań video, shelfmark XXII-518, Henryk Wujec.

161 APMM, Zbiór nagrań video, shelfmark XXII-7, Janina Buczek-Różańska.

162 APMM, Zbiór nagrań video, shelfmark XXII-127, Anna Brzezińska.

163 W. Fiedorowicz Bułachow, 'Poszukiwania' ('Search'), in *Majdanek. Obóz koncentracyjny w relacjach*, ed. by Marta Grudzińska, pp. 264–6.

CHAPTER TEN

Children and Youth in Auschwitz:

Experiences of Life and Labour

Gideon Greif

At the peak of its operation, there were approximately 100,000 prisoners in the Auschwitz concentration camp system. Children and youth were among these prisoners. Historians are often unable to reconstruct how an Auschwitz prisoner felt even for one second in the camp. Even by listening to their testimonies, it is difficult to understand the immense cruelty and what Auschwitz meant for those who were children, while they were deported to the hell on earth. During the time of their life, in which they should have felt safe and cared for, and experienced schooling, friendship and family life, they were locked in a camp and subjected to the daily brutality of the SS and the brutal reality of the camp. Not only were they forced to witness the cruelty of Auschwitz, they were also its direct victims. This chapter examines the diversity of children's experiences in that camp, focusing on themes of family, labour, medical experimentation and transport.

Children in Auschwitz were allocated to different prisoner categories: Jewish children were at the bottom of the hierarchy, as well as their parents, but in the camp there were also 'Gypsy children', Polish children or children from Belorussia and other parts of the Soviet Union.[1] Children from different prisoners groups were deported to the camp for very different reasons. While Jewish children as well as Sinti and Roma were deported to the camp because of the National Socialist plan to murder all Jews (according to the 'Final Solution of the Jewish Question') and many Sinti and Roma, the deportation of Polish and Soviet children was undertaken for different reasons. They were either deported in the framework of revenge actions against partisan or resistance activities or with their families who were part of these resistance groups or partisan units. The last deportation action happened especially in several regions of Poland.[2]

During the Holocaust, close to 1,500,000 children, most of them Jewish, were murdered by the Nazis and their collaborators. During the 'selections' on the ramp at Auschwitz-Birkenau, Jewish children and youth had very little hope of being admitted to the camp, since they were considered unable to become usable slave labour, and therefore lost their right to live. The number of children and youth in Auschwitz varied from year to year, but never exceeded several hundreds. For the purpose of this chapter, children and youth are taken to be aged between thirteen and eighteen years old.

A main reason for the absence of precise information on the number of children and youth in Auschwitz is the fact that most of the children who had been deported to Auschwitz, were not even registered as prisoners. When the children arrived within the framework of the *Reichssicherheitshauptamt* (Reich Security Main Office, RSHA) transports,[3] they were normally selected directly after their arrival and murdered in the gas chambers. This happened because the SS-physicians conducting the selections considered children as 'not fit for work', namely, not able to become efficient slaves, and therefore sent them to their death. Only those children and youth, who were old enough to work in one of the different work units – usually at an age over twelve – and seemed strong enough, became official prisoners of the camp and were registered as such.[4] Nonetheless, most of the children admitted to the camp died relatively quickly due to their young age. Their underdeveloped social skills meant that they had a diminished capability to improvise and deal with difficult and violent situations. Most of the children were not able to cope with the dehumanizing reality of the camp and hold their ground within it.

A second reason for the absence of precise numbers of children in the camp is the deliberate ambiguity of the registration system: those children who became prisoners in the camp, were not admitted as 'children'. They received the same prisoner numbers as grown-up prisoners and the National Socialist Camp authorities paid attention not to use the word 'children' in official documents.[5] Even for them, it seems, the deportation of children to the camps was not unproblematic, for which reason they tried to hide the fact that there were children in Auschwitz.

It is estimated, however, that among the 1,300,000 people (at least) who were deported to Auschwitz, there were 232,000 children and youth, of which 216,000 were Jews, and 11,000 Sinti and Roma.[6] The first youths arriving in the camp were already on the first transports which arrived from the prison in Tarnow on 14 June 1940. The youths on these transports were fifteen or sixteen years old.[7] In the first transport from Warsaw, on 15 August 1940, almost fifty Polish children arrived in the camp.[8] More Polish youth and children arrived in the camp when Poles were expelled from the Zamosc region and deported. Children such as those arriving for example with transports in

December 1942 and December 1943, were categorized as 'not fit for work' and murdered very soon after their arrival. However, they were not gassed but murdered with phenolium injections in Block 20 in the Main Camp.[9]

Those Polish children and youths who were categorized as 'fit for work' and lived in the camp like the older prisoners had to do the same amount of work. An important exception, however, was Block 5 (later Block 13) in the Main Camp, Auschwitz I. Here, 300 Polish boys were housed together. Initially, they had to do sporadic labour, sports exercises and German lessons before transitioning to hard labour such as learning to lay bricks in the so-called *Maurerschule* (Bricklaying School). This school for bricklayers had been established especially for those 300 boys. The plan of the National Socialists was to 'germanize' this group of Polish boys. This plan is also backed by the testimony of one of the boys: 'We were inculcated with the belief that in the future, as qualified workers living in freedom, we would work for the sake of Germany'.[10] The school stopped functioning in spring 1941 and the boys were sent to different work commandos. Yet, in 1942, the school opened once more and young prisoners continued to learn bricklaying. During this period, Jewish youngsters from several countries including Greece (the first transport from Greece arrived in Auschwitz in March 1943) were 'learning' at the *Maurerschule*.

In addition to attending the bricklaying school, the children and youths had to work at the different work commandos and did the same hard work as older prisoners.[11] In the women's camp, there was a special commando for children, the *Kinderkommando*, where girls younger than fourteen had to work. A former member of this commando describes it as follows:

> The next day after arriving in camp I was immediately assigned to the 'Kinderkommando'. This was a group of very young girls, aged twelve to sixteen. This detail worked in the gardens at Rajsko. We went to work barefoot. There were about fifty girls in our group. The work that we did was tolerable enough in camp conditions. Neither the supervisor nor the prisoner functionaries made us work especially hard. We worked at gardening until the women's camp was transferred from the main camp to Birkenau.[12]

Ruth Elias, who had been deported from Terezin to Auschwitz and allocated to slave labour, describes the prisoners' work as follows:

> Then it was: 'Off to work'. The first days we were led out of the camp, counted very thoroughly at the gate while we had to stand in rows of five, then we were led to a bunch of stones which was located half an hour away from the camp. We had to transport the heavy stones from one place to another, only to bring them back to the first place on the next day. The work was completely senseless and soon we realized that we should not only be killed physically but also mentally. We were extremely

hungry, very soon we had lost our strength, but when somebody did not want to continue his work he was hit with whips by the SS or was kicked by the *Kapo*. To escape those beatings we concentrated all our forces and continued to transport the stones. Up to the present day I do not know where we got our strength from. Our food was mostly water. Coffee and tea in the morning, watery soup at noon, and if we were lucky there were some cooked carrots swimming in there.[13]

As stated, Jewish children were not the only youth group deported and victimized at Auschwitz. The deportation of Soviet children to Auschwitz began in 1943 and continued until 1944. Most of the Soviet children in the camp were alleged to have connections to resistance groups or partisans. But children were also randomly deported in the framework of revenge actions. This was the case of some transports from the Soviet Union, for example of children deported from Vitebsk and Minsk. On a transport from Vitebsk on 9 September 1943, 458 children arrived in Auschwitz,[14] and at least sixty children arrived at the camp in 1944 on transports from Minsk.[15]

Most children deported to Auschwitz, however, were Jews. Since it became clear that Auschwitz developed as the biggest and most important extermination camp in the framework of the 'Final Solution of the Jewish Question', it is no surprise that so many Jewish children were deported there. Of course, children were not excluded from the deportations aimed at the complete annihilation of European Jewry. As already emphasized, the majority of those children were murdered directly after they left the trains. Small children and toddlers were sent to the gas chambers as well. Their mothers, with whom they were selected, had to carry them into the gas chambers and were murdered with them. These Jewish children came from different parts of Poland, as well as from France, the Netherlands, Belgium, Slovakia, Yugoslavia, Germany, Austria, Greece, Hungary and Italy.[16]

There were witnesses to the killing of children. The survivors of the *Sonderkommando*, who were intensively interviewed by the author of this article, include details in their testimonies on the automatic murder of babies and infants with their mothers.[17] The arrival experience for children was extremely traumatic. Many Jewish children and youth arrived at Auschwitz on transports from Terezin. They have vividly recalled the emotional feelings of separation in their memoirs and testimonies. Ruth Elias remembered that:

It was especially hard, when we passed a place and somebody in the train car said: 'I was born there. This was my home!' It also happened to me when we passed Ostrau. Next to the train station is the house of Uncle Hugo. So close and so far away. I could not stop my tears. The children in the train car were crying, the sick were groaning and very soon the bucket with water was empty and we became thirsty. For the night we organized ourselves as good as possible. The one half stretched out their limbs and the other half laid down very close to each other. It was extremely cold in this December night, some degree below zero and at least the tight squeeze helped us to warm each other. We tried to help the children and the sick as much as we could but it was extremely difficult with empty hands. We only had good words which of course could not ease the pain.[18]

Elias was also a witness to the traumatic experiences of others, describing the arrival of the children and the other prisoners from Terezin in the Auschwitz camp as follows:

'Auschwitz'. But this name did not mean anything to me. For me it was the name of one of the many cities of Poland. At that time I did not [know] how deeply this name would engrave itself in me. This sad queue of people, grouped in rows of five – because everything has to be in order –, begins to walk, flanked by the SS with sharp guns. No word is said, completely frightened we walked forward automatically. Only one thought guided us: We have to stay together, Koni and I, we cannot lose us. In front of a building we stopped and were ordered to undress ourselves. It was unthinkable to follow this order because women, men and children were among us. Only after the SS started to whip us, we followed the order. All this at 10 to 15 degree below zero. It was shortly before Christmas. We were led in a big room with showers on the ceiling. Cold water rained down on us. We could not escape from this ice-cold stream because we were jammed together.[19]

The deportees in transports from Terezin arriving between September 1943 and May 1944 were not selected after their arrival, but were registered completely as prisoners. All those Jews on these transports became prisoners in the so-called 'Familienlager' (the Family Camp). This was also the reason why young children who were not able to work became prisoners of the camp. The purpose of the 'Familienlager' was to deceive the free world and to create fake 'good' camp conditions in Auschwitz, and accordingly the children were allowed to live with their parents.[20] A 'Family Camp' existed for the 'Gypsies' as well. In the 'Theresienstädter (Jewish) Familienlager', 756 children were housed after the arrival of the first three transports; one of these children was only two months old.[21]

For children, life in the 'Familienlager' was very different to the normal conditions in the other parts of the camp. Not only were they allowed to live together with their parents, but they also enjoyed other privileges. Fredy Hirsch, who had already taken care of children in Terezin and accompanied them to Auschwitz, managed to establish a special block (No. 31) for the children where they could receive lessons and take part in several different activities, such as children's theatre and plays. One of these theatrical events took place on the birthday of Fredy Hirsch, whom the children honoured for his great work. Hirsch also managed to improve the sanitary conditions in the 'Familienlager'. This initiative aimed at making life more bearable and bettering the chances of survival for the children and youths. According to the account of Ruth Elias, the 'Familienlager Birkenau B2b':

> [c]onsisted of two rows of wooden barracks and a camp street in between them. At this street we were allowed to meet our husbands for half an hour after work. Every one of the barracks had a big entrance gate and after one entered there were two rooms on both sides, where the *Blockältesten* and their deputies were housed. We were not allowed to enter these rooms. Inside the barrack, which was called block, were wooden three-story beds, always in groups of three. We had to sleep in one bed with five people because the camp was filled with people. A 60 cm wide bench built with bricks was located in the block. The bench was hollow and could be heated. But this 'oven' never was used because there was no heating material. One side of these barracks the women were housed, on the other side the men were housed. Men and women each had one washing room and latrine barrack.[22]

But the 'Familienlager' did not exist for long. As the National Socialists had planned from the very beginning, it was liquidated in July 1944 and the prisoners living there were murdered in the gas chambers, and, along with them, the children living in this part of the camp.[23]

Additionally to those children who were deported to the camp, some children were also, remarkably, born inside the camp walls. These children were born by mothers who had already been pregnant when they arrived in the camp. Officially, pregnant women were not admitted to the camp but it is obvious that this 'official' rule was broken several times. There is no precise information on how many children were born in the camp, but there were several such cases. The first official documents of a birth in the camp however are from 18 September 1943. In this case, a birth certificate was issued by the registry office of the camp and the child received its own prisoner's number. The child was Maria Romik, daughter of the female prisoner Stefania Romik. Maria Romik was born on 22 July 1943.[24] However, this case has to be regarded as an extreme exception: Normally, children born inside the camp were not registered as prisoners but murdered immediately after their birth.

In her book *Die Hoffnung erhielt mich am Leben. Mein Weg von Theresienstadt und Auschwitz nach Israel* (*Triumph of Hope: From Theresienstadt and Auschwitz to Israel*), Ruth Elias, who arrived in Auschwitz while several months pregnant, describes her fear during a selection by Mengele:

> A panic came upon me, I did not know what to do, a pregnant woman in the eighth month? How could I save my life with nothing? Suddenly the

thought came up in me, which might help me. I asked some of my friends who were standing behind me to move in front of me. My thought was, that maybe Mengele would see the young female bodies and would not pay attention to my pregnant body.[25]

The plan worked. Elias passed the selection and kept her unborn child safe. Later, however, the *Blockälteste* told the officials she wanted to improve the living conditions for Ruth and prevent her from hard work. As a result, Ruth and another pregnant prisoner were brought to Ravensbrück but were again returned to Auschwitz some days later. This was when Josef Mengele heard of the two pregnant prisoners. After Elias gave birth to her child, Mengele came for the daily visit. Ruth recalled that:

> He looked at the new-born for a long time and after giving it some thought he called for a female physician and ordered her to bandage my breasts. In my naivety at first I did not think that this was anything evil but I was deeply shocked when I heard that my child should not be suckled. Why was I forbidden to suckle my child? ... Only one of the other prisoners thought about the correct reason: 'Mengele wants to make an experiment how long a new-born can survive without food'.[26]

After Elias told a prisoner physician named Marca that she would be gassed together with her child as Mengele previously had told her, Marca wanted to help. She offered Ruth an injection to kill the child, an unthinkable act that would likely save Ruth's life:

> Ruth, you are young, you have to live. Look at your child. It is not able to live. It will die in some hours anyway. But it has to die before Mengele comes to get you two. If the child is still alive at that time he will take the two of you. You have to live, you are young. ... You have to kill your child to save yourself. Please give him the injection, do it, do it![27]

Elias finally gave her child the injection which killed it and saved her own life. In most cases children born in the 'Familienlager' were not murdered after their birth, but children from other parts of the camp were. Nonetheless, there is no exact documentation on how many children were born in the 'Familienlager'.

In addition to older prisoners children were victims of medical experiments conducted by the SS-physicians in Auschwitz. Dr Josef Mengele, in particular, conducted experiments with children, both Jewish and non-Jewish. Since Noma, the disease on which Mengele was conducting research, was a particular problem amongst the children in the 'Zigeunerlager', he selected children for his experiments in this part of the camp on a regular basis. Some of these children were murdered after orders by Mengele, and their corpses were brought to the SS-Institute for Hygiene in Rajsko.[28]

Many children were also mistreated through Mengele's experiments on twins. For these experiments, Mengele selected the children directly at the arrival ramp. Mostly Jewish children were selected for these experiments on 'Zwillinge'.[29] They were housed in Block 31 in the 'Zigeunerlager'. As long as Mengele needed the children for his experiments, he was especially kind to them and even gave them gifts or sweets. Yet, for the sake of his research, he took the children to the laboratory and murdered them during the different 'operations' or 'experiments'. The remaining children were shot by Mengele himself when the 'Zigeunerlager' was liquidated.[30] It is estimated that roughly 350 pairs of twins died due to Mengele's 'experiments'.[31]

In the middle of January 1945, the Soviet Red Army approached the camp complex and this hastened the major evacuation of the camp. Children and youths were moved the same way as the other prisoners. Some of them already left the camp with the early evacuation transports in autumn and early winter 1944, which brought the prisoners to other concentration camps in the German-held areas. Other children and youths had to march on what survivors, due to the terribly harsh conditions of distance, terror and climate, would eventually term 'death marches'.

On the death march of those prisoners who had been housed in Section BIId in Auschwitz-Birkenau were 100 boys who had been captured during the Warsaw Ghetto Uprising and brought to Auschwitz.[32] Pregnant women were forced on the death marches as well. If we can imagine how great the suffering of normal prisoners was during the death marches, we can also imagine how children or pregnant women suffered during them.[33] For example, in his Auschwitz chronicle *Landschaften der Metropole des Todes. Auschwitz und die Grenzen der Erinnerung und der Vorstellungskraft* (Landscapes of the Metropolis of Death), the historian Otto Dov Kulka recalls:

> This journey had many facets, but mostly one facet, maybe one color, a nightly color which I remember stronger than anything else and which outweighs everything else. This intensity or maybe better this nightly color, which outweighs everything, represents this journey one later called 'Death March'. It was a way to freedom which led us out of the gates of which no one had thought that we would ever walk through them. What I remember – I remember basically everything about this journey – but the most impressive is the color of this long, black column which only proceeds very slowly and suddenly – black spots on the side of the road: A big black spot and another big black spot and one more spot – at first I was like drunken by this blending white, by this freedom, by the fact that we had left the terrain of the fences, by the nightly landscape and the villages we crossed. I looked at one of the black spots and I understood what this was, this spots became more and more the longer we were walking; the dead became more and more. The longer the march lasted I became weaker and weaker and I fell back in the column to the end of it, who was left behind was shot and became a black spot on the side of the

road. The shots became were heard more frequently and the black spots became more and more until, it was like a miracle, the column finally stopped at one morning.[34]

Since many children had already been murdered before becoming prisoners of the camp, and many of those children who were registered as prisoners, died relatively soon, only a few testimonies of children in Auschwitz exist. Additionally, they were not considered that important for historical research, because the testimonies given by children were considered, due to age, trauma and other factors, less authentic and reliable than those given by adults. Nonetheless, impressive testimonies by children who were prisoners in Auschwitz exist. They reveal an impression of the life of children in Auschwitz and the way children perceived Auschwitz's horrible reality. This becomes evident in one of the best known testimonies about a childhood in Auschwitz, titled *Youth in Chains*.[35] Under the pseudonym Thomas Geve, a Jewish survivor describes his childhood in Auschwitz:

> It was the evening of June 27th 1943, the place Brzezinka, near the town of Oswiecim. Our familiar police guards had been relieved long ago, for this was a secluded world not fit to be watched by outsiders. 'Out, you bastards!' 'Faster, Schweinehunde!' 'Run, you snow hounds!' yelled our new masters, the supermen of the super race. A whole SS company was drawn up along the station. Both ends were guarded by machine-guns. Blood-hound, threateningly tugging their leashes, barked out a warning welcome.[36]

Geve also talks about the general situation of young prisoners in Auschwitz:

> The main camp of Auschwitz had a comparatively large number of young prisoners. Out of every hundred inmates about two were between the ages of 13 and 18. In 1943, nearly all of them were either Russians, Gypsies, from Czecho-Slovakia, Germany, Austria and Poland, Greek Jews or Poles. It was surprising how much we youngsters differed from our grown up compatriots. We had not yet absorbed all the national prejudices and illusions that hate thrives on. There was no particular way of life that we had become accustomed to, for throughout the years of our teens there had been war. Now we were facing our fate as one unit: youth. Differences among us never caused serious troubles, but they provided entertainment. Ukrainians, proud of the muscles, did acrobatics, inviting those who still had sufficient energy to challenge them. Wherever those skillful Eastern performers may have come from, they were just as capable of friendship as the boys I had grown up with. Gypsies were harder to understand, but once you had proved that you respected them as your equal, they would even reveal the secrets of Romany to you, the language that kept them together. This was the greatest honor possible for an outsider, accorded only to the few true friends who

succeeded in gaining their confidence. Other acquaintances of theirs were merely treated to sessions of clairvoyance. Jews, proving themselves to be workers just as good and skillful as anyone else, adapted themselves to the new surroundings best of all. Proud to show their knowledge, quite a few of them had been nicknamed 'professor'. We could not help being impressed by this hopeful atmosphere that youth had created for itself among the holocaust of its elders. Perhaps the block-elder was right in his cruel threats against those who might have disturbed it.[37]

These previous extracts describe the feeling of solidarity amongst the youths in Auschwitz. We can also understand one important point that helped children and youths in Auschwitz to survive even if their bodies were weaker than those of the adult prisoners. They did not have much life experience to draw upon. Due to their young age, they did not yet have a well-established reference framework for how the world should function. In contrast to the adult prisoners, the norms and values of the old world were not known to child prisoners. For this reason, they might have coped with the absurd, perverted and extremely dysfunctional world of Auschwitz in a different way than the adult prisoners. Children were exposed and socialized to an Auschwitz morality that some adults found difficult to understand or accept.

Many youths managed to cope relatively well in the camp and to find different possibilities to increase their chance of survival. But Geve's memories also show how the world of Auschwitz changed the children and how the hard work they had to undertake stole from them what normally should have been their natural right: their childhood. The theft of innocence was also accompanied by painful hard labour, as Geve recalled: 'After a few weeks of seemingly senseless work, dominated by constant shouts of "Keep moving", I was exhausted enough to feel that I could not go on any more. My hands blistered, my feet sore'.[38]

In the memories of Kulka, we find another traumatic experience described that was common to most children and youth in Auschwitz: the loss of their parents. Some had already lost them before they arrived in Auschwitz or – as in the case of Kulka – they had to witness the 'selection' of their parents for the gas chamber during their time in Auschwitz. Kulka's recollections provide a vivid image of the experience children and youth were subjected to in Auschwitz:

I return to July 1944: to the last picture, in fact the only one, when I said goodbye to my mother. It was some days after the final liquidation of the family camp BIIb, which means, it was the liquidation of those which were left over after the previous selections. I was brought to the men's camp BIId with some other youths while my mother was brought to the other side of the grey brick-building of the women's camp. That was where I saw her for the last time when I came to say goodbye. To see her one last time before she would be gone. I knew she would go. Where? I did not know. It was before she went on that train whose tracks seemed to run only in one direction until they vanished in the crematoria or in the net of the camp buildings.[39]

Many children were hardened by their time in Auschwitz and had an extremely difficult time after liberation. Their childhood experience was strongly defined by the rules of daily life in Auschwitz, and they found it difficult to get used to the new-found freedom. Alwin Meyer describes this orientation to life with reference to the fate of Kola Klimczyk, who had been one of the youngest prisoners of Auschwitz:

> At first Kola was sent to the hospital. After that he was often very sick, very thin, he almost did not grow. He had to be treated over and over again. The physicians diagnosed a 'calcification of the lungs'. [In] 1949 the boy had tuberculosis, he was sent to Bielsko for treatment. . . . The family was in constant sorrow due to his condition. In the first time Kola's behavior was very strongly influenced by the time in the camp. He obviously remembered that his feet were frozen and put them into an unsecure position to ensure that he did not have to tread with the whole foot. When his fingers were cold, he contracted his fingers in a very special way as the prisoners had done in the camp. He paid attention on cleanliness and order very strictly. He could not stand it if someone touched one of his things or put it elsewhere. And very often he simply stood there deeply in thoughts. Everything was new for Kola. For food he only knew 'Kartoszki', potatoes. He was used to smell at everything before he ate it. The boy spoke a mixture of Russian, Polish and German words. Orders he always gave in German. About the food he talked in Russian. Feelings were expressed in Russian or Polish. . . . He was very nervous, very often he was struck by cramps. He could not stand the view of uniforms. . . . One day, Kola saw a guard who worked at the smeltery of Jawiszowice. 'Buy me a gun and a knife', he said to his adoptive mother. When asked what he wanted to do with it he said: 'I want to shoot this guy in the uniform and cut him up'.[40]

The fate of Kola Klimczyk as described by Meyer shows that the lives of the children who were prisoners in Auschwitz were indelibly marked by this traumatic experience. After the liberation they had to learn how to live once more. And they had to prepare for an uncertain future in freedom.

A Jewish child, which constitutes a world of its own, as renowned educator Dr Janusz Korczak explained, was not respected by the Germans as a human being in Auschwitz. The German perpetrators perceived Jewish children as a threat for the future of Germany and Europe, bearing the seeds of an alleged Jewish-dominated world. Accordingly, they treated the Jewish child as inferior and contemptible. Jewish children's right to life was taken immediately after arriving at the camp because his meagre power did not allow exploiting it for the war aims of Germany. Jewish life had no value in the National Socialist ideology. Therefore, the Jewish children and youth, as the biological future of the Jewish People, had to be exterminated. They were the first in the row of the 'Final Solution'. The fact that some hundreds escaped the death verdict and survived the gas chambers of Auschwitz is just a miracle, and sadly, one of the few miracles that happened to Jews during the Holocaust.

Notes

1. See Waclaw Dlugoborski and Franciszek Piper, *Auschwitz 1940–1945. Central Issues in the History of the Camp*, vol. II (Oswiecim: Auschwitz-Birkenau State Museum 2000), p. 204.
2. Ibid.
3. Transports organized by the *Reichssicherheitshauptamt* (Reich Security Main Office) in Berlin.
4. Waclaw Dlugoborski and Franciszek Piper, *Auschwitz 1940–1945*, p. 205.
5. Ibid.
6. Ibid. Everyone younger than fourteen was counted as a child and everyone younger than eighteen as a youth.
7. Irena Strezelecka, 'Die ersten Polen im KL Auschwitz', *Hefte von Auschwitz* 18 (1990), pp. 68–9.
8. Helena Kubica, 'Der erste Transport aus Warschau', in *Comité International d'Auschwitz. Informationsbulletin* 10/211 (1978), p. 79.
9. Waclaw Dlugoborski and Franciszek Piper, *Auschwitz 1940–1945*, p. 209.
10. Ibid., p. 245.
11. Ibid., p. 248.
12. Accounts by former prisoners Ruth Milarova and Wanda Marossanyi, APMAB, Collection of Testimonies, vol. 47, p. 32, vol. 14, p. 87, as quoted in Waclaw Dlugoborski and Franciszek Piper, *Auschwitz 1940–1945*, p. 248.
13. Ruth Elias, *Die Hoffnung erhielt mich am Leben. Mein Weg von Theresienstadt und Auschwitz nach Israel* (Munich: Piper 1988), p. 139.
14. Waclaw Dlugoborski and Franciszek Piper, *Auschwitz 1940–1945*, p. 216.
15. Danuta Czech, *Kalendarium der Ereignisse im Konzentrationslager Auschwitz-Birkenau, 1939–1945* (Hamburg: Rowohlt Verlag 1989), p. 439, p. 523, p. 669, p. 782, p. 786, p. 790.
16. Waclaw Dlugoborski and Franciszek Piper, *Auschwitz 1940–1945*, pp. 217–31.
17. Gideon Greif, *We Wept without Tears. Testimonies of the Jewish Sonderkommando from Auschwitz* (New Haven: Yale University Press 2005). See the testimony of Jacob Gabbai, p. 193.
18. Ruth Elias, *Die Hoffnung erhielt mich am Leben*, p. 132.

19 Ibid., pp. 133–4.
20 Hans G. Adler, *Theresienstadt. Das Antlitz einer Zwangsgemeinschaft 1941–1945* (Göttingen: Wallstein Verlag 2005); Miroslav Kárný, 'Das Theresienstädter Familienlager (BIIb) in Birkenau (September 1943–Juli 1944)', *Hefte von Auschwitz* 20 (1997), pp. 133–237; Nili Keren, *The Familienlager in Auschwitz-Birkenau*, in Yisrael Gutman and Michael Berenbaum, *Anatomy of the Auschwitz Death Camp* (Bloomington: Indiana University Press 1998).
21 Miroslav Kárný, 'Das Theresienstädter Familienlager (BIIb) in Birkenau', *Hefte von Auschwitz* 20 (Verlag Staatliches Auschwitz-Museum 1997), pp. 133–237.
22 Ruth Elias, *Die Hoffnung erhielt mich am Leben*, p. 137.
23 Miroslav Kárný, 'Das Theresienstädter Familienlager (BIIb) in Birkenau', pp. 133–4.
24 Waclaw Dlugoborski and Franciszek Piper, *Auschwitz 1940–1945*, p. 240.
25 Ruth Elias, *Die Hoffnung erhielt mich am Leben*, p. 156.
26 Ibid., p. 185.
27 Ibid., p. 189.
28 Waclaw Dlugoborski and Franciszek Piper, *Auschwitz 1940–1945*, p. 262.
29 The 'Zigeunerlager' was the sub-camp BIIe in Birkenau, in which from February 1943 until August 1944 about 25,000 Roma and Sinti were kept as prisoners. Most of them died because of horrible living conditions and the others were gassed in August 1944 when the camp was liquidated.
30 Waclaw Dlugoborski and Franciszek Piper, *Auschwitz 1940–1945*, p. 263.
31 Ibid., p. 264.
32 Ibid., p. 282.
33 On the conditions at the death marches, see Joseph Freeman and Donald Schwartz, *The Road to Hell: Recollections of the Nazi Death March* (St Paul, MN: Paragon House 1998); Michael R. Marrus, *The End of the Holocaust* (Westport, CT: Meckler 1989); Andrzej Strzelecki, *The Evacuation, Dismantling and Liberation of KL Auschwitz* (Oswiecim, Poland: Auschwitz-Birkenau State Museum 2001); Elie Wiesel, *Night* (New York: Hill and Wang 2006).
34 Otto Dov Kulka, *Landschaften der Metropole des Todes. Auschwitz und die Grenzen der Erinnerung und der Vorstellungskraft* (Munich: DVA 2013), pp. 17–18.
35 See Thomas Geve, *Youth in Chains* (Jerusalem: Rubin Mass 1958).
36 Ibid., p. 42.
37 Ibid., pp. 68–70.
38 Ibid., p. 106.
39 Otto Dov Kulka, *Landschaften der Metropole des Todes*, pp. 89–90.
40 Alwin Meyer, *Die Kinder von Auschwitz* (Göttingen: Lamuv 1992), pp. 52–4.

CHAPTER ELEVEN

The Legend of the Ghetto Fighters:

Zionist Youth Movements and Resistance during and after the Holocaust

Avinoam J. Patt

On 10 December 1945 a kibbutz of young Holocaust survivors from Bytom and Sosnowiec in Poland – recent arrivals at the Landsberg Displaced Persons (DP) camp in Germany – learned that their kibbutz group now had a name: *Kibbutz Lochamei HaGetaot al shem Tosia Altman* – the Ghetto Fighters Kibbutz named after Tosia Altman. The young survivors, most of them between the ages of sixteen and eighteen, had not been participants in the wartime resistance or underground movements, nor had they heard of Tosia Altman – or Josef Kaplan, or Mordecai Anielewicz, or Shmuel Breslaw – but as members of a newly formed *Hashomer Hatzair* kibbutz, they would learn about the heroism of the ghetto fighters, a heroism that would form a key part of the postwar identity of the Zionist youth movements. At its first postwar movement conference in Germany on 10 December 1945, *Hashomer Hatzair* decided to name its kibbutz groups – the foundation of the movement's future in Europe – after the ghetto fighters. As part of their Zionist immersion, a process that would involve instruction in Hebrew language, Jewish history, culture and tradition, and agricultural training, all geared to preparing them for their future lives in

Israel, the young survivors would also absorb the ethos of heroic resistance that had become the defining feature of the wartime transformation of the youth movements – from an elitist organization focused on training pioneers for settlement in the Land – to the leaders of a broader Jewish public that would play a key role in postwar political developments among the Surviving Remnant.

This chapter examines the evolution of the concept of 'resistance' during and after the Holocaust among Zionist youth movements in Poland and the Jewish DP camps in postwar Germany. What led the youth movements to shift their focus from educational activities to underground work and eventually armed resistance during the war? And how was the leadership role of the youth movements in resistance during the war transformed into a claim for political leadership of the broader Jewish public after the Holocaust? What was the pedagogical function of 'resistance' in the process of Zionist immersion for children and youth after the war? While most studies of Jewish resistance during the war have focused on debates over Jewish behaviour during the war or the nature of Jewish responses to Nazi persecution,[1] an examination of the choice by Jewish youth to engage in resistance during the war can prove instructive in attempting to understand the success of Zionist youth movements in organizing the Jewish public, and the young survivors in particular, in the aftermath of the war.[2]

Whereas before the war, Zionist youth movements had been focused on training the 'elite' among Jewish youth to make *Aliyah* and become pioneers, during the war, the Zionist youth movements began to transform themselves from elitist organizations dependent on the movement centre in Palestine to self-reliant groups with a focus on the wider Jewish public. This broader focus would eventually lead groups like *Hashomer Hatzair*, *Dror He-Halutz* and *Betar* to take the initiative in determining political and social action underground, maintaining contact between ghettos, writing the underground press and, eventually, leading the ghetto resistance. While most of the official Polish Jewish leadership (including the leaders of the *Bund*, the *General Zionists*, *Poalei Zion* (Zionist Socialists) *Mizrachi*, *Poalei Zion Left*, *Agudat Israel* and the *Revisionist Party*) either fled Warsaw and the other major cities of Poland for the USSR or abroad or were captured, imprisoned and executed at the beginning of the war, a number of Zionist youth leaders who had managed to flee to the East made the decision to return to occupied Poland.[3] Leaders of *Hashomer Hatzair*, *Dror* and *He-Halutz*, such as Mordecai Anielewicz, Zivia Lubetkin, Yitzhak Zuckerman, Josef Kaplan, Frumka Plotnicka, Tosia Altman and Shmuel Breslaw chose to return to Poland voluntarily after several months spent in Russia and Lithuania.[4] The youth movement leaders who returned to Warsaw were motivated by a sense of responsibility as local leaders, not only to their young *chanichim* (movement members), but to the Jewish community as a whole.[5] As one leader of *Hashomer Hatzair* suggested at the movement conference of Polish refugees in Vilna in 1940:

[o]ur eyes are inevitably riveted to Palestine . . . This direction towards Palestine does not mean that we have given up as lost the three million Jews who are still in Poland. Quite on the contrary. As long as there are still Jewish masses, even if only in the physical sense, we must be with them in the struggle for national survival . . . we cannot abandon Polish Jewry in its distress . . .[6]

The leaders of *Hashomer Hatzair* (including Haim Holtz, Zelig Geyer, Josef Shamir, Yitzhak Zalmanson and Tosia Altman who made it to Vilna) decided that 'as long as there is a Jewish community in Poland, the movement must be there'.[7] Likewise, the *Dror* movement decided at a secret conference in Lvov on 31 December 1939 to send Zivia Lubetkin to Warsaw; she was followed several months later by Yitzhak Zuckerman.[8] While much of the leadership of the *Bund* fled Warsaw, Abraham (Abrasha) Blum was one of the few *Bund* leaders who remained in Warsaw. These youth movement leaders would play a key role in the formation of the ghetto underground, and eventually the *Jewish Fighting Organization* (Żydowska Organizacja Bojowa, ZOB).

All the same, it would be a mistake to see the success of the youth movement leaders in creating an alternative underground leadership as simply the result of the vacuum created by the departure of the prewar Jewish leadership. Likewise, as historian Raya Cohen has argued, the choice to resist was the outcome of an ideological evolution before and during the war that led the Zionist youth to see themselves as leaders of the Jewish public.[9] In the case of *Hashomer Hatzair*, Cohen argues, cut off from the *Yishuv* in Palestine, the movement drew closer to the hope for Soviet intervention from the East and forged a connection with *Poalei Zion Left* locally as the movement grew increasingly politicized among a Jewish public in Warsaw suffering from 'ideological disorientation'.[10]

Jewish youths in Warsaw were left disoriented and shattered by the privations of life under the occupation. Writing in Warsaw in the summer of 1940, a *Dror* youth movement activist, using the pen name, R. Domski, described the dire situation facing Jewish youth 'at the present time' as 'one of the saddest in human history':

> All of the foundations of life as we have known them until now have been shattered. And new ones have yet to be established. The younger generation, whose responsibility it is to live and breathe in this transitional time, cannot find the source from which will flow, from a spiritual perspective, and has begun to experience a spiritual crisis, leading to degeneration and a dangerous anarchy in every aspect of thinking and feeling of the youth . . .[11]

The author, Tuvia Borzykowski, sensing the spiritual calamity facing the Jewish youth, prescribed what he saw as the appropriate cure, first, to provide them with basic elementary education, but most importantly:

> To remove the children of the street to a warm, friendly environment, to imbue in them as much as possible a concern for their own fate. To instill the feeling of solidarity and responsibility. With song and games to create the youthful atmosphere for the children who have been aged too soon ... to awaken in them national feeling, give them a socialist consciousness, to activate them socially to all aspects of Jewish life, to familiarize them with all of the spiritual creation, which the Jewish people have formed throughout time. And finally, to concentrate the best segment of the Jewish youth, which have already received their instruction in our branches, as a front-line avant-garde of the Jewish youth ... .[12]

Borzykowski, who would continue to organize for *Dror* in Warsaw and escaped to the 'Aryan side' after the April 1943 Warsaw Ghetto Uprising, prescribed these cures for the lost and demoralized Jewish youth less than one year after the German invasion. As part of their educational efforts in the ghettos, Zionist youth movements established kibbutz groups, underground schools, and an underground press in ghettos, large and small, throughout occupied Eastern Europe. The underground press of the youth movements also served as a key source of information on events throughout Poland, conveying information gathered by intrepid youth movement members who journeyed secretly between ghettos, offering news that was otherwise denied to the ghetto inhabitants. Access to information about the scope of the Nazi annihilation of the Jews of Eastern Europe after the summer of 1941 played a key role in the formation of the resistance groups in the Warsaw ghetto.

The leaders of the pioneering youth movements who had returned to occupied Poland from Vilna after the start of the war (in the case of *Hashomar Hatzair*, Tosia Altman, Josef Kaplan, Mordecai Anielewicz and Shmuel Breslaw) sought to maintain contact with the movement in Vilna, the leadership in Israel, and the *He-Halutz* office in Geneva. Female members of the underground, like Tosia Altman, Frumka Plotnicka or Chajke Grossman, for example, played a key role travelling to the various movement branches in the General Government and Galicia to assist in organizing the movement and sharing information between parts of occupied Poland. They risked their lives to smuggle material and information, as well as people, in and out of ghettos, undermining prevailing gender stereotypes which kept women out of positions of leadership in other domains.[13]

After the German invasion of the Soviet Union in June 1941, contact between Warsaw and the movement leadership became increasingly difficult. In the case of *Hashomer Hatzair*, after receiving reports of systematic slaughters of Jews taking place to the East, Tosia Altman travelled to Vilna in December 1941, entering the Vilna ghetto on Christmas Eve together with Chajke Grossman.[14] While Altman argued to the movement members there that the movement should focus its efforts on saving the activist core of the movement located in Warsaw, Abba Kovner, leader of *Hashomer*

Hatzair in Vilna, argued that the Nazi slaughter of the Jews in Lithuania and Poland was not local in nature, but part of an overall systematic plan bent on the total slaughter of the Jews of Europe. As Ziva Shalev describes, Tosia Altman was told that a decision had been made among the leadership of the various youth movements in Vilna that the Jews should not go to their deaths without a fight ('Let us not go like sheep to the slaughter', in the words of the manifesto composed by Abba Kovner).[15] Shalev speculates that Altman may have even delivered the Vilna underground's manifesto before the *Hashomer Hatzair* members following her return to the Warsaw ghetto.[16]

In Warsaw, the leadership of the Jewish public – both the alternate leadership of the youth movements and the official *Judenrat* leadership – initially met the reports of systematic extermination sceptically. Still, *Hashomer Hatzair* began to focus its efforts increasingly on organizing armed resistance. At the last ideological seminar of *Hashomer Hatzair* held at the end of 1941, the historian and ghetto archivist, Emanuel Ringelblum, noted the evolution in his journal:

> Once, during a break between classes in the Ha-Shomer seminar (I lectured on the history of the Jewish labour movements), Mordechai Anielewicz and Josef Kaplan called me down into the yard of the building at 23 Nalewki Street. They let me into a special room and showed me two revolvers. These revolvers, the members of the central leadership explained to me, were to be employed to train youth in the use of arms. This was the first step taken by *Hashomer Hatzair* even before the Fighting Organization was founded.[17]

At this point, the youth movements began to change the focus of their activities in the Warsaw ghetto – from maintaining an underground organization directing educational and cultural activities for youth in the ghetto to raise morale to a concerted effort to begin preparations for armed resistance in the ghetto. Ideologically, the movement leadership presented the choice to resist as a means of 'breaking out of their forced isolation of the past two and a half years, to end their passivity, and to try and influence their situation within a broader framework while still acting as Jews'.[18] Such a position would distinguish the youth movements as an alternative leadership to the *Judenrat*, which by and large continued to attempt to reassure the Jews and encourage them to work for the German war machine. *Hashomer Hatzair* and other underground groups that began to prepare for an armed struggle disseminated propaganda that opposed policies serving the needs of the German military.[19] At the same time, as Raya Cohen notes, *Hashomer Hatzair* pivoted to a position that enabled it to speak for the people of the ghetto as a whole, even switching the language of its weekly bulletin to Yiddish from Polish, and changing the name of the bulletin from *Przedwiosnie* (Before Spring) to *Der Oifbroise* (Outpouring of Rage).[20]

Meanwhile, in the spring of 1942, the Nazis had begun to implement the so-called 'Final Solution' in the General Government within the framework of Operation Reinhard, sending transports of Jews from the ghettos of Poland to the newly constructed killing centres at Belzec (where killing began in March 1942), Sobibor (May 1942) and Treblinka (July 1942). On 22 July 1942, the great deportation from the Warsaw ghetto to Treblinka began, as German SS and police authorities initiated the process that led to the deportation of approximately 275,000–300,000 Jews from the ghetto by 12 September 1942. Adam Czerniakow, Chairman of the Warsaw ghetto *Judenrat*, decided to commit suicide on 23 July 1942 rather than comply with the deportation order, writing in his final note: 'They are demanding that I kill the children of my people with my own hands. There is nothing for me to do but die'.[21]

In the context of the great deportation from the Warsaw ghetto, on 28 July 1942 the ZOB was founded by three Zionist youth movements, *Hashomer Hatzair*, *Dror* and *Akiva* to organize Jewish self-defence and advocate armed struggle against the Nazis. The command of the newly established organization consisted of Shmuel Breslaw, Yitzhak Zuckerman, Zivia Lubetkin, Mordecai Tenenbaum and Joseph Kaplan.[22] There was, however, little that the initial group of approximately 200 members could do, aside from evade deportation and acquire a few pistols and hand grenades from the Polish Communist underground.[23] Eventually, the command of the ZOB would include Mordecai Anielewicz (*Hashomer Hatzair*), commander; Yitzhak Zuckerman (*Dror He-Halutz*), deputy commander; Marek Edelstein (*Bund*), intelligence chief; Yochanan Morgenstern (*Poalei Zion* ZS), finances; Hirsch Berlinski (*Poalei Zion Left*), planning; and Michael Rosenfeld (Communist rep.).[24] By late September 1942, following the Great Deportation of Warsaw Jews to Treblinka between July and September 1942, the ghetto population had dwindled to approximately 40,000 Jews working in the remaining workshops; the ZOB comprised an estimated 600 members, but by this point had acquired almost full support of the remaining ghetto population who both understood the nature of Nazi policy and came to respect the leadership of the youth movements and fighting organizations.[25] In conjunction with the six-month anniversary of the Great Deportation, the ZOB planned retaliation against the *Jewish Police* for 22 January 1943, calling on the remaining Jews of Warsaw:

> Jewish masses, the hour is drawing near. You must be prepared to resist, not give yourselves up to slaughter like sheep. Not a single Jew should go to the railroad cars. Those who are unable to put up active resistance should resist passively, meaning go into hiding. We have just received information from Lvov that the Jewish Police there forcefully executed the deportation of 3,000 Jews. This will not be allowed to happen again in Warsaw. The assassination of Lejkin demonstrates that. Our motto should be: All are ready to die as human beings.[26]

At the same time, the Jewish Military Union (*Zydowski Zwiazek Wojskowski*, ZZW) and the Revisionist Zionist Fighting Organization, issued a parallel call for resistance; before either the ZOB or the ZZW could act on their plans for 22 January 1943, however, SS and police units launched a new Aktion seeking to round up approximately 8,500 Jews. On the second day of the round-up, the ZOB, under the leadership of Anielewicz, managed to mount several attacks against German soldiers, in some cases embedding themselves with Jews being marched to the 'Umschlagplatz' for deportation. Although the January revolt failed to prevent the deportation of approximately 5,000 Jews, it did teach the resistance several important lessons, notably that the ghetto inhabitants would support the ZOB in its efforts to engage in armed resistance against the Germans, having learned from the previous summer that 'deportation' likely meant death.[27] As Dr Lensky, a physician in the ghetto wrote in his memoirs:

> Unfurling the banner of revolt enhanced the underground's stature in the eyes of the remaining Jews. Many who did not even know that an underground existed now saw concrete proof of its deeds. They sensed that the ghetto has an organized force other than the community council [*Judenrat*]; a moral force that is fed up with the old methods which brought a 'holocaust' down upon the Jews. This organization has chosen a new way of dealing with the Nazis. Hope was revived in the hearts of the doomed. Perhaps the Germans will really not expose their soldiers to danger and will stop sending them to execute operations because Jews are prepared to resist . . .[28]

Even as it worked to apply the lessons of the January 1943 encounter to the next phase of resistance in April 1943, the ZOB was all too aware of the enormous power differential that existed between their meagre force and the Nazi war machine. The decision to engage in a last act of resistance against the German soldiers was not made out of hope that, in some way, lives might be saved, but as a final declaration of human dignity on behalf of the Jewish community, a refusal to 'go like sheep to the slaughter', and out of a sense of duty to lead what remained of Jewish Warsaw. Inspired by Yitzhak Lamdan's epic poem *Masada* (1926), which imagined a return to the desert fortress surrounded by the Romans in the year 73 CE and its call that 'Masada shall not fall again', the ghetto fighters were determined to make a historical statement in their last struggle against the full force of the mighty German Reich.[29]

The final liquidation of the Warsaw ghetto began on Passover Eve, 19 April 1943 (14 Nisan 5703). While the ghetto fighters enjoyed some success employing guerilla tactics in the first days of the uprising, by the end of the first week of the revolt, the German soldiers had managed to destroy most of the points of resistance fighting, as the ZOB dug itself underground. Even so, on 23 April 1943, in the midst of the fighting, Mordecai Anielewicz appreciated the tremendous significance of the moment on a historical level. As he wrote to his comrade Yitzhak Zuckerman stationed on the German occupiers' side: 'Keep well, my dear. Perhaps we shall meet again. Most importantly: the dream of my life has become true. I have been privileged to witness Jewish self-defence in the ghetto in all of its greatness and glory'.[30] On the twentieth day of fighting (8 May 1943), the central command bunker of the ZOB at Mila 18 was discovered and the Germans began to pipe poison gas into the bunker to flush the Jewish fighters out. Arieh Wilner called upon the fighters to take cyanide pills they had prepared rather than submit to the Germans; most of those in the group, including Anielewicz, did so when they could no longer fight off the gas. A group of six fighters, including Tosia Altman, who had managed to breathe through a concealed opening in the bunker, were found that night by Zivia Lubetkin and Marek Edelman, who helped the group escape from the ghetto via the sewers.[31] Most of the remaining fighters were killed in the ghetto. While the uprising was ultimately unsuccessful in preventing the liquidation of the ghetto in Warsaw or the subsequent deportation of the remaining Jews to Treblinka and Majdanek, the event came to occupy great significance after the war, particularly among the Surviving Remnant in postwar Poland and Germany.

While there is not space to discuss in greater detail the role of the youth movements – *Hashomer Hatzair, He-Halutz, Dror* and *Betar*, as well as the *Bund, Poalei Zion* and the communists in organizing the resistance and the uprising in Warsaw and in the ghettos and forests of Eastern Europe – it is clear that their collective wartime work in organizing the Jewish public and forming an alternative leadership to the *Judenrat*, as well as their youth, their lack of responsibility to caring for family and their willingness to take risks, placed them in an ideal position to lead the resistance. After the war, this legacy of wartime leadership and their role in leading the resistance placed the youth movements in the ideal situation to assume leadership of the Jewish public, both in their own eyes and in the eyes of other survivors. Interestingly, the models for reaching youth during the war, for providing a warm home and a surrogate family, would prove quite effective in the postwar situation as well. In a remarkably short period of time after the liberation of Europe, the Zionist youth movements – *Hashomer Hatzair* noteworthy among them – managed to build a system that enabled them to organize Jewish youth more successfully than any other organization. Jewish youth after the Holocaust found the Zionist movements to provide welcoming homes that could provide them with the camaraderie, education and, above all, the emotional warmth, that they sought after the war. Despite the emerging success of the kibbutz model the youth movements offered, leaders of *Hashomer Hatzair* were quite aware that the movement had shifted its focus in the task of *Aliyah* from training the elite of Jewish youth to enlisting as many followers as possible for departure. Still, the movements depended on these 'broken youths' to reconstitute their decimated movements; in this way, the enlisting of the young survivors in the kibbutzim after the war, their absorption into the movement, and the effort to turn them into worthy *shomrim* were part of the larger transformation of the Zionist youth movements in Europe which had begun during the Holocaust in Poland. In accord with the *Bricha*'s effort to organize willing segments of the Jewish public for departure after liberation, the *Hashomer Hatzair* youth movement, in unison with *Dror*, began to organize kibbutzim in a number of cities in Poland in the spring and summer of 1945, including Warsaw, Lodz, Sosnowiec, Bytom and Krakow.[32] Other movements followed suit, finding the kibbutz model an effective means of recruitment. In truth, most of the young survivors who joined the movements had very little understanding of the ideological differences that divided the movements, as the promises of shelter, security and departure meant more than the vision of what the future Jewish state might look like.

The Ghetto Fighters Kibbutz named after Tosia Altman was typical in this regard. The kibbutz, which kept a collective diary of its travels from Poland to Germany to Cyprus and ultimately to Israel, was led by two *madrichim*, Baruch and Miriam Yechieli, who had spent the war in the USSR. Youth movement activists encouraged *madrichim* to understand the obstacles faced by the young survivors in adapting to the collective lifestyle of the movement (lack of education, absence of a normal childhood, stunted mental development, general demoralization and distrust in man).[33] In order to deepen loyalty to the movement, Shaike Weinberg, author of a guide for *madrichim*, encouraged leaders to engage the youth in agricultural work, service work, general education, the teaching of Hebrew, Jewish history, the history of Zionism and the *Hashomer Hatzair* movement, and socialist education. And indeed, such educational techniques were put into place by the *madrichim* of the movement in Poland and in Germany, and reinforced in the *Hashomer Hatzair* movement press and in educational materials made available by the central movement leadership. In this vein, the identification of kibbutzim and youth movement members with the wartime heroism of their namesakes was of particular value. From the perspective of the youth movement, the leadership believed that Zionism, specifically *Hashomer Hatzair* Zionism, had the power to heal this 'broken youth' by turning them into ideologically committed Zionists (and such training was an ideal use of time while kibbutz youth waited to leave Europe). Based on their entries in the diary, however, it is also clear that they had very little understanding of what the movement stood for – but were more than willing to be educated. In their time in Poland the youths began the process of Zionist immersion designed to 'heal their souls'. The kibbutz framework – with its psychologically therapeutic social value, its offer of food, shelter and structure, and its promise of departure for the Land of Israel – succeeded in drafting over 33,000 young people into the framework of the *Bricha* from Poland.[34] When Kibbutz Tosia Altman arrived in the American zone of Germany in November 1945, the kibbutz in fact preceded much of the *Bricha* from Poland, with the majority of the 'infiltrees' into the DP camps arriving in the summer and early fall of 1946 following the Kielce pogrom in July of the same year. Although Kibbutz Tosia Altman eventually spent its last eight months in Germany on a farm, the majority of the 280 kibbutzim (with over 16,000 members) were to be found within the DP camps of the American zone of Germany, where there were a total of 156,000 Jews by June 1947.[35]

The time spent by the kibbutzim of *Hashomer Hatzair* in Germany also enabled the movement to continue the process of creating good *shomrim* as the youth waited their turn for departure from Germany – often up to two years of waiting. In many cases, *Hashomer Hatzair* had to struggle just as hard in Germany to maintain membership and not lose kibbutz members to other frameworks and emigration options, thus needing to adjust its product to the demands and desires of its new constituency. Still, the process of Zionist immersion helped to avoid boredom and demoralization in Germany as the wait dragged on.

What did it mean to be good *shomrim* in Germany? It meant to be *lochamim* (fighters), *halutzim* (pioneers), *ma'apilim* (immigrants conquering the shores of Palestine), *khayalim* (soldiers) and more. The daily activity notes of the kibbutzim and the youth movement press highlight the activities of the youth in the kibbutz groups and the focus on training or *hakhsharah* designed to prepare the youth for *Aliyah*. All the same, a central part of the ideological transformation the movements meant to inculcate in the youth was their part in a shared legacy of wartime heroism.

The archives of the *Hashomer Hatzair* movement in Germany have records on at least fourteen different kibbutzim in the American zone. The decision to name many of the kibbutzim after the movement's resistance fighters who had died during the war was only taken at the first *Hashomer Hatzair* movement conference in postwar Germany at Biberach on 10 December 1945.[36] There several of the kibbutzim were renamed after *Hashomer Hatzair* resistance fighters like Mordecai Anielewicz (the first groups from Sosnowiec and Bytom), Chaviva Reik, Josef Kaplan (first from Warsaw and Krakow), Tosia Altman, Aryeh Vilner and Zvi Brandes.[37] Other kibbutzim carried symbolic names like *LeShichrur* (Toward Liberation), *BaDerech* (On the Way), and *BaMa'avak* (In the Struggle).[38]

The identification of the kibbutzim and the youth movements with the resistance played a key role in fostering the new identities of the survivor youth. The diary of *Kibbutz Lochamei HaGeta'ot al shem Tosia Altman* portrayed the excitement of the members of Kibbutz Tosia Altman when they learned of their new kibbutz identity. Mordechai Rosman, who had been a member of a prewar kibbutz with Tosia Altman, told them stories about her life and her heroism in the ghetto. 'We were all enchanted by her personage... and thus the kibbutz decided in an *asefa* to accept the decision of the meeting and call our kibbutz from now on *Kibbutz Lochamei HaGettaot al shem Tosia Altman*'.[39] The movement, by linking the identity of the individual kibbutzim with the heroism of wartime resistance fighters, cemented the identification of *Hashomer Hatzair* with leadership in the ghetto resistance in the minds of the young survivors.

Within DP society as a whole, political leaders and the historical commissions also attempted to elevate the place of the ghetto fighters, as the Warsaw Ghetto Revolt 'enjoyed an uncomplicated place of honor' within the collective memory of the *She'erit Hapletah*.[40] As noted by historian Ze'ev Mankowitz, the valour of 'the ghetto fighters, the dedication of the underground movements and the heroism of the partisans' was marked at every opportunity, perhaps, he suggests, as a means of lightening the burden of victimhood and 'the torment of helplessness'.[41] As suggested by Levi Shalitan, a survivor from Shavli and editor of *Undzer Veg*, at a meeting to commemorate the Warsaw Ghetto Revolt in 1946, 'a people cannot live off Treblinka and Majdaneks – only thanks to Warsaw can this people live on'.[42]

The Zionist youth, who embraced the legacy of wartime heroism, thus played a central role as the living heirs of the ghetto fighters for the rest of DP society. While in Germany, waiting for selection for *Aliyah*, the youth engaged in the cultural work and the process of Zionist immersion designed to transform them from broken youth into *shomrim*. A look at the movement newspaper is instructive in also suggesting what the movement desired these youths to become. In addition to noting the connection to *Eretz Israel* and making members feel a part of the community there (in time if not in space), a greater part of the newspaper continued to emphasize the wartime heroism of *Hashomer Hatzair* in leading wartime resistance. As was noted in volume two of the newspaper (April 1946) dedicated to the three-year anniversary of the Warsaw Ghetto Uprising, 'our movement was among the first to make the call for rebellion'.[43] The cover was graced by a drawing of the ruins of the Warsaw ghetto, and the first page profiled Mordecai Anielewicz, including a selection from his last will and testament to the world: 'How happy am I that I am one of the first Jewish fighters in the ghetto'.[44] The volume also included part of Abba Kovner's appeal to the Jews of the Vilna ghetto 'not to go like sheep to the slaughter', as well as the hymn of the United Partisans Organization (*Fareinigte Partizaner Organizatsye*), 'Zog Nit Keyn Mol'.[45] Articles by ghetto fighters Ruzhka Korczak, Abba Kovner and Chaya Klinger detailed their wartime activity in the resistance. Later editions of the newspaper continued this emphasis with profiles of other resistance leaders after whom *Hashomer Hatzair* kibbutzim were named, including Josef Kaplan and Tosia Altman (volumes 3 and 4), as well as leaders like Frumka Plotnicka and Abba Kovner. The profile of Tosia Altman in the July 1946 volume described her wartime heroism in great detail, highlighting her role as an underground courier and as a fighter during the last days of the ghetto revolt:

> On May 8, 1943 she was in the bunker at Mila 18 where the majority of the resistance organization was killed. She was among the fourteen who remained alive and made her way to the bunker at Franciszkanska 22

and from there crawled through the sewers to the Aryan side of Warsaw. After two weeks she found herself at another house of the fighting organization on 11th November Street in Praga; on May 24, 1943 a fire broke out there and she was among eight who died in the fire . . .[46]

Other holidays, like the 11th day of the Hebrew month of Adar, *Yom Tel Hai*, the day commemorating the death of early Zionist hero Josef Trumpeldor at the Battle of Tel Hai in 1920, were again opportunities to educate the kibbutz members about the heroism of earlier Zionist leaders, who also typified the Zionist goal of shaking off the passivity of Diaspora Jewry.[47] Kibbutz Tosia Altman spent the evening of *Yom Tel Hai* learning about the heroism of Trumpeldor and singing songs; as was generally the case on such occasions, the focus of the discussion was on the concept of bravery.[48] *Yom Tel Hai* was followed a few days later by a more light-hearted celebration of the Jewish holiday of Purim with a comical rendition of the kibbutz's play, *Haganah* (Defence).[49] The Föhrenwald camp newspaper noted the celebration of a '*Purim-Ownt*' (Purim evening) with the *Hashomer Hatzair* kibbutz in which the

> *madricha* of the kibbutz, Mirjam, . . . gave a speech on the heroes of the present-day Purim, the fighters from the Warsaw, Vilna, Białystok, and Częstochowa ghettoes, as well as the partisans and the front-line fighters, who with their blood defended the honor of the Jewish people just as once before did Mordecai and Esther defend Jewish honor before King Ahashuerus.[50]

The celebration of holidays within the kibbutzim tended to blend Jewish and Zionist motifs; in many cases, Jewish traditions were appropriated by the movement in order to emphasize wartime heroism. On the last night of Chanukah, Kibbutz Tosia Altman held a party to celebrate the holiday (with guests from the *United Nations Relief and Rehabilitation Administration* (UNRRA) and representatives of the camp) and to bid farewell to the first *olim* from the kibbutz departing for the Land of Israel. The activities within the kibbutz combined a focus on the future with constant reminders of the past, especially *Hashomer Hatzair*'s leading role in wartime resistance. As the holiday commemoration 'reminded [members] of their fathers' homes',[51] speeches on heroism were given by Baruch and Mordechai from Kibbutz Tosia Altman. The kibbutz sang songs from the ghetto:

> Before the eyes of everyone arose memories of the dark days in the ghetto, in the forests, and in the hiding places. The songs described the many graves in which our families were buried. The songs told the stories of the Jewish child, on the Jewish home in Poland and Lithuania, on Janusz Korczak, who went to his death without abandoning the children he

taught. The songs told the stories of the ghetto fighters whose deaths in bravery rivaled the deaths of the Maccabees.⁵²

Over the course of 1946, as kibbutz groups moved out of the DP camps and onto one of the approximately forty farms or *kibbutzei hakhshara* that had been created in the American zone of postwar Germany, they continued the process of Zionist immersion and the identification with wartime heroism although now, their acts of revenge were symbolic, as they farmed German soil, waiting to farm actual soil from the Holy Land. Although their contact with Germans was probably more limited than if they had lived in cities, they were still confronted with the reality of having to reside among their former enemies. The DP youth on the Nocham movement Kibbutz Nili in Pleikhershof linked farming to revenge, finding satisfaction in working the land of Julius Streicher's estate as he stood trial in nearby Nuremberg. There could be no mistaking the symbolic value of this gesture by a kibbutz named 'Nili', based on the acronym of the initial letters of the verse '*Netzach Yisrael Lo Yeshakker*' ('The Glory of Israel will not lie'; I Sam. 15:29). The renaming of farm buildings and livestock with Hebrew names were part of a consciously symbolic revenge on the part of youth empowered by membership in a kibbutz and the Zionist youth movement. While Zionism could allow them to transcend their current situation by focusing on the future, when they did face Germany and Nazism, they were now armed with the tools to confront them. At the same time, the young farmers could take pride in their collective accomplishments in Germany, because their farming yielded tangible results as they awaited their departure for Palestine.

Nonetheless, by 1947 after almost two years in the DP camps, Jewish DPs in Germany faced the future with a declining sense of hope for immediate *Aliyah* and increasing willingness to explore other migration options, although even these were limited.⁵³ Although some youth in kibbutzim managed to leave Germany between liberation and the beginning of 1947, they were a minority of the total Jewish DP population, most of which remained stuck in the DP camps. Between the end of the war and spring 1947, only 9,500 people managed to leave the US Zone via illegal immigration, the majority of them in kibbutzim shepherded by the *Bricha*.⁵⁴ As of August 1946, the British policy of sending illegal immigrants to Cyprus, rather than to the detention centre in Atlit near Haifa, diminished DP hopes of reaching Palestine even more as prospects for legal immigration from the American zone continued to be as slim as they had been before the war. Between 1945 and 1948 fewer than 1,000 *Aliyah* permits were given to Jewish DPs in the US Zone.⁵⁵

As DPs began to despair over the prospects of ever finding a solution to their stateless condition, the Zionist youth movements and the Zionist leadership of the Central Committee as a whole, turned the focus of their political energy to *Ha'apalah* as a form of resistance to British tyranny. Feeling cut off from the rest of the world, the cause of *Ha'apalah* could focus the energies of the *She'erit Hapletah* on a solution to their plight that harnessed the activism of underground struggle in the face of a powerful foe. As time dragged on, the youth movements tried to keep the focus of DP youth on *Aliyah* and *Ha'apalah* and recounted stories of successful immigration in the DP Press. The youth, who had until now been instructed in obtaining the proper tools to make them suitable pioneers in the Land of Israel, would now be trained to become *ma'apilim,* prepared to conquer the shores of Palestine. In this way, *Ha'apalah* became the new path of resistance advanced by their predecessors during the war. *Nocham* (*United Pioneering Youth*) devoted almost entire volumes of the movement paper to *Ha'apalah*, including pictures of *ma'apilim*, articles on the importance of the illegal immigration movement, stories about individual *ma'apilim*, and letters from movement members who had tried to land in Palestine but were sent to Cyprus.[56] The July 1947 volume of *Nocham* opened with a picture of a *Ha'apalah* ship on the front cover and explained how *Ha'apalah* could 'be the way to save thousands of Jews'. The youth who had survived the war had a duty to 'lead the way and hold the flag that floats over the ships on the ocean'.[57] The same volume also included a profile of the *Kovshei HaYam hakhsharah* in Deggendorf, whose members learned subjects such as boating, motor construction, electrical work on the ship, as well as lessons on rudders, swimming and ship signalling.[58]

Like *Nocham* and *Dror, Hashomer Hatzair* sought to repair declining Zionist enthusiasm with a renewed focus on the prospect of *Ha'apalah*. The movement had renamed itself *Hashomer Hatzair Be-Ha'apalah* at a 'founding conference' on 14–15 February 1947 in Bad Reichenhall. The name of the new party was significant: this was part of an effort to redefine the character of the *She'erit Hapletah* as immigrants to Palestine, standing at the forefront of *Ha'apalah* (clandestine illegal immigration) and the struggle for the state. The party's slogan was *HaBonim Yibanu, HaMeginim Yagenu, Ha-Ma'apilim Ya'apilu* (the builders will build, the defenders will defend, and the *ma'apilim* (clandestine immigrants) will conquer the shores of Palestine). It was more than symbolic that this youth movement now viewed itself as the political leader of the *She'erit Hapletah* in this struggle. The movement saw its leadership in the wartime struggle against Nazism as justifying its postwar leadership of the *She'erit Hapletah* in the struggle against the British blockade – the new form of underground resistance. Thus, the *Hashomer Hatzair* newspaper of 20 March 1947 linked the current struggle against the British with the wartime suffering of the Jewish people: 'we protest in the strongest terms against the white book – the reason from the annihilation of millions of our brothers! LIQUIDATE THE CAMPS! OPEN THE DOORS TO THE LAND OF ISRAEL!'[59]

On the fourth anniversary of the Warsaw Ghetto Uprising, the *Hashomer Hatzair* newspaper, dedicated its cover to the 20th anniversary of the Kibbutz HaArtzi and featured an Arthur Szyk painting 'The Repulsed Attack', depicting heroes of the Warsaw Ghetto Uprising inside the periodical. As in past years, the volume included photos of Mordecai Anielewicz, Josef Kaplan, Tosia Altman and Aryeh Vilner, accompanied by the poem, *Ashrei HaGafrur* by Hannah Szenes. The final page of the volume included a message from the leadership to all of the *shomrim* – the fighters who preserved the honour of the people of Israel. This year, however, the commemoration of resistance was linked with the plight of the *She'erit Hapletah*:

> Now the entire Yishuv is enlisted in the struggle to save the surviving remnant, to open the gates of Israel, for Aliyah and settlement . . . [just as our comrades (struggled in Israel)] will we continue and struggle, out of a faith in the ideological path and the pioneering tradition on Hashomer Hatzair . . . We are one camp . . . we will not forget the heroes of the people, our heroes in the ghettoes, the camps, and the forests we will not forget. We will remain faithful to their testament and to their flag – our flag. Hazak ve-ematz![60]

Most dramatically, the voyage of the *Exodus 1947* on 11 July 1947 with 4,052 men, women and children reflected the drafting of young survivors into the *Ha'apalah* movement.[61] In brief, the ship of Holocaust survivors attempted to break the British blockade of Palestine, was intercepted by British warships, and the passengers fought until they were subdued. Rather than allow the passengers to disembark in Palestine or even Cyprus, the British government decided to force the DPs to return to France (and eventually Germany) to discourage such attempts in the future. The transfer of the DPs to prison ships in Haifa harbour took place within full view of the *United Nations Special Committee on Palestine* (UNSCOP) commissioners touring Palestine at the time, a notable diplomatic coup on the part of the Zionist enterprise. Although the prison ships were returned to France, the passengers refused to disembark and the French government refused to force them to do so. The passengers even went so far as to stage a hunger strike to arouse sympathy for their plight. The ship's passengers were finally returned to Hamburg, a practical defeat for the DPs in their effort to depart German soil, but one of the greatest victories for the Zionist movement in their ongoing diplomatic struggle against the British blockade. The symbolic value of Holocaust survivors being forced to return to German soil was not lost on the world press or on the UNSCOP commissioners debating the future of Palestine.[62] In fact, a closer look reveals that a substantial number of the over 4,000 passengers on *Exodus* were members of Zionist youth movements from the German DP camps, who had been trained and waiting for just such an opportunity to leave German soil. Of the more than 4,000 passengers on the ship, an estimated 1,000 were deemed eligible for *Aliyat Hanoar* (*Youth Aliyah*) and hence under the age of seventeen.[63] Of these 1,000, 813 were counted as belonging to the Zionist youth movements in Germany.[64] They played a critical role in the manifestations of Zionist enthusiasm on board the ship, and their enthusiasm was emblematic of the DPs' willingness to leave Germany at almost any cost by the summer of 1947. This was in a sense a re-enactment of what they were unable to do in 1939.

Subsequently, the *Exodus* affair received a great deal of attention in the DP camps and was highlighted in the youth movement newspapers. Coverage in the movement papers focused on the heroism of the youth movement members and the passengers of the ship who stood up to British tyranny and refused to surrender their Zionist passion. *Hashomer Hatzair BeHa'apalah* reported that the episode 'open[ed] a new black page in British Labour government treatment of the victims of Nazism'.[65] The August 1947 volume of the movement paper included a profile of the ship and educational instruction in teaching the episode to movement branches. An editorial on the incident proclaimed that 'we will follow in their path until we achieve complete liberation'.[66] The movement papers also recounted with pride the participation of their members in the affair. *Nocham* listed 450 members who took part (November 1947 issue), while *Hashomer Hatzair* highlighted the starring role played by Mordechai Rosman in the affair.[67] The central role played by Rosman emphasized *Hashomer Hatzair*'s struggle to enable Jewish immigration to Palestine.

The October 1947 volume of *Nocham* argued that 'after *Yetziat Eyropah* we must continue with Ha'apalah at all costs'.[68] The episode demonstrated 'the stubbornness of She'erit Hapletah ... that no means can stand in the way of our desire to reach Eretz Israel ... and nothing can stand in the way of our one and only land of the future: Eretz Yisrael'.[69] The episode was linked both with the recent tragedy of the Jewish people in the Holocaust and the distant past, as a new attempt at *Exodus* from slavery. Following the passage of the UN partition plan on 29 November 1947 and the outbreak of hostilities in Palestine even before the onset of the May 1948 war, the DPs, and the members of youth movements in particular, would be called upon again to take up arms, this time unfurling the banner of resistance in defence of a homeland they had never seen.

The very nature of the Zionist youth movements, which sought to shape the DP youth in their own image, was transformed after the war as a result of direct contact with the survivor youth. This was, however, a transformation that had begun during the war as youth movements shifted their focus to the broader Jewish public. The call to resistance not only functioned as a choice of last resort for the ghetto fighters, it also emanated from an assessment of their role as the avant-garde of the oppressed Jewish public and the duty to lead them in battle against the Nazi oppressor. After the war, this leading role in resistance would serve the youth movements well. Many of the young survivors had joined the kibbutz with next to no knowledge of Zionism drawn instead by the offers of camaraderie, shelter, food and the therapeutic value of the kibbutz framework; by the time they left Germany, many were prepared to take up arms to defend the homeland they had never seen. The wartime model of reaching a broader Jewish public to rescue the youth from the physical and spiritual crisis described by Tuvia Borzykowski in 1940 continued to be effective after the war. But the Zionism of the youth movements and the emphasis on resistance in the kibbutzim filled another function for the young members: the traumatic individual past of the

FIGURE 11.1 *Cover page of the collective diary kept by Kibbutz Lochamei HaGetaot al shem Tosia Altman.*
Kibbutz Gazit Archive, Israel.

survivors was replaced with the shared experience of wartime heroism in the ghetto revolts. Regardless of what members' experiences had been in the war, whether in the forests, in hiding, in the Soviet Union, in concentration and labour camps, or in the ghettos for that matter, the kibbutz members now adopted the collective heroic identity provided by membership in the group. The kibbutzim of *Hashomer Hatzair* and other movements were named after fallen resistance heroes and celebrated holidays commemorating ghetto uprisings. Members learned about the bravery of their predecessors in the movement, whose legacy they now continued through participation in the struggle to create the Jewish state. In this way, the postwar activities of the youth as pioneers, as *ma'apilim*, and as soldiers defending the Jewish people, continued the wartime resistance of their new heroes.

Notes

1 The literature on this topic is extensive. For a recent helpful overview of these historiographical debates, see the introduction to the volume by Nechama Tec, *Resistance: Jews and Christians Who Defied the Nazi Terror* (Oxford: Oxford University Press 2013). Tec references in particular debates between Raul Hilberg, Hannah Arendt and Isaiah Trunk over Jewish behaviour during the Holocaust.

2 For a more extensive analysis of this topic, see Avinoam Patt, *Finding Home and Homeland: Jewish Youth and Zionism in the Aftermath of the Holocaust* (Detroit: Wayne State University Press 2009).

3 Israel Gutman, *The Jews of Warsaw, 1939–1943: Ghetto, Underground, Revolt* (Bloomington, IN: Indiana University Press 1982), p. 121. Among the leaders who fled at the beginning of the war were the leaders of all of the major Jewish political parties and movements in Poland; from the General Zionists, Moshe Kleinbaum (Sneh), Apolinary Hartglas and Moshe Kerner; from the *Bund*, Henryk Erlich and Victor Alter; from *Poalei Zion C. S.*, Anshel Reiss and Abraham Bialopolski; from *Mizrachi*, Zerah Warhaftig and Aaron Weiss; from *Poalei Zion Left*, Yitzhak Leib and Nathan Buksbaum; from *Agudat Israel*, Yitzhak Meir Levin; and from *Betar* and the Revisionist Party, Menachem Begin.

4 Moshe Arens, 'The Jewish Military Organization (ZZW) in the Warsaw Ghetto', *Holocaust and Genocide Studies* 19 (2005), pp. 201–25, here p. 205.

5 See Aharon Weiss, 'Youth Movements in Poland during the German Occupation', and Israel Gutman, 'The Youth Movement as an Alternative Leadership in Eastern Europe', in *Zionist Youth Movements During the Shoah*, ed. by Asher Cohen and Yehoyakim Cochavi (New York: Peter Lang Publishing 1995).

6 Cited in *Youth Amidst the Ruins* (New York: Hashomer Hatzair 1941).

7 Cited in Moshe Arens, 'The Jewish Military Organization (ZZW) in the Warsaw Ghetto', p. 205.

8 Ibid. See also Yitzhak Zuckerman, *A Surplus of Memory: Chronicle of the Warsaw Ghetto Uprising* (Berkeley, CA: University of California Press 1993), pp. 36–40.
9 Raya Cohen, 'Against the Current: Hashomer Hatzair in the Warsaw Ghetto', *Jewish Social Studies* 7/1 (Autumn 2000), p. 70.
10 Rachel Manbar, 'Hashomer Hatzair be-Varsha, 1940–1942', *Yalkut Moreshet* 23 (1977), pp. 93–134. In this context, *Hashomer Hatzair* sought to respond to the void that had been created in the absence of political leadership, shifting its focus to the broader Jewish public. Cited in Raya Cohen, 'Against the Current: Hashomer Hatzair in the Warsaw Ghetto', *Jewish Social Studies* 7/1 (Autumn 2000), p. 67.
11 Tuvia Borzykowski, *Between Tumbling Walls* (Tel Aviv: Ghetto Fighters' House and United Kibbutz Movement 1976). See also Yitzhak Zuckerman, *A Surplus of Memory*, p. 49.
12 'Di yidishe yugnt in itstikn moment', article published in *Dror* underground newspaper in Tammuz 1940. Analysis of the state of Jewish youth with recommendations for helping them. USHMM archive, RG 15.079M, Ring I-705.
13 For more on the role of women as couriers in Occupied Poland and in the resistance more generally, see Lenore J. Weitzman, 'Living on the Aryan Side in Poland: Gender, Passing, and the Nature of Resistance', in *Women in the Holocaust*, ed. by Dalia Ofer and Lenore J. Weitzman (New Haven, CT: Yale University Press 1998), pp. 187–222, and Nechama Tec, *Resilience and Courage: Women, Men, and the Holocaust* (New Haven, CT: Yale University Press 2003), pp. 263–5.
14 Ziva Shalev, 'Tosia Altman', http://jwa.org/encyclopedia (accessed 17 February 2014).
15 See for example Jürgen Matthäus and Mark Roseman (eds), *Jewish Responses to Persecution: 1941–1942* (Lanham, MD: Alta Mira Press 2013), Document 9-6, p. 340.
16 Ziva Shalev, 'Tosia Altman', http://jwa.org/encyclopedia (accessed 17 February 2014).
17 As cited in Israel Gutman, *The Jews of Warsaw, 1939–1943: Ghetto, Underground, Revolt* (Bloomington, IN: Indiana University Press 1989), p. 165. See also Emanuel Ringelblum, *Ksovim fun Geto* (Warsaw: Wydawnictwo 'Idisz Buch' 1961), p. II, p. 147.
18 Raya Cohen, 'Against the Current', p. 73.
19 Ibid., p. 75.
20 Ibid.
21 For a detailed account of the deportation, see Barbara Engelking and Jacek Leociak, *The Warsaw Ghetto: A Guide to the Perished City* (New Haven, CT: Yale University Press 2009), pp. 698–730.
22 Israel Gutman, *The Jews of Warsaw*, p. 236.
23 Saul Friedländer, *The Years of Extermination: Nazi Germany and the Jew, 1939–1945* (London: Weidenfeld & Nicolson 2007), pp. 520–1.
24 Israel Gutman, *The Jews of Warsaw*, p. 291.

25 Ibid., p. 293.
26 'Call to Resistance by the Jewish Fighting Organization in the Warsaw Ghetto, January 1943', *Archiwum Zydowskiego Instytutu Historycznego w Polsce* (Archives of the Jewish Historical Institute in Poland), ARII/333 (cited in Israel Gutman, *The Jews of Warsaw*, p. 305). See also Joseph Kermish (ed.), *Mered Geto Varshah be-Einei ha-Oyev* (Jerusalem: Yad Vashem 1966), p. 589.
27 See Martin Dean (ed.), *USHMM Encyclopedia of Ghettos*, vol. II, 'Warsaw', and Gutman, *The Jews of Warsaw*, p. 312; pp. 316–17.
28 Israel Gutman, *The Jews of Warsaw*, p. 319; Dr Lensky MS, in YVA, o-33/13-2, o-33/257, p. 116.
29 David Roskies notes that the *Dror* movement anthology published in 1940, which would later serve as a 'blueprint for the revolt', included Lamdan's famous poem. David Roskies, *Against the Apocalypse: Responses to Catastrophe in Modern Jewish History* (Cambridge, MA: Harvard University Press 1984), p. 207.
30 See *Sefer Milhamot Ha-Getaot*, p. 158 (Yad Vashem Archives, O-25/96), translated slightly differently in Israel Gutman, *Resistance: The Warsaw Ghetto Uprising* (Bloomington, IN: Indiana University Press 1994), p. xx.
31 Altman died on 26 May 1943 as a result of a fire that had broken out in a celluloid factory where she was hiding with the surviving fighters from the ghetto on the 'Aryan side' of Warsaw; described by Shalev, 'Tosia Altman', http://jwa.org/encyclopedia (accessed 24 February 2014).
32 See Avinoam Patt, *Finding Home and Homeland*, p. 80.
33 From Levi Arieh Sarid, *Be-Mivchan He-Anut*, Hashomer Hatzair archive (1) 2.31, proposal written by Shaike Weinberg, pp. 284–6.
34 See table from Yochanan Cohen, *Ovrim kol Gvul: HaBrichah, Polin 1945–1946*, p. 469. Summary of 'HaBricha' from Poland according to movements July 1945–6. The *Bricha* Archive, Efal, Hativah Z. Netzer, Box 3, Folder 4.
35 YIVO, MK 488, Leo Schwarz papers, Roll 16, 159, 1108, Muentz report, May 1947.
36 *Yoman Kibbutz Lochamei HaGettaot al shem Tosia Altman* (hereafter *Yoman KLGTA*) *Yoman KLGTA*, p. 69.
37 The above-mentioned kibbutz groups were named after individuals who participated in the Jewish resistance during the war.
38 Information on these kibbutz groups is available at the *Hashomer Hatzair* archives and in the Ha'apalah Project, Haganah Archives (123/Hashomer Hatzair/410).
39 *Yoman KLGTA*, p. 69.
40 Ze'ev Mankowitz, *Life Between Memory and Hope: The Survivors of the Holocaust in Occupied Germany* (Cambridge: Cambridge University Press 2002), p. 209.
41 Ibid., p. 209. Ze'ev Mankowitz cites an editorial from the DP newspaper *Undzer Veg*, 'Zakhor', vol. 32, 10 May 1946, p. 1.

42 Levi Shalitan, 'Warsaw as a Symbol', in *Dos Fraye Vort*, vol. 29–30, 3 May 1946, p. 7. Cited in Ze'ev Mankowitz, *Life Between Memory and Hope*, p. 209.
43 *Hashomer Hatzair*, vol. 2, April 1946. YIVO Library.
44 Ibid.
45 Hersh Glik, *Zog nit Keyn Mol* (*Never Say*), Song of the Partisans.
46 *Hashomer Hatzair*, vol. 4, 15 July 1946, p. 11.
47 See for example Kibbutz Josef Kaplan report, Haganah Archives, Ha'apalah Project (HAHP, Tel Aviv), 123/Hashomer Hatzair/410, #176.
48 *Yoman KLGTA*, p. 92.
49 Ibid.
50 *BaMidbar*, 20 March 1946, #4 (6), p. 7, YIVO, Jewish DP Periodicals Collection, Reel 15–11.
51 *Yoman KLGTA*, p. 67.
52 *Yoman KLGTA*, pp. 67–8.
53 Had immigration to the United States been a realistic immigration option after the war, it is quite conceivable that a majority of Jewish DPs would have made the choice to move there. According to AJDC calculation, the emigration of Jews from the US zone in Germany during the year of 1946 totaled 6,871, with 4,057 sponsored by the AJDC. Of these 4,135 went to the United States (2,708 sponsored by Joint), 793 to Palestine (16 sponsored by Joint), and 1,430 to South and Central America (850 by Joint). YIVO, MK 488, Leo Schwarz Papers, Roll 9, Folder 56, #524, G.H. Muentz, AJDC Statistical Office to Dr Leo Schwartz, AJDC zone director.
54 See Ze'ev Mankowitz, *Life Between Memory and Hope*, p. 272; Emmanuel Sivan calculates that 21,500 immigrants managed to reach Israel in 1947; two-thirds of these were *ma'apilim*. 36.2 per cent of the total 1947 arrivals were between the age of eighteen and twenty-five; 62 per cent of the 1946–7 arrivals were between the ages of nineteen and twenty-five. See Emmanuel Sivan, *Dor Tashakh: Mitos, Diyukan ve-Zikaron* (Israel: Ministry of Defense 1991), p. 81; News of the statistical branch of the Jewish Agency (30 August 1947), p. 5; also Jewish Agency statistical bulletin (1946–7); M. Sikrun and B. Gil.
55 See Aviva Halamish, *The Exodus Affair: Holocaust Survivors and the Struggle for Palestine* (Syracuse: Syracuse University Press 1998), p. 5.
56 *Nocham* newspaper, 20 May 1947, Number 7 (2), YIVO, Jewish DP Periodicals Collection.
57 *Nocham*, 8 July 1947, Number 3–4 (8–9), YIVO, Jewish DP Periodicals Collection.
58 *Nocham* survey of movement activity, 16 July 1947, HAHP, 123/Maccabi/0014, #66–72.
59 *Hashomer Hatzair* movement newspaper, vol. 3 (13), 20 March 1947, Munich.
60 *Hashomer Hatzair* movement newspaper, vol. 4–5 (14–15), 1 April 1947, Munich, pp. 14–16.

61 See Aviva Halamish, *The Exodus Affair*, p. 72.
62 While the historian Idith Zertal has raised questions as to whether these survivors were manipulated by the Zionist movement to further their political goals, it is clear that the survivors played an active role in the dramatic events aboard the ship. See Idith Zertal, *From Catastrophe to Power: Holocaust Survivors and the Emergence of Israel* (Berkeley, CA: University of California Press 1998).
63 *Inyanei Aliyah* (Items related to *Aliyah*), 10 August 1947, Central Zionist Archives (CZA), S53/586. *Aliyat Hanoar* was a branch of the Zionist movement founded for the purpose of rescuing Jewish children and young people from hardship, persecution or deprivation and giving them care and education in Palestine. The agency started its activities in Germany at the end of 1932. For more on its activities in Germany in the 1930s, see the dissertation by Brian Amkraut, 'Let Our Children Go: *Youth Aliyah* in Germany, 1932–1939' (New York University 2000).
64 List of *Aliyat Ha-noar* (*Youth Aliyah*) on *Exodus*, 23 February 1948, *Inyanei Aliyah* (Items related to *Aliyah*), CZA, S53/586. The 23 February 1948 letter to members of the Directing Committee for Aliyah of Children and Youth, Number of youth eligible for *Aliyat Ha-noar* in *Yetziat Eyropah* counted 230 members of *Hashomer Hatzair*, 189 in *Dror*, 83 in *Noar Zioni*, 107 in *Mizrachi*, 28 in *PA"Y*, 7 in *PH"H*, and 50 in *Betar* eligible for *Youth Aliyah* on *Exodus* for a total of 713.
65 *Hashomer Hatzair Be-Ha'apalah*, Circular #10, 27 August 1947, YIVO, MK 483, DP Germany, Roll 97, Folder 1374, #173.
66 *Hashomer Hatzair* movement newspaper, #8 (18), August 1947, YIVO Library.
67 *Nocham* movement newspaper, #6 (11), 14 November 1947, YIVO, Jewish DP Periodicals Collection. See also *Hashomer Hatzair*, #10 (20), October 1947, p. 3.
68 *Nocham* newspaper, 1 October 1947, Number 5 (10), YIVO, Jewish DP Periodicals.
69 Ibid.

PART THREE

Postwar Displacement:

War Childhoods in an Unforgiving World: Memory, Rehabilitation and Silence

CHAPTER TWELVE

The Kinder's Children: Second Generation and the *Kindertransport*

Andrea Hammel

The *Kindertransport* (1938–9) to Britain is one of the best-known rescue movements of children from Central Europe. Research, though by no means exhaustive, has been carried out since the 1990s. This chapter will provide an overview of the history of the *Kindertransport* to Britain in 1938–9 followed by a focused analysis of the experiences of the descendants of former Kindertransportees.[1] It investigates the social history of the Second Generation group experience, namely, the experiences of the children and possibly also the grandchildren (Third Generation) of former Kindertransportees who fled to Britain in 1938–9 organized in specific groups. It outlines its interrelationships with other Second Generation groups but also its distinct specificity.

As is widely known, children with a Jewish background suffered discrimination and persecution during the National Socialist regime in Germany from 1933 onwards and in Austria after 1938. It is difficult to analyse what effect the National Socialist anti-Semitic policies had on children as compared to adults. Marion Kaplan outlines the growing exclusion of Jewish children from mainstream schools in Germany following the implementation of the law euphemistically called *Gesetz gegen die Überfüllung der deutschen Schulen und Hochschulen*, a law against the overcrowding of schools and high schools, in April 1933.[2] A quota for the admission of Jewish children to German schools was set and many Jewish children were explicitly asked to leave their schools, while others left after becoming more and more ostracized. Even for those who were still enrolled in mainstream German schools, everyday life was affected by exclusion from school trips and other extra-curricular activities. These changes must have been difficult to understand, especially for younger children, and even more so for those who had not been aware of their Jewish background before the National Socialists' rise to power. Consequently, more and more children were sent to Jewish schools. This trend did not completely cushion the children from discrimination and persecution, as public life in general, and the public sphere of children in particular (for example, on their journeys to and from school), was littered with discriminatory incidents or even violent situations. Thus, it could be argued that children were even more prone to experience everyday violence because of their Jewish background than adults. Because of the threats experienced, most children understood their parents' efforts to find a way for them to emigrate, even if they were scared to leave their families. Martha Blend (born in 1930) remembers:

> When my parents broke this news to me, I was devastated and burst into hysterical sobs at the mere thought. ... I felt as though some force stronger than myself was dragging me into an abyss and I had no power to prevent it. Although I was still very young, I had seen and understood the build-up of terror in the last two years, so I knew very well that my parents were doing this out of sheer necessity.[3]

Relatively soon after 1933, it had become clear to the *Reich's Deputation of the German Jews* (*Reichsvertretung der Deutschen Juden*) that leaving Germany was the only way to save the lives and livelihoods of many German Jews, thus facilitating emigration became the main task of the organization.[4] Most families tried to stay together when attempting to emigrate, but often this was not possible. Sending children abroad unaccompanied, however, was not a popular option until the November Pogroms in 1938.[5]

Although the courage of the parents who sent their children abroad to save them is generally acknowledged, postwar researchers have sometimes argued that not enough was known about the effects of parent–child separation,[6] which might have made such a course of action easier to follow for the parents. Publications of the *League of Jewish Women* (*Jüdischer Frauenbund*) make it clear that this was not the case and that a discussion about the negative sides of children emigrating without their parents was in the public domain in the 1930s.[7]

However, as archival research shows, many families tried to put their children on a *Kindertransport* to keep the family together. The Jewish community in Vienna had pre-printed application forms in which parents could state that they had obtained a domestic permit to enter the UK and thus wished their child to be considered for a *Kindertransport*.[8] Clearly parents wanted their children to be in the same country as them, possibly hoping for a speedy reunion. Domestic permits were another route of entry into the UK, for women or couples who were prepared to work as domestic staff. Nearly always they were not allowed to have their children live with them.

The eruption of violence towards the Jewish population in Germany during the November Pogroms of 1938 was not only a turning point for German-Jewish organizations and individuals. It also showed the international community that the German Jews were in an absolutely desperate situation. The government of Great Britain reacted with a public avowal of assistance for the German Jews. At a Cabinet Committee Meeting discussion on Foreign Policy on 14 November 1938 various possible reactions to the events were discussed, and the Prime Minister Neville Chamberlain stated that 'something effective should be done to alleviate the terrible fate of the Jews in Germany'.[9] He alluded to the public consciousness, which shows that the British population and media were aware of the situation and that there was a certain pressure on the government to be seen to be doing something. However, although various suggestions for helping the German Jews leave Germany were discussed, none was decided on during this particular meeting. The next day a group of Anglo-Jewish leaders met with Prime Minister Chamberlain, and at this meeting the idea of temporarily admitting a number of unaccompanied children for the purpose of training and education seems to have been discussed. Just a week later, the Home Secretary Sir Samuel Hoare announced the government's new refugee policy, which included the directive that all children whose maintenance could be guaranteed by private individuals or charitable organizations were allowed to be admitted to Britain 'without the individual checks used for older refugees'.[10] This was the official go-ahead for the *Kindertransport*.

The speed of organization and the magnitude of this immigration movement are two of the reasons why the *Kindertransport* is often mentioned with admiration. But this admiration needs qualification: although the government gave permission to admit the refugee children, almost all the financial support came from charitable bodies and private individuals. Neither swiftly organized emigration of large numbers of people nor child immigration to Britain was without precedent: during the Spanish Civil War, about 4,000 unaccompanied Basque children found refuge in the UK, and during the First World War a large number of Belgian child refugees were admitted to the UK. Nevertheless the extremely short period of time of two weeks between the decision to admit unaccompanied child refugees in late November 1938 and the arrival of the first ferry on 2 December 1938 at Harwich with around 200 child refugees on board shows the determination and excellent organizational skills of all involved.

On the German side, a department for child emigration (*Abteilung Kinderauswanderung der Reichsvertretung der Deutschen Juden*) had already been established by the *Reich's Deputation of the German Jews* in 1933. This meant that there were people with experience available, who could deal with the formalities and organization of a large group of Jewish children to be sent to the UK. In Austria, the situation was different, as there had been no initiative to send unaccompanied children abroad before the 'Anschluss' in March 1938. In Germany, the department for child emigration, which had its offices in Berlin, collected all the applications from Berlin and from provincial Jewish organizations and community offices. The department pre-selected the applications and sent them on to London, where they were received by the *Movement for the Care of Children from Germany* which was renamed *Refugee Children's Movement* (RCM) in 1939 and located in *Bloomsbury House* in London. There the children who were deemed to be suitable for emigration were chosen and this was then communicated back to the department for child emigration of the *Reich's Deputation of the German Jews*. The children and their parents were subsequently informed of the decision and were notified of their likely departure. They were allowed to take a small amount of luggage, which had to be labelled. No valuables and only a small amount of money were to be taken out of Germany. The age of the children ranged from two to seventeen, though there are some reports of even younger children.

Trains left from Berlin or Frankfurt on the Main, and the children were either asked to board the trains there or picked up at stations en route. A small number of adults accompanied the trains. The most likely route from Germany to the UK was via Bentheim and the Dutch Hoek of Holland, where the parties boarded the ferry to Harwich. There were also transports that took the train route to Hamburg or Bremen and from there a boat to Southampton. Upon arrival in the UK the children were either put in holding camps – a number of empty holiday camps had been put at the disposal of the RCM, the largest being Dovercourt – or transferred straight onto trains to London, either arriving at London Liverpool Street Station or Victoria Station. Eventually children were either accommodated in hostels or with foster families. The first call for foster parents put out by public appeal in Britain elicited 500 immediate responses from those willing to accommodate children.

In the beginning of the *Kindertransport* movement a sizeable number of children were selected according to the urgency of them having to leave Germany, i.e. boys aged fifteen to seventeen were seen as particular urgent cases as they were at danger of arrest. Also children who were living in children's homes were perceived to be urgent cases as were others living without one or both of their parents and those in particularly straightened circumstances. As mentioned above, all children had to be 'guaranteed', i.e. someone had to indemnify the UK government from financial responsibility for the child. Some of the money – £50 per child – came from the so-called Baldwin fund, a national appeal by the former Prime Minister Lord Baldwin, which was launched in December 1939 and eventually managed to collect £500,000. Half of this money was used to finance the immigration of Jewish child refugees.[11] Other guarantors were private individuals who were either identical with the child's prospective foster carers or people who just guaranteed the upkeep of the child refugee while they were placed elsewhere. Until about March 1939, an unspecified number of children who were sent to Britain did not have an individual guarantor, but were supported by a pool of guarantees to be distributed by the RCM as they saw fit. In spring 1939, this pool of guarantees from general funds was restricted to 200 cases, which meant that only if one of the 200 individuals was not in need of a guarantee any more, could another child refugee come to Britain in his or her stead. From March 1939 onwards, in the majority of cases, only children who had an individual guarantor could enter Britain. This led to a complicated relationship between the German department for child emigration and the RCM. Potential guarantors and foster parents in the UK were most keen to foster girls between seven and ten, which was not the largest group of child refugees waiting to leave Germany. The RCM forcefully rejected the German and Austrian child refugee departments' attempts to ask for further children without individual guarantees to be allowed entry into the UK:

> The Movement for the Transport of Children [*sic*], again, cannot bring over more unguaranteed children, until those already here have been placed. I regret that it is no use to continue to ask for more help than we are giving, because it is not in our power to grant it.[12]

Not all children who came to Britain on a *Kindertransport* were Jewish. About 20 per cent of the *Kindertransport* child refugees were so-called 'non-Aryans', children with a combination of Christian and Jewish parents or grandparents who either had no religious affiliation or were in fact Christians. The Quakers, also known as the *Society of Friends*, had offices in Berlin and Vienna and there were also specific organizations connected to the Protestant and Catholic Church.[13] The RCM in Britain was an interdenominational organization and took care of all the different groups of children. Not unsurprisingly, a certain amount of wrangling is reported between the representatives of the different groups about the numbers of places allocated to each group.

As mentioned above, the situation in Austria was less organized, but the department of child emigration of the Jewish community in Vienna nevertheless managed to put together the first transport to the UK in December 1938, which included 500 child refugees and remained the largest single transport. Research shows that there were constant debates between the parents of potential child refugees and the RCM in the UK, with the department for child emigration of the Viennese Jewish community positioned in the middle.[14] Parents were clearly eager to place their children on a transport and stressed their individual plight. The RCM was eager that only those children who had no special needs and were well-behaved should come to the UK, thus making their placement easier and creating a positive precedent which might encourage more people to come forward in aid of future child refugees. The Viennese department was dependent on the goodwill of the RCM, but also most immediately aware of the needs of the Austrian children. It seems that in the beginning the social workers in the department gave an honest account of a child's needs to aid the preparation of a foster placement in the manner of modern social work professionalism. When it became known to the RCM that a child had special needs, it often meant that they excluded the child from the transports. Sometimes even those who had an individual guarantor were excluded. The consequence of this was 'less thorough' medical examinations, which in turn made the RCM suspicious and led to accusations that the Viennese department was not working as well as required.

To conclude, one can only emphasize the difficult circumstances all agencies were working under and that tensions were structural rather than based on failures on one side or the other. Behavioural problems were clearly an understandable reaction from the children placed under stress, but they were seen as a problem that might jeopardize the whole operation. For the British public, the media and the government, refugee children had to be portrayed as helpless victims grateful to Britain for their rescue.

Because of time pressure, very little effort was made to match up the potential foster families with the children. This led to many unsuitable situations which ranged from a mismatch in cultural and religious backgrounds between foster families and child to situations in which the children suffered physical and sexual abuse.[15] Also, as nobody could have predicted the events of the Second World War, many foster parents had not realized the length of time they would be required to look after their charges. As the children got older and entered adolescence, their relationship became more difficult with their foster parents. Those who had arrived as adolescents were often accommodated in hostels with other young refugees. Overall, this seems to have been a preferable option for older Kindertransportees as they felt more comfortable in the company of other young people with a similar background. Some of the older Kindertransportees were very disappointed when they were not allowed to follow the educational path they had originally anticipated. They encountered prejudices that a basic education should be 'good enough' for a refugee and that they should earn their own money as soon as possible. Many older Kindertransportees played their part in the British war effort, either joining the army or working in a variety of jobs that were considered useful. There are as many *Kindertransport* stories as there are Kindertransportees and it seems that it depends on a wide variety of factors how individual Kindertransportees remember the war years and use this narrative to construct their identity.

Although the British government could perhaps be described as a rather reluctant partner in the *Kindertransport* rescue effort, after 1945 it decided to offer naturalization to almost all refugees that had spent the war in the UK and most former Kindertransportees who had reached the age of maturity by then, became naturalized. There has been some debate on how many of the Kindertransportees who came to the UK were reunited with their parents after 1945. As no reliable statistics are available for many years it had been assumed that 90 per cent of children lost both their parents. However, in 2008 the *Association of Jewish Refugees* (AJR) in the UK sent out questionnaires to over 1,500 surviving former Kindertransportees and over 1,000 were returned. Although the survey cannot claim to be reliably representative, there are a number of striking overlaps between statistical data known from contemporary sources of the 1930s and 1940s and statistical data of the *AJR Kindersurvey*. Thus we can assume that the survey's authors' assumption that about 60 per cent of the former Kindertransportees never saw their parents again is a reasonable estimate.[16] This trauma of separation and loss affected the former Kindertransportees for the rest of their lives. But even those who were reunited with one or even both parents had a very difficult time. Ruth Barnett, born January 1935, describes the adjustment difficulties of both herself and her mother who had last seen her as a four-year-old and met her again as a teenager after the war.[17]

For a number of decades after the war, former Kindertransportees did not identify as such in public, some even did not do so in private. There were those who had been very young when they fled to the UK. Some of the foster parents had tried to keep their foster children's memory of their parents and their background alive, others had not done that. This was in keeping with the policy regarding fostered or adopted children at the time: it was considered easier for their adaptation process if they were not reminded of the past. A sizeable number of this group knew very little about their background, some were adopted by British families and did not even know they had come on a *Kindertransport*. Even those who were well aware of their background concentrated on efforts to establish themselves in life after 1945. There is every indication that the former Kindertransportees achieved a higher educational standard than the average British person and were successful in their chosen professions.[18] Additionally, although most former Kindertransportees stayed in the UK, a sizeable number emigrated again after the end of the war, mainly to the US and Israel and today there are *Kindertransport Associations* in both countries.[19]

The relative obscurity of the *Kindertransport* as a refugee movement and of the fate of individual Kindertransportees changed in the last quarter of the twentieth century. In Britain today, the former Kindertransportees are a high profile group who are celebrated and accepted by the British establishment. This manifested itself in a knighthood for the chair of the *Association of Jewish Refugees' Kindertransport* group, now Sir Erich Reich, and a number of receptions hosted by the Royal family. The latest took place in June 2014 at St James' Palace attended by His Royal Highness Prince Charles. This happened in conjunction with the latest reunion meeting organized by the UK-based AJR in London.

It is the *Kindertransport Reunion Movement* (*Reunion of Kindertransports*: ROK) that can largely be credited with raising the profile of the *Kindertransport* in Britain and even abroad. The first *Kindertransport* Reunion took place in London in 1988. Thanks to the organizer Bertha Leverton, a large number of people who fled to Britain in 1938–9 came together to remember the events of their youth. Quite a few former Kindertransportees, especially those who had been very young when they escaped, only realized through these first reunion meetings and the public attention that surrounded them, that they had been part of a large refugee group. Some had very limited memories of their own early life. The term *Kindertransport* also only became common in the late 1980s. Ruth Barnett confirms this:

> I only discovered this interest in myself in 1989 when Berta Leverton organised the first Reunion of Kindertransport. Up until then the word Kindertransport had not entered my vocabulary and I was shocked to discover that there were nearly 10,000 of us brought to England in 1938/39.[20]

By this time, even the youngest of the former Kindertransportees were in their mid-fifties and many had children and grandchildren. Many of these had attended some reunions with their parents, a practice that would become increasingly common as the former Kindertransportees aged. In 2013, the former Kindertransportees were said to be in the minority at the reunion meeting, with the rest of the attendees mainly made up from the second and third generation.

To understand the *Kindertransport* Second Generation, we must first understand the development of the Holocaust Second Generation. According to Alan and Naomi Berger 'The Jewish Second Generation emerged as a distinct group in the mid-seventies, and gathered momentum in the eighties and early nineties'.[21] For those involved with Second Generation groups or publications it is apparent that there is such a thing as a Second (and Third) Generation experience and identity. The essence of this experience is the fact that the children of survivors had to live with the intensely traumatic experience of the Holocaust without ever having experienced the Holocaust first hand. One of the special generational aspects of the *Kindertransport* is the fact that some of the trauma of the First Generation often relates to the parent–child relationship. Because of the fact that about half of all Kindertransportees lost their parents to the Holocaust and the fact that even for those who did meet their parents again, the parent–child relationship was irretrievably changed by the events of the Holocaust, Kindertransportees' trauma is located in this relationship and thus it affected their own parenting. The psychologist Gaby Glassman who specialized in working with Second Generation survivors and refugees explained the challenges experienced by individual members of these groups:

> When very young children wanted unconditional love from their parents, parents were not always able to give it. I have heard some Second Generation say, 'My mother doesn't do love'. Our generation seems to be much more aware of the importance of receiving unconditional love. ... Separation issues were common. Children often found it hard to express their own feelings and to think and act independent. Consequently, some children skipped adolescence altogether while others went through 'adolescence' at a later time than usual, often only after they started therapy.[22]

At the same time, many members of the Second Generation report that their parents were unable or did not wish to speak about their experience to the children.

> For this generation, the Holocaust means the *eternal presence of an absence*, that is those who were murdered in the Shoah. The legacy of the Holocaust is present in a variety of ways for the Second Generation, issues of intergenerational communication, parental enmeshment and separation concerns.[23]

While many members of the Second Generation were glad to be accepted as such and were happy to develop spaces where they could express themselves, children of survivors are a heterogeneous group and some were not keen on the way the Second Generation identity was defined. Menachem Rosensaft, who was elected the first chair of the *International Network of Children of Jewish Holocaust Survivors* in September 1981,[24] was initially not sure whether he wanted to join any Second Generation group but when he heard how others defined their experience, he decided that the Second Generation needed to organize and present and represent itself:

> I changed my mind in the fall of 1979 at a New York Conference on Children of Holocaust Survivors. Organized by a well-meaning Jewish organization, this conference featured psychologist after psychologist after psychiatrist after psychiatrist after an array of other mental health specialists who considered themselves authorities on survivors and their children. In turn each of them publicly dissected our supposed pathology, trauma, guilt complexes ... I was appalled. I did not recognise myself or any of my friends in the collective psychobabble to which we were subjected.[25]

While children of Holocaust survivors had initially been considered by some as 'replacement children'[26] and pathologized, it was soon apparent that the children of Holocaust survivors were a very heterogeneous group. It also became clear that it was problematic to deduce general trends of mental well-being from those members of the Second Generation who had entered treatment for mental health conditions and generalize for the wider Second

Generation group. There is an obvious tension between wanting to acknowledge the difficulties Second Generation experiences bring and not to assume that all members suffer from mental health problems.

The transgenerational transmission of trauma became an established concept in the 1990s, but the focus was moved towards how families worked rather than on mental health problems and treatment.

> Families provide the socialization of children. Children learn values, beliefs and attitudes through direct teaching or indirect observation. The results of the present day study strongly support the transgenerational submission of depression, guilt and shame from Holocaust survivors to Second Generation and their children (third generation).[27]

Most recently, a number of studies were published arguing that there is no increased occurrence of depression and other associated problems among the children of Holocaust survivors. This development points to the complexity of the issues, which is true for Second Generation Kindertransportees as well.[28]

In Britain the Second Generation was mainly organized in the *Second Generation Trust*, a publication called *Second Generation Voice(s)*, the website secondgeneration.org and in therapy groups. All of these were not specific to the *Kindertransport*, but children of former Kindertransportees were increasingly involved. Whereas in the US, the *North American Kindertransport Association* (KTA) has a very prominent Second Generation and people define themselves as KT, KT2 or KT3,[29] this seems less common within the *Association of Jewish Refugees' Kindertransport Section* in the UK.

The first issue of *Second Generation Voice* was published in January 1996 for 'children of Jewish Holocaust survivors and refugees'. The editors stated the publications' intentions:

> With Second Generation Voice we aim:
>
> - to provide a forum for discussion of topics of interest to the Second Generation;
> - to provide the Second Generation with information on organizations, events and projects of interest to them;
> - to foster contacts between members of the Second Generation, especially outside London and where contacts are less developed;
> - to encourage the formation of a national body for the Second Generation.[30]

The editor for this first issue was David Bernheim, and Barbara Dorrity was assistant editor. The founding of the magazine follows a Second Generation Conference in summer 1995. As is made clear from the aims and intentions, the magazine was not aimed at children of Kindertransportees specifically. However, even at this stage they appear as an important section. It is reported that subgroups are to be set up, and one is for 'Children of Kindertransportees'.

The first volume contains statements by children of survivors and refugees where they outline how and why they had been affected by their parents' experiences. Susan Budnik writes in her contribution 'The Experience that Began in the Womb':

> I believe that my experience began in the womb and was later absorbed through my mother's milk. The Holocaust experience passed down in diluted form to my innocent lips and through me to my children.... Both my parents were deported from ghettos in Hungary and transported in cattle waggons to Auschwitz.[31]

Not all members and correspondents would agree with this narrative of essentialist embodiment of the Holocaust experience. Most describe their experiences of difference and the difficulties of growing up with survivor parents when defining their identity as Second Generation Holocaust survivors and refugees. For example, in 'Search for Identity', Barbara Dorrity, the daughter of a Kindertransportee, writes: 'Having always been acutely aware of being different from other children at school, because my parents were not born in England, I suppose I have only ever felt partially British, whatever "feeling British" means'.[32]

Dorrity's father, Rolf Dresner, fled to the UK on a *Kindertransport* from Leipzig and arrived in his host country at age thirteen on 27 June 1939. His parents were trapped in Poland, the father was shot by the Gestapo in Krakow in 1941, Dresner's mother was murdered in Belzec.

One of the problems for the children of Kindertransportees was to overcome the implicit hierarchy of suffering regarding different Holocaust experiences. Kindertransportees were often deemed to have suffered the least. Doris Bader Whiteman discusses the perception of those who had escaped National Socialist persecution before the 1940s as 'those to whom "nothing happened at all"'.[33] If these attitudes were brought to their logical conclusion, the children of Kindertransportees might be seen by some as a group that was so removed from the experience that it should not consider itself affected. This perception is often not from outsiders but is the self-perception of the Second Generation themselves. Compared to survivors who lived through the horror of a concentration camp experience, refugees often feel that it is difficult to talk about their suffering. In many cases refugees feel they do not want to call themselves Holocaust survivors. An intense debate on this issue was carried out in the Letters pages of the AJR journal on this topic. Thus, the children of former Kindertransportees sometimes feel the need to justify their inclusion in a Second Generation Holocaust experience. However, as Dorrity's description of her family's background shows, it is a very complicated issue because Holocaust and refugees experiences are almost always intertwined in one family. Also, it is clearly impossible to generalize every individual's reaction to their individual experiences. Some former Kindertransportees feel they were unaffected by the experience: 'a man who arrived on a *Kindertransport* to England in 1938 stated that he was lucky to be reunited later on with his parents. They had fled to Shanghai and come to England after the war. He said he felt "neutral, untraumatised"'.³⁴

Additionally, children of refugees found themselves in an emotionally difficult conundrum: because of their background, many were brought up with a Central European culture in the family. Especially for those families from a German or German-language background this often entailed a love–hate relationship to this culture and was difficult for the children to work out. Furthermore, not an insubstantial number of families were made up of one parent with a German-Jewish refugee background and one parent with a German background who came to the UK after 1945. For example, Barbara Dorrity's mother was a non-Jewish German who met her father when he was in the RAF and followed him to Britain in 1948.³⁵ This very specific situation is reflected in the May 1997 issue of *Second Generation Voices* when a conference is announced entitled 'The Presence of the Holocaust in the Present: the Intergenerational Transmission of the Holocaust and Communication Between Descendants'. This conference to be held in Berlin on 26 and 27 January 1997 was organized by Katherine Klinger of the *Second Generation Trust*, London, and Christian Staffa of the Institute for Comparative History, Berlin and its aim was to bring together children of survivors and the children of perpetrators.

Soon after the founding of the newsletter the editorial committee of the Second Generation publication recognized the varied experiences and the different opinions. By September 1996 *Second Generation Voice* had become *Second Generation Voices*:

> Names are important to us. The name of our newsletter has been changed – expanded if not altered, according to the original intention of the founding editorial group. Henceforth the newsletter is to be called Second Generation Voices. It is a minor but salutary correction.³⁶

Clearly, there is an acknowledgement that there is not one voice, but, rather, different voices by Second Generation members. At the same time, being able to speak about the *Kindertransport* experience was still considered difficult:

> Too many voices have been too silent for too long in respect of Second (and First) Generation Experiences. While respecting these silences, we feel they may also be probed, opened up and spoken of if a receptive ear (or form) is available for them. We hope you may feel closer to responding with your own voices to these views.³⁷

As in the case of the US *Second Generation Survivor Groups* there was a 'presence of an absence'. In *Second Generation Voices* Ruth Selwyn writes:

> The atmosphere of silence surrounding the Holocaust created a very particular environment for the Second Generation. Group members often describe having been aware of pain, grief, sadness in their homes. In that sense they were 'born' into the Holocaust. However there was nothing clear they could get hold of. A fear of triggering a parent's overwhelming pain prevented many children from asking about their parents' Holocaust past.[38]

However, it was not always the parents' unwillingness to talk about painful experiences. Because of their young age when they lived through Holocaust-related trauma and the separation from their own parents, some of the First Generation Kindertransportees had unclear memories of their own experiences. The psychotherapist and former Kindertransportee Ruth Barnett writes about this in an article entitled 'Breaking the Silence: Mending the Broken Connection' in *Second Generation Voices*: 'That reunion made me realize not only that I knew very little but that I must have been shutting out, or relegating to the back corners of my mind, an awful lot of knowledge that was available to me'.[39]

Other members of the Second Generation describe an atmosphere where things were generally understood between the two generations although they were not explicitly articulated. Karen Goodman, a social worker and the daughter of a Kindertransportee from Czechoslovakia, writes about the communication with her mother on the occasion of the Winton Train Memorial event:

> Our journey 70 years later was full of fun and tears, markedly more comfortable than for the original passengers. As my mother so poignantly remarked when I explained what I was doing: 'Hmm we sat on wooden benches, the trains were sealed, we were not allowed off the train. We only had what we brought with us to eat and drink . . .' The remainder of the realities, as ever, were unsaid but fully understood. (like most of the untold stories and truths about her history had been throughout my childhood). . . . I am one of the 5,000 descendants of the people whose lives were saved by the Winton trains.[40]

All of these instances can be defined as communication challenges within the families of former Kindertransportees. From our position in the twenty-first century there seems little point in putting responsibility for addressing these challenges on anyone or any generation in particular, but they have to be acknowledged in order to understand the situation of the children and grandchildren of former Kindertransportees more fully.

The *Second Generation Voices* newsletter did not only publish the texts of those writing articles, editorials and features. There was often a lively discussion in the letters pages and *Second Generation Voices* also actively sought the opinions of its readership in a survey. In the same number as Ruth Barnett's article, a 'Letter from Derbyshire' by a daughter of a Kindertransportee from Germany, appeared in response to the survey:

> There are other things I don't care for quite as much. Firstly and foremost there is an overall impression that the Second Generation contributors all seem to have taken the mantle of suffering from their First Generation ancestors. There is a lot of looking backwards and grieving. I personally find this very difficult to deal with on several fronts. Yes, to shape what we are and will be, we have to understand where we come from; but the past is the foundation of the future – where is the mention of the third generation? I think if the Second Generation invested time into the third generation, instead of 'Oi Vehing' about the first generation, their experiences and how they affect us, it would be a positive and healthy approach. . . . Let the hangups of the past rest. I believe that you honour the dead by living positively.[41]

Caring about the future and how to transfer the lessons learned from the *Kindertransport* experience of their parents are important recurring themes and demands in the newsletter. Overall, it cannot be said that the Second Generation as represented in *Second Generation Voices* is too inward looking. There are numerous articles calling for assistance and solidarity with present-day refugee groups and for education campaigns to be set up. Members of the Second Generation of the *Kindertransport* were involved in an education resource *The Last Goodbye* aimed at teaching British school-children about the *Kindertransport*, which was developed by *The Jewish Museum* in London and the AJR.[42] A group of social workers also developed an education pack to help others in the caring profession to understand older survivors and former refugees and their specific needs. There are debates about conflict in Israel and about the British government's attitude to present-day refugees and asylum seekers. Reviewing a *Kindertransport* Reunion publication entitled *Kindertransport – 60th anniversary*, Jenny Alexander writes:

> Despite my interest in the book, in my opinion, its principal weakness lies in its inability to move on, or to offer more than many similar texts have in the past. It does not address the present, and probably in its defence never had any intention of doing so. It seems to me that, whilst this is enough for the Kinder generation, it is important for those in the second and third generation to see beyond the memories of their parents.[43]

In a feature entitled 'Network News' discussions about the tension between looking at their own experiences and sharing these with others and the need to work with others outside the Holocaust survivors' and refugee circles is discussed frequently:

The committee is now reviewing our aims and objectives to reflect on our experiences. Much of our efforts so far have turned inwards, reflecting on individual, family and communal experiences. It may now be the time to look outwards as well, sharing our stories and making connections with other groups – this may in turn shed new light on our own experiences.[44]

The sixteen-year-old grandson of a survivor, Jacob Engelberg makes the obvious connection to today's situation: 'I left the seminar in awe of the rescue operation and all who partook in it, and grateful that my grandfather was one of the lucky few. I also left with the message that those fleeing from authoritarian regimes and genocide should be given every right to asylum'.[45] Others criticize reunion meetings for a lack of contemporary relevance. Anne Overton writes about the reunions which took place in November and December 2008:

> I was sorry that the day's programme did not make a link with people from other ethnic groups whose lives are currently threatened by oppression. ... My experience as a Second Generation member of a Holocaust refugee family has been mostly one of being on the edge of majority culture, of having a history that is on the margins of the mainstream. At the reunion we were not at the edge but at the centre of a story that is still in the making. For me, the reunion played a part in the shaping and re-shaping of the narrative that binds the refugee and the host country, and the past with the present and the emerging future.[46]

Since the 2008–9 seventieth anniversary meeting, the question of legacy and how to continue the memory of the *Kindertransport* has become more and more prominent. David Clark wrote about a lack of energy because the First Generation had either passed on or was now too old or ill to be involved in a major way:

> All went fine: but it lacked something; it was too much of a show, but no real guts; the formula was there; honours had been done; but it was all stage managed. . . . the spirit from the grass root was lacking; many of the Kinder were no longer there, or could not make it to the reunion, and for many much of the energy was gone, well it is 70 years on. For how much longer can they be expected to turn up to such occasions?[47]

This is indeed a difficult issue and one that many stakeholders in the memorialization and education processes surrounding the Holocaust and, especially in the UK, the *Kindertransport* struggle with. The *Kindertransport* Reunion meeting organized by the AJR which took place in London in 2013 was criticized by some members of the Second Generation for its lack of sensitivity to the First Generation, both in practical matters (lack of comfort and accessibility) and as regards to the content of the programme. The programme included a performance by students reading out fragments of letters from parents to their children who had fled on a *Kindertransport*. These performers were dotted around the audience and started speaking at irregular intervals. It was felt that these 'surprise' narrations were not sufficiently sensitive to the First Generation Kindertransportees in the room who were suddenly and in such an inescapable and immediate manner reminded of their childhood trauma.[48] Menachem Rosensaft warned about becoming desensitized to the trauma the First Generation suffered: 'As our knowledge of the Holocaust increases, we must be careful not to become desensitized. As we perpetuate memory we must also prevent it from becoming commonplace'.[49] This is an issue that both the Second and the Third Generation as well as others working in this area would be well advised to remember.

Notes

1 I would like to thank the staff at the Wiener Library, London, and especially Kat Hübschmann and Howard Falksohn for their assistance in the research for this article. I am also grateful to Barbara Budrich for permission to use passages for the historical overview of the *Kindertransport* in this article, which have been published in Andrea Hammel, 'Child Refugees Forever? The History of the Kindertransport to Britain 1938/39', in *Diskurs Kindheits-und Jgendforschung*, Nr. 2 (Leverkusen: Verlag Barbara Budrich 2010), pp. 132–6.

2 Marion Kaplan, *Der Mut zum Überleben. Jüdische Frauen und Familien in Nazideutschland* (Berlin: Aufbau 2001), pp. 140–56.

3 Martha Blend, *A Child Alone* (London: Vallentine Mitchel 1995), p. 32.

4 Claudia Curio, *Verfolgung, Flucht, Rettung. Die Kindertransporte 1938/39 nach Großbritannien* (Berlin: Metropol 2006), p. 31.

5 Ibid., pp. 39–42.

6 See Ute Benz, 'Traumatisierung durch Trennung. Familien-und Heimatverlust als kindliche Katastrophen', in *Die Kindertransporte 1938/39. Rettung und Integration*, ed. by Wolfgang Benz, Claudia Curio and Andrea Hammel (Frankfurt/Main: Fischer Taschenbuchverlag 2003), pp. 136–55.

7 D. Edinger, 'Ver Sacrum? Fragen einer Mutter', *Blätter des jüdischen Frauenbundes*, November 1933, pp. 1–2.

8 Completed form 'O', dated 14 June 1939, Collection Israelitische Kutlusgemeinde Wien, XXII. Fuersorge- und Wohlfahrtswesen, F. Jugendfuersorge, 7. Kinderauswanderung, Korrespondenzen ueber bereits abgereiste Kinder, 1938–1939, A/W 1962, Box 560, Central Archive for the History of the Jewish People, Jerusalem.

9 Cited in Louise London, *Whitehall and the Jews 1933–1948. British Immigration Policy and the Holocaust* (Cambridge: Cambridge University Press 2000), p. 99.

10 Ibid., p. 104.

11 Ibid., p. 122.
12 Cited in Rebekka Göpfert, *Der jüdische Kindertransport von Deutschland nach England 1938/39* (Frankfurt/Main: Campus 1999), p. 92.
13 See Claudia Curio, *Verfolgung, Flucht, Rettung* and Jana Leichsenring, *Die Katholische Kirche und 'ihre' Juden* (Berlin: Metropol 2003).
14 Claudia Curio, *Verfolgung, Flucht, Rettung*, pp. 83–92.
15 See Vera K. Fast, *Children's Exodus: History of the Kindertransport* (London and New York: I.B.Tauris 2011), pp. 41–59.
16 http://www.ajr.org.uk/kindersurvey (accessed 18 February 2014).
17 Ruth Barnett, *Person of No Nationality: A Story of Childhood Separation, Loss and Recovery* (London: David Paul Books 2011).
18 http://www.ajr.org.uk/kindersurvey (accessed 18 February 2014).
19 For the *North American Kindertransport Association* (KTA), see http://kindertransport.org/ (accessed 18 February 2014), and article on Kindertransportees in Israel, 'Special Gathering of Kindertransport Children at Yad Vashem', http://www.yadvashem.org/yv/en/about/events/event_details.asp?cid=167 (accessed 18 February 2014).
20 Ruth Barnett, 'Breaking the Silence: Mending the Broken Connection Part 2', *Second Generation Voices* 19 (January 2002), p. 12.
21 Alan L. Berger and Naomi Berger (eds), *Second Generation Voices: Reflections by Children of Holocaust Survivors and Perpetrators* (New York: Syracuse University Press 2001), p. 3.
22 'Establishing a Separate Identity', Gaby Glassman in an interview with Leonie Grayeff, *Second Generation Voices* 51 (October 2012).
23 Alan L. Berger and Naomi Berger (eds), *Second Generation Voices*, p. 1.
24 Menachem Z. Rosensaft, 'I was Born in Bergen-Belsen', in *Second Generation Voices*, ed. by Alan L. Berger and Naomi Berger, pp. 188–207, here p. 202.
25 Ibid. p. 201.
26 Alan L. Berger, *Children of Job. American Second-Generation Witnesses to the Holocaust* (Albany: State University of New York Press 1997), p. 13.
27 Susan Weisz Jurkowitz, 'Transgenerational Transmission of Depression, Shame and Guilt in Holocaust Families: An Examination of Three Generations', unpublished PhD thesis (California School of Professional Psychology, Los Angeles 1996), p. 196.
28 For example, Lotem Giladi and Terece S. Bell, 'Protective Factors for Intergenerational Transmission of Trauma Among Second and Third Generation Holocaust Survivors', *Psychological Trauma: Theory, Practice and Policy* 5/4 (2013), pp. 384–91; Ayala Fridman, Marian J. Bakermans-Kranenburg, Abraham Sagi-Schwartz and Marinus H. Van IJzendoorn, 'Coping in Old Age with Extreme Childhood Trauma: Aging Holocaust Survivors and their Offspring Facing New Challenges', *Age & Mental Health* 15/2 (2011), pp. 232–42.
29 At the *Kindertransport* Conference in November 2012 in Irvine, California, participants were identified as KT, KT2 and KT3 on their name badges.

30 Alan L. Berger and Naomi Berger (eds), *Second Generation Voices*, January 1996, p. 1.
31 Ibid., p. 6.
32 Ibid., p. 7.
33 Doris Bader Whiteman, *The Uprooted: A Hitler Legacy* (New York and London: Plenum Press 1993), p. 2.
34 Alan L. Berger and Naomi Berger (eds), *Second Generation Voices* 27 (October 2004), p. 17.
35 Ibid., p. 7.
36 Ibid., 1 (September 1996), p. 1.
37 Ibid., p. 1.
38 Ibid., 7 (January 1998), p. 3.
39 Ibid., 8 (May 1998), p. 12.
40 Karen Goodman, 'The Winton Train 2009', in *Second Generation Voices*, ed. by Alan L. Berger and Naomi Berger, 45 (October 2010), p. 15.
41 Alan L. Berger and Naomi Berger (eds), *Second Generation Voices* 8 (May 1998), p. 3.
42 Ibid., 24 (September 2003), p. 2.
43 Ibid., 23 (May 2003), p. 20.
44 Ibid., 24 (September 2003), p. 2.
45 Jacob Engelberg, 'My Grandfather's Plight', *Second Generation Voices*, ed. by Alan L. Berger and Naomi Berger, p. 5.
46 *Second Generation Voices*, ed. by Alan L. Berger and Naomi Berger (January 2009), p. 18.
47 Ibid.
48 Karen Goodman, in an interview with Andrea Hammel, London, 28 November 2013.
49 Menachem Z. Rosensaft, 'I was Born in Bergen-Belsen', in *Second Generation Voices*, ed. by Alan L. Berger and Naomi Berger, pp. 188–207, here p. 204.

CHAPTER THIRTEEN

Remembering the 'Pain of Belonging': Jewish Children Hidden as Catholics in Second World War France

Mary Fraser Kirsh

> For my soul, my mind, have been twisted in so strange a direction. That no part of me is home, here or there. And I shall forever be left to wander.[1]

In 1943, nine-year-old Renée Fersen-Osten and her sister were baptized into the Catholic Church with the consent of their parents. Willing to sacrifice their daughters' Jewish identity to ensure their survival, the parents entrusted them to the Church, promising to raise the children as Catholics if they returned home after the war. In silence, the parents watched the baptism, and at the close of the ceremony, the mother burst into tears. Fersen-Osten remembers her mother crying: '"I sold you!" And she ran out of the church. And she ran from us. We didn't belong to her anymore'.[2] This marked the beginning of Fersen-Osten's lifelong struggle with her religious and cultural identity. She accepted a religion and adopted an identity that promised her security, but the price paid was a repression of her former self.

Fersen-Osten, along with thousands of other Jewish children in France during the Second World War, actively negotiated the categories of Jewish and Christian. However, due to a scholarly focus on the heroics of adult rescuers and the impact of trauma upon children, the actual voices of child survivors have been overlooked until recently.[3] One way to change the focus on the Holocaust's hidden children from passive subjects to active agents is through a closer look at their memoirs. Although historians have often shied away from memoirs as source material due to their subjective nature, the unreliability of memory and the change of perceptions over time, they provide intimate insights into how ordinary children responded to anti-Semitism during an extraordinary time. Children's reactions to persecution were largely determined by parental decisions, but when it came to their inner spiritual life, children demonstrated a remarkable degree of autonomy. I draw upon over fifty of these testimonies by children hidden under assumed Catholic identities to explore the ways in which children from secular homes[4] perceived their religious identity before, during and after the war.[5]

These testimonies represent a small fraction of the approximately 70,000 Jewish children who survived in France. Hidden children have only begun to define themselves as survivors and bear witness in the past few decades. Even after the term 'survivor' became widely used, it was generally applied to those who had been deported and interned in camps in other countries. As Sarah Gross recalled: 'I felt that since I had not ... lived through the unimaginable horrors of camps ... I had not suffered'.[6] A hierarchy of suffering is a common theme in their testimonies. Odette Meyers explains: 'I felt that the right responsibility of bearing witness belonged to those camp survivors who were older than I'.[7] The *First International Gathering of Children Hidden during World War II,* held in 1991 and attended by 1,600 survivors, has inspired many hidden children to speak out about their wartime experiences.[8] Since 1993, members of *Aloumim*, an association of hidden child survivors from France, have been publishing their wartime reminiscences and hosting support groups. Through these relatively new avenues for self-expression, hidden children have analysed their individual identities and established a common identity. The voices are distinct, but as a collective, they 'bear "family resemblances" in tone, genre, and emotional or narrative content that place them in significant dialogue with each other'.[9] Hidden child memoirs have become a specialized subsection within the wider canon of Holocaust literature.

Hidden children experienced a splitting of identities, because of their dual religious affinities. It was difficult to 'be at one' with Judaism's future, because Jewish life was precarious during the war years, but to associate with Catholicism's future implied that their parents were not returning for them. As the children struggled to reconcile their past Jewish identities with their new Catholic ones, they experienced a crisis of self-understanding, which was further exacerbated when the Jewish community expected them to return to Judaism at the war's end.

By actively exploring the categories of Jewish and Catholic, these children participated in a historic process of finding a balance between religious, social and civic identity. A new generation of hidden Jews was born, as the historic challenge to be a 'man on the streets and a Jew at home' was transformed into the challenge to be a Catholic on the streets, in school, in church, and at home, and a Jew in memory only. While the children had moments when they identified one religion as more authoritative than another, the inner conflict that is expressed in testimonies illustrates the impact that assimilation had upon religious identity. The children, particularly those of foreign parents, had juggled multiple identities before the war, learning to be Jewish at home and 'French' in public so that they could win their classmates' acceptance. Even younger children expressed an awareness of the flexibility of the definitions of Jew and Christian. While in hiding, eight-year-old Claude Morhange-Bégué felt ambivalence towards weekly Mass: 'I say my prayers – I don't mind doing it at all. Has any of that anything really to do with me? Indeed, I believe that in this period I also learned about the relativity and the flexibility of manners and customs'.[10]

Hidden children such as Morhange-Bégué were unknowingly participating in what Yirmiyahu Yovel understands as a rich tradition of secular Jews: the tradition of Marranism, of negotiating the categories of Christian and Jewish to determine public and private behaviour. Scholar Elaine Marks argues that Marranism occurs when 'Jewish and Christian cultures mingle, in which both are recognized as being present, albeit in different degrees, and neither is denied'.[11] *Marrano* is the term historically used in Europe to refer to crypto-Jews, individuals who adopted Catholicism in public while secretly continuing to practise Judaism within their homes. Both crypto-Jews of fifteenth-century Spain and the crypto-Jewish children of the Holocaust ensured their survival by concealing their identities, but the latter faced a significant disadvantage. While the secrecy of Judaism played a large role in the familial and social life of Spanish crypto-Jews, hidden children were cut off from the rest of the Jewish community, and younger children had little memory of Jewish beliefs and practices. Without communal support, the children's hold on Judaism was tenuous.

Prewar, Jewish children raised in secular homes understood Judaism in more ambiguous terms than their observant counterparts. Marks argues that such children were already 'marranos', because they had been taught early on that Jewishness was private, something only expressed inside the home or synagogue.[12] Their parents' struggles to reconcile religious and secular worlds shaped the children's identity. Isaac Levendel notes: 'Having already broken away from the Orthodox interpretation of the Jewish religion before they left the Polish shtetl, my parents were awkwardly striving to behave like the French. Inside, however, they remained ferociously Jewish'.[13] As a result of synthesizing the religious and the secular, Judaism became a culture, part of the family's heritage, rather than a religion; assimilation was thus facilitated. Jacqueline Wolf recalls that while her father 'had given up organized religion', he also taught his children 'to be proud of [their] heritage, that the only way to fight discrimination was to assimilate'.[14] Such ambiguous messages left the children with a complex legacy. Children from secular homes carried vague understandings of Judaism into the war years, expressed through fragmented memories, such as dusting before sundown on Friday and *matzo* in the spring.[15] French Christiano-centrism further superseded Jewish identity.[16] While Judaism was a private religion, marked by domestic details such as kosher foods and *mezuzot*, Catholicism was a public religion, pervading French culture and society. The most secular Jewish children may have known nothing of Judaism, but Catholicism was not entirely foreign.

The physical marking of individuals as Jews challenged the notion that affiliation could be determined by the self. For secular children in the Northern Zone, 7 June 1942 changed the way they understood their identity: Jews over the age of six were required to wear a yellow star on their outer clothing. The suddenness of this externally imposed label was alarming. Renée Roth-Hano recalls: 'I went to bed one night as an ordinary eight-year-old and woke up the next day as a Jew'.[17] For Sarah Gross, the mandate to wear the star marked the end of innocence, because it triggered anti-Semitic comments from previously kind classmates: 'Because I wore a star, even though I was the same Sarah, someone had taunted me as a "dirty Jewess". From that day on, my small happy world was gone'.[18] The star was particularly frustrating for children who had never thought of themselves as being Jewish. Joseph Joffo writes: 'All of a sudden they stick a few square inches of cloth on me, and I turn into a Jew. A Jew. What does that mean? What the hell is a Jew? I feel anger rising up in me, along with the helpless rage of not understanding'.[19] The pronounced emphasis on difference, made public by the wearing of the star, led to an obsession with identity.[20] The implication of this tangible star was the recasting of the self.

The star also created an enormous sense of vulnerability. Before Roth-Hano left home each morning, she counted the remaining minutes of her privacy: 'I am ashamed. I no longer walk: I skim the walls'.[21] The discrimination the children faced at school compounded their vulnerability. 'Lazare' recounts: 'I was bullied by the teachers, slapped at random . . . no one defended me'.[22] Testimonies such as Levendel's emphasize the fierce desire to disappear. He recalls wishing that the earth would swallow him up when his schoolmates called him a 'dirty Jew' on the playground.[23]

Many children made a conscious effort to hide their Jewish identities, even before they formally adopted new ones. Simon Jeruchim considered his Jewishness a 'shameful secret'; he tried to conceal his star under his scarf while walking to school.[24] Psychologist Mary Gallant explains that public stigmatization, coupled with the changing dynamics at home and in school, 'meant that there was no automatic safe haven possible with others or within the self'.[25] The war led them to associate Judaism with something that needed to be hidden in order to prevent humiliation. If no safe haven could be found as Jews, a new identity would have to be forged in order for them to remain secure in a country under anti-Semitic legislation.

One month after the mandate to wear the yellow star, French Jewry reached its crisis point, when French police arrested 13,000 Jews in the

Occupied Zone. Of the 8,000 Jews detained at the Vélodrôme d'Hiver, half were children, who would be brutally separated from their parents and deported to Auschwitz alone. The public violence of the summer round-ups, which extended to the Unoccupied Zone in August, sent an alarm through the Jewish community. Relief societies such as *Amitié Chrétienne* and *Service Social des Entrangers* worked feverishly to smuggle youths out of camps. By mid-1943, a network of volunteers orchestrated by Georges Garel placed over a thousand children within Christian schools, orphanages and farms.[26]

When the children formally went into hiding by adopting Christian identities, their names were the first things the parents changed; this caused fear for some, relief for others. Claudine Vegh recalled: 'I wanted to keep my name. I was going to grow, change: and what if [my parents] did not recognize me?'[27] Saul Friedländer, hidden in a boarding school near Vichy, best sums up the confusion many children felt: 'Paul-Henri could only be French and resolutely Catholic, but that did not yet come naturally'; consequently, 'it was impossible to find my way, which struck me as an adequate expression of a real and profound confusion'.[28] Conversely, Roth-Hano greeted her name change with welcome relief: 'I'm ashamed of my name now ... I've been feeling ashamed ... of not being like everybody else'.[29] In some families, children had always been addressed by two different names: a Yiddish or Hebrew name at home and a French name outside the home. Ruth Hartz registered at school as Rénee,[30] and Jeruchim responded to Zizi at home but became Simon at school; they all learned to 'dance the waltz of names with mastery'.[31]

Suppressing identity went hand in hand with the new names; the children had to replace their past with a fabricated history. They could no longer talk of the people and experiences that had formed their identity up to this point; silence was their greatest protection, but the fragility of this shield was apparent. Ruth Hartz was acutely aware that a mere lie was all that protected her: 'There had been constant reminders that I was also a Jewish child: the round-ups, the suspicious looks, the fear. Now, all that had been erased. I was not Jewish. I was going to be protected by a false piece of information'.[32] The children's resiliency and their impressionable age helped them to adapt to the values of the new environment, but thoughts of their past lives remained, even as they strove to live within the framework of their new identities. Despite carefully hiding her past, Pnina Spitz unconsciously betrayed herself: 'I guess it was the constant stress that pushed me one day while I was doing my homework, to take a piece of paper and draw a yellow star with the word "Jew" right in the middle. Maybe it was to remind me of who I really was'.[33]

Once safely ensconced in institutions and families, hidden children expressed an intense attraction to Catholicism, as well as a need to cling to whatever fragments they remembered of their Jewishness. This neatly fits into the tradition of Marranism, in which Judaism and Christianity 'are recognised as being present albeit in different degrees, and neither is denied'.[34]

The majority of the memoirs evoke conflicted loyalties.[35] Catholicism provided comfort, security and protection; Judaism offered a link to the parents who were no longer physically present. These two needs – to protect oneself with a 'safer' religion and to maintain ties with a familiar past – exacerbated the children's search for religious identity.

Posing as Christians induced guilt, even if they hailed from secular families. Several survivors mention that they expected to be struck by lightning the first time they entered a church or took communion.[36] Wolf worried that her father would think less of her for pretending to be a Catholic: 'To me, a religious masquerade was the ultimate hypocrisy ... I thought I'd be committing an act for which he could never forgive me'.[37] When Roth-Hano was assigned the role of Judas in a pageant of the Last Supper, she feared that the other children would 'realize that I'm Jewish, too ... and that I'm a traitor as well, since I'm passing for a Catholic'.[38] Her only consolation was that Judas betrayed Christ 'because he wanted to. I, for one, don't have any choice'.[39]

All of the children clung to some aspect of their Jewishness, since it provided a tie to their parents. Upon separation, some parents imparted biblical stories to help the children remember their heritage.[40] As parents searched the past for something to impart to their children, the children accepted these stories and accessed the narratives when they felt homesick. Before being sent to a convent, Ruth Hartz's parents urged her: 'Remember that you are Jewish. Don't speak of it to anyone, but never forget it. Be proud of it, as Queen Esther was'.[41] While Hartz remembered this instruction, the story that her father told her of Ruth and Naomi had more meaning, since she shared the matriarch's name. Each night, Hartz would address her absent parents, using the words that Ruth spoke to Naomi: 'Wherever you go, I will go. Wherever you live, I will live. Your people shall be my people, and your God my God'.[42] This passage brought strength to Hartz, and she 'thanked Papa a thousand times for telling me the story'.[43] Not all children were armed with such stories, however. Roth-Hano grappled to find Jewish prayers and stories in the recesses of her memory as a way of fighting the Catholic indoctrination, but she could remember none.[44]

Over time, the children appreciated the haven that the Catholic Church provided. Today, they recall Mass as 'comforting', 'soothing' and a 'refuge'.[45] For Roth-Hano, singing 'made me feel like I belonged ... At least when I was singing, there was hope coming from my heart'.[46] The predictability of a life dominated by ritual brought solace. Many children spent time praying for their families. Frankie Paper hung pictures of Jesus and prayed that he would reunite her with her parents.[47] With so much uncertainty, the church was the one place where simplicity reigned and the children did not live in fear. As Friedländer reflected: 'Straight-forward faith, which was inculcated into us, this was what I needed. Was not literal Christianity directed, first of all, to the disinherited and the abandoned of the world?'[48]

The children also sought comfort from tangible things in the church. Josie Martin felt safe surrounded by the crucifixes in the convent and sent her parents a paper cross so that they would be protected as well.[49] Statues of saints became confidants in a world where talking to people could cost children their lives. Fersen-Osten recalls: 'After Mass, I would go to Saint Francis and I'd tell him everything. He was made of stone but he would hear every word and would never tell anyone'.[50] The Virgin Mary played the most significant role. For many children, the Virgin reminded them of their mothers. Roth-Hano explained: 'When everything is gray inside – I like to sit by the Virgin. She is a mother, and she must surely understand'.[51] Odette Meyers associated the Virgin Mary with Madame Marie, her godmother who secured her hiding place. Meyers was delighted upon learning that 'Madame Marie' was the peasants' term of affection for the Virgin Mary. Before the war, Meyers had respected the wisdom of her godmother; now in rural France, far from the protection of Madame Marie, she discovered a surrogate godmother in the Holy Mother. 'Madame Marie was with me. She was in the church. She was in every statue, every picture of the Virgin Mary. She would take care of me'.[52] At Friedländer's baptism, he received the name Marie; for him, this was an invocation of the 'protection of the Virgin, the heavenly mother who sheltered me from the storm, less vulnerable than my early mother who, at that very moment, had already been carried away by the whirlwind'.[53] Like Roth-Hano, Friedländer would sit at the base of the statue, thinking of his absent mother. Catholicism eased the desperate void left by the removal from their homes and the sudden departure of their parents.

The price that the children paid for the solace of Christianity was an increasing spiritual distance from their family and heritage. During her third month in the convent, Martin's father came to visit; after watching his daughter gather a bouquet to place at the foot of a cross, he lamented: 'She's already become a little Catholic'.[54] Martin recognized that she was 'not their little girl anymore'.[55] While Hartz missed her parents, the nuns assured her that 'we had a new family – our brothers and sisters in Jesus'.[56] Roth-Hano worried that she was betraying her parents with her indoctrination into the Church, but she felt powerless to stop its growing influence. Loyalty towards Judaism equated with loyalty towards her parents, and her love of the Church created a moral dilemma for her: 'How can you adopt a new family without betraying the old one?'[57]

As the children's memories of Judaism grew dim, they turned against their former religion. Wolf 'started to think that perhaps Jews were bad; otherwise, why would God allow anyone to persecute them?'[58] Hartz mirrored this thought: 'It would be better if we could forget altogether about being Jewish. Jewish people got into trouble and were taken away. If Haman had tried to get rid of the Jews, and now the Nazis had the same intention, there must be something terribly wrong with being Jewish'.[59] Faced with the dichotomy of Christians as holy and Jews as evil, Meyers worried that the messages of the sermons were true: that Jews were 'in a league with Satan and that he was using us to hurt true Christians'.[60] Some children blamed their heritage for personal weaknesses. Frida Weinstein attributed her periods of doubting 'to the fault of my origins; they stand in the way of my path to sainthood'.[61] Isabelle Riff, unable to distance herself from the guilt of being Jewish, was aware that something within her was 'wrong': 'This is a terrible feeling, to be aware that what you are is a reason that you have to hide it ... This is to feel ashamed for what you are'.[62] Attachment to Catholicism was thus facilitated by the fact that participating in a 'safe' collective identity was a mechanism for spiritual and physical survival.

Rather than simply deny their Jewishness, it was more constructive for the children to use their relationship with the Church to create a new identity. They began by adopting new names and learning new prayers, but over time they became enmeshed in their new environment, building a new sense of self that contained elements from past and present lives. The children were moved from one institution to another, rarely staying in one place long enough to establish lasting relationships with children and adults around them. However, their relationship with religion was 'portable', a part of the newly forged identity framework that could be used throughout the war, no matter where they lived.

When the children wished to convert to Catholicism, they sought the ultimate assimilation. Historian Debórah Dwork claims that the 'sincere embrace' of Christianity was 'an infrequent occurrence' among these hidden children.[63] However, many children experienced intense periods during which they felt extremely close to the Church and wanted it to be a permanent part of their lives. Weinstein was furious when her mother refused to let her be baptized: 'I am thinking very hard that it is not my mother's business – it's my soul. But she is no longer my mother: I want to be a daughter of the Church'.[64] Should her mother not return, Weinstein comforted herself with the knowledge that the Church would offer her a replacement family.[65] Martin was alarmed that she needed her family's permission in order to be baptized: 'You have to have papers before Jesus can enter your heart and make you pure'.[66] She begged the nuns to ask her parents to send a white dress for Holy Communion. Yvonne Fersen, Friedländer, Roth-Hano and Weinstein all felt the 'calling' to devote their lives to the Church. Roth-Hano was 'totally committed' to becoming a nun after God protected her during the D-Day invasion.[67] Friedländer explains that he had 'passed over to Catholicism, body and soul'.[68] While 'Eva' had wanted to become a rabbi's wife before the war, her wartime religious experience was so profound that she asked to be baptized in 1944. In Christianity, she found order:

> To my anguished questions: 'why, why?' Christ alone was able to respond ... Christianity represents to me the only solution for peace and universal harmony. I thought that the Christian ideal of the union of men

in God was superior to that of the Jews, who more and more lose their faith.[69]

After the war, Eva slowly found her way back to Judaism, but her intense identification with Christianity articulates how older children were not simply attracted to the protection that Christianity offered but to Catholic theology as well.

These immediate postwar years brought with them their own set of problems, and the children continued to struggle with synthesizing an identity. Wolf writes that the 'four years following the war were more destructive to our emotional well-being than all our years of hiding'.[70] During their years of separation, children and parents had become strangers. Orphaned children were shuffled between orphanages, foster homes and distant relatives.[71] Meyers felt that her parents expected her to fulfil one duty: 'to get "back to normal". For those ... who are too young to remember much of "normal" prewar times, it is hard to figure out what it all means'.[72] In the rush to regain normalcy, adults did not encourage children to talk about their wartime experiences. As Charles Zelwer reflected: 'We, who had been hidden, we were the miracle children. When other children had been burned, had been killed, when so many people had died, how could we consider our personal problems?'[73] Instead, adults expected the children to shed the false identities that they had carried throughout the war and resume their place in the Jewish community. The children, however, doubted that the war's end meant they would be safe to live as Jews. Because of their years in hiding, they saw another option: to continue concealing their Jewish identity under a cloak of Catholicism.

In a variety of ways, the children remained in hiding after the war. Even though the story of her biblical namesake brought her private comfort during the war, Hartz wanted to keep her Christian name after the war; she had never used the name of Ruth at school, and she feared renewed discrimination.[74] Levendel took his cue from his father, who resumed attending synagogue but hid his prayer book in a bag: 'My Jewishness ... was becoming a burden: I felt pressed to carry it in a brown paper bag as my father did on his way to the synagogue'.[75] Thus, for hidden children, the need to suppress their Jewishness was an extension of the concealment they had practised during the war. When faced with external challenges to one's identity, the children utilized what they knew about Catholic culture in order to create safer frameworks of identity.

In addition to hiding their Jewishness from the world, the children shielded their Christianity from their parents. The inculcation of Catholicism, a necessary survival mechanism in wartime, was difficult to overcome. Meyers learned to internalize her Catholicism: 'My soul was a castle with many rooms. It was fully portable and conveniently invisible; therefore the highest degree of privacy was guaranteed. I would hide all my treasures in those rooms'.[76] When the children returned to their families, they sensed that their parents did not approve of their thanksgiving prayers to Jesus. Hartz explained:

> I knew that I must not forget my Holy Father in heaven ... yet I felt strange praying the rosary in front of my parents. There was no crucifix on the wall, no figure of Christ or of Our Lady to look at as I prayed ... My own parents looked away. They did not understand, and I did not know how to explain to them.[77]

Martin's insistence upon stopping to pray at each cross along the road alarmed her parents. Their 'child had been saved, but her soul was elsewhere, roaming, lost'.[78] Even the youngest child survivors, who had grown up in a Catholic milieu and who felt like foreigners in the Jewish community, sought to internalize their love of Catholicism so that they would not upset their families. They stashed rosaries and prayer books under mattresses; older children, including Fersen-Osten, Meyers and Roth-Hano continued to go to church leaving early in the morning before their families awoke. Roth-Hano and her sisters attended Mass for five years after the war, driven by an inner conviction that the Church was their home. Others still sought the Virgin Mary when they were feeling troubled. Eventually, as they reconnected with Judaism, they became less dependent upon Catholicism. Martin writes that after a while, her Jewish identity 'was forged, except for secret church visits to see the Virgin Mary. Kneeling before her, I would stare in confused darkness and deep isolation, rushing out almost as soon as I came'.[79]

Interactions with other Jews facilitated the children's return to Judaism. Relief organizations worked to retrieve children from Christian institutions and re-establish them to a Jewish milieu. In cases where the children's parents had not survived, the children were placed in Jewish orphanages.[80] Although the *Oeuvre de Secours aux Enfants* (OSE) oversaw most of the orphanages, each had a distinct character. Some of the homes had overt Zionist agendas and prepared the children for life in Palestine. Thus, these children encountered a political form of Judaism. Fersen-Osten was placed in a Hebrew class because, as the director explained to her: 'We all must speak Hebrew. It will be our national language'.[81] Eric Cahn attended weekly services for the first time,[82] and 'Paulette' became well-versed in Jewish culture.[83] The security provided by these homes allowed the children to explore their forgotten heritage in a safe environment, surrounded by peers in the same situation. Fersen-Osten began talking about her wartime experiences with the other children: 'I felt I belonged. I knew what they wanted. For us to be what we'd been before. To send us to Palestine. To build a new nation. To forget the nightmares of the past'.[84] The children within these homes were encouraged to work towards the goals of building new lives and resurrecting their Jewish identities.

Parentless children living in Jewish institutions after the war enjoyed a safer environment, because the commonality of their experiences in hiding prevented the creation of a hierarchy of suffering, which could be a painful point of contention between hidden children and their parents who had returned from concentration camps. Jeruchim's time in a Jewish orphanage benefitted him, because it provided him with space and time to reconnect with his heritage. A budding artist, he was asked to decorate the walls of the school cafeteria with Hebrew letters. The project had a profound impact upon Jeruchim:

> All along I had been trying to distance myself from a foreign culture in which I felt I had no part. This was the first time I felt some sense of pride in being Jewish, and I wondered whether a mysterious link connected those Hebrew words with my parents' past and the world of their ancestors in Poland?

While he admits that his reconnection with Judaism 'had little to do with God or religion, but rather with the need to come to terms with the Jewish identity I'd worked so hard to keep hidden during the war', he studied for his *bar mitzvah*, and after the ceremony, he felt a sense of belonging.[85] Jeruchim acknowledged the power of Hebrew to link the distant past with the present. While his encounter did not transform him into an observant Jew, it served to meaningfully connect him with his heritage.

Jewish youth groups and summer camps also developed a sense of camaraderie. Sociologist Mary Gallant argues that the forging of a positive Jewish identity within a community of survivors helped to mend the collapse of social worlds that the children experienced during the war.[86] Ruth Hartz recalls that her mother 'wanted me to learn about my religion and not to be afraid of it any longer'.[87] She enrolled in *Les petites Ailes;* all of her friends were Jewish, and 'whatever I did it was always with the Jewish community'.[88] As she attended Hebrew school and celebrated the establishment of the state of Israel, Josie Martin transferred her loyalties to Judaism, and 'my Catholic ways were forgotten'.[89] Many child survivors have positive memories of Jewish summer camps; those organized by the OSE were run by people who understood the children's past, and the atmosphere was remembered as 'friendly and warm ... they did not try to overwhelm us with excessive rules'.[90] The reconnection with Judaism among peers was less isolating than the forging of a Catholic identity that had occurred in relative solitude.[91]

One of the strongest forces that influenced children to abandon Catholicism was the sense of duty they felt – or were made to feel – towards the dead. The Jewish community, anxious to preserve its heritage, expected the children to embody the renewal of Judaism. Family friends reproached Wolf, who dated a Catholic man at the end of the war, for betraying her heritage: 'I was practically accused of committing some sort of religious treason ... How could I even think of marrying a Catholic when Christians had killed my parents merely because they were Jewish?'[92] The idea that her parents might disapprove of her life planted guilt in her mind: 'The last thing

I wanted was to displease my parents, dead or alive. I was convinced that ... they were looking at ... me from heaven'.[93] She eventually ended her engagement, having internalized the pressure from her parents' friends.

A powerful encounter with a camp survivor made Odette Meyers recognize a responsibility to her fellow Jews. While attending a ceremony in the Père Lachaise Cemetery for France's Shoah victims in 1946, a woman approached Meyers and fiercely embraced her:

> Here is this strange woman, hugging me as if she had lost me and found me again. In pain and joy she cries, over and over again: 'I had a daughter like you', I am so overwhelmed by her physical appearance; it's as if all Jewish mothers mourning a child had embraced me at once!

Meyers began to understand that she had an obligation to all of the Jews around her. She was no longer just her parents' daughter; as a child survivor, she belonged to the Jewish community of France:

> I was every Jewish daughter killed in the mass slaughter of innocents. She was every Jewish mother orphaned from her daughter. I was a child of History. True, I belonged to my blood mother ... But all that was secondary. I knew now that I was baptized into a new life, that first of all I belonged to the family of my people – the dead we were burying ... as well as the living.[94]

Months later, when a Jewish classmate suggested they pose as Catholics so that the teachers would not discriminate against them, Meyers was tempted to use the survival skills that she had drawn upon during the war. However, thoughts of the ceremony at Père Lachaise made her hesitate:

> Could I forget that woman who had hugged me during the mass funeral procession, crying, 'I had a daughter like you!' transfusing me with a puzzling identity from which no cross could protect me? When she had left the ceremony she felt that 'my people's dead follow[ed] me – invisible honor guard'.[95]

Meyers could not hide her Jewishness behind a cross any more.

On 21 August 1940, fourteen-year-old Aaron Dov was baptized into the Catholic Church without his parents' blessing. Born to Polish parents who had immigrated to France before the First World War, Aaron found physical and spiritual shelter in a Catholic school during the Holocaust. While his father and sister survived the Holocaust, his mother died at Auschwitz, and as an adult Aaron made pilgrimages to the site of her murder to say *kaddish*. Until his own death, Aaron remembered the Yiddish of his childhood and signed his name in Hebrew in correspondence with Jewish friends. In many ways, his story mirrors that of Fersen-Osten, related at the opening of this chapter. However, unlike hidden children who returned to Judaism, Aaron became a priest in 1954 and served as archbishop of Paris for over a decade. Today he is known as Jean-Marie Lustiger, the only Catholic prelate in modern times to be born Jewish.

Aaron's story is not novel, but he is the most public survivor who retained formal ties with Catholicism. There may be former hidden children who openly embrace Catholicism, but they have chosen to not speak publicly about their decision, perhaps because their dual identity causes unease among the Jewish community. Aaron's position among Jews is ambiguous at best. Some Jewish leaders worried that he would become an advocate for apostasy when he announced in one of his first interviews after becoming archbishop of Paris, that Judaism 'found its fulfillment in welcoming the person of Jesus, the Messiah of Israel; it was in recognizing him, and only in recognizing him, that Judaism found its meaning'.[96] Aaron explained that becoming a Christian was, for him 'a better way of being Jewish'.[97]

Fellow hidden child and director of the Anti-Defamation League, Abraham Foxman, protested when Aaron received the *Nostra Aetate Award* for his work to advance Catholic–Jewish relations: 'I don't think he should be honored because he converted out, which makes him a poor example'.[98] Aaron, however, still considered himself to be a Jew: 'Until the Messiah's coming in glory, the Jew remains, and he remains a Jew, whether he is Christian or not'.[99] His insistence that baptism did not 'make me abandon my Jewish condition – quite the contrary, it would lead me to find it, to receive the plenitude of its meaning'[100] creates unease among Jews. Former Chief Rabbi of Britain, Jonathan Sacks, explained: 'What greater posthumous victory can we give our enemies than . . . cease to be Jews?'[101] The war's end required assimilation back into the Jewish community, because the children's identities did not belong to them alone.

Debórah Dwork writes that the youngest hidden children 'simply grew up as Christians. It was a natural part of the life they led'.[102] Analysis of memoirs, however, illustrates that their assumed identities were neither natural nor simple, and their religious crises continue to compound their sense of identity. Many survivors struggle with theodicy, but the case of hidden children is distinct from camp survivors in one crucial way: those Jews who had been arrested and deported no longer had a reason to hide their Jewishness, and while they may have lost faith in God during the Holocaust, the change in their relationship with God did not have to do with the indoctrination of another religion. Hidden children also struggled with God's role in the Holocaust, but their memoirs are mostly preoccupied with the need to reconcile a religion that tied them to their heritage and their parents with a religion that saved their lives.

Meyers succinctly expresses the inner conflict many children lived both during and after the war: 'You're a bad Catholic because you're a Jew. You're a bad Jew because you're a Catholic'.[103] Neither religion is entirely comfortable. Unlike marranos of more peaceful times, the children did not always enjoy the freedom that could come with being in a liminal place. Yirmiyahu Yovel argues that a Jew who, 'abandoning his Orthodox tradition without being integrated in the Christian world, develops a penetrating eye for both worlds and the ability to free himself from their conventions'.[104] While the children included in this study possessed a 'penetrating eye' for Catholicism and Judaism, understanding the benefits and dangers of declaring membership in each community, they did not have the ability to free themselves from the religions' conventions. As hidden children, their survival depended upon the observance of Catholicism: Catholicism had superseded Jewishness. While the children were living in an overwhelmingly Catholic country after the war, their reclamation by the Jewish community, which desired to resurrect Jewish life in France, meant that the children were expected to abide by the religion's conventions, in some cases to a higher degree than they had in the prewar years.

When the hidden children reached adulthood, they found new ways to express their Jewish identity. Rene Lichtman rejects any notion of God, but he has found a way of being Jewish: 'A cultural Jew, yes, with a strong identification with all the Jews who suffered in Europe'.[105] As an adult he had the power to select a religious community, and Judaism became something to be chosen, not something imposed by the Nazis or the postwar Jewish community. Despite years of uneasy assimilation, despite years of living simultaneously as 'crypto-Jews', and despite a strong affinity for Catholic practices, a recognition of the common destiny of Jews and of a sacred link between the past and future connects hidden child survivors to their heritage.

Jewish history is a history of adaptation and the negotiation of what it means to be a Jew in a secular world. Hidden children's wrestling with Jewish identity must be understood within the context of identity as a historical construct. From Moses and Esther to Jews in Eastern Europe who are just discovering their familial heritage after decades of silence, in the face of persecution, hidden Jews have struggled to reconcile the contradictions between their historical heritage and the culture of the dominant societies in which they live. The hidden children of the Holocaust, uniquely positioned during the war between and within two religions, exercised agency through the negotiation of the categories of Jewish and Catholic, in ways which have not been adequately recognized by historians.

Now that hidden children are identifying themselves as survivors and bearing witness, historians are inheriting a growing literature of testimonies that provide a new dimension to the study of the Holocaust. The importance of testimony lies not in the concrete evidence that they can offer researchers. David Roskies notes that when studying catastrophe in modern Jewish culture, 'what was remembered and recorded was not the factual data but the meaning of the desecration'.[106] Testimonies reveal the social dimensions of survival, as well as the ways in which they battled what Jacques Derrida terms a *mal de l'appartenance*, or a pain of belonging, before, during and after the war. Hidden children's written and oral accounts eloquently express the consequences of religious and cultural negotiations, allowing survivors to reassert their voices in the historical narrative and offering historians insights into the ambiguous legacies of the lonely Marranism of the Holocaust's youngest survivors.

Notes

1. Renée Fersen-Osten, *Don't They Know the World Stopped Breathing?* (New York: Shapolsky Publishers 1991), p. 125.
2. Ibid., p. 54.
3. See, for example, Philip Hallie, *Lest Innocent Blood be Shed* (New York: Harper & Row 1979) and Marion Feldman, 'Psychopathologie des enfants caches en France', in *L'Enfant Shoah*, ed. by Ivan Jablonka (Paris: Presses Universitaires de France 2014), pp. 145–58.
4. 'Secular' will refer to Jews who associate themselves with Judaism primarily in cultural, social and historical ways. The majority of the children in this chapter defined themselves as secular or were too young to have substantial memories of Judaism.
5. While Protestant communities also sheltered Jewish children during the war, the children they cared for were not as engulfed in Christian rituals. Because Jewish children in Protestant communities seem to have had such a different relationship with Christianity, this study only explores Jewish children in Catholic environments.
6. Sarah Gross, *Sarah Dreams of Pitchipoi: A Hidden Child's Memoir of the Holocaust in France* (Margate, NJ: ComteQ 2008), p. 6.
7. Odette Meyers, 'The Return of the Secret Jews', in *Remembering for the Future*, ed. by Yehuda Bauer, vol. I (Oxford: Pergamon 1989), p. 1125.
8. After this gathering, the Hidden Child Foundation came under the direction of the Anti-Defamation League. Its French counterpart is the *Association des Enfants Cachés*, founded in 1992.
9. Susan Suleiman, 'The 1.5 Generation: Thinking about Child Survivors and the Holocaust', *American Imago* 59/3 (2002), pp. 277–95, here p. 292.
10. Claude Morhange-Bégué, *Chamberet: Reflections from an Ordinary Childhood*, trans. by Austyn Wainhouse (Evanston: Northwestern University Press 2000), p. 59.
11. Elaine Marks, *Marrano as Metaphor: The Jewish Presence in French Writing* (New York: Columbia University Press 1996), p. 141.
12. Elaine Marks, *Marrano as Metaphor*, p. xvii.
13. Isaac Levendel, *Not the Germans Alone: A Son's Search for the Truth of Vichy* (Evanston: Northwestern University Press 1999), p. 70 and p. 16.
14. Jacqueline Wolf, *Take Care of Josette: A Memoir in Defense of Occupied France* (New York: Watts 1981), p. 16.

15 *Traqués, cachés, vivants: des enfants juifs en France* (1940–1945) (Paris: L'Harmattan, 2004), ed. Danielle Bailly.
16 See Emmanuel Levinas, *Difficult Freedom: Essays on Judaism*, trans. by Seán Hand (Baltimore: Johns Hopkins University Press 1990).
17 Renée Roth-Hano, *Safe Harbors* (currently written as Safe Habors).
18 Sarah Gross, *Sarah Dreams of Pitchipoi*, p. 42.
19 Joseph Joffo, *Un sac de billes* (Paris: J.C. Lattés 1973), p. 21.
20 Elaine Marks, *Marrano as Metaphor*, p. 111.
21 Renée Roth-Hano, *Touch Wood: A Girlhood in Occupied France* (New York: Puffin Books 1989), p. 97 and p. 106.
22 As quoted in Claudine Vegh, *Je ne lui ai pas dit au revoir* (Paris: Gallimard 1979), p. 83.
23 Isaac Levendel, *Not the Germans Alone*, p. 83.
24 Simon Jeruchim, *Hidden in France: A Boy's Journey Under the Nazi Occupation* (Santa Barbara: Fithian Press 2001), p. 47 and p. 53.
25 Mary Gallant, *Coming of Age in the Holocaust: The Last Survivors Remember* (Lanham: University Press of America 2002), p. 276.
26 Yehuda Bauer, *American Jewry and the Holocaust: The American Jewish Joint Distribution Committee, 1939–1945* (Detroit: Wayne State University Press 1981), pp. 246–9.
27 Claudine Vegh, *Je ne lui au pas dit au revoir*, p. 12.
28 Saul Friedländer, *Quand vient le souvenir* (Paris: Éditions du Seuil 1978), p. 92.
29 Renée Roth-Hano, *Touch Wood*, p. 82.
30 Stacy Cretzmeyer, *Your Name is Renée: Ruth Kapp Hartz's Story as a Hidden Child in Nazi-Occupied France* (New York: Oxford University Press 1999), p. 7.
31 Isaac Levendel, *Not the Germans Alone*, pp. 13–14.
32 Stacy Cretzmeyer, *Your Name is Renée*, p. 60.
33 Pnina Spitz, 'À l'école' in *Aloumim* (February 1999). Retrieved from http://www.aloumim.org.il/temoignages/ecole.html (accessed 11 March 2014).
34 Elaine Marks, *Marrano as Metaphor*, p. 141.
35 Odette Meyers, *Doors to Madame Marie* (Seattle, WA: University of Washington Press, 1997); Stacy Cretzmeyer, *Your Name Is Renée; Ruth Kapp Hartz's Story as a Hidden Child in Nazi-Occupied France* (New York: Oxford University Press, 2002)
36 Debórah Dwork, *Children With a Star: Jewish Youth in Nazi Europe* (New Haven; CT: Yale University Press, 1991).
37 Jacqueline Wolf, *Take Care of Josette*, pp. 84–5.
38 Renée Roth-Hano, *Touch Wood*, p. 196.
39 Ibid.
40 Joseph Weil, who liberated children from Venissieux and placed them in hiding, recalled that at the moment of separation, many parents 'blessed their children with a biblical phrase. They asked them to be brave, worthy of their

Jewishness, and not to forget them'. Vivette Samuel, *Sauver les enfants* (Paris: Liana Levi 1995), p. 98.
41 Stacy Cretzmeyer, *Your Name is Renée*, p. 126.
42 Ibid.
43 Ibid., p. 151 and p. 158.
44 Renée Roth-Hano, *Touch Wood*, p. 160.
45 Elaine Marks, *The Hidden Children*, p. 350; Jacqueline Wolf, *Take Care of Josette*, p. 85; Claudine Vegh, *Je ne lui ai pas au revoir*, p. 133.
46 Elaine Marks, *The Hidden Children*, p. 36.
47 As quoted in Paul Valent, *Child Survivors of the Holocaust*. See more at: http://www.paulvalent.com/publicationtype/child-survivors-of-the-holocaust/#sthash.tvNm3LBi.dpuf p. 79 (accessed 19 August 2015).
48 Saul Friedländer, *Quand vient le souvenir*, p. 114.
49 Josie Martin, *Never Tell Your Name*, p. 39.
50 Fersen-Osten, *Don't They Know the World Stopped Breathing?*, p. 37.
51 Roth-Hano, *Touch Wood*, p. 187.
52 Odette Meyers, *Doors to Madame Marie*, p. 117.
53 Saul Friedländer, *Quand vient le souvenir*, p. 78.
54 Josie Martin, *Never Tell Your Name*, p. 109.
55 Ibid., p. 128.
56 Stacy Cretzmeyer, *Your Name is Renée*, p. 13.
57 Roth-Hano, *Touch Wood*, p. 160 and p. 229.
58 Jacqueline Wolf, *Take Care of Josette*, p. 85.
59 Stacy Cretzmeyer, *Your Name is Renée*, p. 126.
60 Odette Meyers, *Doors to Madame Marie*, p. 153.
61 Frida Weinstein, *A Hidden Childhood, 1942–1945* (New York: Hill and Wang 1985), p. 103.
62 As quoted in Debórah Dwork, *Children With A Star*, p. 104.
63 Ibid., pp. 105–6.
64 Frida Weinstein, *A Hidden Childhood*, p. 50
65 Ibid., p. 82.
66 Josie Martin, *Never Tell Your Name*, p. 67.
67 Elaine Marks, *The Hidden Children*, p. 38.
68 Saul Friedländer, *Quand vient le souvenir*, p. 113.
69 Vivette Samuel, *Sauver les enfants*, p. 207.
70 Jacqueline Wolf, *Take Care of Josette*, p. 161.
71 Postwar, custody disputes were played out inside the courtroom and in private between Jews seeking to reclaim hidden children and the rescuers who did not want to relinquish them. Sarah Kofman relates the conflict between her rescuer and her mother in *Rue Ordener, Rue Labat*. See also Jacob Kaplan, *L'Affaire Finaly* (Paris: Les Éditions du Cerf 1993).

72 Odette Meyers, *Doors to Madame Marie*, p. 258.
73 'Récit de Charles Zelwer', *Traqués, Cachés, Vivants*, p. 49.
74 United States Holocaust Memorial Museum (USHMM), Record Group 50.462*0040, Oral History, Gratz College Oral History Archive Collection, Interview with Ruth Hartz, 1997. A.0441.40.
75 Isaac Levendel, *Not the Germans Alone*, p. 184.
76 Odette Meyers, *Doors to Madame Marie*, p. 200.
77 Stacy Cretzmeyer, *Your Name is Renée*, p. 179.
78 Josie Martin, *Never Tell Your Name*, p. 197.
79 Ibid., p. 198.
80 Renée Poznanski, *Jews in France during World War II*, trans. by Nathan Bracher (London: Brandeis University Press 2001), p. 469.
81 Fersen-Osten, *Don't They Know the World Stopped Breathing?*, p. 113.
82 Eric Cahn, *Maybe Tomorrow* (Colorado: Casan Publishing Company 1995), p. 24.
83 Claudine Vegh, *Je ne lui ai pas au revoir*, p. 82.
84 Fersen-Osten, *Don't They Know the World Stopped Breathing?*, p. 121.
85 Simon Jeruchim, *Hidden in France*, p. 189 and p. 193.
86 Mary Gallant, *Coming of Age in the Holocaust*, p. 14.
87 Stacy Cretzmeyer, *Your Name is Renée*, p. 192.
88 USHMM, RG50.462*0040.
89 Josie Martin, *Never Tell Your Name*, p. 197.
90 Isaac Levendel, *Not the Germans Alone*, p. 173.
91 Some child survivors remained disinterested in Judaism, despite the efforts of the Jewish community. Arnold Rochfeld preferred to identify himself as 'French French': 'My Jewish identity was totally absent . . . I didn't want to learn the Hebrew alphabet. They gave us courses in Yiddish; it wasn't my thing'. *Traqués, Cachés, Vivants*, p. 105.
92 Jacqueline Wolf, *Take Care of Josette*, p. 133.
93 Ibid.
94 Odette Meyers, *Doors to Madame Marie*, pp. 225–6. Vegh echoes this duty to live for others: 'I kept feeling that life had been given to me a second time. So I had to show myself worthy of living this life. It was no longer my own. In some way, I was living by proxy'. Claudine Vegh, *Je ne lui ai pas dit au revoir*, p. 10.
95 Odette Meyers, *Doors to Madame Marie*, pp. 292–3.
96 Jean-Marie Lustiger, *Dare to Believe: Addresses, Sermons, Interviews, 1981–1984* (New York: Crossroad 1986), p. 42.
97 Ibid., p. 38.
98 As quoted in 'Jewish Group Criticizes Honor for Converted Prelate – Cardinal Jean-Marie Lustiger', *National Catholic Reporter*, 6 November 1998.
99 Jean-Marie Lustiger, *Choosing God, Chosen by God* (San Francisco: Ignatius Press 1991), p. 79.

100 Ibid., p. 42.
101 Cited in Gershom Gorenberg, 'A Holocaust? Not Quite', *The Jerusalem Report*, 15 June 1995, p. 54.
102 Debórah Dwork, *Children With A Star*, p. 106.
103 Odette Meyers, *Doors to Madame Marie*, p. 267.
104 Yirmiyahu Yovel, *Spinoza and Other Heretics*, vol. 2 (Princeton: Princeton University Press 1989), pp. 141–2.
105 As quoted in Barbara Kessel, *Suddenly Jewish: Jews Raised as Gentiles Discover their Jewish Roots* (Hanover: University Press of New England 2000), p. 64.
106 David Roskies, *Against the Apocalypse: Responses to Catastrophe in Modern Jewish Culture* (Cambridge: Harvard University Press 1984), p. 35.

CHAPTER FOURTEEN

Unaccompanied Children and the Allied Child Search:

'The right ... a child has to his own heritage'[1]

Susanne Urban

This chapter focuses on child survivors of the National Socialists' crimes, and provides a discussion of the postwar *Child Search* programme. In its first section, the chapter elaborates on the reasons why *Child Tracing*, carried out by the *United Nations Relief and Rehabilitation Administration* (UNRRA) and other Allied and welfare institutions, had to be established after the Second World War and describes the circumstances that affected children in this context. The following section provides a discussion of the process involved in setting up *Child Tracing*, followed by a description of the development of the *Child Tracing Branch* which was affiliated to the *International Tracing Service* (ITS) in 1950. The final section will summarize the actions of *Child Tracing*, with a view to the thousands of individual file cases, and address the question, whether there was a common guideline which assisted the children on their way into a new life, in spite of the many, diverging strategies of care and rehabilitation.

The Allied Forces expected to be confronted with a huge mass of Displaced Persons (DPs) while advancing in Europe. This expectation was confirmed 'In the early spring of 1945, when the Second World War was finished, the land of Germany became a land of movement'.[2] This comment effectively encapsulates the journeys of different groups – the displaced persons, humanitarian organizations in place to manage them in DP camps, and reunification agencies – in the early postwar period, a movement that began even before the war was over. With the end of the Second World War in sight, UNRRA sent personnel to Europe, who received specialized training and manuals on how to provide the estimated 10 million Displaced Persons with food, clothing and shelter.³ As agreed by the Allied Forces at the Yalta Conference of 1945, all DPs were to be repatriated to their countries of origin.⁴ These were the guidelines, and when the Western Allied Armies, accompanied by UNRRA staff entered defeated Germany, they were confronted with various problems and a reality that was much harsher than anything ever imagined. In Germany alone, 6 million DPs, deported and now liberated from Nazi Germany's multiple places of incarceration, concentration camps and forced labour sites, needed care – but also mental rehabilitation and acknowledgement of their suffering.

> It was not an easy aim to be reached, it was just after the end of the war, the borders between countries were still closed, there was no transport and much confusion. Also many of the people themselves were not fit for transportation and repatriation. They were sick, exhausted from under nourishment, almost starving and over worked. They had first to rest and recover.⁵

Unprecedented as Germany's crimes against humanity – especially the Holocaust – were, neither UNRRA nor the other agencies which volunteered and therefore supported UNRRA in its enormous task, expected to find children in the same situation as adult survivors.

Children were not only liberated from concentration camps, but also from forced labour camps and so-called *Lebensborn* homes. The *Lebensborn* programme was established on 12 December 1935 by Heinrich Himmler with the initial aim of offering German women who were deemed 'racially pure' the possibility to give birth to a child in secret. The programme's ultimate goal was to reverse the decline in Germany's Germanic/Nordic population, and to encourage SS officers to have children with 'Aryan' women – *Lebensborn* children who would grow up to lead the 'Aryan' nation.⁶ However, the *Lebensborn* policy was soon expanded to address the need of compensating for war casualties. From winter 1942 onwards, following a decree of Himmler, babies born by Eastern European women deported for forced labour were meant to be examined and, if 'racially not desired', sent to so-called 'nurseries for foreign children' or *Ausländerkinderpflegestätten*. Most of the babies were not 'desired', and the institutions in which they were placed sometimes featured death rates close to 90 per cent because of malnutrition and deliberate neglect.⁷ However, those children who were confirmed as 'racially desired' were meant to be integrated by the *National Socialist People's Welfare* (*Nationalsozialistische Volkswohlfahrt*) in their care programmes, including *Lebensborn*. Such were the children found by the US army in a *Lebensborn* home in Steinhöring in Bavaria, though the full extent of the crimes committed in this institution were only revealed much later.[8] One of the most horrible aspects of *Lebensborn* was the kidnapping of 'racially desired' children from Eastern Europe. In 1942, the SS began searching for such children in Polish and Czech orphanages; later on, children from captured resistance fighters in Slovenia and the Czech lands, as well as a handful of children from Romania and children simply stolen from occupied Poland were brought to the *Lebensborn* homes in order to be 'Germanized'. Their identity was stolen as well; they were given new names and new birth certificates that labelled them as *Volksdeutsche* or ethnic Germans. In April 1947, an UNRRA report emphasized: 'UNRRA was prepared to find people starving, sick, without clothing, displaced and homeless, but they were not prepared to handle a problem of stolen children'.[9]

At the 8th Nuremberg Trial against the *Main Race and Settlement Department of the SS (Rasse- und Siedlungshauptamt der SS)* of 1947–8, the male *Lebensborn* personnel were sentenced only for their role in the SS and not because of the crimes of Germanization.[10] Although UNRRA and the *Child Tracing Section* (CTS) knew about these stolen and oppressed children, as seen above in the April 1947 report, the tracing officers seem to have still doubted the information regarding such crimes. This is evident from another report, written after a *Child Search* conference in February 1947:

> It is interesting to note that although some discovered German documents and interviews with Germans indicate that the theory that children were 'stolen' from foreign countries for germanization, as yet no child has been found to prove the theory. . . . Upon consideration it would seem to be contrary to the Nazi plan of developping [sic] a pure Aryan race to import mass transports of foreign children.[11]

Although the number of children subjected to Germanization across Europe cannot be verified, it is estimated that in Poland there were approximately 20,000 children abducted from their homes. It is also estimated that only 10–15 per cent were located and returned to their families up to the 1950s.

There were other children who fell victim to racial policies of the Nazi regime and had to be cared for or first to be found, such as those relatively few Jewish children in Europe who were not liberated from camps, but had survived with false papers and false identities in orphanages, cloisters or families, and others who had hidden in forests or with partisans. It was mainly soldiers serving in the Jewish Brigade who tried to locate them and, as they were mainly orphans, transferred them to DP camps in the Western Occupation Zones. Since December 1945, 'infiltrees' started to arrive in the Western Occupation Zones in Austria and Germany, often brought in by the *Bricha*.[12] These were also Jewish survivors who after the German occupation had fled to the Soviet Union, returned to Poland after liberation and found that no family members had survived, and, moreover, many of them experienced anti-Semitism and even pogroms such as the Kielce pogrom of July 1946. The 'infiltrees' in the Western Zones were not cared for by UNRRA, even if they lived in an UNRRA camp. They received no food and were therefore totally dependent on supplies distributed by Jewish organizations such as the *Joint Distribution Committee* (JDC, also known as *Joint*). The US policy changed relatively quickly, and from 18 February 1946 onwards, 'infiltrees' were also accepted as DPs, which explains the massive increase in immigration to this zone.[13]

Sometimes surviving relatives sent Jewish children alone – only accompanied by *Bricha* – to the West, and *Child Care and Tracing* was confronted with children who were neither orphans nor unaccompanied, but who refused to return to their home – an attitude which was backed by Jewish emissaries and welfare workers. In autumn 1946, according to a report of an inter-zonal Conference on *Child Search* and repatriation, it was noted that 20,000

> 'infiltree children' had arrived in the US Zone, 6,000 of them were not accompanied, although it was estimated that 75% of them have family members in Germany [meaning: in DP Camps] or in their home countries. In some instances, the children have been sent into Germany first as members of organized groups and the parents or other relatives have come into Germany later. . . . Some members of Jewish organizations feel that if these reunions were allowed they would lessen the children's chances of getting to Palestine.[14]

The *Child Tracing and Repatriation Unit* of UNRRA was faced with many more issues than expected. Although UNRRA gave absolute priority to the four 'R's': Rehabilitation, Repatriation, Reunification and Resettlement, they had to take into consideration various strategies from other agencies, organizations and also psychological and humanistic or political considerations and masterplans.

Other welfare workers and organizations for instance expressed their doubt about the childrens' repatriation or reunification with a distant relative. Various strategies were thus employed and came to collision, although every individual and organization involved in child care underlined that their common goal was 'The best interest of the child':

> The children, it was evident, had lived in an atmosphere of active and purposeful evil. They had quivered and cringed with fear. They had witnessed inhuman cruelty and murder, and many of them had been forced to help every day in revolting and barbarous work. Loathing and hatred and rage; maniacal cravings for revenge; a vile rivalry; ruthless competition for the crust that meant life as against death of starvation – had not these made up the emotional climate in which they lived? How would they react to the gentle and tranquil environment,

the programme of studies, social activities and co-operative living which awaited them?[15]

It was not only an adequate environment that was established for the care of these children, but child survivors of Nazism were also elevated to precious symbols. They were innocent victims, and therefore lights in the darkness of shattered Europe. For nations which had experienced slavery, annihilation and brutal oppression, these children represented survival and an emblem of the future.

Although each party and individual involved in the care and rehabilitation for DPs expected that the management of this humanitarian problem would be a challenge as its scope was unprecedented, the welfare officers and staff involved, even if themselves were DPs, had to rethink and reshape much of the Allied strategies when it came to the care of unaccompanied children – child survivors of Nazi persecution, forced labour, the Holocaust and other crimes against humanity.

> Since 1945, first UNRRA and then the IRO have had to deal with the problem of unaccompanied children. This problem involves the finding of these innocent victims of Nazism, the kidnapped allied children, as well as those non-German children who became displaced and unaccompanied as a result of the war, the identification of the children found, the establishment of their citizenship, their documentation and, if necessary, the tracing of their families so that, in the end, they may be reunited with their parents or relatives.[16]

Furthermore, inquiries by parents, siblings and other relatives searching for children either deported to camps or sent to forced labour were also addressed to the CTS. The distinction between German and non-German citizens was relevant, as the tracing service offered by the Allies did not include care and rehabilitation for children affected by war in general. Historical circumstances, knowledge about Nazi Germany's crimes against humanity, the insight into the Holocaust and therefore a distinction between victims of these crimes and others affected by war was crucial. Care and assistance was offered to Jewish victims and Jewish children of former German nationality, and the Allied tracing mandate did not account for German children who were lost or found alone due to the expulsion of the German population from regions such as Silesia or Bohemia. These cases were registered mainly by the *German Red Cross*.

The Allies integrated into their care programmes German Jews or so-called 'Mischlinge' from mixed marriages, who requested a DP status or qualified as unaccompanied children. In a similar situation were those Roma and Sinti, who were born in Germany, but, after having experienced deportation and the family's annihilation, registered themselves as DPs within the category 'stateless' or 'formerly German'. The number of these DPs – formerly

German-Jewish or with Sinti background – was relatively small, but such cases nevertheless existed.

Disputes about this strategy and the ITS's clear-cut mandate occurred both in educational and academic settings, as it was argued that empathy, especially with children affected by war, is a universal emotion, but historical circumstances need differentiation. This was certainly the right decision with regard to Germany's unprecedented crimes, and the need to differentiate between Nazi victims or survivors of the Holocaust and those who were affected by war remains valid today and in the future. Historian Tara Zahra uses the term 'lost children' for this target group of child care in the postwar period and identifies in her study many more children than those who were included by *Child Search* in its work, thus covering issues relating to children as victims of the Spanish Civil War.[17] The term coined by the Allies – 'unaccompanied child'[18] – is certainly a term that illustrates the tragedy of the children who became victims of Nazi Germany. These unaccompanied children were in the aftermath not classified as orphans or 'war orphans', but rather as children not accompanied by a relative. This designation reflected the extent of the tragedy that affected their families and also trying to hold up hope that relatives could be located somewhere.

Those individuals responsible for the *Child Search Branch* (CSB) also sought to shield family units from the effects of destructive ideological policies. The separation of families through deportations and ideological re-education was practised in for example, the Soviet Union and the Franco Regime in Spain. The Soviet Union separated convicted and deported parents and their children as an instrument of repression against the so-called 'enemies of the state'. The children were placed in orphanages to educate them as 'good Soviet citizens' and to alienate them from their cultural origins and parents. In Spain, the children of captured or fallen Republican Fighters were left in the care of Church Orphanages which sought to 're-catholicize' the children of 'Reds'. This strategy of destroying families was often used to 'stabilize' totalitarian systems and to 'assimilate' as many people as possible. With a view to these unquestionably horrendous crimes (which were also used in Argentina under military dictatorship in the 1970s), Nazi Germany extended these strategies and carried out crimes against children throughout occupied Europe. Not one Jew was meant to survive, let alone Jewish children who were seen by Himmler as possible 'avengers'. The murder of the majority of Roma and Sinti was considered by the Nazis as well as plans to enslave Poles, Slavs and Russians – and with them their children. The intention to 'Germanize' adequate Polish, Czech and other children was also beyond what happened in other countries.

As UNRRA was confronted with these crimes, the term 'unaccompanied children' was deemed the most appropriate for the German context. The deportations from all German-occupied countries had torn families apart, taking family members to various places of forced labour, incarceration and extermination. When the tracing efforts were started with the support of several Zonal Tracing Bureaus, many unaccompanied children were interviewed, and sometimes families could be reunited; in other cases, grandmothers asked about the whereabouts of their grandchildren, knowing that the parents were shot, for example during the Warsaw Uprising of 1944. Mothers wrote desperate letters to the *Red Cross Societies* or the *Tracing Offices* reporting the kidnapping of their child.

Most of the children cared for in children's centres were interviewed by welfare officers who registered them and started the search for relatives or assisted them in repatriation or emigration. Those children interviewed were asked about their parents, their history of persecution, first and other displacements such as deportations, how they came finally to Germany, and other questions which could be traced through official searches. The children's answers were in most cases written down in third person, and only rarely can one find testimonies in the first person, as a personal narrative. The interviewer also shortened the testimony as there are examples from the DP Children's Centre Indersdorf, which report that the children told their stories in full length time and again. Therefore, one has to see these testimonies as abridged texts that were shaped by the interviewer.

From these texts created through the interview of a child survivor one can sense often that, although the children knew that their parents and/or siblings were gassed in Auschwitz or they had witnessed how they were shot in a mass grave, they still hoped that some remote or even closer relative may have survived or that some relative may have emigrated to the USA, Palestine, Great Britain or elsewhere. As long as the tracing process did not reach a dead end, the child was 'unaccompanied', not an orphan. On the one hand, the term mirrored the harsh reality, but on the other hand there was still a spark of hope for UNRRA staff, other welfare workers and, above all, for the children, that perhaps somewhere someone would be alive to accompany the child in its new life, into the aftermath of destruction and desperation.

In 1951, one of the first books on the situation of children in Europe after the Second World War was published, and its author, Dorothy Macardle, interpreted the term 'unaccompanied child' in a different way, as she wrote:

> Everyone realizes that war and occupation have disastrously affected the children in the invaded countries, but the deep and varied nature of the injuries inflicted on them is not easy to comprehend. Official definitions are scrupulously colorless, and one may well fail to guess the misery masked by such terms as 'displaced person', or 'unidentified' or 'war-handicapped', or – supreme understatement to cover total bereavement and desolation – 'unaccompanied' child.[19]

In retrospect, the term seemed to be adequate and the tragedies behind each individual case were written down in each and every individual file. A child liberated or located and brought under UNRRA care in a children's centre was interviewed when old enough, as it seems from age six on. Toddlers or babies were examined to obtain any useful indication of its origin from, for example, special clothing or how the child reacted to lullabies in various languages. These interviews or observations were the first step to collect facts about the parents, the history of deportation, etc. It was often the first time the child was talking about his or her experiences and sometimes these children talked for hours, either very matter-of-fact or emotionally. Those who interviewed the children had to listen time and again to heartbreaking, cruel stories of separation and survival. UNRRA or *International Refugee Organization* (IRO) staff believed that this was also part of the children's rehabilitation. In May 1946, W. C. Huyssoon commented: 'More children are to be interviewed, probably more than we expect and that is our work, our job, a mighty worthwhile job, for we feel we are saving children, we are doing our part in this marvelous work: Rehabilitation'.[20]

Reality broke in on various levels. Traumatized children did not behave appropriately or follow the rules set up in children's camps, and their sometimes extreme behaviour led to negative images or even prejudices of UNRRA and welfare staff – from anti-Semitism to questions about why exactly this child had survived. Furthermore, conflicts about the 'best interest of the child' started to divide the various organizations regardless of their common task. Different views and methods of rehabilitation clashed with diverse psychological, ideological and political backgrounds. This led also to diverging perceptions about how a child should be, what family means and what nations should look like.

> Humanitarian workers, child welfare activists, and government officials across Europe shared a general faith in the rehabilitative powers of both nation and family after World War II. But there was little consensus about what this meant in practice. More often than not, displaced children had some surviving family members, but they had also formed new kinship bonds during the war. They were torn between competing families, nations, and religions.[21]

What did rehabilitation in fact mean? To implement universal, humanistic standards and to neglect nationalities? To repatriate all children to their country of origin if a relative was found? To take all children who were exposed to forcible Germanization out of foster families for repatriation? To unite children with uncles, aunts, or other relatives who lived in the USA or Australia for example, but had no contact with the child for many years? To resettle children for whom no relative was found overseas? Diverse strategies were thought out for these children. Zahra described this situation aptly when stating that each and every welfare organization had its own 'Psychological Marshall Plan':

The postwar campaign to rehabilitate displaced children was far from unified. It openly pitted the collectivist visions of nationalist, Zionist, and socialist child welfare experts against the psychoanalytic and familialist theories of British and American psychoanalysts and humanitarian workers.[22]

Jewish emissaries and organizations aimed not only to reconstruct Jewish life and find new families or even – with a low success rate – reunify survivors, but they also wanted to awaken within survivors the feeling of belonging to the Jewish nation so that they engaged in the creation of the Jewish state. Many Jewish survivors chose Palestine not because they were convinced Zionists, but rather for pragmatic reasons – to share with their own group and people a country, a life and a future. UNRRA acted only during the first months after liberation on a broad scale regarding Jewish children, and then step by step Jewish emissaries and former Jewish youth movement leaders were involved and became instrumental in getting the children out of Europe to Palestine, where they were often cared for by *Youth Aliyah*.[23] Not only because of this, but also because of the specific situation that Jewish DPs and Jewish children found themselves in, UNRRA, and later on IRO and other welfare activists, had to accept that ethnic and national affiliation was much more important than any universalistic approach. The children cared for had experienced persecution, incarceration and murder. After having survived, they started to reconstruct their identities and longed to belong to someone, to form a group of their own, for example, Jewish or Polish. These needs and insights were more or less framed by the superior organizational unit which acted under certain rules that should have underscored nearly each action taken for these children – the *Child Tracing Office*. Registration processes, interviews, examinations, tracing of relatives, assisting in emigration or repatriation – this work all needed to be done in a very structured and organized way. It was a strategic step to concentrate various efforts of tracing, connecting families or sending out documentation on persecution in one institution.

The ITS and its forerunners were established as Allied institutions. While UNRRA carried out the principle task of caring for and repatriating millions of non-German DPs and refugees from the end of the war until 30 June 1947, the *Central Tracing Bureau* (CTB) was already moved from Frankfurt-Hoechst in January 1946 to Arolsen. This remote village was chosen because of its central location between the four occupation zones and its intact infrastructure with enough housing, etc. On 1 July 1947, IRO replaced UNRRA and on 1 January 1948 the CTB was renamed the *International Tracing Service* (ITS). In April 1951, the management of ITS was taken over by the *Allied High Commission for Germany* (HICOG), which was also the year in which active tracing by the CSB – prior to 1948 the CTS – ended. The ITS's future had to be discussed, as in 1954 the statute of occupation was to come to an end for Western Germany and therefore a change in management was foreseen – with the clear aim to pursue ITS activities not as a German institution, but as an international organization that originated in the Allied efforts to assist DPs and survivors of Germany's crimes.[24]

Child Tracing until 1947 was centralized and went through the CTB from where inquiries for missing children were distributed to *Zonal Tracing Bureaus*. If a child was located or found unaccompanied after liberation, all possible information was collected in a file and delivered then to the CTS. From there the search started. The CSB was notoriously understaffed and even slowed down by certain Allied regulations, for example tracing activities in the French Zone were, under UNRRA regulations, carried out only by French Military Government personnel.

> From the beginning of the unaccompanied children's programme, it was thought desirable to have certain policies enunciated by the Allied Control Authority in Berlin. This would have ensured uniform treatment of unaccompanied children in the British, French, U.S. and U.S.S.R. Zones with regard to such basic issues as determination of nationality, guardianship and repatriation. For various reasons, such overall policies were not possible at quadripartite level, and the decisions of major problems were left to the individual zones.[25]

By 1947, problems of heterogeneous tracing methods and even the intensity of these efforts varied from zone to zone even more.[26] *Child Search* was decentralized and *Zonal Bureaus* were made responsible for the 'unaccompanied children': the US Zone handed the mandate to the *Zonal Bureau* there, whereas in the British Occupation Zone cooperation with the *British Red Cross* was implemented, and the French still did tracing through military personnel. The CTS nevertheless was a central filing office where all information was gathered. In addition, during the transition phase to IRO, the Soviet Union withdrew from the tracing activities and for the most part also regarding the exchange of documents and information with the Western Allies. This was a result of the disagreement over the establishment of IRO.[27] It was also a result of the diverging activities concerning DPs and repatriation efforts. The Western Allies registered not only unaccompanied children but also every DP under a nationality the person claimed – and which, in the politics of the Soviet Union, was non-existent: Ukrainian, Polish-Ukrainian, Jewish.

The CTS section was affected by all these developments. At the end of 1947, centralization was again taken into consideration, but it was decided also to end the process of proactive tracing for unaccompanied children and to start activities or to open files only if an inquiry arrived. In the US Zone *Child Search* teams were, regardless of this decision, still active. It was only in 1948 that the *Child Search* was restructured and incorporated, although as an autonomous branch, in the ITS. The *Child Search* kept a relatively independent status and was finally renamed as *Child Search Branch* (CSB). The headquarters was set up in Esslingen.

Child search had not been included in the original plans of the International Tracing Service and no provision had been made for staff to handle the work.... A second conference was held, in order further to clarify the work of Child Search. This conference was attended by representatives of the International Tracing [S]ervice and representatives from Child Search and Child welfare of the three western Zones of Germany and Austria. It was decided ... that a central Child Search Branch of the International Tracing Service should be built up.[28]

With the Provisional order No. 75 from 26 July 1948, the aims and organizational structure of the CSB were finalized.[29] Under IRO, in 1947 and 1948 only eight staff members worked for the CSB – before a budget for the CSB was approved. From 1948 to 1950 the CSB had its own budget to work with: the core staff rose to twelve people with twenty additional administrative assistants and forty-two Child Search Officers, working 'in the field'.[30] This 'field work' included efforts for the *Limited Registration Plan* (LRP) which was implemented in October 1948. The LRP was not only, but also a result from the aforementioned 8th Nuremberg Trial in 1947, against the *Race and Settlement Office of the SS*. The CSB was entitled to collect all data of children in foster families, as well as of adopted children and of those placed in orphanages in the Western Allied Zones after 1939. A Master Index was created 'to include inquiries for missing children, children located repatriated, closed cases, names extracted from documents intelligence; everything which has any bearing on unaccompanied children'.[31] In cooperation with the *German Red Cross* a system was designed to use Hollerith Machines by IBM as it was estimated that around 400,000 cases were to be processed.[32]

> During the year, much public interest was evinced in the problem of the search for unaccompanied United Nation's children. The American film 'The Search'[33] was released. Several radio programmes [sic] covered Child Search and some dozen newspaper correspondents visited the Branch.[34]

The CSB was now in charge of the entire administration and coordinated the tracing activities also outside of Germany. They worked closely with the *IRO Child Welfare Program*, which was responsible for the care of unaccompanied children in the children's centres. These special DP camps for children were already established under UNRRA but taken over by IRO.[35] Although media coverage was raising awareness for the unaccompanied children, the transition from IRO to HICOG again put the CSB under pressure and already in autumn 1949 the change evoked turmoil within the CSB:

> Rumours are going round to the effect that ITS will within a short time be taken over by the International Red Cross, and I therefore wish to acquaint you with the present state of our work and our plans for the

future.... From the point of view of personnel, the International Red Cross would not be able to cope with our work, particularly in the field.[36]

Whether the *International Committee of the Red Cross* (ICRC) was willing to take over ITS or not, is of less significance, the important point here is that neither CSB staff nor journalists familiar with the topic had confidence in the ICRC regarding this specific Child Care and Tracing task:

> But the structure of the International Committee of the Red Cross differs greatly from that of a specialized agency of the United Nations. It is independent, neutral and free to adopt its own methods, and not subject to political considerations. Moreover child search does not come within its normal activities, and it would be unwilling to take over the branch on any terms.[37]

In September 1950 the CSB in Esslingen was closed down and all documents and files transferred to Arolsen. The LRP was never completed due to these changes. On 1 October 1950 the ITS formed a CTB which was then 'downgraded' on 1 April 1951 to a Section[38] and incorporated into the *General Tracing Branch*.[39] Only two staff members worked there,[40] and in 1952 it had four employees handling more than 4,000 inquiries.[41] Closed cases were meant to be either destroyed when children were repatriated – which did not happen – or transferred to the countries of resettlement when demanded from authorities such as Australia, Canada and Israel.[42] Today, in addition to administrative CSB files,[43] more than 65,000 individual case files are stored in the ITS archives. Only a minority of Jewish children searched for by their relatives were found alive, and only a small number were located after having been stolen and 'Germanized'. Moreover, only a minority of those children who were liberated from camps, etc., ever found a relative to live with.[44] *Child Search* registered more than 340,000 children. The ITS collected more than 150,000 birth certificates and over 32,000 death certificates which mirror the fate of non-German children after 1939 on German soil.

A brief examination of several case studies illustrate varying approaches to rehabilitation and repatriation or resettlement. One has to take into consideration, while analysing the CSB work and the efforts taken by the welfare officers and staff in the children's centres, that the children had experienced traumatizing events. Before the case – the child – was dealt with according to its future whereabouts, the child had to develop confidence in those who cared for him. Second, many children had experienced a phase of sudden maturity during persecution, camps, etc., so although they were children by law, they often behaved more grown up than their age was.

> On the whole the children are making a good recovery. They still at times ask whether they now appear like other people or whether they seem

different. Some of them say that they feel very different from people they meet. At times real difference is apparent in their behavior ... They have a tremendous wish to make up for lost time and are very anxious to learn and to be trained for a particular kind of work. In spite of their harsh experiences, they have preserved a real friendliness towards other people and are in the main really cooperative. They enjoy being regarded as independent people and their attitude towards authority needs careful understanding. Their only experience of authority had been a bad one and they have difficulty in accepting authority sometimes can be wise and understanding ... They seem to have little feeling of self-pity in relation to what has happened to them as individuals but their continuing distress at the loss of their families is deep. They are eager for an opportunity in beginning a fresh life and their great need is for real certainty as to the future.[45]

These observations were extremely caring, mirroring psychological insights and showing much empathy for the child survivors. Each case needed individual judging, but there was also the basic idea of what may be 'the best interest for the child'.[46]

In many individual cases of Jewish child survivors one can conclude from the answers given in interviews with UNRRA staff that they were eager to leave Europe. Their options were to resettle in the US, Palestine or to stay with comrades from the camp or the DP group to resettle together first, for example in England, to attend school, learn a profession and then probably immigrate to another country again. Return to the country of origin was usually not their plan for the future – and those who returned, often on their own, came back to the DP centres, as they found no one and nothing left. These children, although longing for their parents and siblings, were much more realistic and disillusioned about the family's whereabouts and knew they had lost them, than non-Jewish children were. Mikal/Michael Dirnfeld, born 1928 in Hungary, gave the interviewer in UNRRA DP Camp Neu Freimann the following information about his life during the Shoah:

First displacement from Sombothaly [*sic*, means *Szambathely*] in June 1944, was deported to C. C. Auschwitz with his parents. His mother and father died there in the 1944 year. Child remained in Auschwitz for one month and was then sent to Buchenwald, Reimsdorf and C.C. Theresienstadt. Russian liberated the camp. Child went back to Hungary in order to look for his family. Michael returned to Germany ... in order to go to U.S.A. Relatives in other countries: UNCLE: Emanuel Birnfeld ... Brooklyn N.Y. ... Family history ... In July 3, 1944 the parents and 7 children were brought to crematorium in Auschwitz and burned, which can be verified by people, who lived in Sombothaly and knew the family Dirnfeld very well. ... After liberation Michael was sick and very weak and lying in hospital in Theresienstadt but now he is already in good health. He has finished 6 years primary school. Since May 1946 he has been attending in a school ort [this is an *ORT Training school*, the author] of a type writer mechanics ... Michael hopes to go to the USA and became a self supporting member of the society.[47]

The children's words, written down by the UNRRA Welfare Officer, show clearly various levels of his experience: loss, trauma, physical exhaustion and finally the perspective of the child to move on and start a new life. Many children's interviews as such which can be found in the CSB's individual case files show that there was, despite the horrible experience, the desire to start life anew and build a future. It seems that sometimes this clear perspective to build a future was also the attempt to fulfil the parent's hopes.

Israel Benedikt, born 1929 in Poland, wrote a letter to UNRRA staff after he emigrated from Children's Camp Indersdorf to England with more than fifty other boys in October 1945:[48]

> Dear Miss Robbins! First I have to thank you for what you have done for all of us. The short time we have been in Indersdorf gave us so much. How much I can only appreciate today, as we live together with youth from Bergen-Belsen and Wohlfratsgausen [means: *Wolfratshausen*, another children's centre] ... We are very satisfied that we live with other Jews because no one can understand us as they do ... We feel very happy and well. The food is very good, we feel that we live with free people in a free country.... Greetings for all employees of UNRRA.[49]

Many Jewish children who were interviewed in Children Centres and then appeared on lists such as Lindenfels DP Camp have a mark on their file – or a whole list bears the note: 'Disappeared' or 'Left for unknown destination'.[50] Most of these children were en route to Palestine, accompanied by the *Bricha*; many of these 'illegal' ships were halted by British soldiers and all passengers, including the children, taken to internment camps, first in Atlit in Palestine and then in Cyprus. The last children left Cyprus in 1948 after the establishment of the State of Israel. Small groups of children were able, with special immigration certificates obtained by *Youth Aliyah*, to get out of internment.

Polish or Ukrainian children who were deported or stranded in the Western Occupation Zones hoped for reunification with relatives or were even searched for by relatives, so that the renationalization and repatriation process was often much more complicated than in the case of Jewish children. One example out of thousands will be mentioned here; it provides a glimpse into Walentina Fedorina's fate, and is based on her interview with UNRRA. She was born in 1930:

> Deported by German Army on June 18th 1942 with her parents WLODIMIR & EUDOKIA FEDORIN from KONSTANTYNOWKA

nr. OREL, UKRAINE, RUSSIA. Arrived in HEILBRONN, Wuerttemberg, Germany, on June 29, 1942.... Separated from her father on arrival in HEILBRONN i.e. on 29.6.42. The father was sent to a camp male slave workers while WALENTINA'S mother have been sent to a camp in HEILBRONN destined for female workers. WALENTINA has never heard from her father again. WALENTINA'S mother died on August 4th 1943 in BISCHELHOF nr. KUENZELSAU.... sent with her mother to BISCHELHOF nr. KUENZELSAU where she worked as a farmer's help for KRISTIAN KERN until 7.7.1945.... 7.7.1945 sent to the Assembly Centre KUENZELSAU ... October 1945 – sent to the Assembly Centre SCHWAEBISCH HALL where she is still living. On arrival to Schwaebisch Hall, Walentina was put under the care of Mrs T. LAPCZYNSKA, Polish school teacher.... Walentina is a pupil of the Polish Elementary School in Schw. Hall, UNRRA 512. She is now in the 5th grade. Her teachers consider Walentina a good and intelligent pupil.... In the opinions of the welfare worker it would be advisable to place Walentina in a Children's centre where she could continue to study under good supervision. She is a bright and intelligent child, well developed physically and mentally. Walentina, herself, would like to immigrate to U.S.A.[51]

Walentina was listed in a letter from UNRRA Team 512 to UNRRA District No 1 as an unaccompanied child of Russian origin. A short handwritten note on the carbon copy says: 'Discharged *23.11.1946* for repatr. to Russia via Prien'.[52] The wish to live in the USA and the guidance of the Polish teacher were overruled by the Soviet Union's intentions, which in this case meant repatriation – but what was the best interest of the child?

Those children who were stolen for Germanization and finally located and returned to their country of origin represent special cases. They were so very changed by these infamous programmes that they had to learn about their families, their original names and often even re-learn their native language. Some of the elder children had to overcome their aversion against Poles which was engraved in them by Nazi ideology. They had to be taught, just like many Jewish children who were hidden under 'Aryan' identities, that being Polish or Jewish was no shame; that they were not 'subhuman'.

The children removed from orphanages, families and villages such as Lidice to be 'Germanized' were sought to be rehabilitated through repatriation and the countries insisted that these children were to return to their homeland. Unfortunately, these children were not welcomed by parents, siblings or loving relatives because many were orphans or because their elder relatives, for example their grandparents, were themselves deeply affected by wartime experiences and not able to care for the children. Therefore many of these children ended up in orphanages, were labelled as 'Germans' or 'Nazis' and did not know where they belonged.[53] Gitta Sereny, as UNRRA officer, was involved in locating these children and remembered this task with ambivalent emotions and thoughts:

As proof of just how effective Germanization had been, this was not true of those who had been 10 years old when taken. It was, though, easier to bring back memories in children that age than in the youngest ones. For the youngest, we found that the most effective reminders were songs. Even though songs were part of German family culture (and group singing a vital part of Nazi youth education), in a number of cases the sound of Polish nursery songs and children's prayers brought back images of home.... This was the question that so often occupied us. What was the 'right' solution to this human conundrum? ... What was in the best interest of the children? ... I have not solved the question of what was the best solution for these children – and I don't think that anyone can.... But what is certain, and what we should not forget, is that their birth parents have not even been able to mourn for them.[54]

UNRRA and its successors, and with them ITS, were certainly not prepared for the various demands and needs of all unaccompanied and traumatized children. Mistakes were made, due to ideological directions or simply out of helplessness. But there were also many success stories: reunifications with relatives, adoptions into loving families, resettlements and thousands of lives built anew. Families were founded, children born by these child survivors, and when they speak about their rehabilitation one main point which is repeated time and again by these former 'unaccompanied children' is that they started to believe in a new life and were therefore able – due to their resilience – to cope with and work through their traumatic past. The first weeks and months after liberation were not only important with regard to physical rehabilitation, but also for regaining confidence in the world around.

Jack Terry, born as Jakub Szabmacher and the youngest survivor in *Konzentrationslager* (concentration camp, KL) Flossenbürg, spoke as a professional psychologist during a symposium on the topic of traumatized children. He summarized what was important in the aftermath for child survivors of the Holocaust and other deported and oppressed children: 'To belong to someone. To be wanted. To have dignity'.[55]

Notes

1 'Report on Removal from German Families of Allied Children, January 21, 1948', 6.1.2/82486419/ITS Digital Archive, Bad Arolsen.
2 'United Nations Relief and Rehabilitation Administration, Area Team 1048, Regensburg. The Beginning of Child Search, April 12, 1947', 6.1.2/82486029/ITS Digital Archive, Bad Arolsen.
3 As this article focuses on surviving children, it will avoid any presentation and discussion of the various stages of DP politics and Allied strategies or on the

inter-Allied tensions on acknowledging nationalities such as Ukrainian or Jewish and the repatriation which came to a halt in 1947; those who still lived in DP camps were mainly integrated in the resettlement programs of IRO. Further recently published studies are: Anna Andlauer, *The Rage to Live. The International D.P. Children's Center Kloster Indersdorf 1945–46* (Wiesbaden: e-lectra Verlag 2012); Suzanne Bardgett, David Cesarani, Jessica Reinisch and Johannes-Dieter Steinert (eds), *Survivors of Nazi Persecution in Europe after the Second World War. Landscapes after Battle*, vol. 1 (London: Valentine and Mitchell 2010), vol. 2 (London: Valentine and Mitchell 2011); Gerard Daniel Cohen, *In War's Wake: Europe's Displaced Persons in the Postwar Order* (Oxford: Oxford University Press 2011); Anna Holian, *Between National Socialism and Soviet Communism: Displaced Persons in Postwar Germany* (Ann Arbor: University of Michigan Press 2011); Holger Köhn, *Die Lage der Lager. Displaced Persons-Lager in der amerikanischen Besatzungszone* (Essen: Klartext 2012); Angelika Königseder and Juliane Wetzel, *Lebensmut im Wartesaal. Die jüdischen DPs (Displaced Persons) im Nachkriegsdeutschland*, second edition (Frankfurt/Main: Fischer Taschenbuch Verlag 1994); Avinoam J. Patt and Michael Berkowitz (eds), *'We Are Here': New Approaches to Jewish Displaced Persons in Postwar Germany* (Detroit: Wayne State University Press 2010); Ben Shephard, *The Long Road Home. The Aftermath of the Second World War* (London: Vintage 2010).

4   See for UNRRA: Malcolm Proudfoot, *European Refugees 1939–1952: A Study in Forced Population Movements* (Evanston: Faber & Faber 1956); Jessica Reinisch, 'UNRRA and the International Management of Refugees', in *Post-War Europe: Refugees, Exile and Resettlement, 1945–1950* (Reading: Cengage Learning EMEA Ltd 2007), http://www.poemfinder.com/pdf/whitepapers/gdc/PreparingForNewWorldOrder.pdf (accessed 2 September 2015); George Woodbridge, *UNRRA: the History of the United Nations Relief and Rehabilitation Administration* (New York: Columbia University Press 1950).

5   'United Nations Relief and Rehabilitation Administration, Area Team 1048, Regensburg. The Beginning of Child Search, April 12, 1947', 6.1.2./82486030/ITS Digital Archive, Bad Arolsen.

6   See for the history of *Lebensborn*: Georg Lilienthal, *Der 'Lebensborn e.V.' Ein Instrument nationalsozialistischer Rassenpolitik* (Frankfurt am Main: Fischer Taschenbuch 2003); http://www.spiegel.de/international/nazi-program-to-breed-master-race-lebensborn-children-break-silence-a-446978.html (accessed 11 May 2013).

7   Bernhild Vögl, *Entbindungsheim für Ostarbeiterinnen. Braunschweig, Broitzemer Straße 200*, http://www.birdstage.net/images/entbindungsheim.pdf (accessed 9 May 2013).

8   See Georg Lilienthal, *Der 'Lebensborn e.V.' Ein Instrument nationalsozialistischer Rassenpolitik*.

9   'United Nations Relief and Rehabilitation Administration, Area Team 1048, Regensburg. The Beginning of Child Search, April 12, 1947', 6.1.2/82486029/ITS Digital Archive, Bad Arolsen.

10   Ines Hopfer, *Geraubte Identität. Die gewaltsame 'Eindeutschung' von polnischen Kindern in der NS-Zeit* (Köln u.a.: Böhlau 2010); Richard C. Lukas, '*Germanization*'. *Did the Children Cry? Hitler's War against Jewish and Polish Children, 1939–1945* (New York: Hippocrene Books 2001); Educational Material on *Lebensborn* and Germanization, in '*Ich bin alleine zwischen fremden Menschen*'. *Unterrichtsmaterial zu Kindern und Jugendlichen als Verfolgte und Opfer des nationalsozialistischen Deutschland*, ed. by Susanne Urban (Bad Arolsen 2013), here: Brochure 5. See also: *Proceedings of the Nuernberg Military Tribunal*, vol. IV, pp. VII–VIII, http://www.loc.gov/rr/frd/Military_Law/pdf/NT_war-criminals_Vol-IV.pdf (accessed 2 September 2015).

11   'Child Search Conference, Bad Wiesee, U.S. Zone on 3rd and 4th February and visit extended to 20th February 47', E. Dunkel, Regional Child Search Officer, 6.1.2/82486021/ITS Digital Archive, Bad Arolsen.

12   See for the *Bricha*, the underground assistance for Jews to Western Europe and Palestine: Yehuda Bauer, *Flight and Rescue: Brichah* (New York: Random House 1970); Asher Ben-Natan and Susanne Urban, *Die Bricha – Aus dem Terror nach Eretz Israel* (Düsseldorf: Droste 2005).

13   See for the topic of Jewish infiltrees, Zeev W. Mankowitz, *Life Between Memory and Hope: The Survivors of the Holocaust in Occupied Germany* (Cambridge: Cambridge University Press 2007).

14   'Minutes of Inter-Zonal Conference on Child Search and Repatriation, October 16th, 17th & 18th, 1946, UNRRA Central Headquarters for Germany, Eileen Blackey, Child Search and Repatriation Consultant', 29 October 1946, 6.1.2/82489976/82489977/ITS Digital Archive, Bad Arolsen.

15   Dorothy Macardle, *Children of Europe. A Study of the Children of Liberated Countries: Their War-time Experiences, their Reactions, and their Needs, with a Note on Germany* (Baltimore: Beacon Press 1951), p. 245.

16   '*History of the search for unaccompanied children*, prepared and submitted by Mr Herbert H. Meyer, Chief, Child Search Branch, in collaboration with Miss Sheila Collins, Deputy Chief, Child Search Branch and Miss Vera Samsonoff, Chief, Child Tracing Section, Esslingen 1950', 6.1.2/82493105/ITS Digital Archive, Bad Arolsen.

17   See Tara Zahra, *The Lost Children. Reconstructing Europe's Families after World War II* (Cambridge: Harvard University Press 2011). The first time the author of this research has found the term 'Lost Children of Europe' was in *The Times*, in an article from 5 November 1949 (stored in the directorate files/press clippings in the ITS). Macardle uses the term as well in her research.

18   The term 'unaccompanied child' was, although used before, finally defined with all limitations regarding age etc., under IRO on 13 April 1948; see: *History of the search for unaccompanied children*, 6.1.2/82493116/82493117/ITS Digital Archive, Bad Arolsen.

19   Dorothy Macardle, *Children of Europe*, p. 11.

20   '"Who is this child". Sample of an Interview with an unaccompanied child, by W.C. Huyssoon, Regensburg, May 1946', 6.1.2/82485973/ITS Digital Archive, Bad Arolsen.

21 Tara Zahra, *The Lost Children*, p. 21.
22 Ibid., p. 116f.
23 Susanne Urban, '*Rettet die Kinder! Die Jugend-Aliyah 1933 bis 2003 – Geschichten von Einwanderung und Jugendarbeit*' (Frankfurt/Main: Kinder- und Jugend-Aliyah Deutschland 2003).
24 See for the ITS' history and aims: http://www.spiegel.de/international/germany/holocaust-tracing-service-in-bad-arolsen-still-reunited-survivors-a-869289.html (accessed 8 June 2015); Bernd Joachim Zimmer, *International Tracing Service Arolsen. Von der Vermisstensuche zur Haftbescheinigung. Die Organisationsgeschichte eines, ungewollten Kindes' während der Besatzungszeit*, vol. 18 (Bad Arolsen: Waldeckische Forschungen 2011). This non-scholarly book was reviewed by Jennifer Rodgers (www.sehepunkte.de/2012/10/21188.html) who will publish in the near future her dissertation on one part of ITS history. All websites last accessed 11 May 2013.
25 *History of the search for unaccompanied children*, 6.1.1/82493113/ITS Digital Archive, Bad Arolsen.
26 Ibid., 6.1.2/82493116–82493121/ITS Digital Archive, Bad Arolsen.
27 Louise W. Holborn, *The International Refugee Organization: A Specialized Agency of the United Nations, its History and Work 1946–1952* (London: Oxford University Press 1956).
28 *History of the search for unaccompanied children*, 6.1.2/Document ID 82493117/82493118/ITS Digital Archive, Bad Arolsen.
29 Ibid., 82493121/ITS Digital Archive, Bad Arolsen.
30 Ibid., 82493152/ITS Digital Archive, Bad Arolsen.
31 'Summary of Discussion at the meeting convened by I.T.S. Headquarters of Representatives from Child Search/Welfare/Tracing Departments . . . 22/23 March 1948', XXX/82486508/ITS Digital Archive, Bad Arolsen.
32 *History of the search for unaccompanied children*, 6.1.2/82493128/Digital Archive ITS, Bad Arolsen.
33 The film was made with support by UNRRA; see also J. E. Smyth, 'Fred Zinnemann's Search (1945–48): Reconstructing the Voices of Europe's Children', *Film History* 23/1 (January 2011), pp. 75–92.
34 *History of the search for unaccompanied children*, 6.1.2/82493126/ITS Digital Archive, Bad Arolsen.
35 In the ITS' holdings we were able to locate a number of children centres and hospitals which existed between 1945 and 1950 in various periods; 22 in the US Zone, 17 in the British Zone and 2 in the French Zone.
36 'Address by Mr Meyer to the employees of ITS Child Search Branch on September 14th, 1949, 16.30 p.m.', 6.1.2/82486313/ITS Digital Archive Bad Arolsen.
37 *The Times*, 5 November 1949 (stored in the directorate files/press clippings in the ITS), p. 2.
38 It is interesting that the overall restructuring of the ITS in 1950 led not only to this important change, but also to the closure of the Documents

Intelligence Section which was replaced by the so-called Historical Unit / Cataloguing Unit, understaffed now, as the Child Search Unit, with only two employees. These changes seem to be the first steps towards a reduction of the ITS' mandate and aims due to the 1955 change to the management of ICRC.

39   *History of the search for unaccompanied children*, 6.1.2/82493154/82493155/ITS Digital Archive, Bad Arolsen.
40   'Child Search Activities after September 30, 1950', 6.1.2/82486331/ITS Digital Archive, Bad Arolsen.
41   'Children's Archives, Yearly Report, 1952', 6.1.2/82486833/ITS Digital Archive, Bad Arolsen.
42   *History of the search for unaccompanied children*, 6.1.2/82493156/ITS Digital Archive, Bad Arolsen.
43   See the finding aid for the administrative files (in German): http://findmittel.its-arolsen.org/ITS1_Child_Search_Branch/index.htm (accessed 5 January 2015).
44   The Child Search Branch Files are only indexed since 2013; therefore valid numbers and more detailed research on quantities and also on certain children's groups can be done only after the indexing is finished, presumably in 2015.
45   'Team News. Unaccompanied children sent to England, Switzerland receive good care, by Gwen Chesters, Child Welfare Specialist, March 15, 1946', 6.1.2/82485890/ITS Digital Archive, Bad Arolsen.
46   See for the case of the Children's Centre Indersdorf as a role model of empathy and care: Anna Andlauer, *The Rage to Live. The International D.P. Children's Center Kloster Indersdorf 1945–46* (CreateSpace Independent Publishing Platform 2012).
47   'CSB Files Individual Cases, Michael Dirnfeld', 6.3.2.1/84203288/ITS Digital Archive, Bad Arolsen.
48   The letter is in German; it was translated for this article. As the German is very plain, the English translation stays true to the style of Israel Benedikt's writing.
49   'CSB Files Individual Cases, Israel Benedikt', 6.3.2.1/84160095/84160096/ITS Digital Archive, Bad Arolsen.
50   See 'Nominal roll of children and adults who have left the Children's Centre Bayerisch Gmain on July 1, 1947 for unknown destination', 3.1.1.2/81966547/ITS Digital Archive, Bad Arolsen.
51   'CSB Files Individual Cases, Walentina Fedorina', 6.3.2.1/84220391/ITS Digital Archive, Bad Arolsen. The letters in the quote appear as such, in capital letters, in the original.
52   Ibid., 84220395/ITS Digital Archive, Bad Arolsen.
53   See the story of Barbara Gajzler, later Paciorkiewicz, who was stolen from Poland and handed over to a teacher couple in northern Germany. This story is told in the ITS' teaching unit: Educational Material on *Lebensborn* and Germanization, *'Ich bin alleine zwischen fremden Menschen'*.

Unterrichtsmaterial zu Kindern und Jugendlichen als Verfolgte und Opfer des nationalsozialistischen Deutschland, ed. by Susanne Urban (Bad Arolsen 2013), Brochure 5.

54 Gitta Sereny, *Stolen Children. The Nazis took 250,000 Children from their Families, Intent on 'Germanizing' them*, http://www.jewishvirtuallibrary.org/jsource/Holocaust/children.html (accessed 5 January 2015).

55 Symposium 'Was hilft Kindern, ihr späteres Leben zu meistern?', 18 July 2011, Greta-Fischer-School, Dachau.

CHAPTER FIFTEEN

Children of Lidice: Searches, Shadows and Histories

J. E. Smyth

In 1946, when Fred Zinnemann and Peter Viertel began developing a film about Europe's displaced children, they knew that they wanted to narrate youth experiences across several European countries. However, the film-makers also believed that the protagonist had to be a child from Czechoslovakia. For many during the war and in the postwar era, the Czech nation and its children symbolized future hopes for a regenerated Europe. In *The Search* (1948), Czech actor Ivan Jandl played Karel Malik, a young boy who had forgotten his name, family and language. United Nations workers try to reconstruct his identity, but, at first, only the audience learns of his horrific past through a flashback. Separated from his father and siblings in Prague, interned in Auschwitz with his mother, and later separated from her, Karel was one of thousands of Czech children whose history was all but obliterated by the Nazis. Behind Karel's mask of fear was the public memory of the Lidice massacre on 10 June 1942 and the abduction and deportation of the town's 105 children. Though the Nazis destroyed other towns during the Second World War, including Grun and Klak in Slovakia, Leskovice and Lezáky in Czechoslovakia, Lidice was the most widely reported wartime Nazi atrocity. As John Bradley notes: 'Even the greatest German atrocity, in France at Oradour-sur-Glane, where some 800 people perished in June 1944, did not shock the rest of the world as much as Lidice'.[1] For the Allies, the European resistance, and the American stateside population, the act of remembering Lidice became an act of historical resistance to the Nazis. It commemorated victims of fascism and genocide when most people were unaware of the Holocaust in Eastern Europe, but it also galvanized desperate international efforts to recover lost European children and restore them to their families.

This chapter examines the textual and visual history of Lidice, its legacy in literature, film and history, and the construction of the Czech war orphan in Hollywood and European cinema. While film-makers in Germany (*Irgendwo in Berlin*, 1946), Italy (*Sciuscià* (*Shoeshine*), 1946), France (*Marie-Louise*, 1945), Hungary (*Valahol Európában* (*Somewhere in Europe*), 1947), and Poland (*Unzere Kinder*, 1948) all produced films about the wartime and postwar fates of their nations' children, until very recently, there was no Czechoslovakian equivalent. Instead, British documentary film-maker Humphrey Jennings' recreation of the massacre in a Welsh mining village (*Silent Village*, 1943) and Zinnemann's international film production, based upon his interviews with child Holocaust survivors and the abducted children of '*résistants*', epitomized Czech child survivors' experience during and after the war.[2] This chapter will also discuss public remembrance of Lidice, postwar communist efforts to suppress Lidice and *The Search* as part of postwar Czech historiography and popular youth culture, and Lidice's uncomfortable status in more recent historiography as a non-Jewish/pre-Holocaust massacre which shaped postwar attitudes toward Europe's displaced and lost children.

On 21 May 1942, Czech partisans attacked *Obergruppenführer* Reinhard Heydrich while he was driving through the streets of Prague. A few days later, he died from the effects of the bomb blast. On the night of 9 June 1942, orders were issued to destroy the small village of Lidice in the agricultural and coal mining district of Kladno, just outside the capital. Early on 10 June, the village's 173 men and boys aged fifteen and over were lined up against the walls of the village and shot. Two women attempting to prevent their separation from their children were also killed. The surviving women were deported to Ravensbrück concentration camp, and the majority of the children, eighty-two in all, were gassed in a van on the way to Łódź. Nine were taken for Germanization and a further eight managed to escape extermination.[3] As one memorial pamphlet on Lidice argues, the village was selected for extermination because it was in the heart of the Kladno region, where miners and families struck for higher wages, an eight-hour work day and the franchise in 1905. It was also a revolutionary area during the First World War.[4] Czechoslovakia was a young nation, born in the aftermath of the Great War, a multi-ethnic nation which granted Germans in the Bohemian Lands equal rights under a liberal constitution. For many people in the interwar years, it fulfilled the aims of the Versailles Treaty to foster a new European community. To others, including the Nazis, Czechoslovakia was 'a freak or whim of fate' which separated too many ethnic Germans from a greater 'fatherland'.

Although in recent years, the discussion of Lidice and lost or displaced Czech children has been put in the service of narratives about postwar ethnic cleansing and Czech nationalism, the international engagement with Lidice should not be minimized.[5] Before the facts were widely known, Heydrich's assassins were imagined in Bertholt Brecht and Fritz Lang's *Hangmen Also Die* (1942) as Czech partisans acting purely within an internal resistance group, patriots Jan Kubiš, Jozef Gabčik and Karel Čurda were a Moravian, a Slovak and a Czech. Following the invasion on the Ides of March, they joined the French Foreign Legion, and then, with 4,000 other Czech soldiers, escaped to Britain after the Fall of France. The Czech army and air force became part of the Allied forces in Britain, and some were invited to join special training as paratroopers. The Anthropoid mission to kill Heydrich was devised and run by the *British Special Operations Executive* (SOE).

Humphrey Jennings was one of millions of Britons to hear about the extermination of Lidice in June 1942. As he noted in an interview for the BBC Home Service, a month after the massacre, he got a film synopsis from Dr Viktor Fischl, a Czech poet and author of *The Dead Village*. Fischl escaped to London in 1939, joining the government in exile as a close associate of Jan Masaryk in the Czech Ministry for Information. Fischl's poem and synopsis became the basis for Jennings' film. It began:

> 'This is the small village of Lidice somewhere in Czechoslovakia, and this is the village of X somewhere in Wales. It is not so long since these two villages were exactly like one another', and then from that draft develops the idea of a short picture paralleling these two villages and showing the difference in their two fates.[6]

Jennings decided that instead of paralleling the two villages' war experience, he would make the Welsh mining village, Cwmgiedd, be Lidice. Though Lidice's name was invoked in projected text and voice-over narration, Jennings' wider concern was in creating a resistant history that lived beyond national borders and could energize the ongoing war effort.

The Nazis were very public in their extermination of Lidice, advertising it on German and Czech radio ('the name of the community has been obliterated'),[7] but the fates of the children remained ambiguous throughout the war. While many historians have pointed out the defining postwar national issue in Czechoslovakia focused on the repatriation and rescue of appropriately Czech children with which to rebuild the nation, these debates were already focused during the war. Heydrich's repressive regime in Czechoslovakia was notorious but as historian Tara Zahra points out, in the months before his assassination, Heydrich was involved in the Germanization of Czech children that in many cases resulted in their forcible removal from parents who refused German education. As Heydrich's office wrote: 'The personal interest of the Czech parent is completely irrelevant'.[8]

Although Jennings did not focus on the fate of the children, in his interview with the BBC about *Silent Village*, he drew some potentially uncomfortable parallels between the Czech resistance to Germanization during the war and Welsh efforts to preserve their culture and language in the face of English control. Jennings' principal shots of the children are of them cuddling with their parents at home and collectively in the school as they learn their lessons in Welsh. The decision of the miners to strike and the Nazi attacks on the resistance leaders are accompanied by the schoolmistress's own struggle to teach the children Welsh culture and language in the schools ('Promise me one thing: do not forget your Welsh. Speak Welsh on the roadside, at your play, everywhere. Will you promise me not to forget your Welsh language?').[9] After the suppression of Welsh, Heydrich is assassinated and the Nazis report it and announce their intention to destroy the village in English.

Yet, what is truly striking about *Silent Village* is Jennings' and the Welsh villagers' belief in the connection between cultures and the solidarity between one agricultural and mining community and another. Jennings also saw the resistance to fascism in an international context. So did his Welsh cast and crew. As he wrote to his wife Cicely:

> I really never thought to live and see the honest Christian and Communist principles daily acted on as a matter of course by a large number of British – I won't say English – people living together. Not merely honesty, culture, manners, practical socialism, but real love ... From these people one can really understand Cromwell's New Model Army and the defenders of many places at the beginning of the Industrial Revolution. The people here are really Tolstoyan figures – or is it a place where Turgenev's *Lear of the Steppes* could have taken place.[10]

Jennings' cast were not the only miners to take action to ensure Lidice would never be forgotten. Miners in Birmingham and Stoke-on-Trent started collecting money for the postwar rebuilding of Lidice, starting the *Lidice Shall Live!* organization in September 1942. Indeed, even after the communist takeover of Czechoslovakia and American abandonment of the Czech nation in 1948, British officials came annually to meet at the new Lidice, fostering cultural links even during the Cold War. One 1957 pamphlet on Lidice featured photographs of Scottish miners coming to lay wreaths on the memorial at Lidice, of Soviet soldiers posting first guard on the tomb, and the mayors of Stoke-on-Trent and Coventry shaking hands with the Mayor of Stalingrad. British concern for Lidice and the lives of the rescued women and children continued. Several cities were renamed Lidice in the aftermath of the massacre: San Jerónimo in Mexico, a barrio in Caracas, Venezuela, and Stern Park, Illinois became Lidice. A square in war-devastated Coventry and a section of Santiago, Chile, were also renamed for the city.

But while Jennings and the Welsh cast of *Silent Village* connected with Lidice through their shared history as miners and members of a politically resistant working class, these discussions did not focus on the child victims of Lidice and their possible victims in Great Britain during air raids. It was left to the wider international community to make these links.[11] Jan Masaryk, son of the first president of Czechoslovakia, made these connections when he wrote an introduction to an edition of Czech fairy and folktales for British children in 1943:

> Here are some stories from Czechoslovakia for English children to read. Some of them, like the Fire Bird, you will probably know already. Others have a counterpart in the folk-lore of other parts of the world . . . But the characters, the setting, and the way of telling these stories is entirely Czech. They show how highly our people have always valued kindness, industry, and truth.[12]

Masaryk ended with the wish that 'you will like them as much as our Czech children do'. This appeal to cross-cultural exchange and understanding, coupled with a reaffirmation of the distinct Czech nation, circulated around the experience of children.

American response to Lidice was widespread and tied to the USA's own uncertainty about its immunity from fascism. Edna St Vincent Millay's poem, reproduced in its entirety in *Life Magazine* in July 1942, articulates this anxiety: 'Careless America, crooning a tune,/ Please think! – are we immune?/ . . . Who, after all, are we? – / That we should sit at peace in the sun,/ The only country, the only one/unmolested and free?' The text became the basis for an extended voice-over narrated prologue in *Hitler's Madman* (1942), produced by the Poverty Row studio PRC and directed by Douglas Sirk. The prologue was complete with text and document inserts, stock footage and voice-over. Lidice, despite Nazi efforts, was put back into history. MGM mogul Louis B. Mayer was so interested in Sirk's production that he bought the film so MGM could distribute it more widely. This was the first time a major studio had been so publicly supportive of another less-known work. Yet children did not figure prominently as victims in the advertising trailers for the film. Instead, studio publicists focused on the deaths of the men and the sexual exploitation of women by Heydrich (John Carradine). Children were not part of *Hangmen Also Die*, the other major wartime Hollywood film to deal with Heydrich's assassination.[13]

Why were children not featured prominently in these early Czech war dramas? First World War histories of German atrocities were encouraged in the relatively unregulated screen censorship a generation before (and subsequently discredited in the 1920s), but the Production Code's regulation of violence and the depiction of children on screen shaped representation during the Second World War. Child war victims were not new to wartime

Hollywood cinema. Both *The Pied Piper* (1942) and *A Journey for Margaret* (1942) were released soon after the extermination of Lidice, and featured stranded, orphaned children helped by internationally (and primarily female) staffed charities, American war correspondents and British tourists. However, children were usually from France, Belgium and Great Britain. In a rare exception to the rule, Katharine Hepburn and Spencer Tracy's marriage in *Woman of the Year* (1942) unravels when Hepburn's character, based on journalist Dorothy Thompson, briefly adopts a Greek war orphan named Chris. The deaths of children in war were not normally subjects brought before the Production Code, but both *A Journey for Margaret* and *Mrs Miniver* (1942) feature shots or references to children killed in German air raids. Jacques Tourneur's *Days of Glory* (1944), which focused on the fate of a group of Soviet partisans, was even more unique in showing the execution of a teenage boy by the Nazis (Glenn Vernon).

Toward the end of the war, European producers realized the value of children in encouraging both foreign audiences and raising public awareness of the *United Nations Relief and Rehabilitation Administration* (UNRRA). Lazar Wechsler was one of the first to be inspired by the photographic work of Therèse Bonney whose book on displaced children chronicled the deprivation of French, British, Finnish and Spanish girls and boys.[14] Although Bonney was unusual in drawing attention to Franco's fascist Spain as a landscape for child abuse and death, the children identified by nation were English, Finnish or French. A handful of other photographs are merely headed 'concentration camp'. Bonney's work had a precedent in the photojournalism of Jacob Riis, a Danish immigrant whose pictures and descriptions of New York's poor (and especially homeless children) made headlines and fuelled Progressive legislation fifty years before.[15] Wechsler found one of Bonney's photographs particularly arresting. It shows a French schoolgirl of perhaps nine or ten carrying a bedroll, rucksack and doll in her arms as she and her mother are sent to an unknown destination after the Fall of France. Bonney writes: 'They tried so hard to save what they loved if only – a doll'. Wechsler then produced the immensely successful *Marie-Louise* (1945), which narrated a refugee child's desperate attempt to protect her baby brother and keep a treasured toy with her during her ordeal.

Appearing in the United States in November 1945, *Marie-Louise* was America's first film import from continental Europe since the war began and critics applauded the film for being 'direct and simple in its graphic assembly of details expressing the heartrending pathos of the impact of war upon a child'.[16] It was refreshingly free of Hollywood heroism and melodrama, and yet again, the children were French rather than Eastern European or Jewish. Swiss writer Richard Schweizer went on to win an Academy Award for his original screenplay. Yet, the film only played to big city, art-house cinemas and had little impact beyond the awards ceremony.

The war was over, but the problems finding and reuniting Europe's lost children had just begun. In 1945, the *Red Cross* estimated that 13 million

European children had lost parents, and within days of the war's end, UNRRA was in charge of over 50,000 displaced children.[17] While over 1.5 million Jewish children were murdered in the concentration camps, thousands of non-Jewish babies were abducted for Germanization as *Lebensborn*, and those younger than five were kidnapped for forced labour, hostages and medical experiments.[18] Older children were often forced recruits for the SS. By 1946, over 200,000 queries for lost children were received by Polish relief organizations alone.[19] Lucky ones, including the future Czech director Miloš Forman, managed to stay in contact with a family member or protector. And against the odds, once UNRRA organized child search teams in 1946–7, over 15,000 children were reunited with their families. As time passed, however, the number of traced children declined to under 2,000 in 1948 despite over 40,000 new tracing requests.[20] For the others, children's homes, including UNRRA's twenty-five children's centres in the British, American, and French zones of Germany, became home before repatriation, adoption, or one-way voyages to Palestine.

When the surviving perpetrators of the Lidice massacre were tried in Czechoslovakia in 1946, Fred Zinnemann kept the article that was covering the trial, in which sixteen Czech mothers faced the men who were responsible for the deaths of their children, to pieces.[21] The report noted that following the destruction of the town and the murder of all male inhabitants in June 1942: '[T]he Gestapo then scattered 104 [*sic*] children to various parts of Europe and that most of them never were found or returned'.[22] It wasn't until later that officials discovered the majority of children were gassed almost immediately after removal. Lidice returned to the headlines as fifteen of the children, including one family of two sisters and a brother, were located in Germany and Prague by *Child Search* teams.[23]

The bulk of Peter Viertel's original story focused upon a little girl and boy from the camp who escape together and plan to return to Czechoslovakia. This idea was developed between him and Zinnemann in the summer of 1946 before Viertel left Hollywood for Wechsler's studio in Switzerland. Viertel shared Zinnemann's interest in Czechoslovakia and wrote to Wechsler: 'We chose Prague because of all the countries that I visited in Europe, this one seemed to be the one with the greatest hope for the future'.[24] Early on in the children's adventures, the little girl, Susan, still has a photograph of her house in Plzen and so 'the photograph became their hope'.[25] Viertel focuses on Carl, an eleven-year-old Polish boy, whose 'young brain was still tortured by a hundred pictures of brutality and fear', who remembered his parents being taken away from him, hunger, and cold. Eventually they meet up with a gang of *Wolfskinder* (wild children) in the woods (the basis for Géza Radványi's (*Valahol Európában* (*Somewhere in Europe*), 1948), then in production). The young leader runs the group like an incipient Hitler and at one point, he makes contact with a former *Wehrmacht* officer, 'a cynical Nazi diehard' and black market racketeer, who runs gangs of thieving children. Carl and Susan escape at last and American soldiers try to protect the children, but the German people are unsympathetic. When Carl tells of their treatment in the gang, the Germans treat the young boy 'as a spy'. One Nazi reminds him that 'Germany is not such a large country and one day the Americans will be gone . . .'.

In his treatment, Viertel tries to show an American officer's development from an uninvolved occupier to a human being concerned with the fate of the two children. As he wrote to Wechsler:

> In many ways America is the hope of Europe today. We have food, materials, and a general welfare which exists nowhere else. We cannot disappoint those Europeans who still think of our country as a paradise from which they are barred by immigration quotas. We cannot be satisfied to be Sir Galahads in shining armor, who kill the dragon and then go home, to forget the battle, for we have learned that this is one world and if disillusionment and cynicism spread again the children who today scurry through Europe's gutters will become new *führers*, new scourges of humanity.[26]

Viertel's words echo the voice-over narration of David Miller and Gene Fowler's *Seeds of Destiny* (1946), an Academy Award-winning documentary produced by the Defense Department of the US Army War Department about the fate of Europe's children. Lidice features briefly as the classic obliterated town, though none of Czechoslovakia's victimized children are shown in the brief segment. Instead, the narrator (Ralph Bellamy) claims: '[A]ll the little children [were] sold for 50 marks a piece to various German families and perhaps lost forever'.

Wechsler had initially suggested to Zinnemann that the project might attract more international attention with the participation of a major Hollywood star. But even before visiting the camps, Zinnemann had been wary of involving even the most potentially dedicated Hollywood actors. In early December 1946, he wrote to Lazar Wechsler, who had hoped to build the role of the soldier around a big Hollywood star like John Garfield, one of the few major Jewish Hollywood stars: 'Would it not perhaps be best to concentrate on writing the story we want, and to say what we want in the most effective way, without committing ourselves a priori to a starring vehicle for Garfield or some comparable Hollywood personality?'[27] Zinnemann argued that although the American connection was important, he did not want the role to diminish the importance of the children's stories, and commented, 'I believe – perhaps wrongly – that in order to interest a star, the story would almost certainly have to be primarily about *him*'.[28] He continued:

> Either we would like to make a film about displaced European kids – and the world as it appears to them – including their friendship with a young GI, or the film could be about a young officer, reluctant and disinterested in Europe, who grows to understand what is at stake through his friendship with the two displaced children.[29]

He also wrote to Viertel, enclosing a copy of his letter to Wechsler, and asked, 'Which character do we emphasize? The kids or the GI? The outline is sort of indecisive ... Personally, I like the kid story much better'.

But after Zinnemann travelled to occupied Germany to meet thousands of children in the UNRRA camps, he decided that any existing Hollywood storylines were an affront to the children's testimony. He conducted many interviews with Jewish and non-Jewish children at the camps, including Christina Zamoyska. She was in a camp in Munich and survived the SS 'clearance' of the Krakow ghetto in 1940. She remembered a horrific incident, and Zinnemann transcribed:

Mother on knees holding baby pointing save baby kill me – SS man one dog and cigar – listening casually, kindly – CZ [Zamoyska] wants to run, take baby, friend holds her back – SS man waits, watches, very kindly takes baby, pats it, smashes brains on wall – shoots mother – walks off – scrapes brains off wall and feeds dog.

At the Prien International Home, there were a lot of young Czech boys from ages six to twelve. Zinnemann took particular note of one: 'George Milon, 4½ – hugs my legs – looks deep into my eyes – touching both my cheeks with his hands ... "Du bist mein Vater", he says to me'.[30] He also took notes on some shocking things done by an *Aglast Evangelical Church* group. Every week the minister 'made selections from list, so many a week to be exterminated ... Kids killed in Karlsruhe and Stuttgart by injections'. He heard children and UNRRA officials tell of Nazis gassing children in ambulances and trucks and that therefore the children would not enter *Red Cross* ambulances, of mothers who strangled their babies so they would not die of hunger in the camps, of tiny children working in slave labour, of teenagers who had to sign 'with a cross' because there 'were no schools in KZ for five years', and was shattered by the narratives.[31] Zinnemann recorded their testimonies and decided to ask the children and UNRRA if the young survivors would recreate their interviews and early experiences in the child camps for the film. And so, hundreds agreed to have their heads reshaved and to wear rags in the centre which was a former SS barracks. Zinnemann, prevented by UNRRA's laws to pay the children in money, gave them chocolate instead. The bulk of the film's cast comprised child Holocaust survivors.

He compiled a photographic archive which would inspire many of the shots from the concentration camps and children's centres. UNRRA also supplied him with their reports since 1946, and he learned about the history of the child-tracing teams and their success. Initially, no one thought of DP children until parents forced to do slave labour told their liberators that their children were still alive in Germany. One UNRRA report described how everything began when 10,000 DP children were found after 'a few of these DPs, unable to contain their paternal and maternal instincts, took matters into their own hands and set out to find their children'.[32] As Zinnemann compiled more and more dossiers, he scrawled, 'Get detailed case histories – the most moving ones – get detail on kids' first reactions upon arrival'.[33] Although he knew that the narrative would hinge on the experience of one child arriving at a new camp, he wanted to cover as many poignant and horrifying histories as possible to show the scale of the crisis. He did not want a 'national' story, which focused on children of one favoured country.

The concept of the geographically and ideologically resilient nation preoccupied not only Nazi Germany, but also the US and many European nations in the postwar era. Even as he worked, European governments were banning international adoptions of DP children and UNRRA's international child centres were disbanded as children returned to the care of their birth nations.[34] In Germany, DEFA and film companies in the Western Zones began to make films like *Irgendwo in Berlin* (1946) that focused on Germany's children and largely ignored the lives of DP children in Germany or any international presence.[35] While *The Search* was in production, Vittorio de Sica's *Sciuscià* (*Shoeshine* (1946)) and Rosselini's *Germany Year Zero* (1948) focused on the child victim in the postwar era as part of a single nation's efforts at postwar reconstruction. Even Géza Radványi and Béla Balázs's *Valahol Európaban* (*Somewhere in Europe*), focuses on the experiences of a group of Hungarian children after the war as a way of envisioning European reconstruction.[36] The children's hilltop community is pitted against the ex-Hungarian Nazis attempting to reconstruct their fascist pasts. Only films such as *Unzere Kinder* (1951) and documentaries such as David Miller's *Seeds of Destiny* (1946) and Jill Craigie's *Children of the Ruins* (1948) look at conditions outside conventional nationalist boundaries.[37] In *Unzere Kinder*, the children are Jewish and actively criticize adults' historicization of the Holocaust. As J. Hoberman argues: '*Unzere Kinder* is not only among the first films about the Holocaust, it is also the first to critique its representation'.[38] Zinnemann would continue to resist the reappearance of nationalism in Europe, opting instead for a uniquely European perspective. He wrote: 'To make the film big it MUST show wandering of kids across the face of Europe – at least 3 countries!'[39] And yet, Czechoslovakian history would determine the identity of *The Search*'s protagonist.

Zinnemann's interest in keeping his young protagonist a Czech was fuelled by reports from UNRRA newsletters describing Czech children who had forgotten their own language since they were interned in Germany. 'There are young children in Czechoslovakia today, children ten and twelve years of age, who are struggling to unlearn German, the only language they know, and re-learn Czech, the language they have forgotten', noted one such report.[40] Most of them were Jewish or children of those suspected of political resistance. The report explained:

> Six-year-old children were often put to work that way and forced to speak only German. They were given German names. Or only numbers

branded on their little arms. And many of them hardly remember their own names or their mother-tongue. The difficulties of tracing such children and reuniting them with the remains of their frantic families after so many years, can easily be understood.[41]

The Nuremberg Trials and the continuing searches for 'displaced' Czech children kept Lidice in the news. In addition, Czech children were particularly vulnerable to starvation and neglect, and in 1945–6 Jan Masaryk had appealed to the Allies for additional emergency relief for the children.[42] According to his research notes, Zinnemann considered restructuring the film to focus on war and postwar fates of Czech children in a Lidice-like situation: 'Possible story: Kids caught in Czech village on street – put into institute – one can't make grade in slave labour – one resists – experiment'.[43] But the wider statistics remained in his mind as he annotated UNRRA worker John Troniak's report on Lidice and kidnapped Czech children: '1449 Czech kids taken to Germany; 390 dead; 289 found and sent home; found 73 = 697 missing'.[44] In his research notebooks, Zinnemann kept the *Jewish Agency for Palestine Child and Youth Immigration Bureau* notes on a Czech boy called Jichak Grosz who was born in Galanta, Czechoslovakia before being separated from his parents. He was sent to Deutschkreutz and survived, but the fate of his parents unknown.[45] Could he have served as a basis for Karel Malik?

One of the few professional actors involved in the project was famed Czech soprano Jarmila Novotná, who played Karel's mother. She was very close to the Masaryk family and in 1942 recorded a series of *Songs of Lidice* accompanied on the piano by Jan Masaryk. Several years later, it was Masaryk who convinced the singer to take on the unglamorous role of a DP mother.[46] Ivan Jandl was another of the handful of 'professional' actors involved in the film, although as a Czech radio actor, he had had very little professional experience prior to meeting Zinnemann. They met during the director's research trip to Czechoslovakia. But historian Atina Grossmann has argued that in making *The Search*'s child hero 'the child of anti-Nazi Czech intelligentsia parents', the film was part of a pattern of the 'universalization and dejudaization of the Holocaust' in the postwar era.[47] Tara Zahra has made a similar claim, arguing that relatively few Czechoslovakian children were in UNRRA camps and even fewer would have been non-Jewish Holocaust survivors: 'Lingering anti-Semitism in the United States and Europe after the Second World War, a middle-class Czech child made for a more sympathetic protagonist than a Jewish child or even the more exotic Poles or Ukranians who populated Europe's refugee camps'.[48] Pursuing her revisionist portrait of Czechoslovakia and Nazi Germany's shared interests in race and national purity during the 1930s, Zahra has pointed out the Nazis' recognition of Czechs as racially acceptable for Germanization; yet, the statistics do not really support the idea that the Lidice children were deliberately taken into the German system for that purpose. Only nine of the original 105 children were taken for the *Lebensborn* programme. Six others would join them, but the remaining eighty-two were executed as racially unacceptable.

Historians' assessments of *The Search*, largely ignorant of its production history, oversimplify Zinnemann's position. In addition to the wide variety of Jewish and Eastern European children at the camp and interviewed by Mrs Murray (who were played by DP children from the Rosenheim children's home), *The Search*'s other child protagonist is a Jewish child. Both Grossman and Zahra ignore Jarmila Novotná's close relationship with Joel (Leopold Borkowski), the Jewish child who appropriates Karel's identity and who the mother saves from anti-Semitic abuse at the hands of non-Jewish UNRRA children. Zinnemann was himself Jewish, interviewed and cast many Jewish child survivors,[49] and wanted to focus on the unique plight of Jewish children, but was well aware that there were tens of thousands of non-Jewish child victims under the care of UNRRA as well.[50] As many as 1.5 million Jewish children were killed in the Second World War, but another million children died in Europe between 1938 and 1945, including tens of thousands of German children killed by bombing raids on major German cities. Thousands more perished from famine and neglect in 1946–7, and the UN reported that in 1947, 20 to 30 million children were at risk of starvation.[51] Zinnemann was equally 'guilty' of universalization and particularization simply because he wanted to accommodate the stories of as many European child victims as possible. Karel, as a non-religiously affiliated son of Czech intellectuals, was part of a resisting group that experienced some of the longest oppression of the war. Although not a Lidice child, the separation from his mother, miserable silence, and lack of memory attest to a national psyche overpowered and nearly obliterated by the Third Reich.

Karel has a unique and tragic past, but he represents a mixture of many horrific events in the lives of Europe's children. Though unlike his parents and sister, Karel is blond and pale-eyed, so were many Polish and Eastern European Jews (recall Sol's/Rod Steiger's golden-haired children in *The Pawnbroker*, 1964).[52] Initially, Karel is not identified as Jewish or Gentile. Only later, after discovering that a Jewish boy attempted to assume Karel's safe identity while in a camp, Mrs Murray mentions that Karel is not Jewish. But, in the flashback, Karel's home is presented as middle class and prosperous, and heavily invested in music, something common to Zinnemann's own background in Vienna and the representation of many European Jewish homes in film (*Golden Boy*, 1939; *Humoresque*, 1946).[53] Karel's knitted cap may be treasured because his mother made it for him and kept it in good repair even in the concentration camp, but the small cap has visual connections to both the *kippah* worn by Jewish men and boys and the ubiquitous cap of a schoolboy. More broadly, in the initial filmed interviews, the UNRRA officials avoid designating the children as Jewish. Instead, their parents' names, original country and fate in the concentration camps identify them only as victims of the Nazis. Yet, Karel's complex amalgamation of Jewish and Gentile elements resonates ironically with the experiences of two prominent Czech-American immigrants, director Miloš Forman and former US Secretary of State Madeleine Albright. As both reveal in their memoirs, their families concealed their heritage and for many years they had no idea of their Jewish parentage.[54] Being Czech and Jewish involved an ongoing suppression of history and identity in the postwar era.

Despite the massive US interest in Lidice and the fate of Czechoslovakia's children, the tragedy for Karel and for Ivan Jandl was that the fluidity of language and culture did not permeate geographical boundaries. Steve's (Montgomery Clift) efforts to adopt Karel are met with sympathy from the female UNRRA worker (played by Aline MacMahon, who also supplies the film's voice-over narration), but at the end of the film, had Karel not been reunited with his mother, Steve would have had to leave him at an UNRRA camp with no guarantee that he could arrange his emigration. But Steve cares about what happens to Karel, and delays his return to the US in order to facilitate adoption. His ability to truly see Karel in the rubble of Munich and not simply run away after tossing him the remains of his lunch was a telling metaphor for what American commitment to Europe could mean. It was significant that Zinnemann changed Steve's occupation from army journalist (intent on using Karel's story for career advancement) to an engineer (in the business of German reconstruction).[55]

Ivan Jandl's fate was grimmer than Karel's fate. With the assassination of Jan Masaryk and the Soviet takeover of Czechoslovakia, Czech immigration to the USA ceased. The United States had been the slowest nation to offer DPs asylum, and the DP Act/Public Law 774 (1948) had exclusions that effectively barred Czech immigrants (since refugees from the communist regime would have left after December 1945). When Jandl won a special Academy Award in 1948 for his performance as a child actor, the regime ended his acting career. He was barred from the film industry, from the theatre, and from immigrating to the USA. The communists even smashed his Golden Globe and confiscated his Academy Award. Zinnemann arranged to send him another. As he wrote Margaret Herrick, secretary to the Academy:

> Ivan is very unhappy because to date he has not received the award ... You can well understand how strongly a child feels about such things ... I would be glad to pay personally for a replica of the Award – because I feel very strongly that a joy such as this should not be withheld from a child who may not be leading a very joyful life at present.[56]

Soon, even his letters to Jandl were confiscated.[57] Jan Masayrk, who had strong ties with the USA and supported the international film production, was killed in Prague by Soviet agents. Peter Viertel and Fred Zinnemann's original hope – that Czechoslovakia was the future of European regeneration

– was over. Novotná was more fortunate and remained in the USA. Her affiliation with the film may have been one reason why she was denied a visa to attend her mother's funeral years later. But her recordings, particularly the *Songs of Lidice* with Jan Masaryk, were unavailable in Czechoslovakia until the 1990s.

The perception of Czechoslovakia as Europe's most international country may have contributed to the predominantly international character of its wartime and immediate postwar experience. Zdeňka Bezděková's historical children's novel, *They Called Me Leni* (1948) was inspired by the author's reaction to the public return of Hana Spotová, one of the Lidice children, whose return to her mother on 2 April 1947 was witnessed by crowds of journalists and UNRRA officials.[58] It was translated into nine different languages and went through several Czech editions. But many years would pass years before a Czech film could be made about Lidice and its children. The first Czech scenario on Lidice was written by František Kropáč in 1946; it was never made.[59] Ten years later, a script, *Bez Názvu* (*Without a Name*), was written about the massacre, but was stopped by censors.[60] Miloš Forman and Jiří Sehnal's script, entitled at various points *Lidice budou žít* (*Lidice Shall Live*), *Pět mužů* (*Five Men*) and *Lidice*, went through several drafts in 1961 before the production was stopped by censors.[61] Forman's work in Czechoslovakia would remain firmly focused on contemporary material, and to this day, histories of Czech cinema focus overwhelmingly on the contemporary material of the New Wave, avoiding discussions of Barrandov, Prague's huge international studio during the 1930s, and the dearth of historical productions following the communist takeover in 1948.[62] Later in life, Forman would reflect that it was only upon coming to America and becoming part of the Hollywood system that he was able to explore historical issues and indulge his 'yearning for authenticity'.[63] It is tempting to speculate why the dramaturgs in the Czechoslovakian film industry would have suppressed Forman and Sehnal's script and then supported *Práče/The Slingshot Bearer* (dir. Karel Kachyňa, 1960) and *Atentát* (dir. Jiří Sequens, 1965) a few years later. Forman's film focused on the massacres and deportations of Czech men, women and children by the Nazis, but by the late 1950s, revelations of de-Stalinization and ongoing Soviet actions in Eastern Europe showed that the Germans no longer had a monopoly on atrocities. But *Práče*'s story of a Czech boy (Michal Koblic) rescued by Soviet soldiers and then given to Czech soldiers as a mascot cemented postwar Czechoslovakian and Soviet 'cooperation' and *Atentát*'s wartime fight against the Nazis was a 'national' history that both the Soviet and Czech governments could support.

Additionally, a film about Lidice and Czech children in the postwar era ran the risk of drawing attention to *The Search* and what had happened to its child star, Ivan Jandl. For a number of years, Zinnemann received appeals from students studying at the Prague Film School asking for information about Ivan Jandl. They all planned documentaries about the actor's tragic life, but unsurprisingly none of them made it to the screens. Films about Jandl, like films about Lidice's children, could be an embarrassment to the communist regime.[64]

Atentát was the first Czech film to depict the assassination and the hunt for the Czech partisans. It won the Golden Prize at the Fourth Moscow International Film Festival (Bondarchuk's *War and Peace* and Zoltán Fábri's *Twenty Hours* won the Grand Prix). Fred Zinnemann was one of the judges, the only representative from the United States.[65] Ten years later, the British co-production *Operation Daybreak* (1975), starring American Timothy Bottoms and Briton Anthony Andrews, largely recreated Sequens' production for an English-language audience. Both films are suspenseful reconstructions of the resistance network's killing of Heydrich. They culminate in the cellars of the cathedral in a final confrontation with the Gestapo. The tragic aftermath of Lidice, and the fate of the children, is not covered. However, popular British and American television series about the Second World War make references to Lidice; in *Secret Army* (BBC, 1977–9), memory of the children of Lidice is what stops partisans from assassinating Gestapo Chief Ludwig Kessler in Brussels. In Dan Curtis's definitive Second World War period drama, *War and Remembrance* (1983), Herman Wouk's teleplay recreates the horrors of Babi Yar, but does not show Lidice. However, Czechoslovakia is central to the script's consideration of war children. Byron and Natalie Henry's only child, Louis, escapes from Theresienstadt with the help of Natalie's uncle (Chaim Topol) and Czech partisans, but is nearly killed in the woods by Nazis. He joins a group of *Wolfskinder* before being rescued and flown to Britain to a children's camp. Byron's search for Louis begins with Jewish war relief organizations and UNRRA in France and Germany, and eventually leads him to a silent Louis, who, like Karel Malik years before, cannot speak or remember his past.

The first major Czech feature film to focus on Lidice was only released in 2011.[66] Yet, the film's international title, *Fall of the Innocent*, hints that worldwide recognition of Lidice is not what it once was. *Lidice* belongs to a growing cluster of post-*Schindler's List* war films, novels and histories to focus on the war via the child victim. The Nicholas Winton story in *All My Loved Ones* (Czechoslovakia, dir. Matej Mináč, 1999), *Lebensborn* drama *Spring of Life* (Czech, dir. Milan Cieslar, 2000), Vélodrôme d'Hiver narratives *Sarah's Key* (dir. Gilles Paquet-Brenner, 2010) and *La Rafle* (dir. Rose Bausch, 2010), all focus on the historical and sometimes fictional escapes of children from Nazi extermination. Yet, these films often truncate the postwar experiences of the survivors and their place within the reconstructed nation. Winton's on- and off-screen association with the Kindertransport in histories of Czech child victims has been criticized for over-emphasizing British (and international) efforts to save the children while diminishing efforts of Czech resistance groups. Jennings's female schoolteacher and Mrs. Malik in *The Search*, at least play active roles in asserting 'Czech' resistance and efforts to locate lost children.[67] *Lidice*, although a fairly accurate reconstruction of the details of the massacre (it even includes shots of the Nazis filming the destruction of the village), is seen principally through the eyes of a male inhabitant of the village who escapes death only because he is serving a prison sentence. Two recent novels about surviving Lidice children focus on the *Lebensborn* process, but while Joan Wolf's *Someone Named Eva* minimizes the postwar conflicts over their repatriation, making protagonist Milada's reunion with her mother a happy event, Maureen Myant's *The Search* takes a more critical look at the story.[68] Jan's life in the village is far from idyllic and his mother beats him. Although his mother survives, Jan is not particularly happy when they are reunited. His younger sister Lena, who has been adopted by an older German farmer and his wife, is miserable at the prospect of leaving her new parents. The UN worker who forces them back to Czechoslovakia is a nasty, red-faced, impatient woman who has no sympathy for the children.[69]

Recent historiography on the subject of the child war orphan has moved on from Dorothy Macardle's international studies of war deprivation and relief; in Zahra's accounts of postwar repatriation, the efforts of Czechoslovakia and other European nations to reconstruct the nation

FIGURE 15.1 *Montgomery Clift, Fred Zinnemann and Ivan Jandl (right) on location in Munich, 1947.*

Courtesy of the Academy of Motion Picture Arts and Sciences.

אויבן: א געזעגענונגס־קוש דורך די דראָטן.
פאַרשפּאַרטע יידן אין דער לאָדזשער געטאָ־תּפיסה אויף מּשאַרניעצקענגאַ גאַס בעת דער „אויסזידלונגס־אַקציע".
איבערגעגעבן דורך פּנחס שוואַרץ.

אונטן: קאַוונע. דער וויאַדוקט וואָס האָט פאַרבונדן דעם גרויסן מיטן קליינעם געטאָ.
איבערגעגעבן דורך וואָלף גליקסמאַן.

FIGURE 15.2 *A page from Zinnemann's research dossier on the Holocaust, which he put together in late 1946–early 1947. The top image inspired the parting kiss between Karel (Jandl) and his mother (Jarmila Novotná).*
Courtesy of the Academy of Motion Picture Arts and Sciences.

through appropriately pure families look as unpleasant as some of the Nazis' clumsy efforts at Germanization. But arguing that international attention on Czechoslovakia and the enduring power of films such as *Silent Village* and *The Search* are really sops to latent anti-Semitism and avoidance of 'more worthy' war victims distorts the wider significance of Lidice, Czechoslovakia's potential ties to a new Europe, and the efforts of filmmakers like Humphrey Jennings and Fred Zinnemann to see beyond national myths and postwar ideologies of national purity.[70] In addition, however tempting it may be to view postwar cinematic efforts to restore young Czechoslovakia and a democratic Europe as political platforms for American capitalist 're-education', Jennings and postwar Britain's faith in transnational working-class socialist identities and Zinnemann's commitment to his young Jewish survivor cast offer a strikingly different perspective. Lidice's children would live in these two films, inextricably linked to wider searches for Jewish, European, and international collaboration and survival.

Notes

1. John Bradley, *Lidice: Sacrificial Village* (New York: Ballantine Books 1972), p. 143.
2. For more on Jennings, see Keith Beattie, *Humphrey Jennings* (Manchester: Manchester University Press 2010) and Philip C. Logan, *Humphrey Jennings and British Documentary Film: A Reassessment* (Farnham: Ashgate 2010), and on Zinnemann, see Fred Zinnemann, *An Autobiography* (London: Bloomsbury 1992) and J. E. Smyth, *Fred Zinnemann and the Cinema of Resistance* (Jackson: University Press of Mississippi 2014).
3. Seventeen children were returned to Lidice after the war, *Lidice Shall Live!* (Prague: The Association for the Restoration of Lidice 1947), p. 18.
4. Lidice pamphlet (Nase Vojsko – SPB – Prague 1962), pp. 8–9.
5. Tara Zahra, *Kidnapped Souls: National Indifference and the Battle for Children in the Bohemian Lands* (Ithaca: Cornell University Press 2008) and *Reconstructing Europe's Families after World War II* (Cambridge: Harvard University Press 2011). See also Kateřina Čapková, *Czechs, Germans, Jews: National Identity and the Jews of Bohemia* [2005] (Oxford: Berghahn 2012); Jan Láníček, *Czechs, Slovaks, and Jews: Beyond Idealization and Condemnation* (London: Palgrave 2013); Tomas Sniegon, *Vanished History: The Holocaust in Czech and Slovak Historical Culture* (Oxford: Berghahn 2014).
6. Humphrey Jennings, 'The Silent Village', transcript of interview on the BBC Home Service, 26 May 1943, p. 67.
7. Extract from Czechoslovakian News Broadcast, 10 June 1942, European Service of the BBC, INF 5/90, Crown Film Unit Files, National Archives, Kew.
8. Tara Zahra, *Kidnapped Souls*, p. 197.
9. Humphrey Jennings, *Silent Village*, script A141CFU, INF/1916, Crown Film Unit Files, National Archives, Kew.

10 Humphrey Jennings to Cicely Jennings, 10 September 1942, in *The Humphrey Jennings Reader*, ed. by Kevin Jackson (Manchester: Carcanet Press 2012), p. 61.
11 Nevertheless, the publicity for the film (which included a large uncaptioned photo of the children) and the *New York Times* review of *Silent Village* did focus on the children, 'the same children that will walk in a dismal file through the sun-streaked playground to the waiting Nazi trucks, which will scatter them forever'. *Silent Village: A Memorial to the People of Lidice*, INF/1916, Crown Film Unit Files, National Archives, Kew.
12 E. J. Erben, *The Fire Bird and Other Selected Czech Folk and Fairy Stories* (London: P. R. Gawthorn Ltd. 1943).
13 Gerd Gemünden, *Continental Strangers: German Exile Cinema, 1933–51* (New York: Columbia University Press 2014), pp. 102–25.
14 Thérèse Bonney, *Europe's Children: 1939–1943* (New York: Thérèse Bonney 1944).
15 Jacob Riis, *How the Other Half Lives* [1890] (London: Penguin 1997).
16 Bosley Crowther, 'From The War's Fringe: Marie-Louise (1945)', *New York Times*, 13 November 1945.
17 Dorothy Macardle, *Children of Europe* (Boston: Beacon Press 1950), p. 231, p. 305.
18 Isabel Heinemann '"Until the Last Drop of Blood": The Kidnapping of "Racially Viable" Children and Nazi Racial Policy in Occupied Eastern Europe', in *Genocide and Settler Society: Frontier Violence and Stolen Indigenous Children in Australian History*, ed. by A. Dirk Moses (New York, Oxford: Berghahn Books 2004).
19 Mark Wyman, *DPs: Europe's Displaced Persons* (Ithaca: Cornell University Press 1998), p. 93. See also Tara Zahra, *Reconstructing Europe's Families after World War II*.
20 Dorothy Macardle, *Children of Europe*, p. 296.
21 'Lidice Women Face Accused As Trial Opens', 27 March 1946, AP clipping, box 58, folder 796, FZ Papers. For contemporaneous responses, see Edna St Vincent Millay, *The Murder of Lidice* (New York: Harper & Bros. 1942) and especially Zena Irma Trinka, *A Little Village Called Lidice: Story of the Return of the Women and Children of Lidice* (Lidgerwood, ND: International Book Publishers 1947); for histories, see J. F. N. Bradley, *Lidice, Sacrificial Village* (London: Ballantine Books 1972); Ivan Ciganek, *Lidice* (Prague: Orbis Press Agency 1982); Eduard Stehlík, *Lidice: The Story of a Czech Village*, trans. by Petr Kurfürst (Prague: Kejrová 2004).
22 'Lidice Women Face Accused As Trial Opens', 27 March 1946, AP clipping, box 58, folder 796, FZ Papers.
23 Dorothy Macardle, *Children of Europe*, pp. 234–5.
24 PV to LW, 22 June 1946, 4pp, box 57, folder 779, FZ Papers, AMPAS. Though Tara Zahra, *Reconstructing Europe's Families after World War II*, has argued that Czechoslovakia's predominantly Catholic populace made it a comfortable, non-Jewish state in which the postwar West could imagine

the rebuilt Europe, Viertel and Zinnemann were also drawn to the unique multi-ethnic make-up of the prewar Czech state and its democratic constitution.

25 PV, Outline, 8, ibid.
26 PV to LW, 22 June 1946, ibid.
27 FZ to LW, 2 December 1946, box 57, folder 779, FZ Papers, AMPAS.
28 Ibid.
29 Ibid.
30 FZ, Interviews and Transcribed Oral Testimonies (1947), box 59, folder 801, FZ Papers, AMPAS.
31 Annotations on *Search* Script, box 57, folder 770, FZ Papers, AMPAS.
32 UNRRA Report, 2 June 1946, box 59, folder 801, FZ Papers, AMPAS.
33 Annotations on *Search* Script, box 57, folder 770, FZ Papers, AMPAS.
34 Dorothy Macardle, *Children of Europe*, p. 270.
35 See Robert Shandley, *Rubble Films: German Cinema in the Shadow of the Third Reich* (Philadelphia: Temple University Press 2001) and Marc Silberman, 'What's New? Allegorical Representations of Renewal in DEFA's Youth Films, 1946–1949', in *German Postwar Films*, ed. by Wilifried Wilms and William Rasch, 93–108 (London: Palgrave Macmillan, 2008), 94–8.
36 Constantin Parvelescu, 'The Continent in Ruins and Its Redeeming Orphans: Géza Radványi and Béla Balázs's *Somewhere in Europe* and the Rebuilding of the Post-War Polis', *Central Europe* 10/1 (May 2012), pp. 55–76.
37 Jill Craigie's short documentary for the Crown Film Unit would, like *The Search*, use a female voice-over to comment on its footage of starving children.
38 J. Hoberman, *Bridge of Light: Yiddish Film Between Two Worlds* (Dartmouth: University Press of New England 2010), p. 331.
39 FZ, Annotated UNRRA Report, 2 June 1946, 5, box 59, folder 801, FZ Papers, AMPAS.
40 Eileen Blackey, 'Children Have Forgotten the Czech Language', *UNRRA Newsletter* 9/9 (December 1945), box 59, folder 800, FZ Papers.
41 Ibid.
42 Dorothy Macardle, *Children of Europe*, pp. 58–9.
43 FZ, Notes on Interview with John Troniak, Regensburg, box 59, folder 801, FZ Papers, AMPAS.
44 FZ, Annotations, Excerpts from Report of John Troniak, 3 December 1946, box 59, folder 801, FZ Papers, AMPAS.
45 Folder 795, FZ Papers, AMPAS.
46 Walter Price, 'For Novotná, A Lifetime as Dramatic as an Opera Plot', *Los Angeles Times*, 16 November 1986.
47 Atina Grossmann, *Jews, Germans, and Allies: Close Encounters in Occupied Germany* (Princeton: Princeton University Press 2009), pp. 183–4, pp. 331–2. Gerd Gemünden has pointed out that during the war, director Fritz Lang curbed scriptwriter Berthold Brecht's plans to show Czech hostages exhibiting

signs of anti-Semitism in *Hangmen Also Die*. See Gerd Gemünden, *Continental Strangers*, p. 112.

48   Tara Zahra, *Reconstructing Europe's Families after World War II*, p. 179.

49   This is in contrast to Fritz Lang, who vetoed Brecht's hope of casting exiled German actors in *Hangmen* because he felt the public was more likely to identify with the Czechs if they were played by Americans. See Gerd Gemünden, *Continental Strangers*, p. 113.

50   Among Zinnemann's child cast members from UNRRA child centres were (from Dornstatt): Giza Mebel, Hadassah Neumann, Pinchas Wiszenko, Mordechai Pozniak, Hadassa Warszawska, Tamara Friedman, Marcel Fuchs, Szymon Ivanszczenki, Aron Szuflita, Mordechai Geber, Feige Waldberg, Feiwel Szindler, Boris Kaplan, Josef Gorny, Szmul Finkelstein, Heniek Broda, Leon Kapelner, Sima Feinberg, Chana Torczinek, Jenta Pozniak, Michas Romatansky, Leibel Szipa, David Hildebrand, Fajer Stockmau, Eliahu Waldberg; (from Rosenheim): Sala Akerman, Selig Schumacher, Boris Schneider, Grischa Borok, Zwi Miller, Marek Parchamowski, Abram Mendel, Hevek Trachtenberg, Abram Litman, David Erlichmann, Golda Kros, Feiwel Tonk, David Miller, Fela and Josef Jilisz, Berele Gordon, Hirsch Steinberg, Sala Akerman, Bayr Main, Chaim Katz, Josna Heisler, Raphel Feuster, Gedalja Ladany, Mosze Polachek, Umer Hauser, Mosze Heisler, Chaja Gross, Sosa Reich, Dov Kis, Rahel Presil, Jizchak Pressburger, Zev Bohm; (from Struth): Joel Feldman, Israel Wasil, Josef Bajor, Peter Gang, Dota Reder, Bruno Roth, Jaffa Herman, Benjamin Hahn, Josef Csillaz; (from Indersdorf): Jakob Leiserowicz, Marcel Landsberger, Gabriel Leiserowicz, Szcomo Aftergut, Jizchak Birnbaum, Jechiel Rub, Bejamin Teitelbaum, Jakob Szor, Moniek Orlanczyk, Raja Szklerowicz; (from Prien): Rosalie Goldschak, Margarete Marhardt, Stella Rebryk, Nadya Bozko, Raya Bozko, Johann Merz, Constantin Proniewez, Ary Goldshalk, Franz Marhartd, Wladimir Bozka, Nikilai Goribow, Vera Aboschinowa, Wassily Jvanow, Bruno Buonovicini and Alex Gordoff (folder 774, Casting, FZ papers, AMPAS).

51   Dorothy Macardle, *Children of Europe*, p. 297, p. 301. In 1943, it was estimated that 40 million European children were starving.

52   Allan Zullo and Mara Bovsun, *Survivors: True Stories of Children in the Holocaust* (New York: Scholastic 2004), p. 46, p. 82 and p. 180.

53   Fred Zinnemann, *An Autobiography*, p. 8.

54   Miloš Forman, *Turnaround, A Memoir* (London: Faber & Faber 1994) and Madeleine Albright, *Prague Winter: A Personal Story of Remembrance and War, 1937–1948* (New York: Harper 2012).

55   See 'Treatment by Richard Schweizer' (May 1947), 19, box 16, folder 1, Montgomery Clift Papers, New York Library for the Performing Arts.

56   Ivan Jandl to FZ, Letters, box 58, folder 790, FZ Papers; see also FZ to Margaret Herrick, 18 August 1949, box 57, folder 782, FZ Papers, AMPAS.

57   Ibid.

58   Zdeňka Bezděková, *They Called Me Leni*, trans. by Stuart R. Amor (New York: MacMillan Publishing 1973), p. 6. See also Testimony of Maria Hanfová, 8 October 1947, Nuremburg Military Tribunal, vol. IV, pp. 1033–4.

59 František Kropáč, *Lidice*, [1946], 28 page synopsis, Czech National Film Archive, S-2115-SY, track no. 0006237.
60 *Bez Názvu*, 17pp, date 1950s(?), S-2591-FP, Czech National Film Archive. A 1970s short documentary film by Goran Markovic was released under that title.
61 Miloš Forman and Jethro Spencer McIntosh, *Lidice budou žít* (1960), S-1734-FP-2, track no. 0006175; Miloš Forman and Jethro Spencer McIntosh, *Lidice* (1961), S-1734-FP-2, track no. 0006203, Czech National Film Archive; see also *Pět mužů* (1961), S-1734-LS-2, track no. 0005813, and 2A track no. 0007579. See Jan Lukeš, 'Slovo nevezmu zpět (Nerealizované scénáře šedesátých let)' [1960s Screenplays that Didn't Make It to the Screen], *Iluminace*, Roc 8, c. 1 (21) (1996), pp. 9–46.
62 Peter Hames, *The Czechoslovak New Wave* (Berkeley: University of California Press 1985).
63 Miloš Forman, *Lidice*, p. 286.
64 See Oskar Reif (a student in the documentary school in Academy of Film Art FAMU in Prague) to FZ, no date, box 105, folder 5; FZ Papers, AMPAS; Dagmar Macková-Smižova to FZ, 12 February 1990 and Hana Cielova and Stefan Uhrik to FZ, 12 July 1991.
65 Actress Marina Vlady represented France and Jiří Marek represented Czechoslovakia.
66 Jacky Conforty's documentary, *In the Shadow of Memory* (2007), focuses on the legacy of Lidice through the experience of Jerri Zbiral, whose mother and sister survived the destruction of the village. *Lidice* writer Zdeněk Mahler had worked with Forman as historical consultant on *Amadeus* decades before. See *Nokturno* [2000] (Prague: Labyrint 2011). Allegedly, it was the reluctance of German-run firms in the Czech Republic to finance the film and its unpleasant image of wartime Germans that delayed production (Producer Adam Dvořak, quoted by Christian Falvey, 'Film Producers Look to Public Collection to Save Lidice From Development Hell', *Radio Prague*, 30 April 2010). Ironically, Dvořak argued that Lidice's film-makers 'want to make an international film that's not just about good guys and bad guys'.
67 Anna Hájková and Martin Šmok, 'NÁZOR: Česká pohádka o Wintonovi aneb holocausts happy endem', *DNES*, 9 November 2014.
68 See Joan M. Wolf, *Someone Named Eva* (New York: Sandpiper 2007); Maureen Myant, *The Search* (London: Alma Books 2008).
69 Maureen Myant, *The Search*, p. 309.
70 Michel Hazanavicius' 2014 remake of *The Search*, restaged in war-torn Chechnya, explores a female NGO worker's (Annette Bening) relationship with Kolia (Maksim Emelyanov).

CHAPTER SIXTEEN

Europe's Children across the Borders of Memory

Roger Hillman

The subject matter of this chapter embodies a cross-temporal perspective, as war-affected childhoods are viewed in post-Holocaust representations, during the progressive 'normalization' of the post-Wall Federal Republic of Germany. The focus is on what representations of the Second World War children tell us about our current vantage point and about the historical reception of childhood, especially childhood dislocation,[1] either during or in the immediate wake of the Second World War. This temporal arch is in keeping with memory studies itself and its symbiotic connection to written history: 'Memory is active, forging its pasts to serve present interests'.[2]

The main texts analysed are Cate Shortland's film *Lore* (2012), an adaptation of the central chapter of Rachel Seiffert's three-part novel *The Dark Room* (2001), and W. G. Sebald's novel *Austerlitz* (2001).[3] Their figures are not historical, but fictional (with elements of biography and autobiography in Sebald's novel). Shortland's film, whose style blends surface realism with a moody poetry, is dominated by concrete images of German children of Nazi parents, traversing their multiple fragmented country on foot. Sebald's novel, among much else, reconstructs through the spirallings of an adult mind a Jewish childhood in Prague, a childhood that remains lost from consciousness for much of the title-figure's life. Its psychological intricacies locate it at the opposite end to *Lore* on a spectrum of wartime representations, but also at the opposite end to conventional history on a different spectrum. The imaginative rendering of cultural memories in these two texts complements 'the urgent need' in more scientific approaches 'for further studies on the ageing groups of former children of World War II'.[4] Because recent German stories of grief and suffering (particularly with Sebald and Günter Grass) have only gradually emerged from their hibernation of political incorrectness, they bypass the negative implications of revisionist history, and bear different baggage[5] to the Historians' Debate of the mid-1980s. And the two texts foregrounded here bear a different relationship to domestic German debates, given the self-exiled status of German-born Sebald, and the Australian roots of film-maker Shortland.

In recent years, cultural memory and representations of history in film have both been making progressive inroads on a more conventional, logocentric brand of history. The discipline may never recover from Hayden White's foregrounding of the rhetorical devices involved in writing history, and not just fiction, devices which ignore detached, scientific purity. The relationship between history and fiction has become far more complex, and less antagonistic.[6] The Routledge journal *Rethinking History* has already brought out a fourth special issue in 2013 on a topic inconceivable even a decade ago, 'History as Creative Writing'. Sebald's novel *Austerlitz* could turn that title round and then go still further – it embodies idiosyncratic, chameleon-like writing, as history, or rather writing that fills in some of what falls between the cracks of history. For material like Sebald's:

> [a]rtistic works may be more suited than historical or sociological method to making visible the complex interaction of times and sites at play in memory, as a fundamental feature of imaginative (poetic) works is to overlay meaning in intertextual space and blur the frontiers between the conscious and the unconscious, the present and the past, and the personal and the collective. . . . [They] can open up an alternative history . . . which challenges the compartmentalized narratives that we habitually receive.[7]

But let us start with a more straightforward narrative, the film *Lore* and its literary model. Rachel Seiffert's English-language novel *The Dark Room* (2001) came from a then thirty-year-old author of mixed German and Australian parentage. The second of three segments, titled 'Lore', tells of children traversing their own country from south to north after their parents are interned as part of the Allies' de-Nazification process. The German-language film adaptation by Australian director Cate Shortland premiered in 2012. Almost certainly the only Australian feature film with German dialogue throughout, *Lore* was Australia's official Oscar entry in the category of 'best foreign language film' that year. At the Berlin Film Festival of 2012, however, it was not the only non-German German-themed film premiere. Shortland had already been living in Germany with her South African-born husband Tony Krawitz, and his yet more ambitious film *Dead Europe* appeared the same year. At one stage of *Lore* a man says to the title-figure: 'You smell of death'. In Krawitz's film anti-Semitism (and more generally, bigotry) emits a stench of death that refuses to leave Europe. However, not least through its childhood settings – inherently more transnational, less overtly nationalistic – *Lore* is more successful in challenging notions of national cinema, and in showing how restrictive labels like 'German Cinema' or 'Australian Cinema' have become. EU-funded co-productions are no rarity, but the co-production of *Lore* by German, Australian and British companies is. And a further highly unusual aspect, within and beyond German cinema, is a feature film about children of Nazi parents, whether perpetrators or Party members.

According to an early review, the film 'rather controversially offers up as victims, not those subjected to barbarous anti-Semitic crimes, but the bewildered German civilians struggling in the wake of WWII to comprehend what just happened'.[8] The fact that a novel in English and then an Australian-made film should venture into such territory complements the recent success of Anna Funder's novel *All That I Am*. *Lore* encapsulates Germany's postwar heritage of a discredited parents' generation and a disqualified nationhood, a burden imposed on displaced and traumatized children. Its narrative is a further challenge to German cultural memory, not from the always fraught inside, but in the direction of a more transcultural memory of Germany. Filtered via the Antipodes, that does have its dangers.[9]

For cultural historian Jan Assmann, not 'the past as such . . . counts for the cultural memory, but only the past as it is remembered'.[10] Post-traumatic symptoms were not eclipsed by the gradual 'normalization' of the post-Wall Federal Republic (at grass-roots level, the latter only took off at the 2006 World Cup in Berlin, when initially tentative flag-waving by host-nation soccer fans was welcomed by non-Germans). In interviews, director Cate Shortland acknowledges that for her as a linguistic and national outsider, examination of the Second World War and the Holocaust in a German setting has resonance with apartheid in South Africa, and the Stolen Generations debate in Australia. Viewed this way, the Holocaust is not just a European event of worldwide ramifications, but becomes the paradigm for a 'cosmopolitan memory' culture.[11] But, in this kind of narrative territory, Shortland does have what the Germans call *Narrenfreiheit*, a fool's freedom (fool in the Shakespearean sense of un-blinkered insights through an outsider's perspective).

Released in a (re-)unified and progressively 'normalized' Germany, Cate Shortland's film is full of atmospheric nature shots, even visual poetry. The novel *The Dark Room* conveyed a tangible sense of traipsing, trudging and trekking. The film gives a stronger sense of waiting, of stasis, though a number of sequences feature camera shots at ankle level, with framing cutting off round the knees, to emphasize the way life became focused on the feet. And when the children are on the move, an almost uniformly handheld camera emphasizes the difficulty of their progress. The Germany they wander through is ruined and dispirited, deserted and often soundless. Until their travels take them to the junction with the Soviet occupation zone, all this occurs in the relatively idyllic setting of the Black Forest, rather than the razed landscapes of Berlin or other German cities. The children barter possessions; their mother's wedding ring buys them food. The title-figure, the apple of her Nazi father's eye, is the oldest of the children, and ideologically the least equipped to cope with the new realities. Confronted with concentration camp images at a refugee centre, she is incredulous, and no doubt shares the resentment expressed by an adult voice at the refugee centre: 'I had to look at dead Jews for two hours, just to get stale bread'.

The linguistic simplicity of the novel *The Dark Room* gave it the quality of a fairy tale – often the most threatening genre frame of all in a German tradition.[12] *Lore* is a different sign that Germany's private stories can again be told/imagined, even by non-Germans, while it also brings to the completely German story images that are not in the shadow of German cinema history. Rather than whatever it gains or loses as a film adaptation of a novel, this location in film history is what truly sets it apart, I feel. For a whole lineage of German directors had used intertextuality across movements and genres to create a strong sense of film history *as* history, as one answer to the perennially difficult question of how to approach their own national history.

At the end of the Second World War, hordes of Germans were indeed on the move. Displaced from territories that had once been their home, around 12 million expellees (*Heimatvertriebene*) had lost a *Heimat* that no longer belonged to a defeated and divided Germany, itself divided into the East and West blocs of what was to become Cold War cartography. *Lore* portrays the abandoned children of a Nazi family, who do not belong to the category of territorially dispossessed refugees. But their wanderings are portrayed without any trace of triumphalism. Till the turn of the tide of war, their home life had been privileged. All the greater, then, the chasm between their old and new lives, compared to their historical exemplars, the 'bands of "feral" children [who] roamed the countryside, living in forests, caves and deserted villages . . . Most were orphans or abandoned and had lived lives of terror and deprivation'.[13]

Lore's own ingrained attitudes are much stronger in the film than the novel, where in any case she is twelve, rather than fifteen years old. The Nazi certainties are challenged when a youth named Thomas attaches himself to the group of children – Lore (full name: Hannelore Dressler), her younger sister Liese, two still younger twin boys, Jürgen and Günter, and baby Peter. When American soldiers interrogate them, Thomas passes the Dressler children off as his siblings, and passes himself off as Jewish, his papers predisposing the Americans to assist them. The children, so goes Thomas's story, lost their own papers at Buchenwald,[14] and were subsequently moved from Buchenwald to Auschwitz ahead of liberation. Lore herself is a highly ambiguous figure, with an overload of responsibility. Presumably her (fluctuating) attitude towards the supposed Jew Thomas comes from the ideological heritage of her absent parents. She orders Thomas to avoid bodily contact with her own siblings ('Nicht anfassen!'), yet seeks his sexual touch; she launches a broadside against Jewish scum ('Dreckjuden'), yet also develops a strong symbiotic need of Thomas. Lore's fascist prejudices clash with her emerging identity as a teenager, as she encourages physical approaches, before repelling them.

The single on-screen act of violence is carried out when Thomas murders a man, with Lore more than abetting his act, a complicity from which she never recovers. But this does at least enable the children to reach the train that will take them to their grandmother near Husum, North Germany. This is another significant variation from Seiffert's novel, where Grandma's house on the outskirts of Hamburg has been bombed, but spared the firestorm of the July 1943 air-raid campaign in which over 40,000 civilians were killed and nearly the same number wounded. This event, not at the forefront of Australian perceptions of the Second World War, was referred to even by British sources as the Hiroshima of Germany. Is this a filtering out of evidence (of Royal Air Force bombing)? Or is it simply – not least given the German advisers supporting the director – a matter of a more picturesque setting, like, one suspects, the Black Forest at the beginning? These are not probing issues of adapting literature for the screen, but they are of great interest as a contemporary (commercially driven) vantage point in assessing German history. Shortland's inserted murder scene also evokes German history of the interim. The desperate need to cross a river at the point where zones divide the land must evoke the situation confronting many youths in the German/German division of the Cold War years. The historical weight and guilt borne by the German youths Thomas and Lore, somewhere between childhood and adulthood, is not historically unique.

Thomas also catches the train which takes them north, but he disappears from their lives after a police inspection early in the trip. It emerges that the surviving twin – the other has been shot – has hidden the personal papers Thomas has been presenting at border patrols, and that the papers belonged to another man, a dead Jew. This creates a major ambiguity about a crucial aspect of the film. Their protector Thomas, whom all the children except Lore have unambiguously welcomed as a kind of extended family member, could seem to them to have been operating opportunistically in playing the Jewish card. His violence in killing a man then demands reappraisal; no longer a desperate solution to their increasingly impossible task, it potentially shows the almost innate violence of a youth of unclear location on the German-Jewish spectrum, with the possibility of his being a *Kapo* not completely ruled out. Jürgen claims he only took Thomas' papers so that their protector wouldn't be able to go away. And indeed this central identity issue cannot 'go away' any longer: 'The Americans like Jews. So he pretended to be a Jew'. If this is total pretence – rather than one Jew without identity papers appropriating those of another – then (1) the tattoo on his arm must be understood as cynical performance art, rather than a signifier imposed by a captor; (2) the question is left completely dangling in the air as to the non-Jewish Thomas's relationship to the dead Jew Thomas Weil: prison guard to victim? Is his brutal murder of the boat-owner then a practised after-image? If he really was a German Gentile guard in a concentration camp, then Lore is unable to break a vicious circle described by the two men in her life. On the other hand, Shortland the interviewee does not modify a description of

Thomas as 'a Jewish boy released from the camps'.[15] But this version has narrative problems – wouldn't a Jewish Thomas fear fewer problems with occupying authorities if his own identity papers have been lost?

On the first night after their encounter with the American guards, they all settle down to sleep in the open. Thomas pulls his sleeve down when he realizes that a number seemingly tattooed on his forearm is exposed (in turn, this desire for concealment hardly tallies with another scene when all the children are swimming, without shirts). This fleeting gesture is viewed by us, but not by the children, whereas in the novel, which has no violent murder scene, Lore does see the tattooed numbers a couple of times, without comprehending their significance – bear in mind she is twelve, not fifteen. The film scene's point of view is highly disorienting, with tilt shots showing the characters upside down, like sloths in a tree. Individual frames of Thomas and Lore are edited such that eyeline matches across the characters are ruled out. But then comes a close-up of Thomas pulling down his sleeve to cover a number starting with '16365 . . .' That much is clear to us viewers only. We have no disorienting perspective at this stage of the film, only later, when details of the Jewish identity papers are shown, and they do not match this Thomas.

The converse of Shortland's 'fool's freedom' in handling her German materials is the danger of diffuseness, especially given subject matter that is bound up with the nadir of Western civilization, and that requires unique sensitivity in a German-language film set in Germany. The actual role of the Holocaust in this 'German children's story' (the subtitle of Haneke's *The White Ribbon*, also apt here) is not altogether clear. The film runs less the risk of relativizing the Holocaust, than of blurring it, as the awkward German–Jewish relations embodied by Lore and Thomas extend to crucial plot details such as those catalogued above.

At the end of the film, Lore is caught between twin representations of identity. She cannot reconcile photographic evidence of her father in the killing fields of the Eastern Front with her childhood image of him, just as the surviving family photos of Thomas Weil fail to reinforce the prejudices with which she has grown up. In both cases domestic history, the domain of the family album, is overwhelmed by broader national history. Lore, styled by Shortland to be a *Federation of German Girls* (*Bund deutscher Mädchen*, BdM) prototype, has in a sense lost two 'fathers'. One pillar of this dual stewardship collapses when her mother says: 'He is dead'. Her mother means Hitler, but Lore first understands this to mean her father. And her real father, though not dead, is lost to her.

Thomas, the other ill-fated German youth, is caught between dual embodiments of identity. If indeed his Jewishness has been performative, to appease the conquering Americans, then that has consequences for his German body, for his embodiment of German-ness. While stolen identities and identity papers undoubtedly corresponded to historical reality,[16] the fate of Thomas seems caught up in the sundering of a once-possible German-Jewish identity. Severed here at its most acute historical moment, the immediate aftermath of the Second World War, it remains the further reunification ahead for Germany, a longing for another recombined entity, as a wish-fulfilment in the new Europe.[17] But the difficulties of that path are pre-empted, whether consciously or not, by difficulties with the consistency of Thomas's character portrayal.

The film's mood is somewhat indeterminate, especially given the lack of emotionality of Thomas till towards the end, while its atmosphere is dominantly dark. At all events the account balance at the end of the film is bleak. Lore and Thomas have committed murder, despite having sheltered younger children, including a baby, with a commitment beyond their years. In the desperate straits of immediate postwar Germany, it seems, even their generation is condemned to guilt to survive (giving a different twist to survivor's guilt?). That ongoing trauma[18] transmits at the level of affect when Lore is unable to join her sister's dancing with the housekeeper, a benevolent figure from their happier childhood days. Lore seems incapable of relaxation or joy, almost of feeling altogether, and she moves awkwardly away and looks at photos of the Jewish family whose identity Thomas had adopted (as pro-filmic event, these are real photos of the family of Shortland's partner Krawitz). The one feeling penetrating her anomie is rage, rage at her grandmother's surviving attitude of authoritarianism. She destroys the sole material survivor of their trek, a kitschy china deer, as well as her grandmother's whole collection of such toy animals. But, while that is a potentially liberating gesture in a film made in a far more 'normalized' Germany, we are left rather with a sense of emotional deadness bookending the film's females. Early in the film their mother was virtually unaware of baby Peter suckling at her breast, as her mind progressively wanders at the prospect of her imminent internment. At the end, there remains a traumatized Lore – her future, beyond this ongoing trauma, is completely unclear. What may have been read as an apologetic or even self-pitying tone with a German director, runs no such danger here.

Above all, the family as the natural context of children has disappeared, as a structure. In the social turmoil and the Pandora's Box of immediate postwar horrors this basic faultline in European society could not be a political driver. But an *International Refugee Organization* (IRO) officer based in Germany wrote in mid-1949 that: 'The lost identity of individual children is *the* Social Problem of the day on the continent of Europe'.[19] And prominent in that 'Social Problem' is trauma, the psychological manifestations of warfare, the domain of creative arts rather than standard history books in the first place, and one neglected by more scientific approaches: 'With millions of people affected, the enormity and nature of the problem precluded large-scale studies of the psychological effects of war on children'.[20]

Social infrastructure was fully as ruined as physical infrastructure, with 'a widespread consensus that the Second World War had destroyed the family as completely as it had Europe's train tracks, factories, bridges and roads. The concepts of both family and nation in twentieth century Europe were redefined through experiences and perceptions of mass displacement'.[21] It is precisely the new melting pot of family and nation, ahead of redefined contours, with which Seiffert's novel and then Shortland's film engage. Particularly in the film, the children's story is bookended by the loss of their parents at the beginning, and then the experience of being lost to their grandmother at the end. Their wanderings in between show the perils of nationhood in flux, at the confluence of occupation zones, but above all they show the children as DPs of family-hood. Yet, even this socially orphaned status is challenged by the role of Thomas, who functions both as an 'acquired' brother, and as an almost cryptic gesture in the direction of a reunited German-Jewish national family. In the words of Jacques Rancière:

> So we have to revise Adorno's famous phrase, according to which art is impossible after Auschwitz. The reverse is true: after Auschwitz, to show Auschwitz, art is the only thing possible, because art always entails the presence of an absence; because it is the very job of art to reveal something that is invisible, through the controlled power of words and images, connected or unconnected; because art alone thereby makes the inhuman perceptible, felt.[22]

If ever a novel eluded summarization, it is Sebald's *Austerlitz* (2001). And not just its plot – just absorb the following description of Sebald's texts, not confined to this one:

> [t]hey shift vertiginously between fact and fantasy, between documentary solidity and self-conscious fictionality.... the discourses of history, biography, novel, essay, autobiography and travel writing combine to create hybrid forms.... a lack of paragraph breaks facilitates a free-flowing discourse unconstrained by the discipline of the paragraph, while a refusal to use speech marks means that shifts between speakers are not always marked. Furthermore, the progression of the verbal text is constantly interrupted by the insertion of visual material: photographs, reproductions of paintings, facsimiles of handwritten documents, and so on.[23]

Somehow managing to combine such a range of materials is a quaintly stilted prose, whose luminous quality belies the frequent darkness of its subject matter. With the absolutely non-Marxist Sebald, a spectre is still haunting Europe, but in a post-Holocaust era he grapples with revenants from the graveyard of nineteenth-century Europe.[24] Other than in a strictly formalist sense, his tendency to 'mannerism'[25] does not aestheticize the Holocaust, and he certainly resists any lure of what Susan Sontag called 'fascinating fascism'.[26] What ultimately emerges is a kind of subliminal social history, but a history whose substance defies norms of historical accounts, and one which relies on intermedial representation, in the mix of written and visual materials.

The first half of *Austerlitz* is dominated by descriptions of European architecture, including the secular dome of Antwerp railway station, and the star-shaped fortress of Breendonk in Belgium. The latter witnessed many tortures during the Second World War, among others Jean Améry, a famous Austrian-Jewish intellectual, who committed suicide decades on from surviving the Holocaust.[27] At about the halfway mark of the novel, shadows from the periphery materialize as the title-figure's adult memory of reaching England as part of a *Kindertransport*. This turning point in the novel is closely based on the biography of Susi Bechhöfer, who reached England on her third birthday with a *Kindertransport*, and whose foster parents erased memory of her earlier life.[28] In Sebald's novel the intrusion of memory is long held at bay, but once it catastrophically intrudes, the narrator becomes a historically charged exemplar of Walter Benjamin's *flâneur*:

> For him, every street is precipitous. It leads downward . . . into a past that can be all the more spellbinding because it is not his own, not private. Nevertheless, it always remains the time of a childhood. But why that of the life he has lived? In the asphalt over which he passes his steps awaken a surprising resonance. The gaslight that streams down on the paving stones throws an equivocal light on this double ground.[29]

For Sebald's figure the path also leads downward, into the bowels of Liverpool Street Station, and the involuntary encounter with a childhood lost beyond any nostalgic wistfulness results in the scar of childhood as disorientation. At the broader historical level, nineteenth-century Parisian leisure is eclipsed by the anxieties embodied in the mid-1930s Europe that spawned Benjamin's *Das Passagen-Werk* (*Arcades Project*). Austerlitz the figure thus historicizes Benjamin's *flâneur* as a post-Holocaust Wandering Jew or *Ahasver*. His adult revelation of his real childhood, by turns charmed and accursed, is the mirror image of pre-1930s European Jewry.

With a new identity fleshing out the title-figure's adopted name, he sets out to pursue his parents' traces in Prague and nearby. His mother's takes him to Theresienstadt, another star-shaped European fortress. For the figure Austerlitz the double bind of unwitting survivor's guilt and eternally oscillating identity is crushing. He returns to Marienbad, scene of a happy childhood holiday with his parents and also the setting for further happy days with his only female tie in the novel, till their relationship comes to an end there – a very Kafka-like gesture. (Marienbad also no doubt captures the liminal spaces between two centuries, a spectrum of cultural associations from Goethe's *Marienbad Elegy* through to Resnais' film *L'année dernière à Marienbad* (*Last Year in Marienbad*), scripted by Robbe-Grillet, who in his own literature and film-making searched for an intermediary, intermedial form somewhere between the two. Beyond that temporal hinge, Sebald's Marienbad has become a Cold War ghost town, a once grand spa resort visited by prominent Jewish families till the early 1930s.)

The very end of the novel returns to Breendonk, with the narrator reading a book set in the Lithuanian city Kaunas, and a surrounding belt of twelve fortresses which fell into the hands of German troops in 1941. The last indication of transports still arriving from the West, in May 1944, is an inscription on one wall with the signature 'Max Stern, Paris, 18.5.44'.[30] Austerlitz's search for his father, in the wake of his disappearance after a Nazi round-up in Paris, is effectively over – this man's fate stands for his father's. But far more tellingly, Max was Sebald's own adopted Christian name, 'Stern' in German means 'star', in this context irretrievably weighted by the Star of David, and the date given is the day on which Sebald first entered the world. It is as if the German Gentile author Sebald had fulfilled a death wish for reincarnation as a Jew, with the historical lineage of his grand obsession extinguished the very day he is born. Was ever a European childhood more chillingly stillborn?

Sebald's narrative also raises issues of the capacity of literature and photography to render trauma, as well as both personal and cultural memory. The ongoing processing of the events themselves locates the childhood wounds as unhealed, potentially unhealable. Sebald's narrative world signals the deracination of European culture, in its precarious filtering of long suppressed memories. Assmann's 'past as it is remembered' is the core problem for Sebald's central figure, the incapacity to reclaim a remembered past of any certainty. He is severed not just from his real parents, but from their whole generation, and the one before, as prevailing history dictates the extinction of the Jewish peoples of Europe.

Sebald's blending of photography with written script generates another layer of this dilemma: photographs show what was (once) at the time the photo was taken, and the Proustian search for lost time behind the tantalizing image is what the combination generates as a challenge to reading. Sebald's photos are without captions,[31] meaning that both language and image systems remain self-sufficient, and that the images bear a different, visually embedded, relationship to the written text. The merging of image and text continually foregrounds aesthetic issues of simultaneous presence and absence,[32] the whole dilemma of post-Holocaust memory. For in this situation, Ricœur's dual categories prove inadequate, the categories of 'repetition-memory' ('the true recollection by which the present would be reconciled with the past') and 'recollection-memory' (capable of the 'work of remembering' in critical vein).[33] A typical example is the little girl who lived in a coastal village submerged by a flood.[34] This event haunts Austerlitz like an Atlantis that is somehow the key to his own history, to a parallel world just out of reach (like his own true roots), the photo negative of what we see in developed form. This parallel world gains in materiality, while he becomes increasingly disoriented, drawn in his wanderings through London to Liverpool Street Station, where he experiences or imagines voices behind his back, speaking an alien language such as Lithuanian or Hungarian. Finally, gradually, he reconstructs his childhood origins, his arrival more than fifty years earlier, as a four-and-a-half-year-old boy. And at that point his anachronistic time capsule, perpetuated professionally with his devotion to nineteenth-century architecture, collapses, just as the impossible mid-to-late 1930s hopes of Europe's Jewish peoples evaporated.

A further typical example of photos inserted in the written text is the one of the young Austerlitz as pageboy.[35] In this case, independent of all theorization of photography by Barthes and others, the surrounding text is a wrenchingly accurate rendering of Austerlitz' amnesia and of the history of European Jewry in hindsight:

> One has the impression, she said, ... as if the pictures had a memory of their own and remembered us, remembered the roles that we, the survivors, and those no longer among us, had played in our former lives.[36]

This surface-level anthropomorphization is more precisely an extension of the sustained variations on the darkroom processing of photos, both in negative and positive format. It reverses the roles, while retaining the players, in 'the signifying system of photography', which 'at once depicts a scene *and the gaze of the spectator*, an object *and* a viewing subject'.[37] The child is father of the man in the same way that the chemicals of the subconscious crystallize images already there, which only they can call forth.

Harmonizing perfectly with the novel's themes, and far transcending the surrounding text,[38] is a photo of a bazaar item in Theresienstadt, with the camera peering in through the display case glass. It unites three time levels: (a) the past in the slightly kitschy relic of an old world, forever faded; (b) the present with the houses reflected in the background; and (c) the obscured figure, presumably the photographer, in a no-man's-land between past and present, and certainly not suggestive of a future. As one German critic puts it, what pictures document with Sebald is not reality, but the search of the narrator.[39] They will guide and potentially mislead even a posthumous quest; the narrator realizes that 'the black and white photographs ... one day, would be all that was left'.[40]

The Barthes-type *punctum*, the sting in the tail of these often banal images, lies in a post-Holocaust reading of their collage quality, a visual bric-à-brac not unlike the memories embodied in piles of suitcases, spectacles, photos and much else in, for instance, the relevant section of the Imperial War Museum, London (designed to create momentary panic in the viewer, with no exit in sight). The photos can be monuments to human despair in their subject matter, but also in their deeply personal significance. During Australian bushfires, the first impulse of those evacuating houses is frequently to salvage family photos. Sebald's output has all this flickering ambiguity of attempts to salvage the past. The photos themselves iridesce still further in not always having a clear representational link to the prose, and that relationship in turn blends evocation and documentation.

Sebald has acknowledged the influence of Alexander Kluge, one of the great thinkers of German Cinema since the 1970s. One of Kluge's key notions, as a gloss on his own film essays and their use of photos, paintings, etc., was of the 'Film im Kopf', the film activated in the viewer's head, with individual associations triggered by images. A similar process of activation operates here. Sebald rarely directly names the Holocaust. It is viewed from the perspective of a non-Jewish émigré of postwar years, born in 1944, who first saw his father at age three, since the latter was in foreign captivity till then as a member of the *Wehrmacht*. Even ahead of his late sequence of prose works, Sebald (a Norwich-based academic) wished to locate himself in a diasporic situation *outside* Germany, a mirror image of the involuntary Diaspora of the few survivors of the German-Jewish population. But Sebald also seems preoccupied with the Holocaust in our head, which makes it neither more nor less subjective than historian Alison Landsberg's notion of 'prosthetic memory'.[41] In fact, one of the leading critics of German culture, Andreas Huyssen, describes this novel as 'a reinscription of the trauma by means of quotation. As such, this is the secondary trauma of the "second" generation, always already mediated through literature, images, and representations, and perhaps on that account not susceptible to imagining new beginnings'.[42] The Holocaust itself is increasingly viewed transnationally, i.e. as the nadir not just of German history, but also of Western civilization. Writers of prose or history – or of historical prose – face formidable limits to representation. But these limits, it seems to me, are explored by Sebald no less legitimately than through more conventional channels.

Beyond their representation of history, and of cultural memory, where do these texts stand in the context of European narratives of childhood? Two classic tales of arrested European childhoods are those of Peter Pan, and Oscar Matzerath. The shadow of Peter Pan is that of adulthood, to be held at bay by the charms of fantasy as long as possible. While seemingly remote from historical flux, even this tale serves A. S. Byatt as a central symbol for callow British youths entering the First World War in her novel *The Children's Book* (2009).[43] Günter Grass's novel *Die Blechtrommel* (*The Tin Drum*), filmed with comparable success by Volker Schlöndorff, is much closer to the themes of this chapter's texts.[44] The angst-ridden and amoral Oscar chooses to remain at the level of a three-year-old, as the adult world of the German bourgeoisie blithely adapts to the new political landscape of the mid-1930s onwards. His defence mechanisms evoke contemporary history, though his tin drum resonates to a very different beat to the militarism of German occupation, and the glass shattered by his vocal chords is not that of the 'Reichskristallnacht'.

But for Shortland's Lore and for Sebald's Austerlitz there is no returning to the other, the childhood, side of those historical caesuras. At the end of her story, the still disoriented Lore is crystal clear on this one score, that the porcelain deer salvaged across the faultlines of internal German borders has no symbolic place in her new life. And Austerlitz is pitched into the cataclysmic realization of an irretrievable, charmed childhood which he has survived as a historical aberration, as one of 10,000 rescued by the *Kindertransports* among the graves of millions of European Jews. Inwardly torn ahead of his epiphany, to the point of suffering a mental breakdown, his return to Liverpool Street Station sheds some light on the family tree, but also spotlights the historical darkness which to that point had protectively enshrouded its roots. The curse of postmemory is in his case a pincer movement within the one individual. The adult Austerlitz was originally not connected to the past (his own past, as a child) by traumatic recall, as is the case in classical elaborations of postmemory.[45] His brittle sense of identity is not even 'crowded out'[46] by his parents' recollections, but by the dawning of his own. Through involuntary recall as an adult, he comes to awareness of his own direct involvement in the Holocaust as a child, creating a link between two generations of an existentially and historically sundered existence.

Notes

1. 'UNESCO ... estimated that 8 million children in Germany ... remained homeless in 1946. ... An estimated 13 million children in Europe had lost one or both parents in the war'. Tara Zahra, 'Lost Children: Displacement, Family, and Nation in Postwar Europe', *Journal of Modern History* 81/1 (March 2009), pp. 45–86, here p. 46.
2. Susannah Radstone and Bill Schwarz (eds), *Histories, Theories, Debates* (New York: Fordham UP 2010), p. 3.
3. *Lore*, dir. Cate Shortland(Australia/Germany, 2012); Rachel Seiffert, *The Dark Room* (London: Heinemann, 2001); W. G. Sebald. *Austerlitz*, trans. Anthea Bell, with an Introduction by James Bell (London: Penguin Books 2011).
4. P. Kuwert, Carsten Spitzer, Anna Träder, Harold J. Freyberger and Michael Ermann, '60 Years Later: Post-traumatic Stress Symptoms and Current Psychopathology in Former German Children of WWII', *International Psychogeriatrics* 19/5 (Oct. 2007), pp. 955–61, here p. 955.
5. A current example of this is a German-produced television series (dramatized history) set in the years spanning mid-1941 till 1945, *Unsere Väter, unsere Mütter* (*Generation War*, 2013). The two brothers foregrounded in episode 1, for instance, embody Prussian discipline on the one hand, and a vestige of the 1848 Frankfurt Parliament on the other, Germany as a land of poets and thinkers.
6. See the clarion call by Martin Evans, Professor of Modern History at the University of Portsmouth in the first edition of the *Journal of War and Culture Studies* (1/1, 2008), p. 50: 'the new war studies ... is about both representations and experience. It trains its critical sights on the creative interface between war, history, sociology and cultural studies'.
7. Max Silverman, *Palimpsestic Memory: The Holocaust and Colonialism in French and Francophone Fiction and Film* (New York: Berghahn 2013), pp. 28–9.

8   Megan Lehmann, 'Lore: Film Review', *The Hollywood Reporter*, 11 June 2012. Accessed from http://www.hollywoodreporter.com/movie/lore/review/335897.

9   Contextualizing an interview with the director and producer of *Lore*, Jo Dillon (in *Metro* 174 (Spring 2012), p. 22) finds an all too immediate link between past and present, writing of the EU now with its 'political and economic turmoil that in many regards recalls the crisis that followed WWII'. The situations are so different, that I doubt whether even a qualified comparison like this can help us understand the film's context, or shed new light on Europe's complex history.

10   Jan Assmann, 'Communicative and Cultural Memory', in *A Companion to Cultural Memory Studies*, ed. by Astrid Erll and Ansgar Nünning (Berlin: de Gruyter 2010), p. 113.

11   See Sharon MacDonald, *Memoryland: Heritage and Identity in Europe Today* (London: Routledge 2013), pp. 188–215.

12   Elaboration of this, and insightful analysis altogether, is to be found in a conference paper delivered at a GSAA conference in Sydney in December 2014, and generously made available by author Andrew Webber, 'Passing for Children in Cate Shortland's *Lore*'.

13   L. Shields and B. Bryan, 'The Effect of War on Children: The Children of Europe after World War II', *International Nursing Review* 49/2 (June 2002), pp. 87–98, here p. 92.

14   By the end of the film this, confusingly at a narrative level, seems to have become a non-issue. In the fateful ID check on the train, when Thomas is unable to find his own papers because Jürgen has taken them, the children are not queried.

15   Cate Shortland interviewed by Nick James in *Sight and Sound* 23/3 (2013), pp. 44–6.

16   In the context of the First World War, see the Jeunet film *A Very Long Engagement*.

17   On this issue in relation to the French film *Joyeux Noël*, see my chapter 'From No Man's Land to Transnational Spaces: The Representation of Great War Memory in Film, 2000–2010', in *Memory and Nation: Commemorating the Great War*, ed. by Ben Wellings and Shanti Sumartojo (Frankfurt/Main, New York: Peter Lang Verlag 2014), pp. 61–77.

18   They are twice afflicted: 'a new concept of trauma developed during the Second World War, focused on the separation of family members as much as experiences of violence' (Tara Zahra, 'Lost Children', p. 48).

19   Vinita A. Lewis, as cited by Tara Zahra, 'Lost Children', p. 45.

20   L. Shields and B. Bryan, 'The Effect of War on Children', p. 91.

21   Tara Zahra, 'Lost Children', p. 46.

22   Jacques Rancière, *Figures of History*, trans. by Julie Rose (Cambridge, UK: Polity 2014), pp. 49–50.

23   Andreas Huyssen, *Present Pasts: Urban Palimpsests and the Politics of Memory* (Stanford: Stanford UP 2003), p. 156.

24   To the dawning revelation of his true background, the title figure reacts: 'As far as I was concerned the world ended in the late nineteenth century.' W. G. Sebald, *Austerlitz*, p. 197.

25 Andreas Huyssen, *Present Pasts*, p. 157.
26 Susan Sontag, 'Fascinating Fascism' (her review of two books) in the *New York Review of Books* (6 February 1975).
27 The novel has been viewed as 'a lengthy *hommage* to the writer Jean Améry. Améry's experiences in numerous concentration camps, including Auschwitz and Breendonk, are recorded in the book *At the Mind's Limits* (1966), to which Sebald refers in *Austerlitz*'. Mark Richard McCulloh, *Understanding W. G. Sebald* (Columbia: University of South Carolina Press 2003), p. 133.
28 See Martin Modlinger, '"You can't change names and feel the same": The Kindertransport Experience of Susi Bechhöfer in W.G. Sebald's *Austerlitz*', in *The Kindertransport to Britain 1938/39: New Perspectives*, ed. by Andrea Hammel and Bea Lewkowicz (Amsterdam: Rodopi 2012), pp. 219–32.
29 Walter Benjamin, *The Arcades Project* (Cambridge, MA: Harvard University Press 1999), p. 416.
30 W. G. Sebald, *Austerlitz*, p. 415.
31 Though being framed by Sebald's text, they will be in dialogue with that of the reader, according to Victor Burgin: 'Even the uncaptioned photograph, framed and isolated on a gallery wall, is invaded by language when it is looked at: in memory, in association, snatches of words and images continually intermingle and exchange one for the other: what significant elements the subject recognises "in" the photograph are inescapably supplemented from elsewhere'. Victor Burgin, 'Photography, Phantasy, Function', in *Thinking Photography*, ed. by Victor Burgin (London: Macmillan 1982), p. 192.
32 And of death, a strong motif in Roland Barthes' *Camera Lucida*.
33 Paul Ricœur, *Memory, History, Forgetting*, trans. by K. Blamey and D. Pellauer (Chicago and London: University of Chicago Press 2004), p. 79.
34 Her image appears on p. 73 of W. G. Sebald, *Austerlitz*.
35 W. G. Sebald, *Austerlitz*, p. 258. Photographs are also framed by editing layout decisions. The 2001 Hanser-Verlag edition of the original German text has this photograph occupying a half, rather than a third of the page, affecting both text-image proportions, and any larger than life sense of the young boy. In the Penguin edition, further significance attaches to this image through its occupation of the full space on the front cover.
36 Ibid.
37 Victor Burgin, 'Looking at Photographs', in *Thinking Photography*, ed. by Burgin, p. 146.
38 The image appears on p. 276 of W. G. Sebald, *Austerlitz*.
39 Markus R. Weber, 'Die fantastische befragt die pedantische Genauigkeit: Zu den Abbildungen in W. G. Sebalds Werken', *Text und Kritik* 158 (April 2003), p. 68.
40 W. G. Sebald, *Austerlitz*, p. 293.
41 Susannah Radstone, 'Cinema and Memory', p. 334, in *Histories, Theories, Debates,* ed. by Radstone and Schwarz. 'Theories of cinema as prosthetic memory propose that the experience of spectating certain kinds of films is indistinguishable from lived experience and has the potential to create

long-lasting "memories" with the capacity to remould identity.' This makes of memory studies an extreme bridge between historical events, and their representation in (primarily non-documentary) literature and feature films.

42 Andreas Huyssen, *Present Pasts*, p. 156.
43 A. S. Byatt, *The Children's Book* (London: Chatto & Windus, 2009).
44 Günter Grass, *The Tin Drum* (London: Everyman's, 1993).
45 See Marianne Hirsch, *The Generation of Postmemory: Writing and Visual Culture after the Holocaust* (New York: Columbia UP 2012), p. 5: '"Postmemory" describes the relationship that the "generation after" bears to the personal, collective, and cultural trauma of those who came before – to experiences they "remember" only by means of the stories, images, and behaviors among which they grew up'.
46 Ibid., p. 4.

INDEX

absorption 11, 223
adaptation 52, 91, 245, 270
Adamiak, Daniela 143
adoption 24, 292, 305, 308, 311
agency
   of individuals 4, 154, 270
   and organizations 22, 23, 103, 155, 157, 288, 309
Africa 1, 4, 33, 34, 78, 113–27, 323
AFSC, see American Friends Service Committee
agricultural settlements 52, 55, 58, 127
agricultural training 41, 61, 79, 81, 215
agriculture 4, 41, 61, 135, 137
AJC, see American Jewish Committee
AJDC, see Joint Distribution Committee
AJR, see Association of Jewish Refugees in the United Kingdom
AJW&RS, see Australian Jewish Welfare & Relief Society
AJWS, see Australian Jewish Welfare Society
Albright, Madeleine 311
alienation 44, 159
Aliyah 76, 216, 222, 224–9
Allach, see concentration camp
Allied High Commission for Germany 285, 287
Altman, Tosia 215–31
American Friends Service Committee 16, 19, 20
American Jewish Committee 12
American Joint Distribution Committee, see Joint Distribution Committee

Améry, Jean 329
Anielewicz, Mordecai 215–29
'Anschluss' 3, 14, 32, 35–8, 115, 121, 242
anti-Semitism
   in Australia 2
   in Austria 26, 36–8
   in Brazil 60
   in Czechoslovakia 316
   in DP camps 284
   in Europe 280, 309
   in France 258
   in Germany 322
   in New Zealand 103
   in Poland 280
   in the United States 14, 26, 120, 309
apartheid 323
appeals 14, 23, 26, 73, 74, 77, 80, 161, 225, 242, 303, 309, 312
ARI, see *Associação Religiosa Israelita* (Israelite Religious Association)
Armstrong, Diane 77
assimilation 23, 101, 118, 259, 264, 269, 270
Associação Religiosa Israelita (Israelite Religious Association) 53
Association of Jewish Refugees in the United Kingdom 245, 248, 249, 252–3
atrocity 299
Auschwitz, see concentration camp
Auschwitz-Birkenau, see extermination camp
Australian-Jewish community 74
Australian Jewish Welfare and Relief Society 80
Australian Jewish Welfare Society 73

Australian Jewish Welfare Guardian Society 81–2
Austria 3, 5, 6, 14, 18–21, 31–9, 41–2, 44, 53, 57, 73, 82–4, 95, 102, 105, 115, 121–2, 146, 204, 209, 239, 242–4, 279, 287
Avgustina, V., 145–6
Axis Powers 53, 57

'Balts' 102
baptism 257, 263–4, 268–9
Baral, Marcel 156, 158
Barkman, Frances 72, 80, 84
Barthes, Roland 331
Bartosik, Janina 186
Bauer, Heinz 114–15, 121–3, 127
BdM, *see Bund deutscher Mädchen* (Federation of German Girls)
Belgium 5, 18, 19, 34, 84, 204, 304, 329
belonging 2, 6, 12, 44, 54, 57, 60, 105, 121, 229, 267, 270, 285
Belzec, *see* extermination camp
Benedikt, Israel 290
Benjamin, Walter 329
Bergen-Belsen, *see* concentration camp
Berkovits, Eliezer 81
Berlinski, Hirsch 220
Bernheim, David 248
Beth Rivkah Ladies College 81
Bezděková, Zdeňka 312
Bialystok, *see* ghetto
Blair, Frederick Charles 41
Blashki family 84
Błońska, Stefania 180, 186
Bloomsbury House, London 76, 242
Blum, Abraham (Abrasha) 217
Blumenthal, Elchanan 83
Bo Bardi, Lina 66
Bonadei, Aldo 64
Bonney, Thérèse 304
borders
    between countries 37, 95, 98, 278, 301
    in countries 83, 332
    in ghettos 157, 162
    and patrols 325
Borkowski, Leopold 310

Borzykowski, Tuvia 217, 230
Brand, Vera 83
Brand, Walter 75, 79, 83
Braunsteiner, Hermine 172, 183
Brecht, Berthold 301
Brent, Ellen 83
Breslaw, Shmuel 215, 216, 218, 220
Brill Czapski, Alice 57, 62–5
British Special Operations Executive 301
Brooke, Rupert 119
Bruch, Hans 64
Brzosko-Mędryk, D. 185
Buchenwald, *see* concentration camp
Buchenwald Boys 72, 84, 85
Buczek-Różańska, Janina 175, 186
Bułachow, Włodzimierz 187
Bund deutscher Mädchen (Federation of German Girls) 326
Burenko, Galyna 142
Byatt, A.S. 332

Camberwell House 84–5
Campbell, R.M. (Richard Mitchelson) 99
Canadian Jewish Congress 78
Canadian National Committee on Refugees 41
Catholic institutions 5, 77, 83, 98, 105, 243, 262, 268, 282
Catholicism 5, 258–69
Central Synagogue, Sydney 81
Central Tracing Bureau 285, 286, 288
Chamberlain, Joseph 116
Chamberlain, Neville 241
Chelsea Park training farm, Sydney 79
Child Search Branch 282, 285–8, 290
child survivors 42, 72–5, 78, 85, 114, 147, 155, 157, 163, 258, 266–8, 270, 277–92, 300, 310
Child Tracing Section 279, 281, 285–6
Christianity 26, 261–5
Cibulka, Jenine 83
Cieślak, Zofia 144
CIP, *see Congregacao Israelita Paulista* (Sao Paulo Israelite Congregation)

CNCR, *see* Canadian National Committee on Refugees
Cobel-Tokarska, Marta 160
Cohen, Raya 217, 219
Cold War 1, 77, 302, 324, 325, 329
colonies 57, 113, 116–27
Communism
  and beliefs 95
  and regimes 300, 302, 311–13
  and underground movements 220, 222
concentration camp
  Allach 72
  Auschwitz 5, 33, 71, 138, 172, 201–12
  Bergen-Belsen 82, 290
  Buchenwald 32, 60, 82, 84, 289, 324
  Dachau 32, 72, 93
  Flossenbürg 292
  Majdanek (KL Lublin) 4, 171–4
  Mauthausen 144
confinement 2, 153, 159–62
Congregação Israelita Paulista (Sao Paulo Israelite Congregation) 52, 52–5, 57–8, 66
Costa, Lúcio 66
Costello, Paddy 99
Craigie, Jill 308
CSB, *see* Child Search Branch
CTB, *see* Central Tracing Bureau
CTS, *see* Child Tracing Section
Cyprus 77, 223, 227–9, 290
Cytrynowicz, Roney 56
Czechoslovakia 6, 14, 20, 34, 37, 83, 93, 103, 251, 299, 300–16
Czerniakow, Adam 220
Częstochowa, *see* ghetto

Dachau, *see* concentration camp
Danglow, Jacob 74
death march 72, 208
Deckston, Annie 94, 95
Deckston, Max 94, 95
Deckston children 3, 92, 95, 105
Deckston Home 95, 96, 105
Dembo, Regina 22
deportation 4, 5, 14, 31–3, 41, 100, 102, 135–41

Derrida, Jacques 270
Deskur-Dunin-Marcinkiewicz, Eugenia 175
Dickens, Charles 119
discrimination 102, 124, 158, 239, 240, 260, 265
displaced children
Displaced Persons 3, 26, 72, 92, 99, 100, 102, 11, 146, 215, 277, 278, 283
Displaced Persons Camps 5, 100, 102, 114, 146, 215, 216, 223, 224, 227, 229, 230, 277, 279, 280, 287, 290
displacement 1, 2, 5–7, 26, 104, 115, 137, 145, 283, 289, 328
Djatschenko, Olga Andreewna 140, 142
Dobrowolski, Wiesław 174, 182
Dolecki, Edward 185
Domb, Lucina 183
Dorrity, Barbara 248–50
Dov, Aaron 268
DP, *see* Displaced Persons
DP Camps, *see* Displaced Persons Camps
Drabik, Tadeusz 182
Dwork, Debórah 264, 269

Eastern Europe 12, 26, 114, 135–9, 154, 218, 222, 270, 278–9, 300, 304, 310, 312
Edelstein, Marek 220
educators (*see also* teachers) 25, 55
Ehrich, Elsa 172
Eichbaum, Gisela 62, 64–5
Eichmann, Adolf 32
Einfeld, Sydney David 80, 85
Eisinger, Josef 31, 38–44
Elias, Ruth 203–7
EJCA, *see* European Jewish Children's Aid
emigration 16, 17, 19, 20, 32, 33, 51, 54–7, 60–1, 76, 78, 240–3, 283, 285, 311
enemy aliens 31
Eppelsheimer, Natalie 124, 126
European Jewish Children's Aid 15
evacuation 23, 172, 176, 208

extermination camp
  Auschwitz-Birkenau 176, 202, 203, 205–7, 208
  Belzec 220, 249
  Majdanek (KL Lublin) 171, 173, 182
  Sobibor 33, 220
  Treblinka 95, 220

Fajnwaks, Frania 153
Fajnwaks, Jerzy 153
Fajnwaks (Faynwachs), Paul 153, 155, 158, 159
FAJWS, *see* Federation of Australian Jewish Welfare Societies
Falk, Rabbi Leib Aisack 83
Familienlager (family camp) 205–7
farmers 59, 115, 118, 121, 138, 141, 144, 173, 175, 227, 291, 314
farms 4, 38, 60, 79, 81, 101, 115, 118, 120, 121–3, 139, 144, 175, 224, 227, 261
FDRL, *see* Franklin Delano Roosevelt Library
fear 2, 13, 14, 24, 38, 65, 67, 72, 83, 93, 105, 121, 123–3, 127, 141–5, 159–60, 186–7, 206, 251, 261, 262, 265, 280, 299, 305, 326
Federation of Australian Jewish Welfare Societies 73–5
Fedorina, Walentina 290
Ferber (Finder), Rena 158
Fersen, Yvonne 264
Fersen-Osten, Renée 257, 263, 266, 268
Fink, Leo 80
Fink, Mina 72, 84, 85
Fischl, Viktor 301
Fischler (Martinho), Janina 160
FKL, *see* Frauenkonzentrationslager (women's concentration camp)
Flexor, Samson 64
Flieg, Hans Günter 57, 62, 65, 66
Flight 11, 21, 59
Florstedt, Arthur Hermann 172
Flossenbürg, *see* concentration camp
forced labour camps 1, 6, 97, 138, 145

Forman, Miloš 305, 311–12
foster parents 21, 23–5, 242–5, 329
Fowler, Gene 306
Foxman, Abraham 269
France 5, 16, 18–21, 34, 73, 76, 84, 204, 229, 257–8, 263, 268, 270, 299, 300, 301, 304, 313
Frances Barkman Home 72, 73, 77, 80, 81
Frank, Hans 156, 160
Frant, Henryk 77, 78
Frant, Zofia 77
Franziska, E. 145
Fraser, Janet 97
Fraser, Peter 97, 99
Frauenkonzentrationslager (women's concentration camp) 172
freedom 39, 41, 53, 63, 121, 159, 161, 162, 203, 208, 211, 270, 323, 326
Freud, Anna 35
Friedländer, Saul 261–4
Frieze, Leah 80
Funder, Anna 323
fundraising 3, 72

Gallant, Mary 260, 267
Garel, Georges 261
Germanization 136–8, 176, 279, 284, 291, 292, 300–2, 305, 309, 316
German-Jewish Children's Aid 12
Geve, Thomas 209–10
Geyer, Zelig 217
ghetto
  Bialystok 226
  Częstochowa 226
  Kraków 4, 153–63
  Lodz 4, 33, 71, 154
  Theresienstadt (Terezin) 33, 72, 203–5, 289, 313, 329, 331
  Vilna 77, 216–19, 225, 226
  Warsaw 4, 77, 154, 174, 176, 184, 202, 208, 218–26
Giorgi, Bruno 64
GJCA, *see* German-Jewish Children's Aid
Goethe, Johann Wolfgang von 329
Good, Edwin Dudley 93
Gotthilf family 55

Gotthilf, Francisco 57, 62, 63
Gotthilf, Siegfried 55
Grass, Günter 321, 332
Greece 5, 203, 204
Green, Israel 79
Grinchenko, Gelinada 145
Grischajewa, Ludmilla 142
'Gross Breeseners' 60
Gross Breesen training farm 60, 61, 81
Gross, Sarah 258, 260
Grossman, Chajke 218
Grossmann, Atina 309
Gruner (Gans), Luiza (Louise) 161
Gryta, Marcin 181
guilt 247, 248, 262, 264, 267, 310, 325, 327, 329
Gurfinkel, Estera 183
Gutter, Pinchas 176
'Gypsy children' 201

Halm, Albert 82
Hamburger, Charlotte 54, 55
Hamburger, Hans 55
Haneke, Michael 326
Hartz, Ruth 261–7
Hebrew Immigrant Aid Society 3, 16, 72, 75, 78, 84
Heim, Susanne 119
Heimat 44, 324
Heimatlos – Elternlos – Unterkunftslos (uprooted, orphaned, homeless) 139
Heller, Margarete 35
Heller, Peter 31, 35, 39–42, 44
heritage 62, 64, 65, 259, 262–4, 266–7, 269–70, 311, 323, 324
Hertz, Susie 81
Herzl, Theodor 116
HEU, *see Heimatlos – Elternlos – Unterkunftslos* (uprooted, orphaned, homeless)
Heuberger, Theodor 62
Heydrich, Reinhard 300–3, 313
HIAS, *see* Hebrew Immigrant Aid Society
HICOG, *see* Allied High Commission for Germany

hidden children 258–9, 261, 264–5, 267, 269–71
Himmler, Heinrich 138, 139, 171–4
Hitler, Adolf 11, 15, 16, 26, 51, 52, 58, 63, 92–4, 103, 117, 119, 143, 303, 305, 326
Hitler Youth 143, 145
Hoare, Samuel 241
Hoberman, J. 308
Holtz, Haim 217
Hofmann, Ida 54
homeland 2, 3, 5, 19, 44, 51, 52, 64, 67, 98, 113, 115, 116, 120–1, 125, 127, 146, 230, 291
Hungary 5, 34, 36, 100, 204, 249, 289, 300

Ickes, Harold 14
ICRC, *see* International Committee of the Red Cross
IGCR, *see* Intergovernmental Committee on Refugees
Igel, Amelia 76, 82
immigration 3, 11, 12, 15, 18, 20, 26, 33, 41, 52, 58, 75, 91–3, 99–101, 104, 116, 127, 227, 228, 230, 241, 242, 280, 290, 306, 311
India 34, 78, 118
Indian settlers 123, 124, 127
indigenous communities
  in Africa 4, 117, 122
  in Brazil 59
industry 135, 142, 146, 176, 303, 311
injections 138, 203, 207, 307
integration 52–6, 58, 66, 72, 73, 81, 123
Intergovernmental Committee on Refugees 78, 99
International Committee of the Red Cross 288
International Refugee Organization 101, 102, 281, 284, 285–7, 327
International Tracing Service 6, 277, 285, 287
internees 31, 39, 40, 41, 83
internment camps 83, 98, 290

IRO, *see* International Refugee Organization
Isaacson, Peter 74
isolation 94, 95, 159, 162, 219, 266
Israel 1, 26, 32, 43, 95, 101, 115, 216, 218, 223, 225–30, 245, 252, 267, 269, 288, 290
Italy 5, 18, 34, 36, 37, 59, 83, 117, 204, 300
ITS, *see* International Tracing Service

Jablon, Janek (Ephroim) 158
Jandl, Ivan 299, 309, 311–15
Japan 19
Japanese
  communities 52
  origins 53
JDC, *see* Joint Distribution Committee
Jennings, Humphrey 300–3, 313, 316
Jeruchim, Simon 260, 261, 267
Jewish Council 71, 158–61, 219–22
Jewishness 4, 124, 127, 155, 159, 259–71, 326
Jewish police 162, 220
Jewish Welfare Guardian Scheme 73
Joffo, Joseph 260
Joint Distribution Committee 16, 72–9, 280
Judaism 5, 36, 55, 57, 96, 159, 258–63, 265–7, 269–70
Judenrat, *see* Jewish Council
Judenvermogensabgabe (Jewish Property Levy) 33
JUVA, *see Judenvermogensabgabe* (Jewish Property Levy)
juvenile refugees 41–2, 55, 92

Kacenelebegen, Mosiek 184
Kalińska, Kazimiera 142
Kaphan family 60
Kaphan, Heinrich 60
Kaplan, Josef 215, 216, 218, 219, 224, 225, 229
Karp (Biniaz), Celina 160
Karplus, Grete 66
Kates, Josef 31, 36, 39–42, 44
Katharina, P. 143
Katz, Anna 36
Katz, Bernhard 36

Katz, William 81
Katzenstein (nee Berg), Inge 115, 119, 121, 126
Katzki, Herbert 78
Kaufering labour camp, *see* labour camp
Kaufmann, Gabrielle 13
Keats, John 119
Kibbutzim 118, 222–7, 231, 232
Kiefer, Bruno 62–3
Kielce 224, 280
Kiriszczenko, Piotr 177, 179, 185
KL, *see Konzentrationslager* (concentration camp)
KL Lublin, *see* concentration camp
Klagsbrunn, Kurt 62, 65, 66
Kleemann, Fredi (Alfred) 65
Klimczyk, Kola 211
Klinger, Chaya 225
Kluge, Alexander 332
Koch, Adelheid 55, 64
Koch, Eleonore 57, 62, 64
Koch, Ernst 55, 64
Koch family 55
Koch-Weser, Erich 58
Koch-Weser, Geert 58
Koegel, Otto 172
Koellreutter, Hans-Joachim 63
Kołodziejska-Jedynak, Jadwiga 143
Konietzny, G. 184–5
Konzentrationslager (concentration camp), *see* concentration camp
Korczak, Janusz 184, 211, 226
Korczak, Ruzhka 225
Kovner, Abba 218, 219, 225
Kraków, *see* ghetto
Kraus, Eleanor 16
Kraus, Gilbert 16
Krawitz, Tony 322, 327
Kruh, Anna 37
Kruh, Eric 31, 37, 39, 41–4
Kruh, Isaak 37
'Kristallnacht' 14, 17, 32, 93, 117, 332
KTA, *see* North American *Kindertransport* Association
Kukiełka, Stanisław 173, 177
Kulka, Otto Dov 208, 210
Kurcyusz, Helena 178
Kwiatkowski, Jerzy 184

labour camp
    Kaufering 71
    Majdanek 171, 172
labour education camp 143
Lang, Fritz 301
language learning 21, 24, 53, 56, 76, 81, 85, 91, 94, 96, 115, 119–20, 215, 266, 291
Larino Children's Home, *see* Frances Barkman Home
Leavitt, Moses (Mo) 75
Lebensborn 6, 278, 279, 305
Levendel, Isaac 259, 260, 265
Leverton, Berta 246
Levi, Rino 66
Levine Enzie, Lauren 126
Levy, Hertha 60
Lewinnek, John (Isadore) 77, 84
liberation 6, 84, 85, 145, 187, 211, 222, 223, 227, 230, 279, 285, 286, 289, 292, 324
Lichtman, Rene 270
Limited Registration Plan 287
Lippman, Walter 80
Lithuania 102, 216, 219, 226, 330
Lochore, Reuel 91
Lodz, *see* ghetto
London, Louise 127
love
    of country 121
    of language 119
    of literature 119
    of religion 263, 266
LRP, *see* Limited Registration Plan
Lubetkin, Zivia 216–17, 220, 222
Lustiger, Jean-Marie 269

Macardle, Dorothy 283, 314
MacDonald White Paper 77
Maier family 60
Maier, Mathilde 60
Majdanek (KL Lublin), *see* concentration camp; extermination camp; labour camp
Mankowitz, Ze'ev 225
Markovicz, William 83
Marr, Bill (*see* Markovicz, William)
marrano 259, 269

Marcuse, Lotte 18
Marks, Elaine 259
Martin, Josie 263, 267
Masaryk, Jan 301, 303, 309, 311–12
Masel, Alec 74
massacre 6, 182, 299, 300–2, 305, 312, 314
Matsdorf, Wolf 72
Mauthausen, *see* concentration camp
McEwen, John 73
medical experiments 201, 207–8, 305, 309
medicine 43, 77, 78, 115, 175, 186
Mengele, Josef 71, 206–8
Meyer, Alwin 211
Meyers, Odette 258, 263, 265, 266, 268–9
Michlic, Joanna 155
Miller, David 306, 308
Milon, George 307
Mohalyi, Yolanda 64
Montefiore Home, Sydney 72, 79
Morgenstern, Yochanan 220
Morhange-Bégué, Claude 259
Müller, Stella 159
Myant, Maureen 314

Narodnij Komissariat Wnutrennych Del (People's Office for Interior; Soviet Secret Service 1937–46) 146
National Council of Jewish Women 16
National Refugee Service 15, 18, 23
nationalization 52–3, 56–7, 290
NCJW, *see* National Council of Jewish Women
Neikrug, Lewis 75
Netherlands, the 5, 18, 19, 204
New Zealand 2, 3, 35, 73, 91–105
New South Wales Jewish Board of Deputies 81
Newerly, Igor 184
Niemeyer, Oscar 66
Nikitovitsch, Nikolai 143
Nixdorf, Oswald 58
NKWD, *see Narodnij Komissariat Wnutrennych Del* (People's Office for Interior; Soviet Secret Service 1937–46)

Nobiling, Elisabeth 64
North American *Kindertransport* Association 248
Nourse Rogers, Edith 14
Novotná, Jarmila 309–10, 312, 315
Nowak, Jan 172
Nowak, Julian Oleg 142
NRS, *see* National Refugee Service
Nuremberg Laws 32, 117
Nuremberg Trials 227, 279, 287, 309
Nazi occupation
   in Poland 102, 135, 137, 145, 158, 217, 279
   in the Soviet Union 135, 137

occupation zones 6, 146, 285, 286, 290, 323, 328
O'Day, Caroline 14
Oeuvre de Secours aux Enfants (Children's Aid Society) 15, 16, 18–21, 72, 77, 78, 84, 266, 267
One Thousand Children 18
orphanages 19, 71, 83, 95, 97, 261, 265–7, 279, 282, 287, 291
OSE, *see* Oeuvre de Secours aux Enfants (Children's Aid Society)
Ossowska, Wanda 184–5
Ostarbeiter 137
Ostrowska, Henryka 179
OTC, *see* One Thousand Children
outside world 159–60

Palestine 33, 34, 38, 72, 74–7, 101, 113, 115, 116, 118, 216, 217, 224, 227–30, 266, 280, 283, 285, 289, 290, 305
Palmer, Glen 72, 80
Papanek, Ernst 18, 19, 84
Paradowska, Alina 178
Pastuschenko, Tetjana 145
Pauly (nee Berg), Jill 115, 120–2, 125–6
Perkins, Frances 14
photography 62, 65–6, 330–1
Pickett, Clarence E. 14
Pilpel, Robert 76
Plotnicka, Frumka 216, 218, 225
Pohl, Oswald 173

Polish children 73–4, 92, 95–8, 102, 104–5, 141, 146, 173, 175–6, 201–3
Porush, Bertha 79
Porush, Israel 77
Poty (Napoleon Potyguara Lazzarotto) 64
POW, *see* prisoner of war
prisoner of war 4, 40, 140, 145, 171, 172
psychiatrist 247
psychologist 6, 84, 246, 247, 260, 292

Radłowska, Alina 141
Radványi, Géza 305, 308
Razovsky, Cecilia 12–13, 18
RCM, *see* Refugee Children's Movement
Reading, Fanny 79
Rebolo, Francisco 64
Refugee and Migrant Service 103
Refugee Children's Movement 242–4
refugee testimony 4, 114
refugee organizations 11, 14–16, 25
rehabilitation 1, 2, 5, 6, 84–5, 226, 277–8, 280–1, 284, 288, 292, 304
Reich, Erich 245
Reichssicherheitshauptamt (Reich Security Main Office) 202
religion 13, 26, 35, 60, 96, 102, 159, 257, 259–60, 262–4, 267, 269–70, 284
repatriation 136, 146, 278, 280, 283–6, 288, 290–1, 301, 305, 314
Rescue the Child Fund 79
Rescue the Children Scheme 73
resistance 143–5, 202, 204, 215–16, 218–32, 279, 299, 301–2, 308, 313
reunification 6, 278, 280, 290, 292, 327
Reunion of *Kindertransports* 246
Riff, Isabelle 264
Ringelblum, Emanuel 219
RMS, *see* Refugee and Migrant Service

Robbe-Grillet, Alain 329
Rogers, Will 43
ROK, *see* Reunion of *Kindertransports*
Roma 201, 202, 209, 281, 282
Romik, Maria 206
Romik, Stefania 206
Roosevelt, Eleanor 14
Roosevelt, Franklin Delano 14, 15
Rosenfeld, Michael 220
Rosenheim, Käte 16, 17
Rosenthal, Hans 60–1
Roskies, David 270
Rossi Osir, Paulo 64
Rossler, Honza (Henry) 71–2, 79
Rossler, Peter 71–2, 79,
Roth-Hano, Renée 260–4, 266,
route
　escape 2, 117, 240, 290
　transportation 18, 242
RSHA, *see Reichssicherheitshauptamt* (Reich Security Main Office)
Rumkowski, Chaim 71

Saalheimer, Manfred 79
Sachs, Inge 61
Sauckel, Fritz 137, 139
Save the Children's Scheme 73
Schauff family 58
Schauff, Johannes 58
Schauff, Karin 58–9
Schiff, Otto M. 76
Schlöndorff, Volker 332
Schneider, Dieter Marc 58
Schneider, Mr. 79, 81
schooling 37, 41, 56, 60, 79, 81, 93, 104, 114, 124, 201
Schwartz, Zoltan 79
Schwarz, Egon 56
Schweizer, Richard 304
Sebald, W. G. 321–2, 328–32
Second Generation 5, 239, 246–53
Seiffert, Rachel 321–2, 325, 328
Semple, Bob 101
separation
　of families 14, 43, 139, 140, 204, 240, 245, 247, 251, 262, 265, 282, 284, 300, 310
Sereny, Gitta 291
Shakespeare, William 119, 323

Shalev, Ziva 219
Shalitan, Levi 225
Shamir, Yosef 217
Shanahan, Foss 101
Shuckburgh, John. E 125
Siberia 19, 97
SIBRA, *see Sociedade Israelita Brasileira de Cultura e Beneficencia* (Brazilian-Jewish Cultural and Beneficent Society)
Siejwa, Feliks 182
Sinti 201, 202, 281, 282
Sirk, Douglas 303
Siwek-Ciupak, Beata 174
Skwarko, Krystyna 97
Slovakia 5, 204, 299
Sobczak, Zofia 144
Sobibor, *see* extermination camp
Sociedade Israelita Brasileira de Cultura e Beneficencia (Brazilian-Jewish Cultural and Beneficent Society) 53
SOE, *see* British Special Operations Executive
Sonderkommando 183, 204
Sontag, Susan 328
Sopher, Eva 51–2, 62–3
Sosnowski, Kiryl 138
Souhami, Herta 17
South Africa 34, 323, 78, 113, 115, 117
Soviet Union 1, 6, 96–7, 100, 135–8, 145–6, 171–2, 201, 204, 218, 232, 279, 282, 286, 291
Speyer, Anita 55, 57–8
Speyer, Wilhelm 55, 57–8
Spitz, Pnina 261
Spotová, Hana 312
Springer, Miss 17
SS Derna 77
SS Dunera 83
SS Napoli 83
Stanislawa, R., 141
Sterling, Bryan 36, 39, 40, 42–4
Stern, Hans 62
Stinnes, Dr. (Edmund) 60
Streicher, Julius 227
Symonds, Saul 81

Szenes, Hannah 229
Szeps, David 77

Tarasiewicz, Krystyna
teachers 32, 35, 54, 64, 65, 80, 81, 92, 93, 103, 105, 119, 124, 125, 260, 268, 291, 313
Tenenbaum, Mordecai 220
Terezin, *see* ghetto
Terry, Jack 292
Thackeray, William 119
Theresienstadt, *see* ghetto
Third Generation 239, 246, 248, 252, 254
transit camps 140, 174, 175
Traumann, Else 60
Traumann family 60
Traumann, Michael 60–1
Treblinka, *see* extermination camp
Trumpeldor, Josef 226
Trzasalski, Kazimierz 144

Ullstein, Leopold 55
UN, *see* United Nations
unaccompanied children 12, 19, 101–2, 146, 241–2, 281–7, 292
United Nations 288, 299
United Nations Relief and Rehabilitation Administration 6, 226, 277–92, 304–5, 307–13
United Nations Special Committee on Palestine 229
United States Committee for the Care of European Children 16
United States Holocaust Memorial Museum 115, 119
UNRRA, *see* United Nations Relief and Rehabilitation Administration
USC, *see* United States Committee for the Care of European Children
UNSCOP, *see* United Nations Special Committee on Palestine
US child resettlement law 11
USHMM, *see* United States Holocaust Memorial Museum

Vargas, Getúlio 53, 56, 58, 60
Vegh, Claudine 261
Victory Loan Appeal 74
Vidor, Hans 82
Viertel, Peter 299, 305–7, 311
Vilna, *see* ghetto
Volpi, Alfredo 64

Wächter, Otto 155
Wagner, Robert 14
Wagner-Rogers Bill 14–15, 26, 116
war children 6, 313, 321
War Orphans Project 78
Warchavski, Gregori 66
Wars, John 81–2
Warsaw, *see* ghetto
Watson, 'Pa' 14
Wechsler, Lazar 304–7
Weiller-Bruch, Lene 64
Weinberg, Shaike 223
Weinstein, Frida 264
Weizmann, Vera 74
West Indies 113
White, Hayden 322
Wiedemann, Dorothea 59
Wiedemann, Hilde 59
Wilner, Arieh 222
Windisch, Hans 66
Winton, Nicholas 251, 313
Wirtschafts- und Verwaltungshauptamt (SS Main Economic and Administrative Department) 172–3
Wodzicka, Countess 97
Wodzicki, Count Kazimierz 97
Wojciechowski, John Roy (Jan) 98
Wolf, Jacqueline 259, 262–7
Wolf, Joan 314
Wolff, Paul 66
Woliniewska, Matylda 186
Wollheim, Norbert 17
Wollstein, Kurt 84
Wordsworth, William 119
World Zionist Organization 116
Wrotniak, Józefa (Sr. Stella) 97
Wulf, Dawid 156
Wujec, Henryk 186

WVHA, see *Wirtschafts- und Verwaltungshauptamt* (SS Main Economic and Administrative Department)
Wynn, Samuel (Sam) 74

Yechieli, Baruch 223
Yechieli, Miriam 223
Youth Aliyah 74–5, 229, 285, 290
youth movements 5, 96, 215–32, 285
Yovel, Yirmiyahu 259, 270
Yugoslavia 5, 204

Zahra, Tara 282, 284, 301, 309, 310, 314
Zalmanson, Yitzhak 217
Zamoyska, Christina 307
Zanini, Mario 64
Zelwer, Charles 265
Zilberman, Max 84–5

Zinnemann, Fred 6, 299, 300, 305–16
Zionism 96, 223, 227, 230–1
ZOB, see *żydowska Organizacja Bojowa* (Jewish Fighting Organization)
Zuckerman, Yitzhak 216, 217, 220, 222
Zuquim, Judith 56
Zweig, Jettel 114, 117
Zweig, Stefanie 114, 117, 119
Zweig, Walter 114
Zwerling, Bruno, see Sterling, Bryan
Zwerling, Hermann 36
żydowska Organizacja Bojowa (Jewish Fighting Organization) 217, 220–2
żydowski Związek Wojskowski (Jewish Military Union) 221
ZZW, see *żydowski Związek Wojskowski* (Jewish Military Union)